A Programmer's Guide to COMMON

A Programmer's Guide to

COMMON LISP

DEBORAH G. TATAR

Xerox Palo Alto Research Center

Digital Press

9 8 7 6 5 4 3 2 1
Order number EY-6706E-DP

Cover and text design by David Ford. Typeset from magnetic tape by Waldman Graphics. Printed and bound in the United States of America by Arcata/Halliday.

Painting on cover by Gyorgy Kepes, reproduced courtesy of Clark Abt, Abt Associates.

DEC, the Digital logo, VAX, VMS are trademarks of Digital Equipment Corporation. Mars is a registered trademark of the M&M/Mars Company. Necco is a registered trademark of the New England Confectionary Company. Reeses is a registered trademark of the Hershey Chocolate Company. Twinkies is a registered trademark of the Continental Baking Company, Inc. UNIX is a trademark of Bell Laboratories. ZetaLISP is a registered trademark of Symbolics, Inc.

The lines on pages 178, 179, and 181, from "Ash-Wednesday" and "The Waste Land," are from *Collected Poems 1909–1962* by T. S. Eliot, copyright 1936 by Harcourt Brace Jovanovich, Inc.; copyright © 1963, 1964 by T. S. Eliot. Reprinted by permission of Harcourt Brace Jovanovich and Faber and Faber Ltd.

Library of Congress Cataloging-in-Publication Data

Tatar, Deborah G.
  A programmer's guide to COMMON LISP.

  Bibliography: p.
  1. COMMON LISP (Computer program language)
I. Title.
QA76.73.C28T38   1987   005.13'3   86-16498
ISBN 0-932376-87-8

CONTENTS

Preface   vii

Foreword   ix

1   Introduction to Lisp   1

2   Data Types and Evaluation   10

3   Writing Procedures   38

4   Variables   67

5   Recursion, Iteration, and "PROGN-TYPE" Forms   94

6   Interactions with the Outside World   118

7   Manipulating Data   135

8   Manipulating Procedures as Data   158

9   Advanced Constructs   177

10   Compilation   209

11   Macros   219

12   An Extended Example: A Toy Expert System   233

Annotated Bibliography   273

Appendix: Solutions to the Exercises   275

Index of Defined Procedures and Macros   309

General Index   313

PREFACE

The main purpose of this book is to guide programmers through the difficult first stages of learning LISP, by introducing them to the basic assumptions, style, and, of course, functionalities. A secondary goal is to provide a resource for programmers who are moving into COMMON LISP after working with older dialects.

This is an introductory book; it assumes no prior knowledge of LISP. However, it does aim at giving you a high level of competence by including details that might be tiresome for the absolutely naive programmer. On the other hand, LISP is relatively different from other programming languages, so in some sense almost everyone who studies it is a beginner. A guideline is that if you aren't familiar with words like "data structure," "string," and "array," sitting down and reading through this book without help will be difficult.

The *Programmer's Guide* arose from my experience at Digital Equipment Corporation teaching VAX LISP to students with a wide range of skills and interests. I found that students with experience and a sense of purpose could master the material during the two-week course. Those with good will but no programming experience could learn the material up through iteration (chapter 5) and gain a partial understanding of recursion in the same length of time.

I have adhered to the functions and behaviors specified in Guy L. Steele Jr., COMMON LISP: The Language (Digital Press, 1984), so that you should be able to run the procedures in this book in any implementation of COMMON LISP.

Even experienced programmers learning LISP are strongly encouraged to do the exercises at the end of each chapter. You simply cannot learn LISP without practice, and guided practice can be very fruitful. Also, additional material is introduced in the exercises.

ACKNOWLEDGMENTS

This book has been three years in the making. Many people have contributed to it in one way or another. First of all, I am indebted to my students at Digital Equipment Corporation (especially the one who kept asking, ''But what *is* a value?'') and to Jeff Clanon and Emilie Schmidt, who made it possible for me to teach there. I am grateful to Ralph Cherubini for suggesting that I send my course notes to Digital Press. In the VAX LISP group at DEC, Norma Abel, Paul Anagnastopolous, Jerry Boetje, Gary Brown, and Walter van Roggen all read parts of my manuscript and put up with my use of their system. In addition, Beryl Nelson went over the entire manuscript. Also at Digital, Wendy Mackay, Paul Sawyer, and the rest of the Educational Services Research and Development group deserve thanks for their support and encouragement while I was writing.

I am greatly indebted to Guy L. Steele Jr., who in some sense edited the book and accompanied his careful, astute comments with occasional cartoons that were very encouraging to discover when I was working late at night.

Razmik Abnous, Jim Davis, John Duffy, Mike Eisenberg, Geoff Feldman, Leigh Klotz, Flavio Rose, and Bernard Silver all read through the book at various stages and made helpful suggestions. Mark Eckenweiler provided all-purpose Shakespearean commentary. Kent Pitman's criticism and multiple suggestions were astringent, disinfecting, and most helpful. Hal Abelson, with his unerring pedagogical sense, picked out all the places where I had hoped that little said was enough. He generally suggested that I say more.

Glenn Burke was also very helpful, allowing me to use NIL and clarifying the thinking behind and workings of COMMON LISP on many counts. The folks at Lucid also gave me the occasional use of their machines, which was appreciated.

At Digital Press, I am grateful to Chase Duffy not only for production editing but for making this book pleasant to write, and for many wonderful conversations about management, books, and publishing. I want to thank Nancy Gustavesen, who was my acquisitions editor. John Osborn and Mike Meehan facilitated the process. Geraldine Morse, the manuscript editor, and David Ford, the designer, both contributed many hours and good ideas. Beth French handled the logistics of moving machines and copies of the manuscript back and forth across the country.

At Xerox, Mark Stefik and Mimi Gardner helped me with the final stages.

Last but not least, Patrick Sobalvarro made this work possible, contributing both technical acumen (even to the extent of donating the code for Otto) and personal support. This book is dedicated to him.

Palo Alto, California
June 7, 1985

FOREWORD

LISP has been around a while. Not everyone noticed it at first. Thousands of programming languages have been invented, and hundreds have been implemented and widely used at one time or another. Only a handful, however, have continued to be used for years and years. BASIC, Pascal, and COBOL are of course widely used, but what has happened to MAD, JOSS, COLASL, COMIT, TRAC, and even the elegant and powerful ALGOL 60? The ideas in those languages have influenced their successors; the languages themselves have been left behind.

But LISP has survived. It is the second-oldest general-purpose programming language still in widespread use; only FORTRAN is older. For a decade or two it flourished in only a few places, primarily artificial intelligence laboratories, but in those few places LISP was greatly prized for its power and flexibility, and it evolved to meet the changing needs of researchers. Interactive environments grew up around and within the LISP language system—there is something about the language that encourages tool-building—that greatly increased programming convenience and productivity. Some of the first structured editors, the first pretty-printers, the first interactive cross-reference tools, the first automatic error-correction facilities were developed with and for LISP. And LISP was first and foremost in the development of such automatic storage-management techniques as garbage collection.

In the 1980's LISP has suddenly become much more popular. This is in part because of the new interest in practical applications of artificial intelligence, but also because of the inherent usefulness of the language. Looking over the program schedules of recent academic conferences on such topics as compilers and computer architecture, I see papers about LISP language design and implementation. Five years ago there were none. Looking over the advertisements in computer magazines and trade journals, there are dozens of vendors promoting LISP and LISP-based systems. Looking over news articles and editorial columns, LISP is mentioned over and over again.

ix

I like to think that the development of COMMON LISP has been helpful to this process. I was the editor of the COMMON LISP language specification on behalf of a committee of over sixty LISP experts. Our goal was to make LISP even more useful by making it more portable. LISP had thrived for over two decades despite having dozens of incompatible dialects, despite the obstacles to sharing code between sites, despite the great difficulty of building on the work of others. Thanks to the development of COMMON LISP, which has become a *de facto* standard, there are now dozens of *compatible* dialects.

The COMMON LISP specification, like any language specification, aimed to be complete and accurate, often at the expense of accessibility. To the newcomer such a document frequently seems to spend all its time on protruding trunnions and obscure gray corners rather than sweeping themes and the most useful details. What is needed is a proper introduction to COMMON LISP that tells you what you need to know, rather than everything.

Deborah Tatar has come along at just the right time. The book you have in your hands proceeds in a logical order, emphasizing themes as well as features, demonstrating proper usage, and culminating in the presentation of a toy expert system, the code for which is readable and clearly explained. The examples are fresh. You won't find the factorial function coded in endless different ways, but rather references to Shakespeare, rock and roll, bicycles, and a song that you, too, may have sung on the school bus.

I enjoyed reading this book, and I enjoy working with COMMON LISP. I think you will, too, but the proof of the pudding is in the eating. In the tradition of all LISP dialects, COMMON LISP will succeed only if you find it helpful and useful. Books like this are an important step toward making that possible.

Guy L. Steele Jr.
Cambridge, Massachusetts
May 1986

Chapter 1

INTRODUCTION TO LISP

Something about LISP defies easy classification. A recent article by Alan Kay contained a diagram classifying computer languages.[1] At the bottom were languages called "low-level," at the top, languages termed "high-level," "very high-level," and even "ultra high-level." LISP had a place in every category on the chart except "low-level." Kay was referring to different LISPs, or different aspects of LISP, at each stage. Nonetheless, his statement reflects LISP's remarkable flexibility. LISP has become a higher-level language as people have tried to use it that way. As LISP has changed, it has changed the way people look at problems; it seems to absorb new ideas into its own style. A well known statement, frequently credited to Joel Moses, is that APL is like a perfect diamond: if you add anything to it, it becomes flawed. In contrast, LISP is like a ball of mud—if you add more to it, you get a bigger ball of mud.[2] It is worth pointing out that mud is a very useful substance; it can be shaped into any form you wish.

LISP is a general-purpose computer language, perhaps the most general-purpose language. Although it was originally designed with a specific problem domain (recursion theory) in mind, for twenty-five years it has evolved into a tool for solving the problems of artificial intelligence. Since these problems involve many domains of knowledge, LISP has been used in such diverse areas as:

- expert systems
- symbolic algebra
- VLSI design

---

[1] Alan Kay, "Computer Software," *Scientific American* 251, 3 (September 1984): 52–59.

[2] The correct attribution of this remark is in doubt. Although many people claim to have heard Joel Moses make it at the 1979 APL conference, Professor Moses takes credit for a slightly different remark. He did compare APL to a diamond; however, he claims to have compared LISP to a bean bag—you can sit on a bean bag and squash it, but it will always rise again. Like LISP itself, comments about LISP may have improved with the years.

- robotics (planning, obstacle avoidance, user interfaces)
- machine vision
- computer language development
- natural language understanding

LISP can be used in so many domains because it is a symbol-manipulation language and because symbols are powerful, general-purpose tools for conceptualizing relationships, problems, and solutions. The language supports the large system builder, and the environment makes it easy to program in and easy to debug.

1.1   WORKING WITH LISP

What is it like to work with LISP? A programmer's style of interaction with LISP is different from his interaction with most other programming languages. These differences are partly in the language, partly in the environment, and partly in the style of use that has evolved over the years. Before we plunge into the language itself, here are some points that may help to orient you within this environment.

The single most important feature for the new user is that LISP is interactive. You can type an expression at LISP, and LISP will give you an immediate response. LISP is predictable, and learning to predict its behavior at the interactive level is crucial for mastering its complexities. Chapter 2 identifies some of LISP's fundamental behaviors.

Once you understand the fundamental behaviors, you can write function definitions that rely on them. You can make these definitions interactively by typing them in, just as you can type in simpler statements. In theory, you could simply retype these definitions to LISP each time you started a new session; however, that's not practical. Most LISP programs consist of many function definitions stored in one or more files. People load the relevant files into LISP. Loading files has the same effect as if the programmer had typed each definition in by hand.

As a result, once you attain a certain degree of sophistication, you spend a lot of time in an editor, writing procedures. Most LISPs come with a special editor that allows you to send pieces of code directly to LISP, without saving and loading files. Often, you can switch directly between LISP and the editor. These editors are crucial parts of the LISP environment.

A typical LISP programmer writes procedures in the editor, sends them to LISP (by pressing a key or two), switches to LISP (usually by pressing a key or two), tests them out, and returns to the editor to write some more. In some LISPs, you don't even have to leave the editor to test items.

Testing these procedures may involve debugging. Debugging information is directly accessible from the interpreter whenever there is a problem. Several different kinds of debugging tools are built into LISP. The stepper allows you to watch what LISP is doing step by step. The tracer allows you to get information when specific events occur. The debugger allows you to examine LISP's situation when something goes wrong.

The process of working with LISP is critically important to its actual use, perhaps more important than any single piece of information about the language itself. Writing LISP code is, in general, an interactive experience characterized by the short amount of time between discovering a problem and being able to try an alternate solution. In this, it resembles the real world, where you are used to getting immediate sensory responses and making quick adjustments.

LISP code can and should be compiled for speed. However, in most systems you compile your procedure or program only *after* it has been debugged in its interpreted form. Sometimes people compile a whole file to find syntactic errors like misspelled names or too many arguments to a function; however, essential debugging should be done when the code is interpreted.

A good rule of thumb is that if your interpreted code works, your compiled code should produce the same behavior as the interpreted version. There are a few exceptions to this rule, but it is the goal of the compiler to produce code that behaves exactly like interpreted code.

1.2   COMMON LISP VERSUS OTHER LISPS

Since there has been no standard LISP until now, LISP implementations differ greatly, both in underlying concepts and in specific details. The differences can range from the annoying (the user finds that common operations are called something slightly different) to the seriously troublesome (variable scoping is done differently in different LISPs).

Most (but not all) serious modern-day LISP implementations descend from MACLISP. However, even the dialects that grew out of MACLISP differed owing to variations in machines and individual approaches. Eventually, many researchers who used LISP found that they had to make painful choices about which implementation of LISP to use— since dialects varied, a considerable expense was involved in moving from one implementation to another. Frequently, researchers were forced to stay with obsolete hardware to avoid making drastic changes to software.

The COMMON LISP specification was created by a group of LISP programmers who wanted, among other things, to create a common ground from which different implementations could diverge if necessary. They wished to combine the best elements of MACLISP and of some of its many successor languages, including LISP MACHINE LISP and SCHEME. Additionally, they wanted to incorporate some aspects of divergent strains such as INTERLISP. They tried to make COMMON LISP as compatible as possible with the older languages, but they also wished to exclude "kludges" and system-dependent features.

Since COMMON LISP was designed carefully, over a period of years, and has considerable support from within the artificial intelligence community, it will probably succeed in setting a standard.

The COMMON LISP specification is documented in *COMMON LISP: The Language* by Guy L. Steele, Jr. (Digital Press, 1984). Every implementation of COMMON LISP should have all the functions documented there. Some implementations may have other features as well.

Although Steele's book (hereafter referred to as "Steele") is the ultimate guide to COMMON LISP, it can be difficult to approach all at once because it is a specification rather than a user's guide. Furthermore, it specifies an enormous number of functions (about 800). Even worse for the beginner, the functions vary a great deal in level of use. High-level and low-level constructs are described side by side. The current book is intended as a bridge for programmers coming to COMMON LISP from other programming languages and even from older implementations of LISP.

1.3   PREVIEW OF LISP PROGRAMS

It is good to know what you are trying to learn, even if you are not yet in a position to understand it. Three examples of different kinds of programs or program fragments written in LISP follow. Each of these represents one or more interesting things you may do easily in LISP. The first demonstrates the ease of *recursion* in the language. This program takes a *list* of numbers as argument and *returns a value* that is a list of all the positive numbers in the first list. The second example demonstrates how you can use *data abstraction* in writing a simulation in LISP. It allows you to manufacture bicycles and then "pump their pedals." The third example centers around the concept of a program building another program. In this case, we build a machine that manufactures gumball machines. Each gumball machine comes loaded with an allotment of gumballs. A companion procedure allows you to ask the machines to dispense one gumball at a time.

You are not expected to understand these procedures yet; they are set forth here only as a preview, to spark interest and give you an idea of how to program in LISP.

1.3.1   Filter

Imagine that you have a list, somewhat like a shopping list, containing a bunch of numbers. You can write it down as follows:

(1 2 4.5 −6 20 −3/5 .003)

Suppose you want to write a program that searches a list like this and *filters out* all the negative numbers to produce another list containing only the positive numbers:

(1 2 4.5 20 .003)

Now imagine that you have a program, called FILTER, which does this. Once it is typed into LISP, you can type:

(filter '(1 2 4.5 −6 20 −3/5 .003))

and get back

(1 2 4.5 20 .003)

or you can type:

```
(filter '(−5 −6 −7 8/9))
(8/9)
(filter '(360000 −.4 −6/7 3))
(360000 3)
```

In other words, once you define the procedure, you can call it by name with appropriate arguments and get the response it is supposed to give. Regardless of how they work internally, procedures in LISP make contracts with the outside world of the form, "You give me the right information; I give you what I promised."

This concept of a procedure is somewhat different from the more traditional one of a program as something you create and run once with no surrounding, continuous environment.

How could we implement FILTER? We can describe a process that would produce this behavior:

Get a list of numbers.

If the list is empty, there's nothing to do, so return an empty list.

If the list isn't empty, then if the first element in the list is less than zero, ignore it, and start at number one with the rest of the list.

If the first element in the list is not less than zero, then make a list out of it and the result of going through this process on every other item in the list.

We plunge into the heart of matters with a program that implements the process:

```
(defun filter (list-of-numbers)
  (if (null list-of-numbers) nil
    (if (< (car list-of-numbers) 0)
        (filter (cdr list-of-numbers))
      (cons (car list-of-numbers)
            (filter (cdr list-of-numbers))))))
```

The correspondence between the description and the program, while not exact, is very close. See figure 1-1.

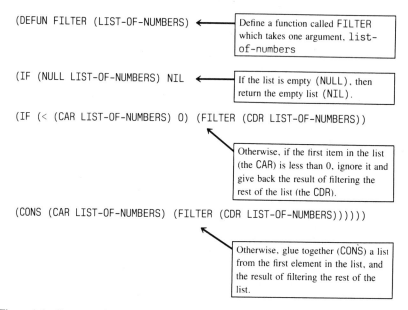

```
(DEFUN FILTER (LIST-OF-NUMBERS)  ◄─── Define a function called FILTER
                                      which takes one argument, list-
                                      of-numbers

  (IF (NULL LIST-OF-NUMBERS) NIL  ◄─── If the list is empty (NULL), then
                                      return the empty list (NIL).

    (IF (< (CAR LIST-OF-NUMBERS) 0) (FILTER (CDR LIST-OF-NUMBERS))

                                      Otherwise, if the first item in the list
                                      (the CAR) is less than 0, ignore it and
                                      give back the result of filtering the
                                      rest of the list (the CDR).

      (CONS (CAR LIST-OF-NUMBERS) (FILTER (CDR LIST-OF-NUMBERS))))))

                                      Otherwise, glue together (CONS) a list
                                      from the first element in the list, and
                                      the result of filtering the rest of the
                                      list.
```

Figure 1-1. Correspondence Between the Code and Algorithm for FILTER

An interesting feature of FILTER is its control mechanism. You may wonder how each element in the list gets processed. FILTER uses a technique called *recursion*. LISP's ability to take advantage of recursive techniques easily is one of its strengths.

FILTER works exactly as written above. If you wanted to, you could type the definition to a LISP interpreter and then call it as it was called earlier with no other details to consider.

1.3.2   *Making Bicycles*

It is easy to model real-world objects flexibly in LISP. For example, suppose we wanted to model a bicycle in such a way that we could ''pump its pedals'' and produce some effect.

First we have to define pumping pedals. Pumping the pedals of the model bicycle should move the bicycle forward by some amount dependent on the radius of the wheel and the gear ratio. The exact relationship is that the new position of the bicycle will be the old position plus ½ the gear ratio times pi times the wheel size. The ½ is because you turn the pedals only one half turn when you pump them. The procedure can be written:

```
(defun pump-pedals (bike)
   (set-x-position
       bike
       (+ (x-position bike)
          (* (gear-ratio bike)
             .5 pi (wheel-size bike)))))
```

This procedure is completely independent of the implementation scheme used. It relies on the set of procedures around it to be consistent with one another. That is, MAKE-BIKE must deliver a bicycle that X-POSITION, GEAR-RATIO, WHEEL-SIZE, and SET-X-POSITION can work on.

Working downward, we could then implement procedures to support PUMP-PEDALS. Many data structures are possible, but here is one set of mutually supporting procedures based on the idea that a bicycle is a list of three elements: an x-position, a gear ratio, and a wheel size, in that order:

```
(defun make-bike (x-position gear-ratio wheel-size)
   (list x-position gear-ratio wheel-size))

(defun x-position (bike)
   (car bike))

(defun gear-ratio (bike)
   (cadr bike))

(defun wheel-size (bike)
   (caddr bike))

(defun set-x-position (bike new-value)
   (setf (car bike) new-value))

(defun set-gear-ratio (bike new-value)
   (setf (cadr bike) new-value))

(defun set-wheel-size (bike new-value)
   (setf (caddr bike) new-value))
```

We do not use all these procedures in PUMP-PEDALS. This is, however, a complete set of primitive functions for manipulating bicycles. MAKE-BIKE is a *constructor*; it constructs bicycles and returns them. X-POSITION, WHEEL-SIZE, and GEAR-RATIO are *selectors* or *accessors*; they select the appropriate information from a particular bicycle. SET-X-POSITION, SET-WHEEL-SIZE, and SET-GEAR-RATIO are *mutators*; they change the value of the appropriate attribute of a bicycle to a new value.

Defining a set of procedures is much like hiring managers—once they are in place, you just talk to them and don't worry about the operation. Here you have seven tiny procedures that work together. We could change the way the bicycle is implemented by changing what the procedures do.

Defining a procedure is also similar to designing an advertising campaign; its purpose is to make a single point. You have to identify what the point should be regardless of the simplicity or complexity of the truth that lies below. Each procedure makes a contract that, given the correct information, it will deliver the correct information.

1.3.3   *Making Gumball Machines*

GUM-MACHINE is another short but powerful program. GUM-MACHINE creates machines, each of which is capable of delivering one gumball each time it is used, until the supply runs out. As each machine is created, it is given a certain allotment of gumballs, of various colors.

First we decide what colors the pieces of gum can be:

```
(defvar *gum-colors*
  '(brown blue red orange purple green yellow speckled))
```

Then we decide how to put together a supply of gumballs for a machine and write a procedure called GENERATE-GUM-SUPPLY which takes one argument—the number of gumballs to put in the package. Then, GENERATE-GUM-SUPPLY picks that many pieces of gum of different colors by making a list containing all the pieces that have been chosen. Since gumballs have only one property in our simulation, we can represent them by that property on the list, i.e., (blue brown green speckled brown):

```
(defun generate-gum-supply (size)
  (if (= 0 size) nil
    (cons (nth (random (length *gum-colors*)) *gum-colors*)
      (generate-gum-supply (- size 1)))))
```

Like FILTER, GENERATE-GUM-SUPPLY is a recursive procedure. It picks one piece of gum, then calls upon itself to create a supply one less than it needed to before. (Remember, this is just a preview. Recursion will be treated in chapter 5.)

Next, we write the procedure that, given a package such as can be created by GENERATE-GUM-SUPPLY, produces fully loaded gumball machines:

```
(defun gum-machine (supply-of-gum)
  (function
    (lambda ()
      (prog1 (car supply-of-gum)
        (setq supply-of-gum (cdr supply-of-gum))))))
```

Each time we call GUM-MACHINE, it returns a GUM-MACHINE ''containing'' the gumballs provided. For example, we can create two machines, the *BARBER-SHOP-MACHINE* and the *GROCERY-STORE-MACHINE*:

```
(defvar *barber-shop-machine*
  (gum-machine (generate-gum-supply 4)))
```

```
(defvar *grocery-store-machine*
  (gum-machine (generate-gum-supply 6)))
```

How can we make these machines dispense gum? The easiest way is to write a procedure called GET-GUM, which will take one argument, the machine to be used, and will return a gumball:

```
(defun get-gum (machine)
  (funcall machine))
```

Now we can use the gum machines to get pieces of gum:

```
(get-gum *barber-shop-machine*)
GREEN

(get-gum *grocery-store-machine*)
BLUE

(get-gum *barber-shop-machine*)
SPECKLED

(get-gum *barber-shop-machine*)
ORANGE

(get-gum *grocery-store-machine*)
ORANGE
```

Each machine has its own private stock of gumballs.

GUM-MACHINE lets us take advantage of LISP's flexibility by allowing us to pass functions just like any other part of the language. GUM-MACHINE, like a machine that creates other machines, is a procedure that creates another procedure.

CHAPTER HIGHLIGHTS

Suggested Reading

The following section in Steele, COMMON LISP, complements the material in this chapter: chapter 1, Introduction, 1.1.

Chapter 2

DATA TYPES AND EVALUATION

The LISP world consists of different types of objects. Numbers, symbols, strings, characters, and lists are the ones introduced in this chapter; others will be introduced later. Each type of LISP object has its own properties, just as objects in the real world have theirs. You usually know whether you want a pat of butter or a piece of bread; so, too, it is usually fairly clear, once you understand their uses and your own purpose well enough, what kind of a LISP object you want. Unfortunately, it takes experience in the LISP world to be sure what uses exist for different kinds of objects.

To learn those uses, you must understand LISP's fundamental operation, *evaluation*, and how it handles each different kind of object. The first task in learning to program in LISP is learning to predict how LISP evaluates expressions made up of objects.

This chapter consists of three parts:

- The first discusses five data types: numbers, symbols, characters, lists, and strings. It is not helpful to separate these data types completely from their use, so they are discussed in terms of what LISP does with them.

- The second part is concerned with using these data types in simple ways, beginning with arithmetic procedures and operations on lists. Then these examples will be used to introduce some LISP conventions (*prefix notation*, *pretty-printing*).

- Finally, comes the underlying construction of lists, and two ways to represent that construction:

  –box-and-pointer diagrams

  –dotted-pair notation

This leads into a brief discussion of a sixth data type: *conses*, or pairs. Lists are constructed from pairs.

For the sake of simplicity, the difference between the printed representation of a LISP object and the object itself will be ignored in this chapter and will not be addressed directly until chapter 6. What is the problem we are deferring? For example, when we talk we use our dog's name, but when we think, we think about the dog itself. In the same way, when LISP prints something on the screen, LISP uses its name, but when calculating it uses the object itself. Programmers share a vocabulary with the machine just as we share a vocabulary with one another and there can be "misunderstandings" in both cases. If you say "Remember the old red chair," it might take much discussion for another to realize that you are thinking of a different old red chair. Such problems don't come up all the time, so we can start by pretending there's no difference. Nonetheless, when they do arise, we must think about how LISP translates between the things it "knows" about and the stuff that appears on the screen.

2.1   SOME OBJECTS IN THE LISP WORLD

Ordinarily, when you write big programs, you create objects explicitly under program control by using special creation operations; however, many objects can also be created implicitly, by typing them in. These latter objects will be treated first.

When you start LISP, you get a prompt that may look like this:

LISP>

The prompt means that you are at "top level." Some LISPs show a prompt every time the LISP interpreter finishes previous computations and is waiting for new commands. Other LISPs show the prompt only at the beginning of the session with LISP and at a few other select times.

Regardless of what you see, the behavior is always the same. LISP attempts to evaluate anything you type at it. When you sit down at the terminal and type something to LISP, it applies a rule for figuring out the *value* of the object represented by what you typed and *returns* that value. Initially, we will look at simple examples in which LISP returns the value by printing it on the screen.

A good rule of thumb is that anything you type in or create under program control becomes a LISP object. Intuitively, a LISP object is a "thing" that exists in LISP's world. Each data type identifies a class of objects, instances of which are acceptable to LISP.

2.1.1   Numbers, Characters, and Strings

LISP has different rules for evaluating objects with different data types. Its simplest rule applies to numbers, characters, and strings: *Numbers, characters, and strings evaluate to themselves.*

This means that if you type a number, a character, or a string to LISP, it returns the object itself to you. If you type the integer 3, LISP returns 3 to you by printing it on the screen.

```
3
3
```

You can produce the same effect by typing a floating point number:

```
3.14
3.14

-9/5
-9/5
```

Negative numbers and all other kinds of numbers are treated the same way. In fact, LISP goes to great lengths (which can be studied in detail later) to make most things that you might think of as a number acceptable as such: 3/4 is treated as a number, but under most circumstances 3g4b is not.[1]

Characters and strings are two data types normally used for manipulating text. Characters are objects that start with a #\ (sharpsign-backslash). There are only a limited number of them, including the ninety-five standard printing characters from the ASCII set, and a newline character, #\newline. If you type #\a at LISP, LISP returns it to you.

```
#\a
#\a
```

Most operations treat #\a as a different character from #\A. Because of this, characters are said to be case-sensitive.

Strings are also used often in text manipulation. At this point, think of a string as an object consisting of a series of characters. The printed representation of a string begins with a double quote and ends with a double quote. Inside a string, the characters are printed just as in normal text. For example,

```
"This is a string."
"This is a string."

"This is also a string."
"This is also a string."
```

Most acceptable characters can be included in strings. For example, the newline character can be included:

```
"This is a string
with a newline inside it."
"This is a string
with a newline inside it."
```

---

[1]If the base were set sufficiently high, even 3g4b would be treated as a number. Some symbols can never be numbers. For example, AB.CD and /9 are always treated as symbols.

Note that the character #\A is not equivalent to the string "A". Later you will learn how to manipulate strings under program control. Then you can examine them in order to determine what characters occupy particular positions and, for instance, extract the character #\A from the string "A".

Thus far, you have been introduced to three data types: numbers, characters, and strings, all of which evaluate to themselves. Now let's turn to symbols and lists, which are somewhat more complicated and which constitute the core of LISP.

2.1.2   Symbols

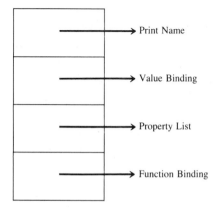

Figure 2-1. A Symbol Has Four Important Parts

A symbol is an object that has room for four parts—the print-name, the value, the function binding, and the property list.[2] See figure 2-1.

Symbols are the "words" of LISP. You can think of the value of a symbol as a noun and the function binding as a verb. The other parts of the symbol represent other "parts of speech" as well. However, the others don't fit into natural language categories as nicely.

The user can define any combination of these parts for any symbol. In ordinary speech some words, like "list," have both noun and verb forms. Other words, such as "character," have only one or the other. Just so, symbols may be used either for one part or several. The other parts need not be specified and may not, in fact, exist.

It is rare to use a symbol without a print name, so that won't be discussed. We will also postpone the subject of property lists. For now, we will concentrate on building LISP phrases by using the print name of the symbol to access its value or function

---

[2]Symbols may not be implemented simply as objects with four parts. Many implementations involve more complex schemes. However, the beginning user finds it most convenient to think of it this way.

TABLE 2-1. Some Possible Symbols and Values

Print Name	Value
APPLE	ORANGE
FOO	3.14159
DOROTHY	(63 BROWN GREEN)
MY-FAVORITE-CHARACTER	#\a
@#$%	$@%!
I-AM-A-SYMBOL	"I am a value"
MY-BANK-BALANCE	2.59

binding. Sometimes we may also want to use a symbol simply for its "face value," i.e., the symbol APPLE has meaning to the human user, in a given context, apart from any computations we might wish to perform by using that symbol.

The value of a symbol may be of any type, including another symbol. For example, although you do not yet know how to create the symbols in table 2-1, they are all possible symbol names and corresponding values.

The rules for determining what constitutes a symbol may be learned later. A good rule of thumb is that something is a symbol if it's not anything else and is followed by a space character, a newline, or a tab. Symbols are most often referred to by their print names. We might talk about "the symbol APPLE," but it is just shorthand for "the symbol whose print name is APPLE."

The symbol A is a different object from the character #\A or the string "A". The symbol is printed without any distinguishing marks such as #\. It is possible to become confused by this, because symbols are printed out more simply by LISP than characters and strings, which, after all, have to do with text (and what appears on the screen, is, after all, text). It might seem like it would make more sense if an A appearing alone were a character and the symbol were written with a special marker. Quite possibly it would; however, symbols are used far more often than characters and strings in LISP and the mechanism or rule by which an object is printed is different than what the object is.

2.1.2.1   EVALUATING SYMBOLS

A number always evaluates to itself; however, instead of returning the symbol itself, LISP uses more complex rules to determine the value of a symbol.

LISP treats symbols in various ways, depending on where it finds them. In general, it attempts to return the contents of the value cell. That is, *if no other rule applies, LISP attempts to return the value of a symbol.*

For example, the symbol with the print name "PI", usually called the symbol PI, is defined by the system to have a long floating point number as its value. LISP retrieves that value by default. Therefore, if you type:

```
pi
```

LISP types back:

```
3.1415926535897932384626433832795035L0
```

or possibly a shorter number, depending on the implementation. Case does not matter for symbols. Words typed different ways, for example, pi, PI, pI, and Pi, all have the same meaning.

There are two more essential situations in which we find symbols in LISP. In particular, *function bindings for symbols are retrieved automatically when the symbol occurs as the first element in a list* that is being evaluated. This topic will be covered in the section on lists. Second, we may wish to use symbols for the meaning of their print name to us. To do this, we must have a way of preventing evaluation. Preventing evaluation is the next topic after lists.

2.1.3   Lists

In COMMON LISP there are many ways of grouping objects together. Strings, for example, allow us to group characters together. However, the most important and versatile way to group objects is the *list*. A list looks like a sequence of objects, without commas between them, enclosed in parentheses:

```
(tables chairs lamps bookcases)
```

The parentheses identify a unit, and that unit can be used for a variety of purposes. In fact, lists provide both the primary way of storing data and the means for defining and calling functions.

A list can have any number and kind of elements, including other lists. A list can be as deeply nested as you wish. A list may also have no elements, in which case it is represented by NIL, and may be written as "()" or "NIL." These two forms are completely interchangeable. NIL is a special symbol, whose print name is "NIL" and whose value is always NIL. Table 2-2 contains some simple lists made up of the kinds of elements you have already seen.

Lists can combine different kinds of elements, as shown in table 2-3.

These lists can be considered ways to store data. For example, you might want to store your inventory as a list, or group together names and phone numbers in a list of lists.

Appropriately constructed lists can also be used to call functions in LISP. If you type any of the lists in table 2-4 to LISP, you will get an appropriate response.

When LISP evaluates a list, it evaluates every element of the list in turn; however, the first element is a special case. For one thing, the first element of a list that is a procedure call has special restrictions. It must be a symbol.[3] Instead of getting the value of the first element, LISP treats it as a verb; it gets the function binding.

In most cases, every other element in the list is treated exactly as if it had been typed in directly at top level. LISP gets the value of the other elements, using its usual rules for elements of that particular type.

Once LISP has evaluated every element in the list, it applies the function binding of the first element to the result of evaluating the other elements.

In part, the evaluation of a list means the evaluation of each element in the list according to those rules. How are these rules applied in the case of the list (sqrt 4)? SQRT is a symbol. When a symbol occurs as the first element of a list, LISP attempts to retrieve its function binding. The function binding of SQRT is code that implements the square root function for LISP. Therefore, LISP accesses this code and puts it aside, as shown in figure 2-2a.

TABLE 2-2. Some Possible Lists

(1 2 3 4 5)	a list of numbers
(A B C D)	a list of symbols
(#\A #\B #\C #\D)	a list of characters
(this is a list)	a list of symbols

TABLE 2-3. More Complex Lists

(this is (also) a list)	a list whose third element is a list
((12 eggs ((large)) (1 bread (whole wheat)) (4 pizzas (frozen with anchovies)))	a list of lists of numbers, symbols and lists
("this is a string in a list" -53)	a list of a string and a number
((beth "555-5834") (pat "555-8098"))	a list containing two lists

TABLE 2-4. Lists That Can Be Used to Call Functions

(sqrt 2)	a list whose first element is the name of a function
(+ 2 3)	a list whose first element is the name of a function
(− 6 5 4)	a list whose first element is the name of a function.

[3]Except in the case of (lambda ...). See chapter 8, Manipulating Procedures As Data.

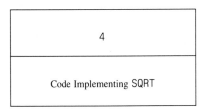

Figure 2-2a. Code Implementing SQRT Set Aside

Evaluation of the first element in a list is governed by a special rule; however, evaluation of other elements proceeds according to the usual rules for that kind of element. For example, since 4 is a number, it evaluates to itself: 4. Figure 2-2b shows how LISP puts this aside as well.[4]

4
Code Implementing SQRT

Figure 2-2b. More Code Set Aside

After LISP has evaluated all the elements in a list, it applies the function binding of the first element to the results of evaluating each of the other members of the list. That is, LISP calculates the square root of 4. Finally, it prints the result on the screen, as shown in figure 2-2c.

```
(sqrt 4)
2
```

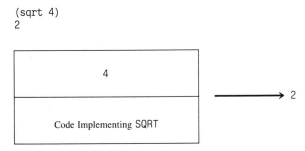

Figure 2-2c. After Evaluation of the Elements, the Calculation Is Done

It is not surprising that the result of typing (sqrt 4) at LISP is 2, but it is worth noting that almost all functions in LISP are evaluated using these rules:

LISP gets the function binding of the first element in the list.
Then it applies the function binding of the first element to the result of evaluating each element but the first one.

[4]LISP doesn't necessarily put these things aside in the same place; however, we can imagine it that way.

These rules result in a prefix notation for arithmetic in LISP. The phrase (+ 2 3) in LISP is equivalent to the arithmetic phrase 2 + 3. Likewise, (+ 2 3 4) is equivalent to 2 + 3 + 4.

How do these rules work out for the phrase (- 6 5 4)? This is what appears on the screen:

(– 6 5 4)
–3

However, we can "walk through" or imagine LISP's behavior, as in figure 2-3.

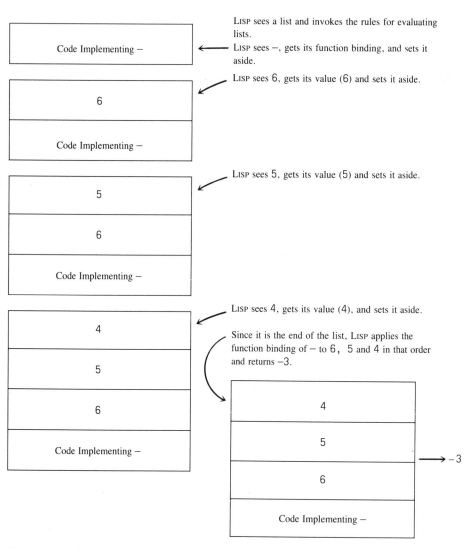

Figure 2-3. Evaluation of (– 6 5 4)

The two rules for evaluating lists in LISP have many implications besides prefix notation for the language. One point to consider is that you know that every item typed at LISP returns a value. Up until now that value has been printed on the screen. However, the values of 6, 5, and 4 are not returned to the screen directly; rather, they are made available to the list, which is the top-level item being evaluated. Only the value of the top-level item is returned to the screen.

Since lists are so central to LISP, it is impossible to discuss every extension, modification, and implication of their use and construction here. However, you have seen some basics and know in principle how LISP evaluates lists. Two more subjects based on lists await you in this chapter: the use of lists as a mechanism for storing data, and a useful model for the interior construction of lists.

2.1.4   Nested Evaluation

LISP would not be very interesting if the only things one could do with it were evaluate simple expressions. Happily, list structure lends itself to more complex expressions. If we think of lists as sentences, we can think of lists within lists as clauses.

For example, we can type in:

(+ (/ 4 2) (* 2 4))[5]

LISP evaluates this expression using the *recursive* application of the two rules for evaluation. The process is said to be recursive because the evaluation of all the smaller lists follows the same rules as the evaluation of the top-level list. (/ 4 2) is evaluated in the same way as the expression as a whole.

Once more, we can imagine the process LISP goes through, as shown in figure 2-4.

If this behavior were not so important, it would not be worth going through it in such detail. However, it is the basis of every program written in LISP. Note that no parsing or precedence rules are necessary, because the outer expression starting with + cannot be evaluated until the inner values are returned.

Every item typed at LISP returns a value; however, + has access only to the value of (/ 4 2) because the call (+ (/ 4 2) (* 2 4)) *contains* the call (/ 4 2). You can tell that the call (+ (/ 4 2) (* 2 4)) contains (/ 4 2) because the outer list defines a unit which, like a fence, encloses all its inner phrases.

2.1.5   Preventing Evaluation

When lists were introduced, you were told that they provided a means of storing data, as well as a way of calling functions. In order to manipulate lists in a useful way, you have to know other commands in addition to arithmetic ones; however, at this point,

---

[5]In COMMON LISP, * and / stand for multiply and divide.

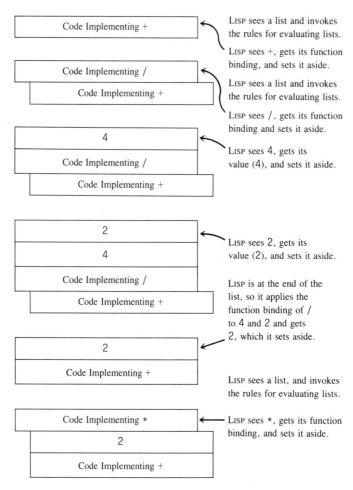

Figure 2-4. Evaluation of (+ (/ 4 2) (* 2 4))

these commands would do you no good, because you don't have a way to type in a list without LISP evaluating it immediately.

For example, CAR is the LISP command that returns the first element from a list. You might like to be able to type:

```
(car (2 3 4))
```

and get back 2. However, that won't work. If you try it, you will get an error message similar to this one:

```
(2 3 4)
 FATAL error in function EVAL
 (signaled with an error).
 Argument must be a function: 2
```

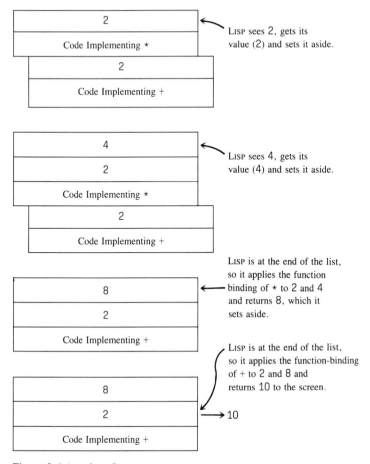

Figure 2-4 (continued).

The problem is that LISP tries to evaluate the list (2 3 4) and you don't want it evaluated. You want it passed to CAR just the way it is.

LISP provides a mechanism for preventing evaluation. Called QUOTE, it has an abbreviation—a single mark '. When this mark is placed before an object, it tells LISP to return the object itself, not its value.

Therefore, typing the following phrase produces the desired effect:

```
(car '(2 3 4))
2
```

You can use the result of this operation as an argument to other operations.

```
(+ (car '(2 3 4)) 5)
7
```

Quoting works, regardless of the contents of the list. Any list can be quoted:

```
'(+ 2 3)
(+ 2 3)

'(apples bananas 3)
(apples bananas 3)

'("This is a string." "Another string" my-favorite-symbol)
("This is a string." "Another string" my-favorite-symbol)
```

You can quote other LISP objects besides lists. The ability to quote symbols is particularly important. In theory, you can also quote numbers and strings, but quoting those objects doesn't make any difference because they always evaluate to themselves anyway.

```
'foo
foo

'apple
apple

5
5

'5
5
```

As with lists, you have to quote symbols whenever you want to prevent their evaluation, that is, to use them literally and not for their value.

Note that the mark ' is really shorthand for the invocation of an operation. That is, 'APPLE is short for (quote apple). '(a b c) is short for (quote (a b c)). Unfortunately, QUOTE is not a function but rather a special form, an item that is treated specially by LISP. Invocations of QUOTE are an exception to the rules just given for evaluating lists, because the argument to QUOTE is (obviously) not evaluated.

Sometimes it can be difficult to decide whether you must quote something or not. One way to figure it out is by analogy with natural language. As in a natural language, in COMMON LISP, there is a difference between a word and its value or meaning. The difference is rarely a problem in ordinary speech; even so, there are times when it can be confusing. For example, the phrase ''Say 'your name','' means something different from the phrase ''Say your name.'' When you say ''Say your name'' to a person, she automatically responds with the value of the phrase ''your name,'' which may be one of many different possibilities: Maria, Donnie, or R2D2, for example. Likewise, if you type only the name of a symbol to LISP, without a quote, it returns the *value* of the symbol. If there is nothing in the value cell of the symbol, LISP signals an error message. In contrast, if you say, ''Say 'your name','' a person who cooperates will respond with the literal words ''your name,'' which is equivalent to quoting in LISP.

2.2   PRETTY-PRINTING

To repeat, if you type a list at LISP, the evaluator attempts to treat it as a function and arguments to that function; it sequentially evaluates the arguments and then calls the function with their results as arguments.

LISP has many arithmetic operators, including +, −, *, /, <, >, =, < =, > =, MIN, MAX, SQRT, and ABS. You have been shown how to nest them according to the rules above. However, suppose you wanted to evaluate the following:

```
(* (/ (+ 64 11149) (− 466 4.58)) (/ 7 9) (+ 10039 234900 (sqrt 4)))
```

According to LISP, that's fine. Nonetheless, it might cause you problems because it's hard to read. To make statements like this one less confusing, LISP programmers use a convention called ''pretty-printing.'' Thus, they would type the above statement like this:

```
(* (/ (+ 64 11149)
      (− 466 4.58))
   (/ 7 9)
   (+ 10039 2349
      (sqrt 4)))
```

This convention helps people read LISP code. Without it, it would be difficult to read even your own code as you are writing it.

The major rule for pretty-printing is that arguments to the same function receive the same amount of indentation. Certain syntactic structures have their own rules for pretty-printing. As you go along, note their presentation in this book.

Pretty-printing is strange, because it is an important part of LISP, yet it is not part of the language. It is up to you to pretty-print your own procedures in the editor. Many editors offer help in doing this; for example, if there is a LISP mode in your editor, typing <LINEFEED> usually causes the cursor to indent to the proper place on the next line.

Typing LISP programs with the pretty-print convention helps you remember where you are in a given procedure. Separately, most LISPs have a program called a pretty-printer, which allows you to print code on the screen nicely when you ask to look at a function binding. Naturally, typing out a procedure inside LISP does not change the contents of your editor buffer.

Pretty-printing does not become fully useful until you know how to create procedures. The expressions mentioned thus far should be typed directly to LISP, not saved in files or worked on in an editor. Files in LISP usually consist of function and variable definitions, and it is when you are working on procedures in those files that you should pretty-print your own code.

2.3   OPERATIONS ON LISTS

Nested lists provide a powerful means of combination for LISP expressions. Thus far, you have seen how to make arithmetic combinations as complicated as you wish. Now that you have been introduced to quotation, you can also make complex lists for use as data.

Just as there are many more arithmetic functions than have been mentioned, there are many more functions for manipulating lists than the one, CAR, already mentioned. Nonetheless, CAR, CONS, and CDR are the three most fundamental list manipulators.

CONS stands for "construct" and, as its name suggests, is used to construct lists. For example,

```
(cons 'apples '(pears peaches cherries))
(apples pears peaches cherries)

(cons 'a '(b))
(a b)
```

CONS takes two arguments, a thing and a list, and returns a list in which the thing occupies the first position.

```
(cons 'a '(b c))
(a b c)

(cons 'a '())
(a)

(cons 'a nil)
(a)

(cons '(beth "555-5834") '((pat "555-8098")))
((beth "555-5834") (pat "555-8098"))
```

The first argument to CONS can be any LISP object. However, the second argument almost always has to be a list. If the second argument is not a list, you get a strange construct called a dotted pair, which will be covered in the following section.

CAR and CDR (pronounced "COULD-er") are selector functions. CAR selects the first item in a list and returns it. CDR returns a list of all the elements after the first. For example, see table 2-5.

TABLE 2-5. Comparisons of CAR and CDR on the Same Lists

(car '(a b))	(car '(a (b c)))	(car '((a b) c))
a	a	(a b)
(cdr '(a b))	(cdr '(a (b c)))	(cdr '((a b) c))
(b)	((b c))	(c)

CAR and CDR decompose lists into the arguments provided to CONS to create that list.

It is possible to decompose any list completely by successive nested applications of CAR and CDR. When evaluating the phrase

```
(car (cdr '(a b c)))
```

LISP sees the first item in the list, CAR, and then evaluates the elements in the rest of the list, which is (cdr '(a b c)). This returns (b c) as the argument to CAR, which then returns b. Thus, the CAR of the CDR is the second element in a list.

It is interesting to note that the list operations just presented reflect the way LISP itself decomposes lists. In other words, the English words ''first'' and ''rest'' can be replaced with the LISP words ''CAR'' and ''CDR'' when you consider how LISP evaluates commands:

1. Evaluate all the elements but the car of the list.
2. Apply the procedure whose name is the car of the list to the results of evaluating each element of the cdr of the list.

2.3.1   **NIL**

The last cdr of a list is always the empty list. By definition, NIL and the empty list () are equivalent, although LISP usually prints NIL. Recall that NIL is a special symbol, defined to evaluate to itself.

Consider the list (a b c). C is the last element of the list, but it is not the last cons, or sublist. To create the list above under program control, you would have to start by consing C with NIL. Then you would cons B onto the product and A onto the product of that. C is the last car in the list, but NIL is the last cdr.

If there were no special item at the end, you would have to guard against references past the end by keeping track of the length of the list. In fact, you must do that with strings. The presence of NIL at the end of every list makes it particularly easy to tell when you have come to the end of the list—you have extracted every element when the cdr of the list is NIL.

```
(cons 'c nil)
(C)
(cons 'c ())
(C)
(car '(c))
C
(cdr '(c))
NIL
(cons 'a (cons 'b (cons 'c nil)))
(A B C)
```

There is nothing to stop NIL from also being a member of the list.

```
(cons 'a (cons nil (cons 'c nil)))
(A NIL C)
```

By fiat, (car nil) is equivalent to (cdr nil), and both are equivalent to NIL. In theory, this could lead to confusion in situations such as the following:

```
(car '(nil))
NIL
(car '())
NIL
```

In practice, it is rarely a problem.

2.3.2   **Shorthand**

You may wonder why LISP uses CAR and CDR instead of mnemonic names. The names CAR and CDR were used in the first implementation of LISP because of the architecture of the IBM 704; the first item in a list was the *Contents* of the *Address Register* while the rest of the list was the *Contents* of the *Decrement Register*. COMMON LISP provides the clearer commands FIRST and REST. However, CAR and CDR persist not only because of history but also because they allow a useful kind of shorthand.

For example:

```
(car (cdr '(a b c)))
```

may be written as:

```
(cadr '(a b c))
```

and

```
(cdr (car '((a b) c)))
```

as

```
(cdar '((a b) c))
```

Also,

```
(car (cdr (cdr '(a (b (c))))))
```

may be written as

```
(caddr '(a (b (c))))
```

The rule is that each ''a'' or ''d'' represents a nested occurrence of CAR or CDR. The inside (or rightmost) occurrences are evaluated first, just as if the functions were all written out. This is permissible for up to four levels of nesting.

2.3.2.1   SITTING DOWN WITH LISP FOR THE FIRST TIME

The purpose of your first session with LISP is to give you an idea of what it is like to type things at an interpreter and get a response. In a normal session with LISP, you would expect to try out different lines of code, just as you can do here; however, in a typical session, you would do it with an eye toward writing larger bodies of code in the editor.

Most LISPs have a prompt, such as LISP>, that appears when you first start up the LISP. Some LISPs, additionally, show a prompt every time they have finished the previous command and are awaiting a new one. In either case, you can type what you want at LISP. It tries to evaluate what you have typed whenever you have typed in *complete* LISP objects (that is, you have a list with balanced parentheses or closing quotation marks on a string). Some LISPs also require that you type a <RETURN> after the end of an expression. When LISP evaluates your statement, it either returns a value or produces an error condition.

You will know when an error is signalled because you will get an error message. In many LISPs, you may have to take some special action to return from the error handler to the normal state, such as typing CTRL-G or q. You should consult the documentation for your implementation of LISP to find out how to exit the debugger.

After exiting the debugger, you can continue as if you hadn't had an error. You can type in your old statement correctly or go on to an entirely different task.

It is extremely important to notice that every COMMON LISP follows the rules presented in this chapter:

Numbers, characters, and strings all return themselves.
A quoted object returns the object.
Unquoted symbols return their values if they have any. Since you don't know how to assign a value to a symbol, most unquoted symbols you try to type in will produce an error message. Exceptions to this include NIL, T, and PI. Read error messages carefully. They indicate the problem LISP is having. As you find out more about LISP, error messages should seem more meaningful.
Unquoted lists are function calls, which are evaluated using the usual recursive rules for evaluation.

To exit LISP, type (exit).

2.4   **CONS CELLS**

We may handle unevaluated lists directly, typing them in and printing them out. However, operations such as CONS, CAR, and CDR allow us to manipulate these lists indirectly, under program control.

Why are CONS, CAR, and CDR the primitive operators, as opposed to all other possible schemes for control? For example, it might seem arbitrary that the selectors CAR and CDR divide the list into the first item and the rest. Why not have primitive operators that divide a list into the front half and the back? This division into the first and everything but the first reflects a particular model of the construction of lists inside LISP.

The function CONS "constructs" an object called a "cons cell." A cons cell has two parts, a "car" and a "cdr." A cell can be represented as a box with a division in it (see figure 2-5). The left part contains a pointer to the car and the right to the cdr.

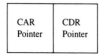

Figure 2-5. A Cons Cell

A list may be thought of as a series of cons cells in which the car points to an element of the list and the cdr to a list containing the rest of the list. For example, (a b c) can be drawn as shown in figure 2-6.

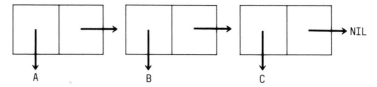

Figure 2-6. The List (a b c) Represented with a Box-and-Pointer Diagram

When CONS was introduced, you were told that it took an element and a list, and returned a list in which the element occupied the first position. That process is perfectly consistent with the idea that CONS creates a cons cell.

Consider the function call (cons 'a '(b c)). The first argument to CONS is the symbol A, the second is the list (b c). They can be drawn as in figure 2-7a.

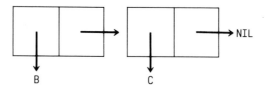

Figure 2-7a. Initial State of (cons 'a '(b c))

Now, CONS causes the construction of a new cons cell. Figure 2-7b shows how the car of this new cell points to the first argument to the function call and the cdr of the new cons cell to the second argument.

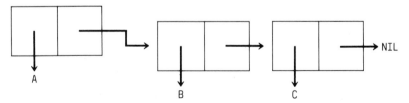

Figure 2-7b. Result of (cons 'a '(b c))

The car of the first cons cell contains an address in memory that points to the symbol A. The cdr contains the address of the next cons cell in the list. The car of the second cons cell contains a pointer to the symbol B, and the cdr contains a pointer to the third cons cell. The third cons cell contains a pointer to the symbol C in its car, and a pointer to NIL in its cdr.[6] In other words, the call to (cons 'a '(b c)) has done exactly what it was supposed to—created the list (a b c).

Box-and-pointer diagrams make explicit the presence of NIL as the last cdr of every list. In fact, a list may be recursively defined as either the empty list, that is NIL, or a cons whose cdr component is a list.

The list ((a b) c) could be represented as in figure 2-8.

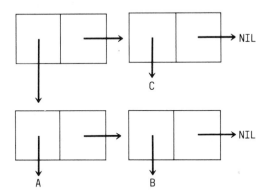

Figure 2-8. ((a b) c) Represented with a Box-and-Pointer Diagram

Again, this is perfectly consistent with the ideas that you could create this list with the call (cons '(a b) '(c)), that (car '((a b) c) is (a b), and that (cdr '((a b) c) is (c).

The box-and-pointer diagram for (a (b c)) is shown in figure 2-9.

---

[6]In LISP, unlike PL/1 or C, the terms "a pointer to an object" and "an object" are interchangeable.

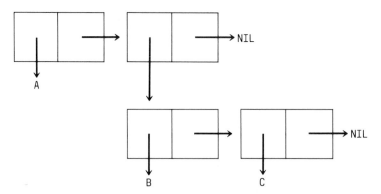

Figure 2-9. (a (b c)) Represented with a Box-and-Pointer Diagram

Thus, dividing the list into the car and the cdr is a natural process in terms of the internal construction of lists. The actual function of CONS is to construct a pair, or cons cell, with two pointers. Those pointers indicate the first and second arguments to CONS. Likewise, CAR and CDR look at a particular cons cell and return the contents of the car or the cdr pointer.

2.5   DOTTED PAIRS

Box-and-pointer diagrams are a useful aid for visualizing lists; however, you can't type a box-and-pointer diagram to the LISP interpreter. There is another way of writing lists that LISP does recognize. If we wanted to, instead of writing lists like this:

(a b c)

we can use a different convention. We can indicate each cons cell explicitly just the way each is drawn in a box-and-pointer diagram. Figure 2-10 shows (a . (b . (c . nil))), which is the list (a b c) written in dotted-pair notation. In this notation, parentheses explicitly indicate each cons cell, including the contents of its car and its cdr. The period, or "dot," indicates the division in the cell between the car and the cdr.

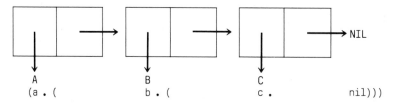

Figure 2-10. The List (a b c) in Dotted-Pair Notation

Like box-and-pointer diagrams, dotted-pair notation forces you to write out the implicit NIL that ends each list. The dotted-pair notation highlights the fact that it is not intrinsically *necessary* for the cdr of the last cons cell in a list to be `NIL`. This is the requirement for a true list; however, conceptually, it is perfectly possible to create a series of conses that do not end in `NIL`.

Not only is such a series conceptually possible, but LISP actually allows you to do it. If you call `CONS` with a second argument that is not a list, you can create a cons cell that is not part of a list. For example:

```
(cons 'a 'b)
(A . B)
(cons '(a b) 'c)
((A B) . C)
```

These constructs are called "dotted pairs." The dot signifies that an actual cons cell, rather than a proper list, is intended. In COMMON LISP the dot must appear with spaces on both sides. Figure 2-11 shows how to draw the dotted pair (a . b).

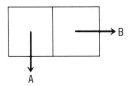

Figure 2-11. The Dotted Pair (a . b)

Figure 2-12 shows a more complex construct—a dotted pair whose car and cdr are both dotted pairs.

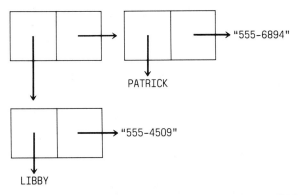

Figure 2-12. ((libby . "555-4509") . (patrick . "555-6894"))

The contents of a cons cell can be any kind of LISP object, including a dotted pair.

As it turns out, you can write combinations of lists and dotted pairs without any ambiguity. Quite often, most of a list can be written as a proper list, and then only one or two cons cells are dotted. For example, LISP would print the list above as ((libby

. "555-4509") patrick . "555-6894"). The dots appear only before a cdr that points neither to the next cons cell nor to NIL.

The construct produced by (cons '(apple ball) 'circus) is ((apple ball) . circus). The car, (apple ball), is a proper list, but the containing cons is dotted, as shown in figure 2-13. Figure 2-14 shows a list that contains two dotted pairs:

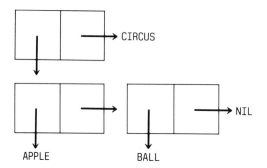

Figure 2-13. The Dotted List ((apple ball) . circus)

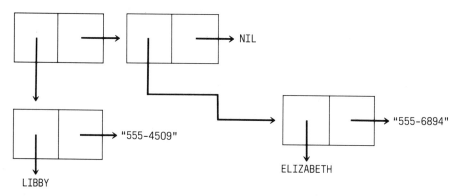

Figure 2-14. ((libby . "555-4509") (elizabeth . "555-6894"))

2.6   RETURNING VALUES

Looking back over the past pages, you will notice that at least one thing has been taken for granted: that every LISP function returns exactly one value as the result of evaluation.[7] This is an extremely important given. Whenever an object is typed to LISP from top level, its value is printed on the screen. Otherwise, the value is passed to the function that called it.

---

[7]If you open Steele to the chapter detailing the arithmetic operators, you will see that some functions return more than one value. Do not be confused by this; LISP is very flexible. It should not be surprising that there is an advanced way to change even the most basic restrictions of the language. However, the essential idea is that one value is returned by each expression, and you can use all those functions as if they return only the first value.

Observe that the expression (car (cdr '(a b c))) is not the same as the two expressions (car '(a b c)) (cdr '(a b c)). In the first case, the value returned by the inner operation is given as an argument to the outer. In the second case, the two operations have absolutely no relationship to each another.

Understanding the manner in which values are returned is the single most important key to understanding LISP.

CHAPTER HIGHLIGHTS

Major Concepts

- Symbols, numbers, characters, strings and lists are all LISP objects.

  –Numbers, characters, and strings evaluate to themselves.

  –All quoted objects evaluate to the objects themselves.

  - Quoting is accomplished by placing a single quote to the left of the object.

  - This is an abbreviation of (quote <item>).

- A symbol evaluates to its value unless:

  –it is quoted or

  –it is the first element in a list.

- Evaluation of a list means evaluation of everything in the list according to the following recursive rules:

  –Evaluate all the elements but the car of the list.

  –Apply the procedure whose name is the car of the list to the results of evaluating each element of the cdr of the list.

- Operations are performed by evaluating lists.

  –Even calls to arithmetic functions are evaluated according to these rules.

  –The rules for evaluating lists result in prefix notation for LISP.

- CONS can be used to *construct* lists.

- CAR and CDR can be used to *select* information from lists.

- Nested operations allow you to perform complicated arithmetic calculations and list decompositions.

- Lists are constructed out of cons cells.

  –Box-and-pointer diagrams are one means of describing cons cells pictorially.

  –Dotted-pair notation is another way of representing cons cells.

–Dotted pairs are cons cells that may not be proper lists. LISP prints conses as dotted pairs when they are not proper lists.

Summary of New Syntax

```
(+ number number ...)
(- number number ...)
(* number number ...)
(/ number number ...)
(sqrt number)
(exit)
(cons obj obj)
(car list)
(cdr list)
(quote object)
'object
(min number number ...)
(max number number ...)
```

Suggested Reading

The following sections in Steele, COMMON LISP, complement the material covered in this chapter: chapter 2, Data Types, 2.1–2.4, 2.5.2; chapter 7, Control Structure, 7.1.1; chapter 12, Numbers, 12.3–12.5; chapter 15, Lists, 15.1.

EXERCISES

1. Each of the following items may be a list, a number, a symbol, a character, a string, or a malformed expression. Identify each accordingly.
   a. ATOM
   b. (this is an atom)
   c. (this is a symbol)
   d. ((a b) (c d))
   e. 3
   f. (3)
   g. (list 3)
   h. (/ (+ 3 1) (- 3 1))
   i.)(
   j. "I am the walrus."
   k. #\k
   l. #\k#\o
   m. "LISP is #\easy"

n. ((()))

o. (mary "328-8195" john "874-6060" gregory "497-8282")

p. (() ())

q. ())(

r. ((ABC

2. What is the difference between typing the following objects to LISP:

a. A

b. 'A

c. #\A

What will LISP do in each case?

3. Evaluate the following expressions:

a. (/ (+ 3 1) (– 3 1))

b. (* (max 3 4 5) (min 3 4 5))

c. (min (max 3 1 4) (max 2 7 1))

4. Evaluate the following expressions:

a. (car '(d g t))

b. (cdr '(p g r s))

c. (car '((purple 1) (green 2)))

d. (cdr '((performances 3) (size-of-hall 250)))

e. (car (cdr '((silver gold) (oil vinegar))))

f. (cdr (car '((#\a #\b) ("c" "d"))))

g. (cdr (car (cdr '((("smith" 35) ("brown" 26))
                    (("jones" 45) ("marsh" 43))))))

h. (car (cdr (car '((1 b) (1 d)))))

i. (car (cdr (car (cdr '((rooms 3.5) (floor 4th)
                         (available "january 1"))))))

j. (car (car (cdr (cdr '((rock "Layla") (opera "Magic Flute")
                         (classical "Handel Flute Sonatas"))))))

k. (car (car
        (cdr '(cdr ((rent (+ (* 1/3 actual-rent) parking-space))
                    (food (+ groceries restaurants))
                    (heat (* 15 avg-temp-of-month)))))))

l. (car (cdr '(cdr (cdr ((a b) (c d)
                         (e f)))))))

m. (car '(car (cdr
              (cdr ((tomatoes (2 bottles)) (pickles (4 bottles))
                    (strawberry-jam (6 bottles)))))))

n. '(car (car (cdr (cdr ((strawberry-protein-drink)
                        (vitamin-d) (acerola)))))))

o. (cadr '((#\esc #\ q) (#\return #\tab)))

p. (+ (car '(1 2 3)) (cadr '(4 5 6)))

q. (caddr '(apples (bananas peaches) pears))

r. (car '(1 2 3))

5. What element of a list is extracted by CADR?

6. Write the sequence of CARs and CDRs that will pick the symbol CHAIR out of the following lists:

a. (table lamp chair shelf)

b. ((table lamp) (chair terminal))

c. (terminal (shelf) ((chair)) (((sofa))))

d. ((((table) file-cabinet) chair) telephone)

7. Which of the following are valid dotted pairs?

a. (x . y)

b. (a . (b . c))

c. A2

d. (x . y2 . z)

8. First draw the following lists as box-and-pointer diagrams; then write them as dotted pairs.

a. (apples bananas strawberries)

b. (values (first-value second-value))

c. ((my-symbol "my-string") #\C)

9. Draw box-and-pointer diagrams for the following lists:

a. (a (b c) d (e (f)) g)

b. (canary (parrot dove) pigeon (chicken (duck)))

10. Draw box-and-pointer diagrams for the following lists, dotted pairs, and combinations.

a. (patrick gregory james)

b. (brian . eric)

c. (marc . (steve . harold)) Note that LISP prints this as (marc steve . harold)).

d. (ruth (myrna . florence))

e. ((marlene . elizabeth) . irene)

f. ((peanut . butter) . (butter . (jelly . bread))) Note that LISP prints this as ((peanut . butter) butter jelly . bread)).

g. (((chocolate . cake) . cinnamon) . icing)

h. ((beth . "555-5843") (patrick . "555-1293"))

    i. ((beth "555-5843") (patrick "555-1293"))

    j. ((x . nil) . (y . (z . nil)))

    k. ((x) y z)

    l. (nil . nil)

11. First write out the dotted pairs shown by the box-and-pointer diagrams in figures 2-15 and 2-16. Then reduce any you can to real list format.

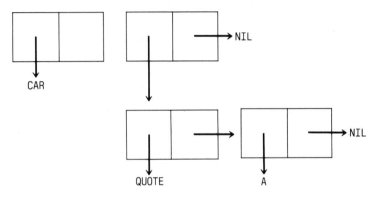

Figure 2-15

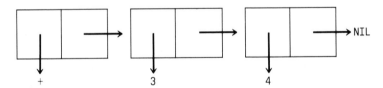

Figure 2-16

Chapter 3

WRITING PROCEDURES

The previous chapters laid groundwork. You should now have a small vocabulary of LISP "words," especially "verbs," or functions, and know how to use those words to make sentences, or commands.

This chapter is concerned with combining commands together in order to write procedures. A procedure is a recipe for accomplishing something.

As you set out to write useful procedures, you will find it necessary to increase your vocabulary of basic LISP expressions. Three general classes of operators—predicates, operators on lists, and conditionals—are introduced in this chapter.

In the course of learning to use these forms, you will encounter exceptions to LISP's rules for evaluation. That is, when calling some of these forms, you will give them unquoted lists or symbols, and yet these will not always be evaluated. Since most of the constructs presented in this chapter are used frequently, it is important to learn how LISP treats each one.

3.1   WHAT IS A PROCEDURE FOR?

A LISP procedure is like a paragraph: a good procedure, like a good paragraph, contains the "right amount" of information. Furthermore, just as in natural language, procedures sometimes stand on their own, and sometimes their content is determined by their place in a larger structure, a "book," or program. For the moment, we will consider procedures in isolation. Later, we will go on to whole programs.

Another similarity between procedures and paragraphs is a stylistic one. A well-written procedure, like a clear, concise paragraph, is devoted to a single "topic." You can write procedures that are as small or as large as necessary for the conceptual structure of your program. The important point is that a procedure should perform exactly one identifiable action.

The analogy between procedures and paragraphs breaks down not when we think about how to write procedures, but when we think about how to use them. LISP procedures differ from natural language paragraphs in two important ways:

- They have names.
- They can be used in more than one place.

In other words, we write procedures in order to enlarge LISP's "vocabulary" by defining new "words," or commands.

New commands are used exactly the same way as the commands that LISP provides, such as CAR, CDR, or *. This is a very important and powerful aspect of the language. Your commands are available anywhere, just as + is available anywhere. The only factor dictating which command you call at a given time is your own sense of purpose.

Since there is no predetermined "main" procedure in LISP, and you are working in an interpreted environment, procedure names are even more important as a means of structuring your thoughts and intentions than they are in other languages. The name of the procedure identifies its single action or purpose.

3.2   DEFINING PROCEDURES

DEFUN (*DE*fine *FUN*ction) is the primitive that allows you to define your own procedures. A function definition has three parts: a function name, an argument list, and a body. Here is a template for DEFUN:

```
(defun function-name (arguments)
       body)
```

You could define your own procedure to return the square of a number as follows:

```
(defun square (x)
  (* x x))
SQUARE
```

What happens when you type in this call to DEFUN? The most important effect is that a symbol, SQUARE, is created, and something appropriate is deposited in its function cell. This "appropriate thing" is not entirely simple, but it is in essence the recipe for performing the procedure, as represented by the body of the procedure.

The call to DEFUN must return a value, just as all LISP objects return a value when evaluated. The value of a call to DEFUN is the symbol whose function binding was defined. You rarely, if ever, use DEFUN because of the value it returns. It is the so-called side effect of function definition that is important.

When writing the body of a DEFUN, you should type each form as you would if you typed it directly to the interpreter. When a procedure defined with DEFUN is called, the body of the DEFUN is executed, in order, as if its elements had been typed in at top level, except that any variables are bound to the values with which the procedure was called.

The value returned by a call to a procedure created with DEFUN is the value of the last form executed in the body of the DEFUN. Since (* x x) is the last form in the body of this DEFUN, when you call SQUARE, you can expect its value to be the result of evaluating (* x x).

Once you have "defined" a function with DEFUN, you can use it just as you would use CAR, CDR, or DEFUN itself:

```
(square 3)
9

(square 2)
4

(square (square 3))
81

(square (+ −4 5 (/ 3 1)))
16
```

During each of these function calls, X is bound to the result of evaluating the second argument in the list (square <something>).

Procedures can have virtually as many arguments as you want. For example, you can use SQUARE to write another procedure, SUM-OF-SQUARES. SUM-OF-SQUARES has two arguments, X and Y.

```
(defun sum-of-squares (x y)
   (+ (square x) (square y)))
SUM-OF-SQUARES

(sum-of-squares 2 3)
13
```

You don't have to have any arguments in a function definition. For example:

```
(defun hi ()
   (print "hello"))

(hi)
"hello"
"hello"
```

PRINT is a function that prints a string on the terminal screen. Again, the list (print "hello") is typed in the definition just as you would type it at top level. When HI is called, "hello" appears on the screen twice. The first time, it is the action of the PRINT command. The second time, it is the value of the function HI. The following function illustrates this point.

```
(defun print-two-return-one (first second)
  (print first)
  (print second))
```

```
(print-two-return-one "hello" "How are you?")
"hello"
"How are you?"
"How are you?"
```

When PRINT-TWO-RETURN-ONE is executed, (print first) is executed with FIRST bound to the value "hello". Therefore, "hello" is printed on the screen. Then (print second) is executed. This prints "How are you?" on the screen. However, since (print second) is also the last form executed in the body of the DEFUN, its value is the value of PRINT-TWO-RETURN-ONE, and "How are you?" appears a second time.

Here is a procedure that takes advantage of LISP's flexibility about symbols. Since 2ND is an acceptable symbol, it is also an acceptable procedure name.

```
(defun 2nd (list)
  (car (cdr list)))
```

```
(2nd '(first second third))
second
```

The variable here is called "list" to remind users that a list is the desired input. It is important to give procedures and variables names that help you keep track of their functions.

Functions can be redefined by calling DEFUN again with the same function name. If you want to, you can even redefine system functions. However, do not be surprised if your LISP system ceases to operate as expected.

3.2.1   **Functions, Macros, and Special Forms**

It is important to remember LISP's fundamental rule for evaluation:

Any unquoted list will be treated by LISP as containing a function call followed by expressions that evaluate to the arguments to that function call.

However, look back at the template for DEFUN. Now consider the definition of SQUARE. There is an important exception to the normal rule about evaluation in a DEFUN. *None of the arguments are evaluated when DEFUN is run.*

You can tell that they cannot be evaluated when DEFUN is run because if they were they would produce errors. The symbol SQUARE isn't quoted; if it were evaluated, LISP would look for its value unsuccessfully. If (x) was evaluated according to the rule, it, too, would produce an error because it's the first item in a list, but X doesn't have a function binding.

In other words, LISP does something special. As with QUOTE, you are facing an exception to the usual rules for evaluation. Here is some terminology:

- A *function* is a procedure that obeys the usual rules for evaluation. Functions are created with DEFUN, although DEFUN is not a function.

- A *macro* is a thing like a procedure in that it is created in a special way according to special rules. Chapter 11 will explain how you can create macros yourself.

- A *special form* is a procedure about which LISP has special knowledge; there are very few of them. You cannot write your own special forms.

- A *form* refers to an expression that, under the appropriate conditions, can be evaluated without error.

The words "procedure" and "operator" are used in this book to refer to functions, macros, or special forms. In LISP, a procedure is a thing that you write to express a process. There is no particular opposition between the terms "function" and "procedure," since everything in LISP returns a value, and functions usually express a process.

The major difference at this point is that a macro or special form may not evaluate all its arguments while all of the arguments to a function are always evaluated. DEFUN is a macro.

Operators that do not evaluate all their arguments may have a special syntax. The effects of these syntactic templates are usually that LISP seems to require "extra" parentheses. The parentheses around the arguments in a DEFUN are a good example of this. If you have trouble learning the syntax of forms with templates, such as DEFUN, COND, DO, and LET, remember that, even in these exceptions, the parentheses usually identify a *unit*. For example, how would LISP know where the variable list ended and the body began if there weren't parentheses around the variables in a DEFUN?

In summary, most operators behave like CAR and +; however, some special forms or macros may want arguments to fit into a certain pattern or template. These differences are all the "syntax" there is to LISP.

Do not deduce from the foregoing that you should memorize which operators are functions and which are macros as the key to understanding LISP. The important issues are behavior, not labeling. The important questions are, "Which arguments to this procedure get evaluated?" and "Does this procedure require a certain template?"

For the truly curious, Steele specifies which procedures should be functions, special forms, or macros in implementations of COMMON LISP.

3.3   OPERATIONS ON LISTS

You've already seen the primitive operators CONS, CAR, and CDR. In addition, there are other useful operators.

LIST is like CONS, except that:

- it automatically makes a list out of its arguments;
- it takes as many arguments as you want.

The essential difference between CONS and LIST is captured in the contrasts shown in table 3-1. CONS creates one cons cell; however, LIST makes a list from whatever it is given.

TABLE 3-1. Comparison of LIST and CONS

(list 'a 'b)	(list 'a nil)
(a b)	(a nil)
(cons 'a 'b)	(cons 'a nil)
(a . b)	(a)

Unlike CONS, LIST can also take more or less than two arguments:

```
(list 'a 'b 'c)
(A B C)
(cons 'a (cons 'b (cons 'c nil)))
(A B C)
(list 'a)
(A)
```

You can always make anything produced by LIST by using enough calls to CONS. However, LIST may sometimes be more convenient.

LIST makes a list containing all its arguments, even if the last argument is already a list:

```
(list '(a b) '(c))
((A B) (C))
```

NTHCDR takes two arguments: an index number and a list, and returns the nth cdr of the list. It is exactly as if you applied CDR n times.

```
(nthcdr 0 '(Jesse Michael Andrew))
(JESSE MICHAEL ANDREW)

(nthcdr 1 '(Jesse Michael Andrew))
(MICHAEL ANDREW)

(nthcdr 2 '(Jesse Michael Andrew))
(ANDREW)

(nthcdr 3 '(Jesse Michael Andrew))
NIL
```

LAST gets the last cons from a list.

```
(last '(Cindi Paul Michael))
(MICHAEL)
```

```
(last '(Cindi Paul (Michael)))
((MICHAEL))
```

All these functions can be built from CONS, CAR, and CDR in a few lines.[1] They are provided in COMMON LISP because they are used so often.

3.4   SEQUENCE FUNCTIONS

In addition to these operators, there is another class of functions, called *sequence functions*, which work not only on lists, but on any ordered sets, including strings. Sequence functions are called *generic* because they work on more than one data type.

LENGTH is a sequence function that counts the number of elements in a sequence.

```
(length '(apples oranges bananas))
3
```

```
(length "apples")
6
```

```
(length '(apples (oranges bananas) pears))
3
```

```
(length "apples (bananas)")
16
```

```
(length 'apples)
Fatal error in function LENGTH, signalled with ERROR.
Argument must be a sequence but received APPLES.
```

In theory, you could use LENGTH to write a definition for LAST:

```
(defun my-last (list)
   (nthcdr (- (length list) 1) list))
MY-LAST
```

```
(my-last '(a b c))
(C)
```

No one would ever actually write LAST this way because it is inefficient. LENGTH has to count the whole list and then NTHCDR has to re-examine it. The reason you have to subtract 1 from the length is that NTHCDR takes a zero-based index number as reference, but LENGTH returns a counting number.[2]

---

[1] You do need some other functions as well. For example, in order to write LAST you have to know where to find the end of a list.

[2] This difference may be confusing at first, but it works nicely in conjunction with iterating over the elements in a string. Since the LENGTH is always one greater than the last index element, the iteration can stop when the counter is equal to the length.

REVERSE takes a sequence as an argument and returns a sequence with all the elements of the original sequence reversed.

```
(reverse '(apples oranges bananas))
(BANANAS ORANGES APPLES)
```

```
(reverse "apples")
"selppa"
```

```
(reverse "madamimadam")
"madamimadam"
```

```
(reverse '(a (b c) d))
(D (B C) A)
```

REVERSE is almost sufficient to write a program that creates palindromes:

```
(defun almost-a-palindrome (list)
  (list list (reverse list)))
```

```
(almost-a-palindrome '(1 3 5 7))
((1 3 5 7) (7 5 3 1))
```

It is considered poor style to use a name for both a function and a variable in such close proximity as to be confusing; however, if you find the use of LIST in the definition of ALMOST-A-PALINDROME incomprehensible, take the time to review what you know about symbols. It is very important to remember that the function binding and value of a symbol are completely separate. ALMOST-A-PALINDROME used the operation LIST, and also the variable LIST. LISP retrieves one or the other, depending on how the symbol is used. If the symbol is the first element in a list, LISP gets its function binding. Otherwise, LISP gets its value.

You can make ALMOST-A-PALINDROME return true palindromes by introducing the function APPEND. APPEND takes two or more lists and concatenates them:

```
(defun palindrome (list)
  (append list (reverse list)))
```

```
(palindrome '(1 3 5 7))
(1 3 5 7 7 5 3 1)
```

ELT returns the *n*th index element of a sequence.

```
(elt '(apples pears peaches) 0)
APPLES
```

```
(elt '(apples pears peaches) 2)
PEACHES
```

```
(elt "why a duck?" 0)
#\w
```

The last example illustrates that when you decompose a string, you get character objects.

Like NTHCDR, ELT uses index numbers. Therefore, you will get an error if you try to do the following:

```
(elt '(apples pears) (length '(apples pears)))
```

If you wish to get the last element, you must write:

```
(elt '(apples pears) (- (length '(apples pears)) 1))
```

3.4.1   *Self-documentation Functions*

You've already been introduced to a number of operators, and there are more to come. You may anticipate some difficulty remembering all of LISP's functions and their arguments and the order of their arguments. Two self-documentation functions in COMMON LISP can be helpful in this task.

APROPOS takes a string or a symbol as an argument and returns a list of every symbol whose name contains that name as a substring. For example, if you give LISP the line (con 'a 'b), you will get an undefined function error. At this point you might check whether you have the name exactly right by typing:

```
(apropos 'con)
```

LISP prints out the name of every symbol whose name contains the string "CON", including CONS, ACONS, CONSTANT, and many others.

DESCRIBE takes any LISP object and prints a description of that object. For example, if you type

```
(describe 'nthcdr)
```

you will get results like:

```
It is the symbol NTHCDR
Value:    unbound
Function: a compiled-function
   NTHCDR number list

     This function returns the nth cdr of the list.
```

Different implementations of LISP give you different amounts of information in response to a call to DESCRIBE. As you learn more LISP, more of the information should seem meaningful but, even at this stage, some of it can prove helpful; for example, here it might be useful to check that the number argument to NTHCDR comes before the list argument.

APROPOS and DESCRIBE are useful when you are trying to find out about forms without having to read the code or look in hard-copy documentation. In this sense, a description is like on-line documentation, a comment that is available inside LISP.

3.5   PREDICATES

So far we have operations on data, but we don't have any way of finding out anything about the data under program control. One class of functions that allows you to find out about data is called "predicates."

Predicates are functions without side effects that return either NIL for false or some non-nil value (often "T") for true. T and NIL are special kinds of symbols—they evaluate to themselves. NIL, incidentally, is also the value of the empty list. The equation of these two meanings of NIL is arbitrary, but convenient.

3.5.1   Simple Predicates

Some important predicates test for the types of their arguments:

- LISTP tests to see if its argument is a list. If so, it returns T; otherwise, it returns NIL.

- NUMBERP tests to see if its argument is a number.

- ATOM takes a LISP object and tells whether it is an atom. In COMMON LISP, the term "atom" refers to any object that is not a cons cell.

A common convention in LISP is to end predicate names with a language-specific symbol. In general COMMON LISP predicate names end with the letter *P* (for predicate). This convention is by no means hard and fast, as you can see by considering ATOM, but adhering to it will make your programs more readable.

The following phenomenon is noteworthy:

```
(listp nil)
T

(atom nil)
T
```

This happens because NIL is both a symbol and the empty list. Another result of NIL's dual role is that there are two cases in which you might like to test whether something is NIL. You might like to be able to look at a list and tell whether it's empty, that is, NIL, or not. You might also like to look at the result returned by a predicate, that is, either NIL or non-NIL, and invert that value. There are two functions, NULL and NOT, that perform the same actions but are used in different circumstances.

Both NULL and NOT take a LISP object as argument and return a non-NIL value if the object is NIL, but NIL if it is anything else. NULL is most often used to test whether or not a list is empty:

```
(null nil)
T

(null '(a b c))
NIL
```

ENDP is also provided for this purpose. ENDP differs from NULL in that it signals an error if it is called on anything but a cons cell or NIL. NOT, on the other hand, is used to invert the value returned by a predicate:

```
(not (equal 'true 'false))
T
(not (= 10 10))
NIL
```

3.5.2   **Equality**

LISP provides different kinds of equality predicates. For example, = tests for equality of numbers, while CHAR= tests for equality of characters.

In addition to type-specific equality predicates, there are four important general tests for equality. These tests take any two LISP objects as arguments, and check to see if they are equal. Naturally, two objects must be of the same type to be equal.

You might wonder why four tests are necessary. Why doesn't one test serve the purpose? The reason is that there are degrees of equality. Most of the time you want to know whether two objects look the same, but sometimes you have to know whether they are actually the same object in memory. That accounts for two of the tests. Then, as it turns out, minor modifications on each of the major tests make two more surprisingly useful functions.

EQUALP and EQUAL are the more general equality predicates. A good rule of thumb is that two objects are EQUALP or EQUAL if they look the same when they are printed on the screen.

Thus, as you might expect:

```
(equal 'true 'true)
T
(equal 'true 'false)
NIL
(equalp 3.14159 3.14159)
T
(equalp "This is a string."
        (cadr '(9 "This is a string." 'what)))
T
```

The difference between EQUAL and EQUALP is that EQUALP is less pure in its definition of equality. Simply because it turns out to be useful, EQUALP ignores differences in case in characters and type in numbers. For example,

```
(equal 3 3.0)
NIL
```

but

```
(equalp 3 3.0)
T
```

Also,

```
(equal "YES" "yes")
NIL
(equalp "YES" "yes")
T
```

The last example demonstrates one of the instances in which EQUALP is useful; if you had solicited user input, you probably wouldn't care whether it was typed in lower-, or uppercase letters, or both.

The other two equality predicates, EQ and EQL, tell you whether you are looking at two objects in memory or at one. Why do we need operators like these? Consider the following calls and returned values:

```
(equal (cons 'a 'b) (cons 'a 'b))
T
(equalp (cons 'a 'b) (cons 'a 'b))
T
```

These might look like good answers, and for many purposes they are; however, consider that CONS is a function that performs an operation. Each time you call CONS, a new cons cell is constructed. The contents of two cons cells may be the same or look the same but they are separate objects, just as twins who have DNA with the same sequence of nucleotides are still separate persons. EQ and EQL test whether two objects not only *look* alike, but whether they are the *same*, that is, located in the same place in memory. In other words,

```
(eq (cons 'a 'b) (cons 'a 'b))
NIL
(eql (cons 'a 'b) (cons 'a 'b))
NIL
```

This kind of test is important when you have the ability to change objects. Then you often need to know whether both items will change, or only one.

As EQUALP is sometimes more convenient than EQUAL, so, too, is EQL a slightly relaxed version of EQ. EQ and EQL can be similar or relatively different, depending on the particular implementation; for example, (eq #\A #\A) may return T, but (eql #\A #\A) always returns T.

One characteristic difference between EQ and EQL has to do with the way LISP handles numbers. EQ returns true only if two numbers are in exactly the same location in memory. Small numbers (called FIXNUMS) have a direct representation in memory, and are always EQ. However, LISP must create a representation for very large numbers (BIGNUMS) and for floating-point numbers each time they are used. Therefore, they may not be EQ. It turns out that much of the time you won't care about exact identity in that case. Furthermore, the number of fixnums is implementation-dependent. EQL is provided as a portable version of EQ. For example, in a given implementation of LISP:

```
(eq 1234567890 1234567890)
```

may return T or NIL, but:

```
(eql 1234567890 1234567890)
```

always returns T.

The difference between EQ and EQL is rather subtle; in fact, the only reason for introducing EQL at this early stage is that it is the default test that LISP functions use to test for equality.

Sometimes it can be difficult to remember what each of these four operators does. A useful observation is that the more letters in the name of the predicate, the looser its demands for equality. EQUALP finds more things equal than does EQUAL. EQUAL is far more accepting than EQL, and EQL is less strict than EQ.

3.5.3   **Other Predicates**

MEMBER is another useful predicate. MEMBER takes two arguments, an item and a list, and searches the list for the item. Like many other predicates, MEMBER is also a selector; if it finds the item, it returns everything in the list, starting with the item. That way, you don't have to search the list twice, once to find out if the item is present and then to retrieve the item.

```
(member 'patrick '(beth "555-5886" patrick "555-0504"))
(PATRICK "555-0504")
(member 'apple '(fruit-list pear peach mango))
NIL
```

MEMBER examines only the top-level list; it does not find objects in sublists.

```
(member 'apple '(fruit-list (apple orange)
                 (pineapple banana) apple mango))
(APPLE MANGO)
```

Notice that MEMBER must do an internal check for the equality of two objects. The test it uses here is EQL, because EQL is the default used by all COMMON LISP primitives that test for equality.

Y-OR-N-P and YES-OR-NO-P are two predicates that print a string (usually a question) on the screen and wait for user input. If the user types Y or YES (depending on which predicate is used), they return T. If the user types N or NO, they return NIL.

In general, use YES-OR-NO-P when you are asking a question with serious consequences and want the user to spend more time answering it. For example:

```
(y-or-n-p "Print this file?")
```

but

```
(yes-or-no-p "Delete all your files?")
```

You can write procedures using predicates:

```
(defun test (input)
  (numberp input))
TEST

(test 'foo)
NIL

(test 3)
T

(defun what-is-it? foo)
   (print foo)
   (y-or-n-p "I don't know.  Is it bad luck? "))
WHAT-IS-IT?

(what-is-it? 3)
3
I don't know.  Is it bad luck? y
T
```

It turns out that predicates alone in procedures that stand by themselves are not very interesting because predicates aren't useful unless you can take different actions based on the results they return. Therefore, the next step will be to introduce constructs that affect flow of control.

3.6   CONDITIONAL AND LOGICAL CONDITIONAL OPERATORS

To use the information that predicates give us, we must be able to alter the behavior of our programs in response to the result of a predicate. Conditional expressions are a means of doing this. Additionally, the logical conditional operators AND and OR can serve this function, although, along with NOT, they are intended for use in an explicitly logical context.

3.6.1   Conditional Expressions

IF, COND, and CASE are the three basic conditionals.

IF is the simplest conditional expression. It consists of three parts: a test; a "then" clause, which is evaluated if the test returns T; and, optionally, an "else" clause, which is evaluated if the test returns NIL. A template for an IF statement follows:

```
(if test then-eval-me else-eval-me)
```

This procedure takes an object and uses IF to tell us whether it is a number or not:

```
(defun feed-me-numbers (object)
  (if (numberp object) "It is a number.  More, please."
    "Hey, that's not a number!"))
FEED-ME-NUMBERS
```

```
(feed-me-numbers 'foo)
"Hey, that's not a number!"
```

```
(feed-me-numbers 3)
"It is a number.  More, please."
```

CONTAINED-IN? returns either TRUE or UNTRUE, based on its finding data in a list.

```
(defun contained-in? (item list)
  (if (member item list) 'true 'untrue))
CONTAINED-IN?
```

```
(contained-in? 9 '(2 4 6 8 ten))
UNTRUE
```

```
(contained-in? 'apples
   '(weight 135 eyes green favorite-food apples))
TRUE
```

If the "else" clause is left out, and the value of the predicate is NIL, the value of the IF statement is NIL.

```
(defun less-than-10 (x)
  (if (< x 10) "Found it!"))
LESS-THAN-10
```

```
(less-than-10 10)
NIL
```

Although IF is very useful when you have to make a binary decision, it has two limitations. IF is not useful when there are more than two alternatives, or when more than one action has to be taken in response to a given alternative.

For example, if you wanted to write a procedure that, given a number, takes one action if the number is less than 10, another if the number is greater than 10, and a third if the number is 10, you would have to do it as follows:

```
(defun guess-the-age-of-my-car (x)
  (if (< x 10) "It's older than that."
    (if (> x 10) "It's younger than that."
          "You got it.")))
GUESS-THE-AGE-OF-MY-CAR
```

This is not too bad, but what happens if you want to add another test? For example, you might want to add a check for numbers over 90, since there are no cars over ninety years old:

```
(defun guess-the-age-of-my-car (x)
  (if (< x 10) "It's older than that."
    (if (> x 90) "That's impossible."
      (if (> x 10) "It's younger than that."
          "You got it."))))
GUESS-THE-AGE-OF-MY-CAR
```

This procedure is already becoming difficult to read. In such situations, you turn to the more general conditional COND. Unlike IF, COND allows any number of predicates with any number of "then" clauses.

COND has a more complex template than IF because more information is carried in the pattern of the construct.

```
(cond (test consequent consequent consequent ...)
      (test consequent consequent consequent ...)
      (test consequent consequent consequent ...)
            .
            .
            .
      (t consequent consequent consequent ...))
```

A COND statement consists of a series of clauses, delimited by parentheses. The first element in each clause should be a predicate. The succeeding elements in the clause are *consequents*. COND evaluates the predicates of each clause in turn. If a predicate returns NIL, it skips the consequents and evaluates the next predicate. When a predicate returns a non-NIL value, COND evaluates all the consequents and returns the value of the last one. If no predicate returns a non-NIL value, then the value of the COND is NIL.

Thus, GUESS-THE-AGE-OF-MY-CAR could be rewritten as follows:

```
(defun guess-the-age-of-my-car (x)
  (cond ((< x 10) "It's older than that.")
        ((> x 90) "That's impossible.")
        ((> x 10) "It's younger than that.")
        ((= x 10) "You got it.")))
GUESS-THE-AGE-OF-MY-CAR
```

Customarily, the predicate for the last clause in a COND is T. Since T evaluates to itself, the consequents of this clause are evaluated automatically if none of the other clauses have succeeded. This allows us to provide an "otherwise" clause, a sort of catch-all.

Like GUESS-THE-AGE-OF-MY-CAR, IS-IT-TALL? takes a number as argument and prints a different message, depending on whether the number is less than, equal to, or greater than 60.

```
(defun is-it-tall? (height)
  (cond ((< height 60) "It's not tall.")
        ((> height 60) "It's too tall.")
        (t "It's just right.")))
```

SIZE-OF-PACKAGE determines the value of its predicates with nested operations:

```
(defun size-of-package (length height width)
  (cond
    ((> (+ length height width) 100)
     (print "The post-office won't mail it.  It's too big."))
    ((= (+ length height width) 100)
     (print "You just made it."))
    ((< (+ length height width) 100)
     (print "No problem."))))
```

You can have as many consequents to a clause as you wish. For example, if you want to print the cubic size if the package is too big, you add a clause to do that:

```
(defun size-of-package (length height width)
  (cond
    ((> (+ length height width) 100)
     (print "The post-office won't mail it.  It's too big.")
     (print (* length height width)))
    ((= (+ length height width) 100)
     (print "You just made it."))
    ((< (+ length height width) 100)
     (print "No problem."))))
```

Now each clause has two consequents.

CASE is another conditional operator. Its syntax is similar to COND's:

```
(case keyform
    (keylist consequent consequent ...)
    (keylist consequent consequent ...)
    .
    .
    .
    (t consequent consequent ...))
```

CASE differs from COND in that, instead of running a series of tests, CASE starts by evaluating the "keyform" to produce a "key object." It then looks for the keylist that *contains* the key object. That is, it takes the first clause, and checks to see whether the keylist contains the key object. If it does, CASE evaluates the consequents; otherwise it proceeds to the next clause, just as COND would.

CASE is useful when you have sets of objects and are trying to classify one object. For example, the following example has two classes of objects: vowels and other characters. You wish to print "an" if the object starts with a vowel, and "a" if the object starts with any other character (i.e., a consonant).

```
(defun a-or-an (string)
  (case (elt string 0)
    ((#\a #\e #\i #\o #\u #\y) "an")
    (t "a")))
A-OR-AN

(a-or-an "cow")
"a"

(a-or-an "avocado")
"an"
```

A-OR-AN takes a word in string form as argument. The keyform is (elt string 0). Therefore, the key object is the first character in the string: #\a for avocado, #\c for cow.

Once CASE has the key object, it checks to see whether it is a member of the first set, which is the set of all vowels. If it is, CASE evaluates the consequents. That evaluation causes LISP to return the appropriate indefinite article for use with words beginning with vowels. If the key object is not a vowel, LISP goes on to the next clause, which is T. Therefore, it returns the indefinite article for use with words beginning with consonants.

Here is an example of CASE used with more clauses:

```
(defun bottom-line-on-Shakespearean-play (symbol)
  (case symbol
    ((Macbeth) "Somebody's head gets cut off.")
    ((Hamlet) "Somebody gets poisoned.")
    ((Titus-Andronicus)
     "Somebody's tongue gets cut off.")
    ((Lear) "Somebody gets hanged.")
    ((Coriolanus Julius-Caesar)
     "Somebody gets stabbed to death.")
    (t "Oh, that must be one of the others.")))
```

Like MEMBER, CASE uses the EQL test for equality. Note that CASE does not evaluate the elements in the key list. In this sense, CASE is a more special purpose construct than COND.

3.6.2   *Error Messages*

Information is the key to debugging. One significant way to get information is through reading error messages. LISP error messages contain several key pieces of information; reading an error message is often enough to give you an idea of what to do next. You can test your hypotheses quickly because most implementations of COMMON LISP give you access to an editor, and the ability to redefine functions easily.

At minimum, LISP error messages supply the name of the function in which the error occurred. They usually give you other information as well. For example, they may tell you whether the error was fatal or continuable and what type of difficulty LISP encountered. It can be hard to decipher error messages at the beginning, because LISP can tell you only what is wrong in relationship to its process of evaluation. It has rules, and you get a message when it can't execute according to its rules. This may not correspond to your perception of the program.

The exact text of error messages differs from implementation to implementation; however, the things that cause the errors generally do not, and a few errors are common. For example, calling an operator on an inappropriate argument:

```
(car 1)
```

generates an error like "The argument to CAR must be a list, but it was 1 instead." The message tells you that the error occurred while LISP was trying to evaluate CAR, and that the problem was that the argument was not a list. It also tells you what the faulty argument was: 1. Frequently this happens when you have called CAR or CDR one more time than you intended to, as in (car (car (car '((why (not)))))).

Some implementations of LISP leave you in a special state after delivering an error message—in the debugger or in a recursive invocation of LISP. You may be able to continue as if nothing was different; however, consult the documentation for your LISP to learn how to return to top level.

Here are more typical LISP errors. Typing:

```
(car '(a) 'b)
```

causes a "Too many arguments, 2, to function CAR." message. Typing:

```
y
```

causes the error "Symbol has no value: Y." This error often means that you meant to use the symbol as the name of a function, but have forgotten to type in one or more parentheses defining the function call, as in (print car '(a b c)). LISP tries to evaluate the form, but finds a reference to a symbol that doesn't have a value. A specially insidious version of this problem occurs when you forget one of the parentheses in a COND, as in (cond (eq x 3) (print "hello")). Likewise, if you have an extra set of parentheses, you usually get a "symbol has no function binding" error message.

Naturally, it is always important to read error messages carefully; however, it is particularly important when you are starting to learn LISP, in order to make sure that you really understand LISP's process of evaluation.

3.6.3 *Logical Conditional Operators*

AND, OR, and NOT are similar to logical operations; however, because they do not necessarily evaluate all their arguments, AND and OR can be used to effect flow of control.

AND takes a series of forms as arguments. It evaluates each one until it reaches one that returns NIL. Then it stops and returns NIL. If every form has a non-NIL value, it returns whatever the last form returns.

```
(and (equal 'apple 'orange) (= 1 1))
NIL
(and (equal 'apple 'apple) (= 1 1))
T
```

You can prove to yourself that AND does not evaluate all its arguments with a side-effecting operator like PRINT:

```
(and (print "At the beginning.") nil (print "At the end."))
At the beginning.
NIL
```

You can take advantage of this property to avoid doing certain tests unless you know that they are appropriate:

```
(and (listp x) (eq (car x) 3))
```

If X is not a list, you do not want to call (car x) because you will get an error.
    BOTH-START-WITH-VOWELS? calls STARTS-WITH-VOWEL-P, which is similar to A-OR-AN:

```
(defun both-start-with-vowels? (string1 string2)
  (if (and (starts-with-vowel-p string1)
           (starts-with-vowel-p string2))
      "Both start with vowels."
    "At least one word didn't start with a vowel."))
BOTH-START-WITH-VOWELS?
(defun starts-with-vowel-p (string)
  (if (member (elt string 0) '(#\a #\e #\i #\o #\u #\y))
      t nil))
STARTS-WITH-VOWEL-P
(both-start-with-vowels? "cow" "avocado")
"At least one word didn't start with a vowel."
```

OR also takes a series of forms as arguments, evaluating each one from left to right. However, when any form evaluates to non-NIL, OR stops and returns that value. If every form evaluates to NIL, OR returns NIL.

```
(or (equal 'apple 'orange) (= 1 1))
T
(or (equal 'apple 'apple) (= 1 1))
T
(or (equal 'apple 'orange) (= 2 3))
NIL
```

OR stops evaluation when it encounters a clause that succeeds:

```
(or nil nil (print "Third one.") (print "Fourth one."))
"Third one."
"Third one."
```

ONE-STARTS-WITH-A-VOWEL? is a variant on BOTH-START-WITH-VOWELS?

```
(defun one-starts-with-a-vowel? (string1 string2)
  (if (or (starts-with-vowel-p string1)
          (starts-with-vowel-p string2))
      "At least one starts with a vowel."
    "Neither starts with a vowel."))
ONE-STARTS-WITH-A-VOWEL?

(one-starts-with-a-vowel? "cow" "avocado")
"At least one starts with a vowel."
```

Conditional statements and logical operators give us the power to write complex procedures. However, as they sometimes have overlapping functionality, initially it can be difficult to decide which construct to use.

For example, let's consider a procedure that gives us the absolute value of a number. We could state the rule we want to implement as follows:

```
if x > 0, return x
if x < 0, return −x
if x = 0, return
```

We could write this quite directly with a COND statement:

```
(defun my-abs (x)
  (cond ((> x 0) x)
        ((< x 0) (− x))
        ((= x 0) x)))
```

However, we need not express this process as a three-way choice because we take the same action in two out of the three cases. Therefore, we could write:

```
(defun my-abs (x)
  (cond ((< x 0) (− x))
        (t x)))
```

This representation suggests an alternate one in an IF statement:

```
(defun my-abs (x)
  (if (< x 0) (− x) x))
```

These three definitions for ABS are equivalent. The last one is preferable because it is easier to read. The fact that an IF is used defines the issue as a binary choice, with one action taken in each case.

Alternatively, we could write:

```
(defun my-abs (x)
  (or (and (< x 0) (- x))   ; poor style
      x))
```

Even though this procedure has the same functionality as any of the conditional statements above, we would not want to use it because it isn't very clear. Someone who knows LISP can read any of the previous definitions of ABS much more quickly than he can read the one that uses OR and AND. Normally, you use logical conditional operators to express logical operations.

3.7   **FORMAT**

Consider the following program:

```
(defun size-of-parcel (length height width)
   (cond
     ((> (+ length height width) 100)
      (print "The post-office won't mail it.  It's too big."))
     ((= (+ length height width) 100)
      (print "You just made it."))
     ((< (+ length height width) 100) (print "No problem.")))))
```

Presently you cannot easily improve this procedure to make it print out the total size of the parcel as part of the message printed on the screen. You could call PRINT several times in a row, but PRINT prints a newline after its argument. What you need is a function that allows you to construct strings, on the fly, out of other kinds of data. FORMAT is just such a function.

Therefore, we redefine SIZE-OF-PARCEL to use FORMAT:

```
(defun size-of-parcel (length height width)
  (cond ((> (+ length height width) 100)
         (format t "The post-office won't mail it.
                 ~a inches is too big."
                 (+ length height width)))
        ((= (+ length height width) 100)
         (format t
           "You just made it.  100 inches is the maximum."))
        ((< (+ length height width) 100)
         (format t
           "No problem. ~a is below The maximum size allowed."
           (+ length width height)))))
SIZE-OF-PARCEL

(size-of-parcel 10 20 30)
No problem.  60 is below the maximum size allowed.
NIL
```

FORMAT is a powerful generalized string manipulation function.[3] FORMAT takes the following series of arguments:

```
(format destination control-string arg1 arg2 ...)
```

There are three kinds of arguments to a FORMAT statement. The first indicates where the formatted string is to be delivered. It can be either printed to the screen or returned as a value.[4] The second argument is a string, usually containing special commands called "directives." The remaining arguments consist of all the information to be used by the directives.

If the destination is T, the string is printed to the screen. If the destination is NIL, the string is returned as a value.

Most directives are like variables or place holders within a string. They start with a ~ (tilde). Most directives look for the next argument in the argument part of the FORMAT command and process that command according to their own rules.

Different directives are used to process different kinds of data to be inserted in the string. For example, ~a keeps a space open for an ASCII string, while ~d causes an integer to be printed in decimal radix. ~S prints a symbolic expression, that is, a LISP object, in such a way that LISP will read it back in correctly. Not all directives take arguments. For example, ~% inserts a newline character inside the string, ~| inserts a form-feed character, and ~<RETURN> tells LISP to ignore any spaces, returns, and tabs until the next character.

The arguments to the directives should occur in order, so that each group of arguments matches up with its directive. For example:

```
(format nil "Look, up in the sky!")
"Look, up in the sky!"
(format nil "It's a ~A!" "bird")
"It's a bird!"
(format nil "It's a ~A!  It's a ~A!" "bird" "plane")
"It's a bird!  It's a plane!"
(format nil "~a~%~a" "who?" "what?")
"who?
what?"
```

Any LISP object may be substituted for a ~A. Therefore, the following returns a string that is similar to the one returned in the previous example:

---

[3] FORMAT is LISP's equivalent of C's PRINTF or FORTRAN's FORMAT, but is more powerful and complicated.

[4] There is a third alternative value for the first argument to FORMAT; the string can be written to something called a stream. Streams are discussed in chapter 6.

```
(format nil "~a~%~a" 'who? "what?")
"WHO?
what?"
```

The symbol WHO? is capitalized because LISP stores the names of symbols as capital letters by default. The directives ~(and ~) convert the characters that occur between them to lowercase:

```
(format nil "~(~a~)~%~a" 'who? "what?")
"who?
what?"
```

For contrast, here are two versions of a program, one that returns the string as a value and one that prints it on the screen:

```
(defun print-something (something)
   (format nil "This is ~a string." something))
PRINT-SOMETHING
```

```
(print-something "your")
"This is your string."
```

```
(defun print-something (something)
  (format t "This is ~a string." something))
PRINT-SOMETHING
```

```
(print-something "your")
This is your string.
NIL
```

It can be difficult to remember whether "T" or "NIL" means "print to the screen" when they occur as the first argument to FORMAT. If you think of NIL as a mnemonic for negation, then it may be helpful to remember that you give an argument of NIL to FORMAT if you do not want to look at the string on the screen and an argument of T if you do.

By employing FORMAT, you can improve the procedure A-OR-AN:

```
(defun select-a-or-an (string)
  (case (elt string 0)
     ((#\a #\e #\i #\o #\u #\y) (format nil "an ~A" string))
     (t (format nil "a ~A" string))))
(select-a-or-an "animal")
"an animal"
```

```
(select-a-or-an "cow")
"a cow"
```

Now, instead of just printing "a" or "an," SELECT-A-OR-AN uses FORMAT to put together a string consisting of the article and the word given as an argument.

3.8   EDITORS AND FILES

Now that you have seen how to write function definitions, and have sufficient knowledge to begin writing programs, you will probably want to start saving your programs.

To keep your programs, you must write them in a file and save the file, using an editor, the way you would any text file. These files consist primarily of function definitions that you may then invoke. Programmers accustomed to languages such as PASCAL or FORTRAN in which one must define a main function to call all others, will probably find files of LISP functions confusing initially but may eventually come to prefer them.

You can load a file into LISP with the LOAD command. The contents of the file are evaluated as if you had typed them in by hand. LOAD takes one argument, a string containing the name of your file in whatever format is appropriate for your system. For example, on a machine that runs the VMS operating system, to load the file "myfile.lsp" you might type:

```
(load "myfile.lsp")
```

Under VMS, files containing interpreted LISP code usually have the second name LSP; other operating systems have other conventions for naming files.

Many implementations of LISP provide their own general-purpose, screen-oriented text editors, which provide a variety of features that make them particularly useful, if not essential, for writing LISP code.

The editors' most important feature is the help they provide with the balancing of parentheses. Whenever you type a right parenthesis, the cursor briefly flashes over the matching left parenthesis. Other important features may include a pretty-printer, which helps with the indentation of LISP code.

Many of these editors can be invoked directly from LISP. Editors with this feature often provide the ability to send code directly to LISP without first saving out the whole file and loading it in. This means that you can easily work on a single procedure contained in a file of other procedures, switching back and forth between the editor and the interpreter for testing and writing. Of course, you still have to save the file if you expect to be able to use the program again.

You should find out what features your editor provides. It is well worth learning to use a new editor for the purposes of writing LISP code if that editor provides you with any of the features mentioned above. Although editors are too implementation-dependent to discuss in more detail here, close association between the editor and LISP is essential to the usefulness and fun of working in the LISP environment. A book cannot demonstrate interactivity effectively, yet as the introduction stated, the single most important aspect of LISP for the new user is the short amount of time between discovering a problem and being able to try a new solution. A convenient editor is crucial to this process.

3.9 MODULARITY

We have covered a lot of ground. At the beginning of this chapter, three or four functions had been presented, but no information about how to write procedures using them had been given. Since then, you've learned not only how to write procedures but also about such aids as predicates, sequence functions, conditionals, and FORMAT.

Procedure writing is the fundamental activity in LISP. Almost everything in this book has to do with writing procedures. However, you don't usually write procedures in isolation from one another. Programs are made up of procedures that use one another, just as SUM-OF-SQUARES called SQUARE.

Why did we make SUM-OF-SQUARES call SQUARE rather than putting the computation (* x x) right there? This is a very small illustration, but it was done that way because it is more modular. SQUARE performs a clear, identifiable, separate action from SUM-OF-SQUARES.

The ability to distinguish between different levels of abstraction is not something that is unique to LISP, but LISP's tools and environment are most helpful to programmers who want aid with that kind of thinking.

Creating modular programs is not easy. It is not merely dividing problems into parts, but rather dividing them into meaningful parts. What information does a particular procedure need to have? What is the one result you want to from it? Since you can call every procedure by name from the interpreter, you can test each procedure in isolation to see if it satisfies its contract. The LISP environment is tailored to support modular debugging.

CHAPTER HIGHLIGHTS

Major Concepts

- DEFUN is used to create functions.
- Predicates are used to find out something about data.
  - Predicates are functions that typically have no side effects and whose values are interpreted as meaning either "true" or "false."
  - In LISP, NIL means "false"; anything else, including T, means "true".

- Conditionals and logical operators decide which forms to evaluate based on values returned by tests.
- Error messages reflect LISP's process of evaluation.
- Most LISP programs are written in editors and saved in files that can be loaded into LISP.
- Functions should be modular and be given accurate, meaningful names.

Summary of New Syntax

```
(defun function-name (argument-list)
      body)
(list obj obj ...)
(nthcdr index list)
(last list)
(length sequence)
(reverse sequence)
(append list list ...)
(elt sequence index)
(apropos string)
(describe obj)
(listp obj)
(numberp obj)
(atom obj)
(not obj)
(null list)
(= number1 number2)
(char= char1 char2)
(eq obj1 obj2)
(eql obj1 obj2)
(equal obj1 obj2)
(equalp obj1 obj2)
(member obj sequence)
(y-or-n-p string)
(yes-or-no-p string)
(case keyform
    (keylist consequent consequent consequent ...)
    (keylist consequent consequent consequent ...)
      .
      .
      .
    (t consequent consequent consequent ...))
(cond (test consequent consequent ...)
    (test consequent consequent ...)
      .
      .
    (t consequent consequent ...))
(if test then-clause else-clause)
(and form1 form2 ...)
(or form1 form2 ...)
(format destination control-string directives)
(load string)
```

Suggested Reading

The following selections from Steele, *COMMON LISP*, complement this chapter: chapter 5, Program Structure, 5.3; chapter 6, Predicates, 6.1–6.4; chapter 7, Control Structure, 7.6; chapter 14, Sequences, 14.1; chapter 15, Manipulating List Structure, 15.1–15.2, 15.5; chapter 23, File System Interface, 23.4.

EXERCISES

Be sure to read over the solutions provided in the back of the book, even after you have a solution that works. Ask yourself whether your solution differs from the model in function or only in format.

1. Predict what the following expressions will evaluate to.

   a. `(= 'foo 'bar)`

   b. `(equalp 'foo 'bar)`

   c. `(equalp 3 4)`

   d. `(defun foo (x)`
      `   (equal (car x) (car '(a b c))))`
      `(foo '(a b c))`

   e. `(foo (cadr '(b (c) d)))`

   f. `(listp '(3 4 5))`

   g. `(numberp nil)`

   h. `(numberp pi)`

   i. `(atom nil)`

   j. `(listp nil)`

   k. `(null (cdar '((d) e)))`

   l. `(null (cddr '(sunday monday tuesday wednesday thursday)))`

   m. `(if t 3 2)`

   n. `(eql #\A #\A)`

   o. `(member 'the`
      `        '(what do you know about (the green one?)`
      `          (the other one?)))`

   p. `(length (member 'the`
      `                '(what do you know about (the green one?)`
      `                  (the other one?))))`

2. Write a procedure that, given the radius of a circle, returns a list containing the radius, the circumference, and the area.

3. Write a procedure that returns the average of two numbers.

4. Draw box-and-pointer diagrams showing each of the arguments to APPEND and the

list that is returned in the following call:

```
(append '(a (b c) (e ((f)))) '((g h) i r))
```

5. Write a procedure called SCHEDULE that takes a weekday as argument and retrieves a list of your commitments on that day.

6. Write a procedure called DRESS-FOR-SUCCESS that takes a list of items or attributes of clothing and gives you advice about what not to wear with the items in the list. For example, if you called it with the argument (shirt pants dress-shoes), it might print out "Don't wear plaids too." and "Don't wear white socks." Write the procedure so that it checks for more than one condition. That is, it should check the list for stripes and for dress-shoes, or for whatever items you can think of.

7. The procedure A-OR-AN takes a string and returns it with the appropriate indefinite article in front of it:

```
(defun a-or-an (string)
   (case (elt string 0)
      ((#\a #\e #\i #\o #\u #\y) (format nil "an a" string))
      (t (format nil "a a" string))))
```

However, it doesn't work for all cases because the character #\a is different from the character #\A. Expand A-OR-AN to check for uppercase letters as well as lowercase ones.

8. Given table 3-2, Postal Rates, write a procedure that takes the weight of a package and the zone of its destination and tells you how much it costs to send it at first and fourth class. Do not hesitate to use support procedures.

TABLE 3-2. Postal Rates

Weight	First Class				Fourth Class				
	Zone 1, 2, 3	4	5	6	1, 2	3	4	5	6
1.0	2.24	2.24	2.24	2.34	1.55	1.61	1.70	1.83	1.99
2.0	2.54	2.70	2.88	3.09	1.55	1.61	1.70	1.83	1.99
3.0	3.01	3.25	3.53	3.85	1.63	1.73	1.86	2.06	2.30
4.0	3.49	3.81	4.18	4.60	1.71	1.84	2.02	2.29	2.61

Chapter 4

VARIABLES

Variables were introduced informally in chapter 3. That was appropriate because, in well-structured LISP programs, variables are created most often in the argument list of a function definition. However, LISP offers a variety of ways to create variables, with very fine control over what part of the program can use them. In this chapter, the subject of variable creation leads to the subject of changing the values of variables already created.

It is necessary to introduce two new terms before talking about variables in more detail. A *binding* is the pairing of a variable and a value. An *environment* is the collection of bindings that are accessible at a given time. These include:

- all the variables in the argument list of the function currently being executed bound to the values with which the function was called, and the variables bound by iteration and such local binding forms as DO and LET, which will be introduced shortly;

- all the bindings that existed in the environment in which the object that uses the variable was defined;

- possibly some other variables, which are called special variables, and their values.

All three items will be discussed in this chapter.

Every time a function is executed, it is executed in a new environment. The new environment consists of:

- the environment in which the function was defined;

- the variables in its argument list bound to the values with which it was called.

The environments of two different functions may be similar. For example, if you define two functions at top level, both are defined in the same environment. Therefore, if one calls the other, the only differences between the environments that exist at the time of execution are the variables in the variable lists bound to their respective values.

4.1   VARIABLES CREATED WITH DEFUNS

Variables created in the argument list of a DEFUN, that is, its *formal parameters*, are usually local to the function. They are bound, whenever the function is called, to the arguments with which it was called. They can be used during the execution of the text of the function but cannot be used after the function call is over or by functions called by the function in question.

A simple function such as the following can be used to demonstrate that the variable STRING is bound during execution:

```
(defun simple (string)
   string)
SIMPLE
(simple "This is a string.")
"This is a string."
```

It is not bound elsewhere:

```
string
Error:  The symbol STRING has no value.
```

In COMMON LISP, variables bound in the argument list of a function cannot be used during the execution of functions called by the current function. For example, calling SIMPLE, as defined below, will signal an error because STRING has no value inside SIMPLE:

```
(defun less-simple (string)
   (simple))
LESS-SIMPLE
(defun simple ()
   string)
SIMPLE
```

This should mesh well with intuitions formed by work in traditional block-structured languages; however, it may seem strange to those who have studied LISP before. In most previous dialects of LISP this example would have "worked."[1]

4.2   LET AND SHADOWING

Variables created inside DEFUNs are local to the function and bound to the values with which the function is called. The variables in the variable list of a DEFUN should hold information that the function must get from the outside world.

LET allows you to add more local variables to the set given when the procedure was called. This is particularly useful when you employ a value, yielded by a calculation, more than once inside a function and do not wish to repeat the calculation.

[1]It is possible to ask for a variable to be scoped dynamically, a topic that will be discussed later in this chapter.

4.2.1   **LET Statements**

Here is a template for a LET statement:

```
(let ((variable-name value)
      (variable-name value) ...)
   body)
```

There are two parts to a LET statement: a variable assignment part and a body. The variable assignment part, like the variable list of a DEFUN, is set off by parentheses. However, the variable assignment clause of LET is somewhat more complex than the corresponding part of a DEFUN.

There is a series of clauses inside the variable assignment section of a LET. Each clause consists of a list containing a variable name and a form to be evaluated. When the LET statement is called, the form is evaluated, and the variable name is bound to the value returned.

The body of a LET is much like the body of a DEFUN. Operations inside the body of the LET are said to be evaluated in the environment of the LET. Variables created this way are *local* to the LET statement. They cannot be used outside the LET statement, just as variables created in DEFUN cannot be used outside the text of the body of the DEFUN.

```
(let ((a 3) (b 4))
  (+ (sq a) (sq b)))
25
```

Like a function created with DEFUN, LET returns the value of the last form evaluated in its body.

Here is a function that, given the diameter of a circle, returns its area:

```
(defun circle-area (diameter)
   (let ((radius (/ diameter 2)))
     (* radius radius pi)))
CIRCLE-AREA
(circle-area 4)
12.566370614359172953850373533118011L0
```

The procedure SIZE-OF-PARCEL, which was an example of COND in chapter 3, can be rewritten to take advantage of LET:

```
(defun size-of-parcel (length height width)
   (let ((total-size (+ length height width)))
     (cond
       ((> total-size 100)
        (print "The post-office won't mail it.  It's too big."))
       ((= total-size 100)
        (print "You just made it."))
       ((< total-size 100)
        (print "No problem.")))))
```

One important thing to realize about LET is that it binds its variables in parallel, not in sequence, which means that if you call ADD-SOME, in the following example, with an argument of 3, Y will have a value of 4:

```
(defun add-some (x)
  (let ((x (+ x 2))
        (y (+ x 1)))
    y))
```

This is not a question of one X taking precedence over another (an issue to be discussed in the next section). Instead the X bound in the LET is invisible at the time that Y's value is determined, because all the value forms are evaluated first, before the assignments are done.[2]

4.2.2   Debugging Aids

LISP provides several ways to find out what is happening during program execution. First of all, LISP's construction provides a great deal of implicit support for debugging. Since the process of LISP evaluation is predictable and LISP is interpreted, it is easy to set up predictions and then test them. You can always type lines of LISP code directly to the interpreter. You can test out particular lines, particular functions, and groups of functions in isolation from the complexity of the entire program. If you have an editor that works with LISP, you can make changes to programs and test the changes easily.

Additionally, the stepper, the tracer, and the debugger are features provided by LISP explicitly for debugging. As with the editor, the exact design of the stepper and the debugger is implementation-dependent; however, they are crucial pieces of the LISP environment.

The step function, or "stepper," is used to execute a program one step at a time, allowing you to examine the sequence of functions called and values returned. Since this highlights the order of evaluation, it is most useful for tracking down flow of control and variable access problems.

Most steppers have a set of special-purpose commands. Typically, you tell the stepper to evaluate the next expression by typing N (for next) or <RETURN>. However, you should check the documentation for your particular LISP system.

Given the function ANY-SHORT-FUNCTION,

```
(defun any-short-function (x y z)
       (print (+ x y z))
       (let ((w 1))
          (print w)
          (print y)))
ANY-SHORT-FUNCTION
```

---

[2]There is a construct called LET* that is just like LET, except that variable bindings are done in sequence. If ADD-SOME were written with LET* instead of LET, Y would have a value of 6.

an interaction with a typical stepper might look like this:

```
(step (any-short-function 1 2 3))
: #11: (ANY-SHORT-FUNCTION 1 2 3)
Step 1> <return>
: : #15: (BLOCK ANY-SHORT-FUNCTION (PRINT (+ X Y Z)) (LET (#)
(PRINT W ...)))
Step 2> <return>
: : : #22: (PRINT (+ X Y Z))
Step 3> <return>
: : : : #27: (+ X Y Z)
Step 4> <return>
: : : : : #32: X ==> 1
: : : : : #31: Y ==> 2
: : : : : #30: Z ==> 3
: : : : ==> 6
6
: : : ==> 6
: : : #21: (LET ((W 1)) (PRINT W) (PRINT Y))
Step 3> <return>
: : : : #27: (PRINT W)
Step 4> <return>
: : : : : #32: W ==> 1
1
: : : : ==> 1
: : : : #26: (PRINT Y)
Step 4> <return>
: : : : : #31: Y ==> 2
2
: : : : ==> 2
: : : ==> 2
: : ==> 2
: ==> 2
2
```

The indentation of each line corresponds to the depth with which the associated expression is nested. When you tell the stepper to go on, evaluation of the phrase it has just printed commences. Notice that function calls and the values they return are lined up vertically.

The stepper allows you to track and control LISP's process of evaluation. Some steppers provide a lot more information than others. For example, the rather mysterious numbers in the output above correspond to items called "frames," which happen to represent each instance of a function call and its associated environment. In this case, the system has tried to suppress irrelevant frames, so that the frame numbers appear to skip. The crucial point, however, when looking at information provided by any debugging tools, is to concentrate on extracting relevant information.

TRACE and UNTRACE are the macros that implement the tracer. TRACE takes the names of the functions you wish to trace as its arguments. After you have called TRACE on a function, whenever that function is called and whenever it returns a value, a message is printed on the screen. For example, define the function TALK, and call it from the function SOCIAL-INTERACTION:

```
(defun social-interaction (mood)
  (if (not (eql mood 'friendly))
      (howl))
    (talk))    ;  doesn't do what author thinks it does
(defun talk () (print "howdy"))
(defun howl () (print "Arghh!!"))
```

Each time you run SOCIAL-INTERACTION it prints HOWDY on the screen. Now you can TRACE TALK and check whether it is being called in situations where you don't expect it:

```
(trace talk)
(TALK)

(social-interaction 'foul)
"Arghh!!"
#12: (TALK)
"howdy"
#12=> "howdy"
"howdy"
```

In this example, the value returned is unimportant, but, in the next chapter, we will consider situations in which that information is valuable. Because TRACE does not evaluate its arguments, you don't have to quote the function name with which you call it.

When you no longer want to trace a given function, you can turn off tracing with UNTRACE:

```
(untrace talk)
```

You have already seen two important debugging tools: STEP and TRACE. In addition, there is the debugger itself, which is a program for examining LISP's *control stack* at the time an error is produced.

The control stack is the place where incomplete function calls and their environments are stored while waiting for other nested functions to be evaluated. As in the stepper, each frame inside the control stack corresponds to a particular function call and its arguments. The control stack as a whole captures the dynamic process that LISP is going through in evaluation.

The top of the stack is the frame containing the most recent function LISP has encountered; the bottom is the frame containing the earliest one.

In most LISP debuggers, as you move up and down the stack, you can query the debugger about the value of variables at every level. You can also return a value or values from any level. When you return a value, you are popped out of the debugger just as if you had returned in the normal fashion from the function whose value you are returning.

Take the time to find out how the debugger associated with your LISP works. You probably won't want to learn every command immediately, but being able to move up and down and pick out relevant features is extremely useful.

One thing to remember when looking at the stack is that it contains only information about outstanding computations. If an item has already been evaluated, and a value returned, the value may be on the stack ready to be used, but there won't be any evidence of the complexity involved in calculating that value.

4.2.3   **Shadowing**

Remember that every time a LISP function is called, a new environment is created. This suggests that it might be interesting to look at the association between particular functions calls and their environments in more detail. Environment diagrams provide a way of representing this relationship.

For example, consider the following function definition:

```
(defun phrase (x y)
  (format nil "his ~a, his ~a~%" x y))
```

We can represent an instance of PHRASE as shown in figure 4-1. One side of this diagram shows the body of the procedure PHRASE, the other, all the bindings accessible to PHRASE.

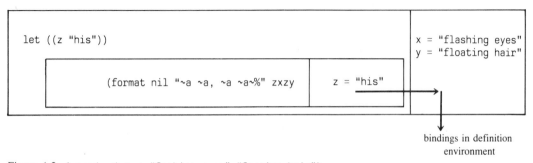

Figure 4-1. (phrase "flashing eyes" "floating hair")

Like a DEFUN, a LET statement also has a variable-value list and a body. However, the values of the variables in a LET statement are specified by the LET statement itself.

Now consider the following modification of PHRASE:

```
(defun xanadu-phrase (x y)
  (let ((z "his"))
    (format nil "~a ~a, ~a ~a~%" z x z y)))
```

Figure 4-2. (xanadu-phrase "flashing eyes" "floating hair")

In this situation, there is a LET that contains references both to Z, which is defined in its own environment, and to X and Y, which are defined in the environment in which the LET was defined. See figure 4-2.

XANADU-PHRASE behaves in a fairly straightforward fashion, but what happens when you have a variable in an inner environment with the same name as a variable occurring in the outer environment?

```
(defun hamlet (phrases)
  (let ((phrase (car phrases)))
    (format t "~a or not ~a~%" phrase phrase)
    (let ((phrase (cadr phrases)))
      (format t "That is ~a.~%" phrase)))))
```

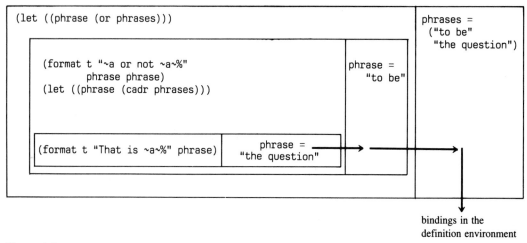

Figure 4-3. (hamlet '("to be" "the question"))

If you create a variable of the same name as a variable outside the LET, the value used in the LET is the value created by the LET. This is called ''shadowing'' and is diagrammed in figure 4-3. The instance of PHRASE inside the inner LET shadows the instance of PHRASE that occurs in the outer LET. Therefore, when you run the call (hamlet "to be" "the question"), the following appears on the screen:

```
to be or not to be
That is the question.
NIL
```

Note that the variable assignment part of the LET is placed outside the environment created by the LET. This corresponds to the fact that the variable assignment inside a LET is done in parallel and outside the environment of its body. This turns out to be useful because it means that you don't have to think about the order of your variable/

value pairs; however, from time to time, it can give surprising results:

```
(defun buggy-hamlet (phrases)
  (let ((phrase (car phrases)))
    (format t "~a or not ~a~%" phrase phrase)
    (let ((phrase (cadr phrases))
          (second-phrase phrase))
      (format t "~%That is ~a.~%" second-phrase)))))
(hamlet '("to be" "the question"))
to be or not to be
That is to be.
NIL
```

This example is worth examining closely because the next time we consider parallel assignment will be in the context of much more complicated syntax, that of the DO-loop. Note that it is implicit that after you exit the body of the LET, you still have access to the environment of the DEFUN.

4.3   VARIABLES: SCOPING AND GLOBAL VARIABLES

The beginning of this chapter listed three kinds of variables that can be referred to in a LISP function:

- all the variables in the argument list of a function, or the variable binding part of any form that creates local variables;
- all the variables that existed in the environment in which the function was defined;
- possibly others, called special variables.

You have seen examples of the first two categories. Variables created in the argument list of a function, or in the variable binding part of a LET, are accessible from within the text of the body of the form. Inside the environment of a LET, you can access variables created in an enclosing function because those variables existed in the environment in which the LET was created.

Sometimes when writing a LISP function, you may want to refer to the value of a variable that is not a member of the argument list of that function. Such a variable is called a *free variable*.

Rules that determine when and where a variable may be referred to are called *scoping rules*.

4.3.1   Scoping

The COMMON LISP specification states that variables, unless otherwise declared, are *lexically scoped*. Lexical scope is the name for the behavior mentioned earlier by which the bindings of the variables in the argument list of a function are visible only within the text of that function. To give another example:

```
(defun my-function (n)
   (1+ n))
MY-FUNCTION
```

In MY-FUNCTION, the argument list is (n), so there is only one formal parameter, N. The fact that COMMON LISP is lexically scoped means that the binding of N may be referred to only within the body of MY-FUNCTION.

Suppose we redefine MY-FUNCTION, and define MY-OTHER-FUNCTION like this:

```
(defun my-other-function (n)
   (my-function))
(defun my-function ()
   (1+ n))
```

Now MY-FUNCTION refers to the variable N, which is not one of its formal parameters but is a formal parameter of MY-OTHER-FUNCTION. Is this reference legal? The COMMON LISP specification says that it is not.

The reference above is illegal if the binding of N created in the call to MY-OTHER-FUNCTION is lexically scoped, because N is bound only while the *text* of MY-OTHER-FUNCTION is being executed. The text of MY-FUNCTION is not contained in the text of MY-OTHER-FUNCTION, so N's binding is not visible while it is being executed.

This differs from some previous versions of LISP, such as MACLISP, in which variables are dynamically scoped. Lexical scoping is generally preferable to dynamic scoping for two reasons: first, because it is easier to think about where bindings are visible in text than when you can refer to them given the flow of the control of the program; second, there is no possibility of the "funarg" problem in lexical scoping. The funarg problem is a condition under which a programmer can, unaware, use a name locally and have the binding conflict with the binding of the same name used locally elsewhere in the program.

4.3.2   *Dynamic Scoping and Special Variables*

Most earlier LISP interpreters were written using *dynamic* scoping. In dynamic scoping, as in lexical, the formal parameters of a function are bound when the function is entered; however, they remain bound continuously until the function returns. This means that the above example would work in a LISP in which formal parameters to functions were dynamically scoped, because N remains bound and visible until MY-OTHER-FUNCTION is exited, even when MY-OTHER-FUNCTION's text is not the text being executed.

COMMON LISP allows us to use dynamic scoping as well as lexical. Variables are lexically scoped unless they are *declared special*, in which case they are dynamically scoped.

We could make the above example run in COMMON LISP as it would in MACLISP by writing it like this:

```
(defun my-other-function (n)
   (declare (special n))
   (my-function)))
MY-OTHER-FUNCTION

(defun my-function ()
   (declare (special n))
   (1+ n)))
MY-FUNCTION
```

The special declaration in MY-OTHER-FUNCTION states that N is dynamically scoped and therefore MY-FUNCTION can legally refer to it, even though N is not one of its formal parameters. Two special declarations are required, one to tell COMMON LISP that N should be set up as a special variable during the execution of MY-OTHER-FUNCTION, and another to state that the references to N in MY-FUNCTION are special. You can think of this more simply as being a result of the scope of declarations: a declare form is usually in effect only in the body of the form in which it occurs. The result is that N is private to MY-FUNCTION and MY-OTHER-FUNCTION. Of course, any other function could declare N special and call MY-FUNCTION as well.

If we wanted to add other function calls between MY-OTHER-FUNCTION and MY-FUNCTION, we could do so:

```
(defun my-other-function (n)
   (declare (special n))
   (yet-another-function)))
MY-OTHER-FUNCTION

(defun yet-another-function ()
   (my-function)))
YET-ANOTHER-FUNCTION

(defun my-function ()
   (declare (special n))
   (1+ n)))
MY-FUNCTION
```

No declaration is needed in YET-ANOTHER-FUNCTION because it does not make any special references.

Both DEFUN and LET have a place for declarations between the variable list and the body of the form.

If you are like most LISP programmers, you will not have to think about the fine points of variable scoping very often, but this knowledge is indispensable for understanding the behavior of certain pieces of code and constructs within LISP. If you find that some of these concepts are at first difficult to grasp, go back and reread them. The implications of scoping rules are among the most difficult concepts to understand in COMMON LISP.

Special variables are not often used in this form. However, there is a generalization of the "special variable" idea which is used frequently. So-called global variables in LISP are, in fact, dynamically scoped special variables.

4.3.3   Global Variables

Free variables are used to communicate information about the state of the program that could be of interest to many functions that are parts of the program. If enough functions need this information, and especially if several functions can change its value, you probably don't want to have to pass it as an argument.

For example, in any program that interacts with real-world conditions, such as a text formatter or a robot arm controller, a series of variables affects the result. In a text formatter, you might want the current value of the left margin to be the value of a variable to which each command routine could refer without having had it passed as one of the routine's arguments. In fact, it would be quite clumsy to have to pass it to each routine.

Sometimes, you want so many functions to know about a variable that you want to declare it special for all functions without requiring separate declarations in each function. LISP provides two forms that do "top-level variable declarations"—DEFVAR and DEFPARAMETER. In addition, DEFCONSTANT provides a way of creating global constants.

DEFVAR, DEFPARAMETER, and DEFCONSTANT can be used at top level to create global variables. Like DEFUN, which defines functions, DEFVAR, DEFPARAMETER, and DEFCONSTANT define top-level objects.

DEFVAR takes either one or two arguments. The first argument, the name of the variable to be defined, is mandatory. The second argument, the initial value of the variable, is optional. Once you create a variable with DEFVAR, you can refer to it from within any portion of code, as long as it isn't shadowed.

```
(defvar *foo* 3)
*FOO*
(defun bar () (sq *foo*))
BAR
(defun sq (x) (* x x))
SQ
(bar)
9
```

It is customary to give a global variable a name with asterisks around it, to make it obvious that it is dynamically scoped.[3]

The first argument to DEFVAR, the symbol, is not evaluated, but the second one is:

```
(defvar *favorite-fruit* (cons 'apples '(pears peaches)))
*FAVORITE-FRUIT*

*favorite-fruit*
(APPLES PEARS PEACHES)
```

DEFPARAMETER is like DEFVAR except that it is intended for use on parameters rather than on variables. Parameters are important system-defining features that will probably not be changed very often. For example, if you were to write a text formatter, you might create a variable with DEFPARAMETER called *HEIGHT-OF-PAGE*:

```
(defparameter *height-of-page* 48)
```

HEIGHT-OF-PAGE is a factor that does change, but usually only once in a given document. DEFPARAMETER differs from DEFVAR in two ways. First, it signals a different intention on your part. Second, if you redefine something defined with DEFVAR, it has no effect, while if you redefine something defined with DEFPARAMETER, the new value is assigned successfully. That is,

```
(defvar *foo* 3)
*FOO*

*foo*
3
(defvar *foo* 4)
*FOO*

*foo*
3
```

whereas

```
(defparameter *bar* 3)
*BAR*

*bar*
3
(defparameter *bar* 4)
*BAR*

*bar*
4
```

---

[3]This is merely a helpful custom and not a requirement of the language. Do not rely on it when reading code.

DEFVAR and DEFPARAMETER both create variables whose values can be altered using the functions that will be introduced in the next section. In contrast, in some implementations of LISP, DEFCONSTANT creates variables that issue warnings when an attempt is made to redefine them. For example, we might say,

```
(defconstant *h* 6.36e-34) ; Planck's constant
```

We would probably want to know if anything in our program was trying to change something as fundamental as Planck's constant. DEFCONSTANT may guard against our changing it inadvertently. More profoundly, using DEFCONSTANT when possible will lead to faster compiled code because the compiler can build in assumptions about it.

4.4   SETF AND DESTRUCTIVE MODIFICATION

You now have a large repertoire of ways to create variables with different properties: DEFUN, LET, DEFVAR, DEFPARAMETER, and DEFCONSTANT. However, you still don't know how to change the value of a variable once it is created, except in the case of DEFPARAMETER.

You may not have noticed this, because you don't usually need to change the value of local variables such as those created with DEFUN and LET. Most often, you call a function with a value, and if you need another value internally, you create a local variable with a LET.

In contrast, the values of global variables persist throughout a session with LISP, so there is a pressing need to have a way of altering them. That way is provided by SETF.

4.4.1   Using SETF to Change the Value of a Variable

SETF can be used to modify the value of a symbol. That is,

```
(defvar *mynumber* 343)
*MYNUMBER*

*mynumber*
343

(setf *mynumber* 259)
259
```

will cause MYNUMBER to have the value 259:

```
*mynumber*
259
```

SETF, like DEFVAR, takes two arguments, in this case a symbol and a form. The first argument, the symbol, is not evaluated. The second argument, the form, is. The value of the first argument is changed to be the result of evaluating the second argument. For example,

```
(defvar *stuffing* (cons 'raisins '(apples bread)))
*STUFFING*

*stuffing*
(RAISINS APPLES BREAD)

(setf *stuffing* (list 'chestnuts 'celery))
(CHESTNUTS CELERY)

*stuffing*
(CHESTNUTS CELERY)
```

You can draw a simple diagram representing the change. Initially, (defvar *stuffing*
(cons 'raisins '(apples bread))) sets up a situation like that shown in figure 4-4.

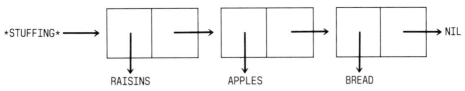

Figure 4-4. *STUFFING*

Then, (setf *stuffing* (list 'chestnuts 'celery)) changes it, as shown in figure
4-5.

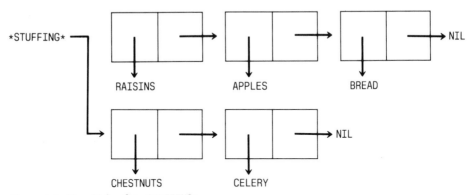

Figure 4-5. New Value for *STUFFING*

One interesting point here is that variables in LISP have pointers to things, not space
for things. They are like pointer variables in PASCAL or C, not like integer, float, or
record variables. You are free to assign objects of different sizes and types to them.

SETF returns the value of the form as its value. However, the programmer is usually
not interested in the value returned, but only in the fact that it changes the value of
some variable. SETF acts differently from most other functions we have seen. It delves
into the actual place in memory where the value assignment is stored, and replaces it.
This is *destructive modification*.

Redefining a function with DEFUN also modifies destructively. When DEFUN was introduced, the term ''side effect'' was also brought up. A function that is not employed merely to obtain a value is said to be used for side effect.

SETF is used in programs to modify variables created by other means. It can also be used at top level to create variables that are widely accessible. However, in modern LISPs, this is considered bad style.

SETF can be used to change the value of a variable based on its previous value:

```
(defvar *aggregate-word* "kinder")

(defun add-to-word (addition)
  (setf *aggregate-word*
        (format nil "~a~a" *aggregate-word* addition)))

(add-to-word "garten")

*aggregate-word*
"kindergarten"
```

SETF can be used to change the values of all kinds of variables: variables created with DEFUN, with LET, with DEFVAR, and with DEFPARAMETER. The value of a parameter may be changed by calling DEFPARAMETER again; however, calling DEFVAR again will neither have an effect nor signal an error.

4.4.2   Using SETF to Change the Value of a Generalized Variable

SETF can also be used to set the values of objects other than symbols, so that these, too, can be treated as variables, that is, places that hold a piece of information.

For example, the list *BOOKS-BY-HOMER*:

```
(defvar *books-by-homer* '(Aeneid Odyssey))
*BOOKS-BY-HOMER*

*books-by-homer*
(AENEID ODYSSEY)
```

can be drawn as in figure 4-6a.

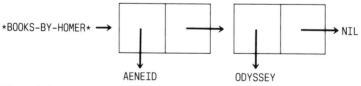

Figure 4-6a. *BOOKS-BY-HOMER*

You can modify it as follows:

```
(setf (car *books-by-homer*) 'Iliad)
ILIAD
```

Now *BOOKS-BY-HOMER* looks like this:

```
*books-by-homer*
(ILIAD ODYSSEY)
```

and can be drawn as in figure 4-6b. The old car has been replaced with a new car.

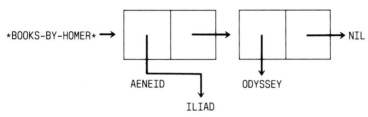

Figure 4-6b. Corrected *BOOKS-BY-HOMER*

4.4.2.1.   GENERALIZED VARIABLES

Consider that a variable is a name that allows us to locate a piece of information. In Lisp, symbols are used as variables. The symbol's value cell holds a pointer to the piece of information. The name of the symbol provides a means of accessing the piece of information. We can use SETF to replace it with another piece of information.

COMMON LISP extends the idea of variables to generalized variables. A generalized variable is any form that allows us to access a particular place in memory, that is, a particular piece of information. For example, the car or the cdr of a list always points to a particular place in memory. The functions CAR and CDR provide a means of accessing the pieces of data stored there. SETF provides a means of altering the value stored in the generalized variable.

4.4.2.2.   SETF IN MORE DETAIL

It is important to remember that SETF does not evaluate its first argument. That is, (setf (car *books-by-homer*) 'Iliad) is completely different from (setf Aeneid 'Iliad). (setf Aeneid 'Iliad) sets the value of the symbol AENEID to ILIAD. (setf (car *books-by-homer*) 'Iliad) uses special information that the operator SETF has about the operator CAR to modify a piece of a list. SETF knows how to use the phrase (car *books-by-homer*) to find the car of a particular cons cell and change it.

SETF has to have special knowledge about any operator that is used in its first argument. Among the operators that you know, SETF can handle CAR, CDR, all compound forms of CAR and CDR, ELT, and NTH.[4]

---

[4]SETF is as efficient in compiled code as the various older functions it replaces and supplements (RPLACA, RPLACD, SETQ, etc.).

Using side effects and destructive modification can be tricky, because you may not always know exactly what you are changing. Side effects should be used with great care.

For example, imagine that you had two lists:

```
(defvar *camping-gear*
   '(sleeping-bag tent insect-repellent toothbrush))
*CAMPING-GEAR*

(defvar *left-to-pack* (cddr *camping-gear*))
*LEFT-TO-PACK*
```

This creates a situation in which information is shared as shown in figure 4-7. If you destructively modify a part of *LEFT-TO-PACK*, you will also modify the list *CAMPING-GEAR* points to.

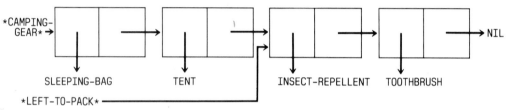

Figure 4-7. *CAMPING-GEAR* and *LEFT-TO-PACK* with Sharing

```
(setf (car *left-to-pack*) 'water-bag)
WATER-BAG

*left-to-pack*
(WATER-BAG TOOTHBRUSH)

*camping-gear*
(SLEEPING-BAG TENT WATER-BAG TOOTHBRUSH)
```

You can test for sharing using EQ:

```
(eq *left-to-pack* (cddr *camping-gear*))
T
```

Sharing is often useful but if it occurs unintentionally, it can present a problem in debugging programs. An alternative is to make a copy of the data before modifying it. For example, if you were to start with *CAMPING-GEAR* in the same state as before:

```
(defvar *camping-gear*
   '(sleeping-bag tent insect-repellent toothbrush))
*CAMPING-GEAR*
```

you could construct *LEFT-TO-PACK* using the function COPY-LIST, which returns a copy of its argument:

```
(defvar *left-to-pack* (copy-list (cddr *camping-gear*)))
*LEFT-TO-PACK*
```

Now you have two independent lists. See figures 4-8 and 4-9. Now changing *LEFT-TO-PACK* has no effect on *CAMPING-GEAR*:

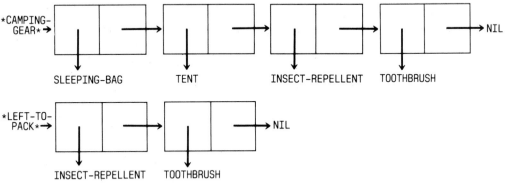

Figure 4-8. *CAMPING-GEAR* and *LEFT-TO-PACK* with No Sharing

```
(setf (car *left-to-pack*) 'water-bag)
WATER-BAG
```

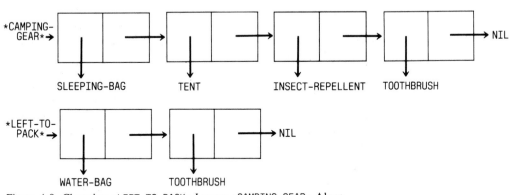

Figure 4-9. Changing *LEFT-TO-PACK* Leaves *CAMPING-GEAR* Alone

The question might arise why anyone ever uses destructive modification as opposed to copying. The reason is that copying takes space and time. One of the strengths of LISP is that you are not forced to think much about memory management as a prerequisite for writing code. However, it is true that any time you have to cons, you are using more space. If it's not being used, the space will be recovered later by the process of *garbage collection*. The garbage collector searches through memory for items that cannot possibly be used, because there are no pointers to them, and deletes them. However, garbage collection takes time and is therefore undesirable. In many LISP systems, it is extremely undesirable because all processing stops while the garbage collector runs. In other systems, the cost is incremental, but still there. Most people choose to use destructive operations when they can to minimize the amount of garbage collection necessary.

Since sometimes you want to copy and sometimes to modify destructively, LISP provides destructive and copying versions of many functions. For example, you have been introduced to the functions REVERSE and APPEND, which copy their arguments. NREVERSE and NCONC are the destructive versions of REVERSE and APPEND. For example, if you have:

```
(defvar alphabet '((a b) (c d)))
```

and you type the phrase:

```
(reverse alphabet)
((c d) (a b))
```

ALPHABET still has the value ((A B) (C D)). However, if you type:

```
(nreverse alphabet)
```

the value returned will be the same, but ALPHABET may have been modified.

4.4.2.3. SETQ, RPLACA AND RPLACD

SETF is a useful abstraction because it allows you to treat different kinds of storage as variables. However, there are also explicit commands that perform the same functions as (setf x value), (setf (car x) value), and (setf (cdr x) value), and you may come across them in programs or occasionally want to use them yourself. These commands are provided for historical reasons and compatibility with older versions of LISP.

SETQ is an operator that changes the value of a symbol. For example,

```
(setq *my-number* 343)
343
```

has exactly the same effect as (setf *my-number* 343). The difference is that SETQ can set only the value of symbols.

RPLACA and RPLACD are two operators that parallel CAR and CDR in function. RPLACA replaces the car of a list with a value:

```
(defvar *fruit* '(apple orange pear))
*FRUIT*
```

```
(rplaca *fruit* 'cherry)
(CHERRY ORANGE PEAR)
```

This has the same effect as (setf (car *fruit*) 'cherry).

RPLACD replaces the cdr of a list with a value:

```
*fruit*
(cherry orange pear)
```
```
(rplacd *fruit* '(mango papaya))
(CHERRY MANGO PAPAYA)
```

This is the same as (setf (cdr *fruit*) '(mango papaya)).

4.5   AN EXTENDED EXAMPLE: BICYCLES

Now is the time to present in more detail a program skimmed over in the introductory chapter. Suppose we wanted to write a program that simulates bicycle behavior. One goal is to be able to "pump the pedals" of the bicycle objects; that is, we would like to be able to make each bicycle move some distance. Eventually, we would like to create a bicycle database and a good, general set of functions for manipulating that database.

We will model only three qualities of a bicycle:

1. its position along an x-axis;
2. its gear ratio;
3. its wheel size.

A bicycle is an object that includes these three qualities. We must decide how to implement them in LISP. There are many ways to do so, but in this example bikes will be implemented as a list of three elements, in a particular but arbitrary order:

```
x-position wheel-size gear-ratio
```

Now we need some basic functions for manipulating the data structure. First, we need a constructor function that will take the values for the three attributes of a bicycle as arguments and produce a bicycle object, the way CONS takes two items and constructs a new cons cell pointing to the items. We then need accessor functions that, when given a bicycle object, will return the various attributes of that particular bicycle, the way CAR and CDR access the parts of a cons cell. Last, we need modifiers, which take a bicycle and a new value and update an attribute of the bicycle to the new value.

Here is the constructor:

```
(defun make-bike (x-position wheel-size gear-ratio)
   (list x-position wheel-size gear-ratio))
```

Any time we want to create a bike, we run the procedure MAKE-BIKE.

If we invoke MAKE-BIKE, we will encounter a difficulty at this point. Typing (make-bike 0 1 2) creates a bicycle object, which is returned, just as typing (cons 'a 'b) creates a list that is returned. However, if we wish to do anything with the bicycle or the list, we must have a way of referring to it. Right now, we know two ways to do so. We can either:

• give it a name (with DEFVAR, for instance);

• put it in a list (we could define a named list containing all the bikes in the world).

Since (for the moment) we are dealing only with one or two bicycles, and not yet writing a driver loop or user interface to perform a given task automatically with our bike objects, we settle for naming each one individually. This is not a strategy that we would use for dealing with more than one or two instances of an object. However, we can create a bicycle object like this:

```
(defvar *my-bike* (make-bike 0 3 5))
*MY-BIKE*
```

```
*my-bike*
(0 3 5)
```

Once bicycles can be manufactured, we will want to extract information about them and update information in them. Therefore, we have to write a set of accessor and update functions.

The first member of the list that is a bicycle object represents its x-position. The selector X-POSITION and the constructor SET-X-POSITION look like:

```
(defun x-position (bike)
  (car bike))
```

```
(defun set-x-position (bike x)
  (setf (car bike) x))
```

The accessor X-POSITION accepts one argument: the bicycle it is supposed to examine. The constructor SET-X-POSITION accepts two arguments: the bicycle it is supposed to modify and the new X value.

Here are the constructors and selectors for the other features of a bicycle:

```
(defun wheel-size (bike)
  (cadr bike))
```

```
(defun set-wheel-size (bike wheel-size)
  (setf (cadr bike) wheel-size))
```

```
(defun gear-ratio (bike)
  (caddr bike))
```

```
(defun set-gear-ratio (bike gear-ratio)
  (setf (caddr bike) gear-ratio))
```

You may have noticed that none of them are more than two lines long. Why bother singling out such small units? The reason is that these units represent important and flexible *abstractions* .

There is nothing in the list that constitutes a bicycle explicitly identifying it as a bicycle object or preventing us from treating it like any other list. However, if we were manipulating it under program control, we would know that it met the criteria for being a bicycle because it was created with MAKE-BIKE. We would refrain from accessing it or changing it except with the defined accessor and update functions for two reasons:

- so that we would be sure of keeping our treatment consistent;
- so that we could change our low-level representation and still use our higher level functions.

Each of these small functions helps create an *abstraction barrier* between the underlying data representation (here, a list) and any procedures and programs that we write to utilize the data structure. No matter what we want to use the bikes for, we will never need any more primitive manipulators. Likewise, we could change the underlying representation of bicycles to be more complex if we wished. For example, we could arbitrarily put every element in a bicycle in a sublist of its own:

```
(defun make-bike (x wheel-size gear-ratio)
   (list (list x) (list wheel-size) (list gear-ratio)))
```

Then, when we made a bicycle like this:

```
(defvar *my-silly-bike* (make-bike 0 3 1))
```

it would look like this:

```
((0) (3) (1))
```

We would have to change all the manipulators to coincide with the new representation. X-POSITION would look like this:

```
(defun x-position (bike)
  (car (car bike)))
```

SET-GEAR-RATIO would look like this:

```
(defun set-gear-ratio (bike gear-ratio)
   (setf (caaddr bike) gear-ratio))
```

However, both the old procedures and the new take the same information as arguments and deliver the same information, in the same form, as values. Even when we change the underlying data structure that implements bikes, as we have done here, if we have built a good abstraction barrier, we don't have to alter procedures built on top of that barrier.

We might want to make the modifiers for the bicycle structure parallel those for data structures built into COMMON LISP. That is, we would like to be able to write:

```
(setf (x-position *my-bike*) 35)
```

instead of

```
(set-x-position *my-bike* 35)
```

We could do this by using DEFSETF to tell SETF how to treat the accessor X-POSITION as a place holding information:

```
(defsetf x-position set-x-position)
```

This means that when we type (setf (x-position *my-bike*) 35), LISP automatically calls SET-X-POSITION with the argument to X-POSITION and the new value argument provided to SETF directly.

To demonstrate what we might do with our bicycle abstraction, here is a procedure that "pumps the pedals" of a bicycle:

```
(defun pump-pedals (bike)
   (setf (x-position bike)
           (+ (x-position bike)
             (* (gear-ratio bike)
                .5 pi (wheel-size bike)))))
```

Whenever we call PUMP-PEDALS on a given bike, the X-POSITION is updated by the amount of ground covered. The amount of ground covered is dependent on the GEAR-RATIO and the WHEEL-SIZE of the bike.

PUMP-PEDALS does not care what the underlying representation of a bicycle is, as long as it is handed a bicycle object that matches the specifications implicit in the accessor and update functions used in PUMP-PEDALS.

A possible next layer for this system is a data structure that groups bicycles together, and a series of functions that allow us to manipulate that structure. One operation we might wish to implement for this structure would extract an instance of a bicycle, so that, for example, we can pump its pedals. However, in order to do these things, we need the more sophisticated flow of control ideas introduced in chapter 5.

CHAPTER HIGHLIGHTS

Major Concepts

- A variable can be used to give a name to a value and is needed if you wish to refer to the value in more than one place.

- Some forms, such as SETF and SETQ, are used primarily for their side effects; others are used for the values they return.
- Variables in the argument list of a function are local and bound to the values with which the function is called.
- Variables created in a LET statement are local to the body of the LET statement.

  –Variables inside a LET statement *shadow* variables outside.
- Global variables created with DEFVAR or DEFPARAMETER can be accessed anywhere in the program (unless they are shadowed).
- A reference to a variable that is not one of the formal parameters of the current function or bound in a lexically enclosing form, such as a LET, is called a *free variable reference*.
- Variable references are governed by *scoping rules*.
- The default rule is *lexical*.

  –In lexical scoping, a variable cannot be referenced unless it is defined within the text of the construct that creates the binding.
- Global and special variables are *dynamically* scoped.

  –In dynamic scoping, a variable can be referenced if it was defined in any of the chain of procedures that called the current procedure. However, a lexically apparent declaration of the variable as special must be made unless DEFVAR, DEFPARAMETER, or DEFCONSTANT was used to define it.

Summary of New Syntax

```
(let ((name value)
      (name2 value2) ...)
    body)
```

```
(step form)
(trace form)
(untrace form)
```

```
(declare (special variable))
```

```
(defvar name value)
(defparameter name value)
(defconstant name value)
```

```
(setf place value place2 value2 ...)
```

```
(copy-list list)
(nconc list1 list2)
(nreverse sequence)
```

```
(setq name value name2 value2 ...)
(rplaca a-cons obj)
(rplacd a-cons obj)
```

```
(defsetf selector modifier)
```

Suggested Reading

The following sections in Steele, *COMMON LISP*, complement this chapter: chapter 3, Scope and Extent; chapter 5, Program Structure, 5.3.2; chapter 7, Control Structure, 7.1.2, 7.2, 7.5; chapter 9, Declarations, 9.1-9.2; chapter 15, Lists, 15.3; chapter 25, Miscellaneous Features, 25.3.

EXERCISES

1. Assume that you have typed (defvar x 3). What will the following expressions do?

   a. ```
      (if (and (> x 3) (< x 5)) "Just right" "Oh no!")
      ```

   b. ```
      (let ((apples 'oranges))
         (format nil "I want ~a ~a" x apples))
      ```

   c. ```
      (let ((x 4)(y x)) y)
      ```

   d. ```
      (let ((y 3))
         (defun apple-statistics ()
            (format nil "I have ~a Cortland apples" y)))

      (let ((y 4))
         (apple-statistics))
      ```

2. Identify what each of the steps does in the following sequences of expressions:

   ```
   (defun test1 ()
      (let  ((a 3))
         (let ((a 4) (b 1))
            (print (+ a b)))
         (print a)))

   (defun test2 ()
      (let ((a 3))
         (let ((a 4)(b 1))
            (setf a 16)
            (print (+ a b)))
         (print a)))
   ```

   Which binding of ''a'' did the SETF inside the LET change?

3. Draw a diagram of the environments in the call (my-function 3 4 5). What will be printed on the screen during execution of this call?

   ```
   (defun my-function (x y z)
      (print (+ x y z))
      (let ((w 1)
            (y 2))
         (print w)
         (print y))
      (print y))
   ```

4. What happens if you put a DEFUN inside another DEFUN? Write a procedure called BOW, which takes one argument, ARROW. Internally BOW should contain another DEFUN,

SHOOT, which takes no arguments. SHOOT should print the value of ARROW on the screen. What does BOW return? Try pretty-printing SHOOT. Now call SHOOT. Call it again.

5. Evaluate each of the following expressions, in order.

   a. `(defvar *ice-cream* '(vanilla chocolate strawberry))`

      `(defvar *my-favorite-ice-cream* (cadr *ice-cream*))`
      `*my-favorite-ice-cream*`

   b. `(setf (cddr *ice-cream*) (list (caddr *ice-cream*)`
      `                                'mint-chocolate-chip))`

      `*my-favorite-ice-cream*`

   c. `*ice-cream*`

   d. `(let ((newest-flavor (last *ice-cream*)))`
      `   (setf *my-favorite-ice-cream* newest-flavor))`
      `    *my-favorite-ice-cream*`

6. In chapter 7, you will see data structures that can be modified easily. However, one drawback to the way the current bicycle system is designed is that adding another attribute to a bicycle is not an automatic process. First change the bike abstraction by adding a new quality: color. Then write appropriate selectors and constructors. There is one easy and several hard ways to go about this. What are they?

Chapter 5

RECURSION, ITERATION, AND "PROGN-TYPE" FORMS

There are two basic strategies for making operations repeat: recursion and iteration. Recursion is accomplished without special syntactic constructs. Iteration is supported via the constructs DOTIMES, DOLIST, and DO, among others.

This chapter considers recursion and iterative constructs, as well as the useful grouping constructs PROG1, PROG2, and PROGN.

5.1   SIMPLE RECURSIVE FUNCTIONS

By the end of chapter 4, you knew enough about LISP to write the following procedure:

```
(defun guess ()
   (format t
     "Think of a number and I'll try to guess what it is.~%")
   (cond ((y-or-n-p (format t "Is it ~a?~%" (get-guess)))
          (format t "See how smart I am!"))
         (t (format t "Oh well, you can't win them all."))))
GUESS

(defun get-guess ()  7)
GET-GUESS
```

An interaction with GUESS might look like this:

```
(guess)
Think of a number and I'll try to guess what it is.
Is it 7?
n
Oh well, you can't win them all.
NIL
```

This procedure could be made more interesting if it repeated. We can make it repeat until the user says that the number is 7, as follows:

```
(defun newguess ()
   (format t
     "Think of a number and I'll try to guess what it is.~%")
   (cond ((y-or-n-p (format t "Is it ~a?~%" (get-guess)))
          (format nil "See how smart I am!~%"))
         (t (format t "Oh well, you can't win them all.~%")
            (newguess))))
NEWGUESS
```

NEWGUESS differs from GUESS in that, when Y-OR-N-P returns NIL, it makes a *recursive* call to NEWGUESS. In other words, NEWGUESS calls itself, the same way it calls COND or FORMAT.[1] An interaction with NEWGUESS might look like this:

```
(newguess)
Think of a number and I'll try to guess what it is.
Is it 7?
n
Oh well, you can't win them all.
Think of a number and I'll try to guess what it is.
Is it 7?
y
"See how smart I am!"
```

The addition of this one small function call to the program has changed its behavior considerably.

As with GUESS, the sophistication of the guess that NEWGUESS makes depends on GET-GUESS and not on the control structure. That is, we could make either program give more interesting guesses by rewriting GET-GUESS. For example, we could employ the function RANDOM, which takes a number as argument, and generates a number between 0 (inclusive) and the number (exclusive):

```
(defun get-guess ()
   (random 10))
GET-GUESS
```

Now GUESS generates different numbers from 0 to 9 instead of always printing "Is it 7?".

We might want to separate out the initializing part of this game as well, so that it wouldn't restart every time:

```
(defun start-guess ()
   (format t
     "Think of a number and I'll try to guess what it is.~%")
   (newguess))
```

---

[1]Strictly speaking, any call to any function from within another function is a recursive call. However, it has become customary to use the term ''recursion'' to refer to the situation in which functions directly or indirectly invoke themselves.

```
(defun newguess ()
   (cond ((y-or-n-p (format t "Is it ~a?~%" (get-guess)))
          (format nil "See how smart I am!~%"))
         (t (format t "Oh well, you can't always be right.~%")
            (newguess))))
```

Now this runs:

```
(start-guess)
Think of a number and I'll try to guess what it is.
Is it 7?
n
Oh well, you can't always be right.
Is it 5?
y
"See how smart I am!"
```

MY-COUNT is a recursive procedure that takes a number as an argument:

```
(defun my-count (number)
   (cond ((= number 0) nil)
         (t (print number) (my-count (- number 1)))))
```

MY-COUNT prints its argument on the screen, and then calls MY-COUNT recursively, with an argument decremented by 1. Calling MY-COUNT produces the following items on the screen:

```
(my-count 4)
4
3
2
1
NIL
```

This sequence of recursive calls is diagrammed in figure 5-1. The top of each box in

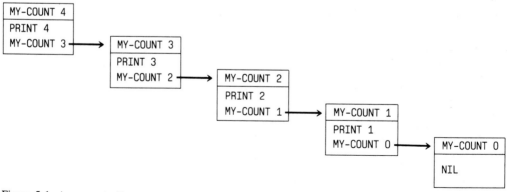

Figure 5-1. (my-count 4)

the diagram contains the current call and the value to which the argument is bound in that call. The bottom of the box contains the clause of the COND invoked, including the recursive call and the argument that call receives. The arrows point to what happens when the recursive call is evaluated. MY-COUNT 4 is not complete until MY-COUNT 3 has finished. In the same way, MY-COUNT 3 is not finished until MY-COUNT 2 is finished, and so forth.

We call a procedure like MY-COUNT for the side effect of getting numbers printed on the screen. Each print command is executed inside the environment of the procedure that calls it. However, we often want to run recursive procedures for the values they return rather than for side effects. Let's look at the flow of control in the recursive calls.

When (MY-COUNT 0) is called, it returns NIL to (MY-COUNT 1). Since (MY-COUNT 0) is the last form in (MY-COUNT 1), (MY-COUNT 1) returns the value that (MY-COUNT 0) returned to it. (MY-COUNT 2) hands NIL to (MY-COUNT 3), and so on up the chain, until we get to (MY-COUNT 4), which returns NIL to the screen as the value of the whole process. This sequence is illustrated in figure 5-2.

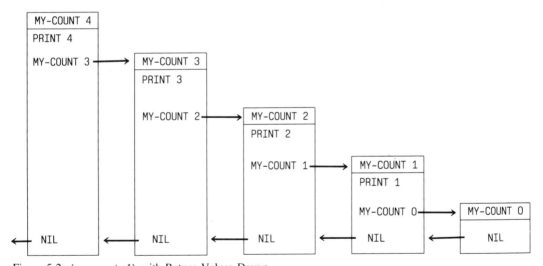

Figure 5-2. (my-count 4) with Return Values Drawn

5.1.1   **More Complex Recursive Functions**

If we think only about the side effects of MY-COUNT, it is possible to think of the MY-COUNT program as looping or iterating; this is because, although the environments are kept, the information stored in them is not used when control is returned to them.

Here is an example of a recursive program that can*not* be thought of as a loop, but only as a function calling other functions:

```
(defun backward (number)
   (cond ((= number 0) nil)
         (t (backward (- number 1))
            (print number)))))
```

When you call BACKWARD with an argument of 3, you get a sequence of recursive calls, as shown in figure 5-3. Instead of printing:

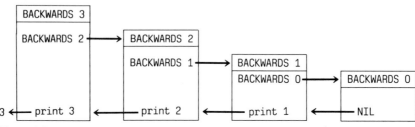

Figure 5-3. (backward 3)

```
3
2
1
NIL
```

BACKWARD prints:

```
1
2
3
3
```

The top-level call to BACKWARD returns 3, not NIL. This is because the last form evaluated in BACKWARD is not a recursive call to BACKWARD but rather a call to PRINT, and PRINT returns the object that it prints.

People learning about recursion in LISP often find the idea of a function calling a different instance of itself confusing. At one level an answer to this confusion is to remind the programmer that every function call is different. Every function call creates a unique environment with the function variables bound to the values with which they were called. Calling BACKWARD from BACKWARD is just like calling = from BACKWARD.

Likewise, calling (backward (- 10 1)) is like typing (= (- 10 1) 4) which is like typing (= 9 4). In all cases, the calling function, whether BACKWARD or =, receives 9 as the result of evaluating its arguments. When the text of the procedure employs variables instead of numbers directly, we might ask, "If NUMBER is NUMBER, then how can it be

(NUMBER – 1)?'' Again, every instance of BACKWARD binds the argument with which it was called to its own particular instance of the variable NUMBER. There are many bindings of the variable NUMBER, but only one for each call to BACKWARD.

5.1.1.1.   DEBUGGING: USING TRACE AND STEP, DRIBBLE

The stepper and tracer can be particularly helpful to your understanding of recursive functions. For example, look at the flow of control in BACKWARD by tracing calls to it:

```
(trace backward)
(BACKWARD)
(backward 3)

#8: (BACKWARD 3)
. #21: (BACKWARD 2)
. . #34: (BACKWARD 1)
. . . #47: (BACKWARD 0)
. . . #47=> NIL
1
. . #34=> 1
2
. #21=> 2
3
#8=> 3
3
```

Tracing allows you to look at that particular function in isolation. Stepping allows you to look at all the subfunctions.

DRIBBLE might assist you in conjunction with either STEP or TRACE. DRIBBLE allows you to record an interaction with LISP in a file, which you can then print out and look at as a whole.

Type DRIBBLE with a file name as argument to begin recording the session:

```
(dribble "test.txt")
```

Then use LISP as usual. When you don't want anything else recorded, call DRIBBLE without an argument. It returns T, and the file is closed.

Here is an example of a sample session as recorded by DRIBBLE:

```
Dribbling to TEST.TXT
NIL

pi
3.14159265358979323846264338327950

(truncate pi)
3 ;
0.14159265358979323846264338327950

(dribble)
```

5.2   WRITING RECURSIVE FUNCTIONS

MY-COUNT and BACKWARD are two procedures that are implemented recursively. How do you go about writing procedures like them for yourself? The first element in finding a recursive solution to a problem is to try to reduce it to a simpler problem of the same sort.

For example, you can specify the behavior for a function called GET-LENGTH. GET-LENGTH should take a list as argument and return the number of elements in the list. It turns out that you can reduce the problem of finding the length of a list to the simpler problem of finding the length of a list that is one element shorter, and adding 1 to it.

```
(get-length '(a b c)) <=> (+ 1 (get-length '(b c)))
```

Likewise,

```
(get-length '(b c)) <=> (+ 1 (get-length '(c)))
```

The second element in finding a recursive solution is to identify the end tests. In this case, you know that it's time to stop when the list is empty; you can simply return 0 at that point, because the length of the empty list is 0.

These two observations constitute an algorithm, and you can implement that algorithm directly:

```
(defun get-length (list)
   (if (null list) 0
      (+ 1 (get-length (cdr list)))))
```

A more complex function, COUNT-EVERYTHING, counts elements not only in the top-level list, but also elements in nested lists. This requires that every list be (recursively) decomposed in the same manner as the top-level list.

Here's how you would go about trying to find a solution to that problem. Suppose you have a LISP object; either it is a list or it is not. If it is a list then either it has elements or it is the empty list. Since you have three potential situations, you have to have three potential actions:

• If it is not a list, then you want to count it, that is, to return 1.

• If it is the empty list, then you don't want to count it. You want to return 0.

• If it is a list, then you want to simplify it. You can simplify the problem of counting a list to the problem of counting the car of the list plus the problem of counting the cdr of the list. Therefore, you can decompose the list by recursively calling COUNT-EVERYTHING on the car of the list and on the cdr of the list, and adding together the results.

We can translate this description almost line for line into code:

```
(defun count-everything (list)
    (cond ((null list) 0)
          ((not (listp list)) 1)
          (t (+ (count-everything (car list))
                (count-everything (cdr list)))))))
(count-everything '(a b (c d)))
4
```

Another example: the factorial of n is defined as being $n * (n - 1) * (n - 2) * (n - 3) \ldots 3 * 2 * 1$. For example, the factorial of 4 is $4 * 3 * 2 * 1 = 24$. This definition can be rewritten:

```
n! =  n * (n - 1) * (n - 2) * (n - 3) ... 3 * 2 * 1
   =  n * (n - 1)!
```

In other words,

```
4! = 4 * 3 * 2 * 1 = 4 * 3!
```

We can say that we define 0! to be 1, or, in other words, we want to stop when $n = 0$. Otherwise we want to multiply the number by the factorial of the number minus one.

This statement of the problem can be converted into LISP code fairly simply:

```
(defun factorial (n)
  (if (= n 0) 1
    (* n (factorial (- n 1))))))
(factorial 5)
120
```

A recursive function normally consists of two parts:

- one or more end tests (possibly including what to compute for one or two simple cases);
- what to compute for the function, given the result of one or more other computations with that function.

In GET-LENGTH and COUNT-EVERYTHING, the input was a list. Therefore, the end tests related to lists or elements of lists. They checked whether the list was empty, or whether an atom was found. In FACTORIAL, the input was a number, which we were decrementing, so we checked whether it had reached a low enough value.

In all three cases, the output was a number. That meant that we wanted to combine the outputs of recursive calls using an arithmetic operation: + or *. These operations are the "glue" for the returned values of the recursive calls.

In the following case, the input is, once again, a list, but the output is another list. Therefore, we use "list glue" instead of "arithmetic glue."

FILTER-OUT-THE takes a list of symbols and returns a list from which all instances of the symbol THE have been removed. We can reduce the problem of filtering out the instances of THE from a list to the problem of examining the first element in the list, and examining the rest of the list. If the first element is THE, we ignore it. Otherwise, we glue it to the result of the recursive call.

```
(defun filter-out-the (list)
  (cond ((null list) nil)
        ((equal (car list) 'the) (filter-out-the (cdr list)))
        (t (cons (car list) (filter-out-the (cdr list))))))
```

It is easy to change FILTER-OUT-THE to make it remove other items from lists.

5.2.1   **Lists as Trees**

Recursive functions are particularly useful in tree searches. A tree is an information structure that looks like figure 5-4. A tree has two kinds of parts—nodes and leaves. Each node has branches. In general, a tree search consists of choosing a branch at every node until we come to the piece of information that we want.

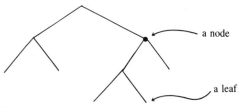

a node

a leaf

Figure 5-4. A Tree

Tree construction is particularly easy in LISP because trees can be represented as lists and vice versa.[2] In fact, the rules that you learned for LISP's recursive evaluation of lists treat LISP commands as if they were trees. For example, we can represent the phrase

(* ([+] 2 4) (− (/ 4 8) 6))

with the tree in figure 5-5. Each node contains a function and two branches. The leaves contain data that can be simply evaluated to produce arguments to the functions.

The process that is generated by running this code is drawn in figure 5-6. LISP uses simple rules for walking this tree. First of all, it always walks the tree completely

---

[2]The only exception is that we may have circular lists, which cannot be represented as trees.

(unless a special form or macro, like COND, is involved). Second, LISP must walk the tree in a *depth-first* manner. That is, at every node a given LISP might first turn left or right, but it must always walk down to the leaves before returning to the node.

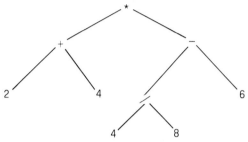

Figure 5-5. Decomposition of (* ([+] 2 4) (- (/ 4 8) 6))

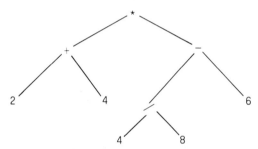

Figure 5-6. LISP's Process of Walking the Tree

Let's consider another example. The tree shown in figure 5-7 represents a data structure for a data base about animals. It is part of a program presented more fully in chapter 6, Interactions with the Outside World. This program assumes that you have an animal in mind and tries to "guess" what it is.

Each node has a string containing a question. The leaves consist of the symbols representing the names of animals. By answering the question at each node with a yes or no, you are able to choose a path to travel along in order to find the animal that is closest to the one you have in mind in the data base. The tree in figure 5-7 can be represented as the following list:

```
("Does it sing?"
    (canary)
    ("Could it have spots?"
        ("Does it bark?" (dog) (leopard))
        ("Does it lay eggs?"
            (chicken)
            (dolphin))))
```

Each nested list represents a node including a question, a yes-branch, and a no-branch. Generally, a leaf is a node without any yes- or no-branches. Specifically, in this representation, it is a list whose car is a symbol.

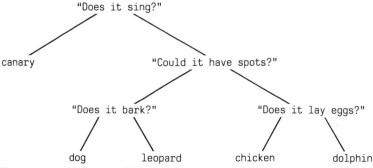

Figure 5-7. The ''Animal'' Tree

You can write very simple selectors to determine where you are in this tree or extract the yes-branch or no-branch at any given point. And, at any given point, you can tell whether you are at a leaf or a node by checking whether the car of the list is a string or a symbol:

```
(defun question (tree)
  (car tree))
```

In this example, being at a question and being at a node are exactly the same thing.

Lisp evaluation walks down a tree with a simple rule about which way to turn at every node. You would walk the animal tree differently. Instead of examining the whole tree, you would walk down only the branches that the user chose. Without writing the whole control structure just yet, note that you can operate on this data base by extracting the yes- or no-branches, perhaps for further recursive decomposition:

```
(defun yes-branch (tree)
  (cadr tree))
(defun no-branch (tree)
  (caddr tree))
```

A powerful technique in the field of artificial intelligence is to imagine that the set of possible states for a system is a tree, and that the solution to a particular problem is a path along that tree. Then, the goal of the program is to find the best path while devoting the least amount of effort to determining which one that is. Determining which path to explore next is itself often a problem that involves tree searches.

5.2.2   **Tower of Hanoi**

The Tower of Hanoi is a famous recursive problem that can be solved elegantly in LISP. Imagine that you have three pegs. On one of the pegs, you have sixty-four disks of different diameters, the smaller ones on top of the larger. Your goal is to move all of the disks to another peg without ever putting a larger disk on top of a smaller. You may never move more than one disk at a time.

Let's name the three pegs; A is the leftmost peg, C is the one on the right, and B is in the middle. A is currently the FROM peg because we are trying to move disks from it; C is currently the TO peg because we are trying move disks to it; B is currently the SPARE peg. We are trying to move N disks. Figure 5-8 shows the start and goal states for this system. The key to solving this problem is finding the right way to reduce it to a simpler problem.

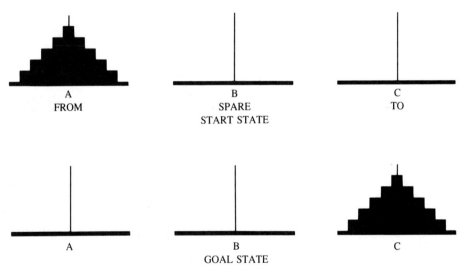

Figure 5-8. Start and Goal States for Tower of Hanoi

The problem of moving N disks from A to C can be reduced to a three-part problem:

- Moving (n − 1) disks from A to B
- Moving 1 disk from A to C
- Moving (n − 1) disks from B to C.

Figure 5-9 shows how to get to the solution state if we know how to solve the step before solution. We now have the subproblem of moving (n − 1) from A to B. Examining this, we see that it can be reduced to a three-part process on (n − 2) similar to the one above, except that the roles of the pegs involved have switched:

- Move `(n - 2)` disks from `A` to `C`.
- Move `1` disk from `A` to `B`.
- Move `(n - 2)` disks from `C` to `B`.

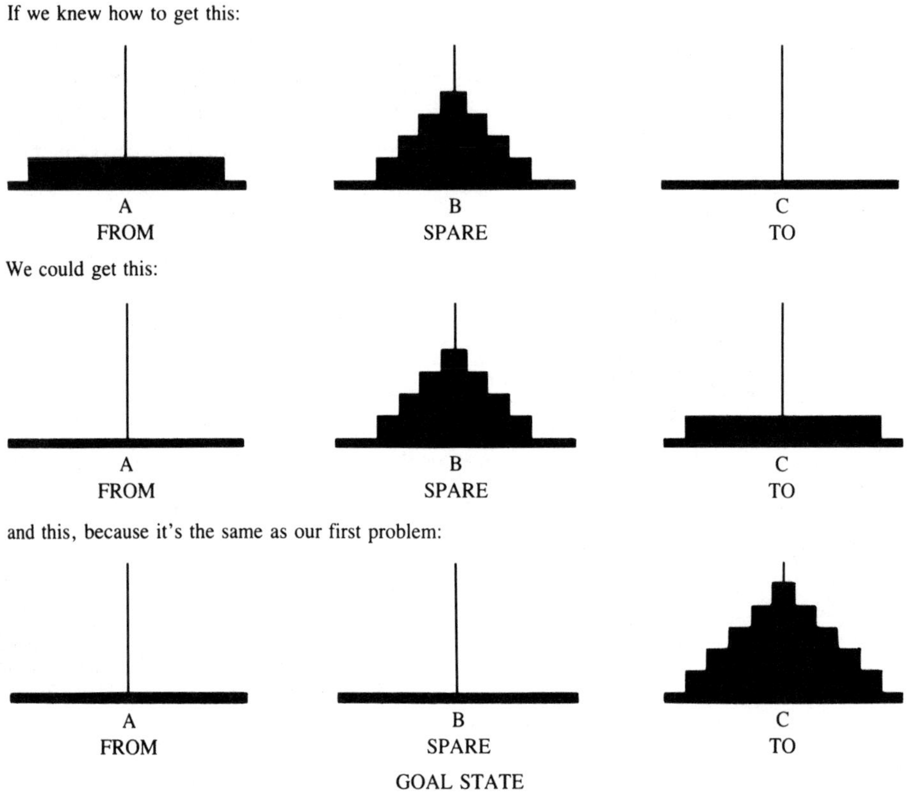
If we knew how to get this:
A
FROM
B
SPARE
C
TO
We could get this:
A
FROM
B
SPARE
C
TO
and this, because it's the same as our first problem:
A
FROM
B
SPARE
C
TO
GOAL STATE

Figure 5-9. The Step Before Solution to Tower of Hanoi

This is drawn in figure 5-10. Within the context of the subgoal, the terms `FROM`, `TO`, and `SPARE` have pairings or values different than they do within the context of the overall goal.

Likewise, the subproblem of moving `(n - 1)` disks from `B` to `C` can be written:

- Move `(n - 2)` disks from `B` to `A`.
- Move `1` disk from `B` to `C`.
- Move `(n - 2)` disks from `A` to `C`.

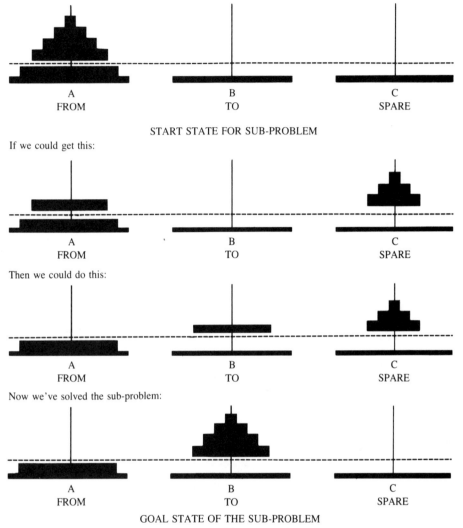

START STATE FOR SUB-PROBLEM

If we could get this:

Then we could do this:

Now we've solved the sub-problem:

GOAL STATE OF THE SUB-PROBLEM

Figure 5-10: Working Another Step Backward in Tower of Hanoi

Again, the values of FROM, TO, and SPARE are different in this subprocess than they are in the top-level goal.

These subgoals can be generalized in the following procedure:

```
(defun tower-of-hanoi (n from to spare)
   (cond ((= n 1) (move-disk from to))
         (t (tower-of-hanoi (- n 1) from spare to)
            (move-disk from to)
            (tower-of-hanoi (- n 1) spare to from)))))
```

Now a definition for MOVE-DISK must be written. The procedure does not in fact move anything, but rather prints a message on the screen indicating which disk would have been moved:

```
(defun move-disk (from to)
  (format t "~%Move a disk from ~a to ~a." from to))
```

A simple call to TOWER-OF-HANOI runs as follows:

```
(tower-of-hanoi 3 'a 'b 'c)
Move a disk from A to B.
Move a disk from A to C.
Move a disk from B to C.
Move a disk from A to B.
Move a disk from C to A.
Move a disk from C to B.
Move a disk from A to B.
NIL
```

Movement takes place only at the leaves, after a considerable amount of calculation about what to move where. This solution is hard to think of because it captures the process of planning rather than the process of moving. The problem of Tower of Hanoi is deceptive because it seems like a problem about moving disks, when it is really a problem about which disk to move. This solution is modularized so that the action of moving a disk is entirely separate from the process that determines which disk is moved. This means that in theory you could substitute a program that actually sends a message to a robot arm for the simple procedure that prints a message on the screen.

5.3   TAIL RECURSION AND ITERATION

You have already seen procedures, such as MY-COUNT, that may be thought of as using an iterative or looping *process*; however, they had a recursive form. You saw a picture of MY-COUNT that looked like figure 5-11. This diagram shows the fact that the calls to MY-COUNT 4, MY-COUNT 3, MY-COUNT 2, and MY-COUNT 1 all stay around, occupying space, until MY-COUNT 0 finishes execution. In BACKWARD, and other recursive functions, you were shown how to use that state information profitably.

However, in a case like MY-COUNT, all that information is superfluous. It is never used again. The recursive call is the last item in the function.

It would be much better to have a MY-COUNT that looked more like figure 5-12. There are two possible ways to achieve this:

- Some implementations of LISP know how to recognize these *tail recursive* situations and do not use more space than they really have to.

- All implementations of COMMON LISP have iterative constructs.

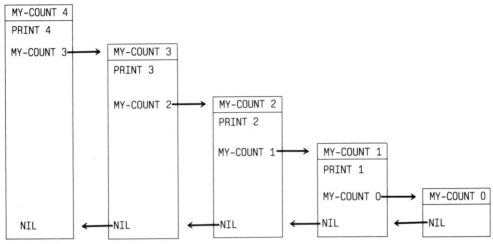

Figure 5-11. (my-count 4) as a Recursive Procedure

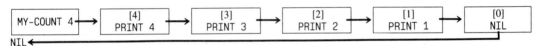

Figure 5-12. (my-count 4) as an Iterative Procedure

In LISPs with tail-recursion optimization, you have a choice. You can program efficiently by using recursive techniques all the time or you can employ special iterative constructs. Recursion is often the most elegant and straightforward way to write the solution to a problem.

In LISPs without tail-recursion optimization, you must be careful to identify processes that recur deeply, but are essentially iterative, and implement them by using the iterative constructs.

The square brackets in figure 5-12 could stand for MY-COUNT, DO, or DOTIMES.

5.3.1   DOTIMES and DOLIST

DOTIMES is a simple iteration construct that performs a series of actions a specified number of times. The user must specify a variable, a form that evaluates to a number, possibly a form to be evaluated and returned as the value of the DOTIMES, and a body, with the following syntax:

```
(dotimes (variable countform result-form) body)
```

DOTIMES binds the variable to 0, and evaluates the countform to get a number. Then every time it executes body, it increments the variable by 1 until the variable is equal to the result of evaluating the countform. For example:

```
(defun print-number ()
  (dotimes (i 2) (print i)))
PRINT-NUMBER

(print-number)
0
1
NIL
```

DOTIMES also takes an optional argument, a form that is evaluated after all the iterations have been completed. The result of evaluating this form is returned as a value:

```
(defun print-number ()
  (dotimes (i 2 "Done") (print i)))
PRINT-NUMBER

(print-number)
0
1
"Done"
```

DOLIST is similar to DOTIMES, except that it iterates over every item in a list:

```
(defun print-squares (list)
  (dolist (x list)
      (print (sq x))))
PRINT-SQUARES

(print-squares '(1 2 3 4))
1
4
9
16
NIL
```

5.3.2   DO

DO is an important function that supports iteration. It is powerful, but its compact syntax requires some study. A DO-loop has three parts: iteration variables, an end test, and a body, in that order. On every iteration, DO performs the following operations:

- assigns new values to the iteration variables;
- evaluates the end test; if it evaluates to anything but NIL, execution stops;
- and then executes the body.[3]

Each part of the DO loop has sufficiently complex syntax to merit a separate discussion.

---

[3]Because it performs the test before executing the body, it is like the ''while . . . do'' forms of other languages, *not* like the ''repeat . . . until'' forms.

Iteration-Variable Specifiers

Each iteration variable specifier has three parts: a name, an initial value form, and a stepping form.

The first time around the DO-loop, the variables are bound (in parallel) to the results of evaluating the initial-value forms. Each subsequent time, variables are, again in parallel, set to the result of evaluating the stepping forms.

If no initial value is given for a variable, the default is NIL. The value of a variable can be set as usual by SETF or SETQ from the body of the DO. Because of the syntax used, you cannot specify a stepping form without specifying an initial value.

The stepping form is used to change the value of the variable at each iteration. If no stepping form is specified, then the variable's value is not changed by DO. (This is useful if you want a local variable but want to change its value yourself, or don't want it to change at all.)

End Test

The end test is a list of two parts: the test itself should be the first item in the list, and consequent or result forms should follow it. In other words, anything that you want to happen when the iteration finishes should be enclosed in the parentheses with the end test. For example, you might want to print the final value of an accumulated variable. The value of the DO is the value of the last result form, or NIL if there are no result forms.

The Body

The body is a sequence of forms that are executed in order on every iteration of the DO. Forms inside the body can use the variables defined in the iteration-variable part of the construct.

Often the entire action of the DO is accomplished within the iteration-variable specifiers and the end test, and the body remains empty.

For example, you could rewrite MY-COUNT using DO:

```
(defun my-count (number)
   (do ((counter number (- counter 1)))
      ((= counter 0) nil)
      (print counter)))
```

This DO-loop contains one variable, COUNTER, which is initialized to the value of NUMBER. After the first time, COUNTER is set to the value of (- COUNTER 1) each time around the loop. This has the effect of decrementing it.

The end test is a check to see if COUNTER is 0. If it is, the consequents to the end test are evaluated. In this case, T is evaluated and returned.

Finally, the body of the DO-loop contains one expression, (print counter).

You can represent the process involved as shown in figure 5-13. Every iteration of the loop contains all the information that the function needs to complete.

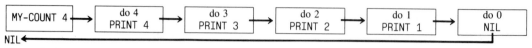

Figure 5-13. (my-count 4) using DO

It is also possible to implement GET-LENGTH as an iterative function.

```
(defun get-length (list)
   (do ((current-list list (cdr current-list))
        (counter 0 (+ counter 1)))
      ((null current-list) counter)))
```

Here we have two variables: CURRENT-LIST and COUNTER. CURRENT-LIST is initialized to the value of LIST and is stepped by being set to the value of (cdr current-list). COUNTER keeps track of how many elements have already been counted. It is initialized to zero and incremented each time around the loop.

When the end test is NIL, the iteration continues forever—or at least until the form RETURN is called. RETURN is also useful when you have two conditions upon which you wish to exit the loop:

```
(defun look-for (list)
   (do ((rest-of-list list (cdr rest-of-list)))
      ((null rest-of-list) nil)
      (if (member (car rest-of-list)
                  '(den-of-thieves barrel-of-monkeys))
         (return (car rest-of-list)))))
```

5.4   PROGN-TYPE FORMS

PROG1, PROG2, and PROGN are all constructs that provide ways of grouping LISP expressions together; each one takes a series of forms and evaluates the forms in order. They differ from one another in that each returns the value of a different form. PROG1 returns the value of its first form, PROG2 returns the value of its second form, and PROGN returns the value of its last form.

In other words, evaluation of every form except the one whose value is returned is done for side effect, rather than for value. All values except for the one returned remain inaccessible from outside the PROGN-type form.

PROGN takes a series of forms, evaluates them, and returns the value of the last one. Sometimes you use PROGN when you have a binary choice (and so want to use IF, not COND) but want to have multiple consequents to the predicate:

```
(defun find-greater (a b)
   (if (> a b) (progn (format t "~%The first argument to
FIND-GREATER, ~a, was greater than the second, ~a~%." a b)
                     a)
            (progn (format t "~%The second argument to
```

```
FIND-GREATER, ~a, was a greater than or equal ~
to the first, ~a~%." b a) b)))
```

PROGN groups expressions together so that they look like one entity to the IF statement.

The body of a DEFUN is an "implicit PROGN." All its forms are evaluated in turn, and the value of the last one is returned. Many other LISP functions contain implicit PROGNs, including LET, COND, WHEN, UNLESS, and DO (the consequents to the end test).

PROG1 and PROG2 keep the calculated value of their first and second forms, respectively, while evaluating the rest of the forms. This means that they can be used for preserving that information even while other forms perform operations on it.

PROG1 can be used to return a value after setting the variable that holds it; therefore, it can be used to exchange the values of two variables conveniently, as in:

```
(defvar a 3)
A
(defvar b 5)
B
(setf a (prog1 b (setf b a))))
5
```

PROG2 is just like PROG1, except that it returns the value of the second form inside it.

5.5   CHOMPER: A "CYBERNETIC" EXAMPLE

Chomper is a simple cybernetic animal that lives in a one-dimensional world of zeros and ones. Ones represent things to eat, and Chomper seeks them out and eats them until none are left.

An interaction with CHOMP might look like this:

```
(chomp '(0 1 0 1 0 0 0 V 1 1 0 0))

(0 1 0 1 0 0 > 1 1 0 0)
(0 1 0 1 0 > 0 1 1 0 0)
(0 1 0 1 > 0 0 1 1 0 0)
(0 1 0 > 0 0 0 1 1 0 0)
(0 1 > 0 0 0 0 1 1 0 0)
(0 > 0 0 0 0 0 1 1 0 0)
(0 V 0 0 0 0 0 1 1 0 0)
(0 < 0 0 0 0 0 1 1 0 0)
(0 0 < 0 0 0 0 1 1 0 0)
(0 0 0 < 0 0 0 1 1 0 0)
(0 0 0 0 < 0 0 1 1 0 0)
(0 0 0 0 0 < 0 1 1 0 0)
(0 0 0 0 0 0 < 1 1 0 0)
(0 0 0 0 0 0 0 < 1 0 0)
(0 0 0 0 0 0 0 0 < 0 0)
(0 0 0 0 0 0 0 0 V 0 0)
That's all, folks.
NIL
```

This fundamental activity is represented in the following loop:

```
(defun chomp (list)
  (do ((list (chomp-once list) (chomp-once list)))
      ((null list) (format t "~%That's all, folks.~%"))
    (print list)))
```

CHOMP takes a list as argument and calls CHOMP-ONCE on the list until CHOMP-ONCE returns NIL. Each time around the loop, CHOMP prints out the list.

Chomper itself is represented in one of three ways, depending on its current state. If Chomper is not currently moving in a direction, it is represented as a V. If it is moving left, it is represented as a >, and if it is moving right, as a <.

Thus the list fed to CHOMP consists of a series of zeros and ones and one instance of Chomper in one of its three states.

CHOMP-ONCE looks at the current direction of Chomper, checks to find out whether that is still appropriate, and, if so, moves Chomper:

```
(defun chomp-once (list)
  (let ((chomper-direction (chomper-going-where? list)))
    (case chomper-direction
      (> (if (anything-to-chomp-left list) (move-left list)
             (chomper-point 'V list)))
      (< (if (anything-to-chomp-right list) (move-right list)
             (chomper-point 'V list)))
      (V (cond ((anything-to-chomp-left list)
                (chomper-point '> list))
               ((anything-to-chomp-right list)
                (chomper-point '< list))
               (t nil))))))
```

Chomper always continues in the direction it is already going if there is any food at all in that direction.

CHOMPER-GOING-WHERE? is the function that determines the current direction of Chomper. It recursively examines the list until it comes to a representation of Chomper:

```
(defun chomper-going-where? (list)
  (case (car list)
    (< '<)
    (> '>)
    (V 'V)
    (t (chomper-going-where? (cdr list)))))
```

ANYTHING-TO-CHOMP-LEFT and ANYTHING-TO-CHOMP-RIGHT are Chomper's ''sensors.'' They determine whether there is any food in the direction that they examine. ANYTHING-TO-CHOMP-LEFT recursively examines the list as long as it keeps finding zeros. If it finds a one, it returns T to signify that there is something to chomp to the left of Chomper. If it finds Chomper, then it has not succeeded in finding any one to the left of Chomper, and so returns NIL.

```
(defun anything-to-chomp-left (list)
  (case (car list)
    (1 t)
    (0 (anything-to-chomp-left (cdr list)))
    ((< > V) nil)))
```

ANYTHING-TO-CHOMP-RIGHT calls a help procedure, FLUSH-UNTIL-CHOMPER, that returns the list starting after Chomper. It then examines this list, using the predicate MEMBER to test for the presence of ones:

```
(defun anything-to-chomp-right (list)
  (let ((list (flush-until-chomper list)))
    (member 1 list)))
(defun flush-until-chomper (list)
  (if (null list) nil
    (case (car list)
      ((> < V) (cdr list))
      (t (flush-until-chomper (cdr list))))))
```

MOVE-LEFT and MOVE-RIGHT do the actual movements. That is, they return lists in which Chomper has been moved. Since they are the last functions called in CHOMP-ONCE, the value they return is bound to the iteration variable LIST in CHOMP, and then printed on the screen.

```
(defun move-left (list)
  (cond ((eql (cadr list) '>) (cons '> (cons 0 (cddr list))))
        (t (cons (car list) (move-left (cdr list))))))
(defun move-right (list)
  (cond ((eql (car list) '<) (cons 0 (cons '< (cddr list))))
        (t (cons (car list) (move-right (cdr list))))))
```

Finally, CHOMPER-POINT changes the direction of Chomper by returning a list in which the new direction is substituted for the old, using the sequence function SUBSTITUTE:

```
(defun chomper-point (direction list)
  (let ((old-direction (chomper-going-where? list)))
    (substitute direction old-direction list)))
```

One nice thing about Chomper is that the list that is passed as data from procedure to procedure captures all information necessary to determine the future behavior of the system.

CHAPTER HIGHLIGHTS

Major Concepts
- Functions are recursive if they call themselves directly or indirectly.

- There are two kinds of recursive programs:

–those that can be thought of as "looping" or iterative;

–those that cannot.

- Recursive functions usually consist of two parts:

  1. one or more end tests and simple cases;

  2. a general case that involves recursive reduction of the problem to a simpler case of the same problem.

- LISP provides special constructs for compact iteration.

- DOTIMES iterates over its body a specified number of times.

- DOLIST iterates over its body once for every item in a list.

- DO is the major vehicle for iteration.

  –A DO-loop has three parts:

  1. a variable-value list;

  2. an end test with consequents;

  3. a body of forms to be executed each iteration.

- PROG1 returns the value of the first form evaluated in its body.

- PROG2 returns the value of the second form evaluated in its body.

- PROGN returns the value of the last form evaluated in its body.

Summary of New Syntax

```
(random number)
(do ((variable initial-value increment)
     (variable initial-value increment) ...)
    (end-test consequent-of-end-test consequent-of-end-test ...)
    (body-executed-each-loop))
(dotimes
    (variable count-form result-form) body-executed-each-loop)
(dolist (variable list result-form) body-executed-each-loop)
(prog1 form-whose-value-is-returned form ...)
(prog2 form form-whose-value-is-returned form ...)
(progn form form ... form-whose-value-is-returned)
```

Suggested Reading

The following sections in Steele, *COMMON LISP*, complement this chapter: chapter 7, Control Structure, 7.4, 7.8.2–7.8.3; chapter 12, Numbers, 12.9.

EXERCISES

The implementations of some of the following functions in COMMON LISP are more general than the implementations you will write. For example, rather than operating only on lists, most of these functions operate on any sequence. Likewise, some of them can take an indefinite number of arguments.

1. TRACE a call to TOWER-OF-HANOI.

```
(defun tower-of-hanoi (n from to spare)
  (cond ((= n 1) (move-disk from to))
        (t (tower-of-hanoi (- n 1) from spare to)
           (move-disk from to)
           (tower-of-hanoi (- n 1) spare to from)))) 

(defun move-disk (from to)
  (format t "~%Move a disk from ~a to ~a." from to))
```

2. Write MY-NTH as a recursive procedure. It should retrieve the *n*th item in a list. Note that this is not the same as NTHCDR, which retrieves the *n*th cdr of the list, not the *n*th element. Do not use NTHCDR in your implementation.

3. GET-MEMBER should take two inputs: an object and a list, and check to see if the object is a member of the list, using an EQL comparison. If so, it should return all of the list starting with the matched item. Otherwise, it should return NIL.

4. Write a procedure called FILTER, which takes a list and an item. It should return a list with all instances of item removed from it. The comparison test should be EQL.

5. MY-APPEND takes two lists and copies the first one into one list. Write MY-APPEND as a recursive procedure.

6. MY-REVERSE takes one argument, a list, and returns a list with all the elements reversed. Write it recursively.

7. Write an iterative procedure that takes a list and returns its reverse.

8. Write a procedure that takes a list of numbers as input and returns their average.

9. The following procedure pumps the pedals of every bike in a list of bicycles. There is a bug in it. Find the bug and correct the error.

```
(defun pump-all-pedals (bike-list)
   (do ((current-list bike-list (cdr current-list)))
       ((null current-list) nil
     (pump-pedals (car current-list)))))
```

10. Now use the procedure PUMP-ALL-PEDALS as a basis for writing a procedure that races the bicycles on the list by pumping each one's pedals a random number of times. (Use the RANDOM command, which takes one argument, a number, and returns a random value between zero and that number.)

Chapter 6

INTERACTIONS WITH
THE OUTSIDE WORLD

Most interesting programs require interaction with a user, interaction with a file system, or both. This chapter is about input and output. It introduces the LISP reader and printer and a new data type, the *stream*, which is a generalized mechanism for I/O in LISP.

6.1   GETTING USER INPUT

You have been introduced to two operators, Y-OR-N-P and YES-OR-NO-P, that allow you to get very specialized user input. These two predicates pose a question and solicit a response. Each returns either T or NIL, depending on the user's answer.

Of course, LISP also provides more general mechanisms for reading user input. READ, READ-LINE, and READ-CHAR are the three functions most commonly used for getting input. By default these functions read input from the keyboard; however, they can also be used to read from other sources, such as files.

READ-CHAR reads a character and returns it as a LISP character object.

```
(defun musical-taste ()
   (format t "~%Do you like rock 'n' roll?~%")
   (case (read-char)
     ((#\y #\Y)
      (format t
        "~%Great! We'll have to take in a concert sometime.~%"))
     (t (format t "~%Nice weather, isn't it?~%"))))
MUSICAL-TASTE

(musical-taste)
Do you like rock 'n' roll?
n
Nice weather, isn't it?
NIL
```

Each call to READ-CHAR reads exactly one character:

```
(defun read-two-chars ()
   (format t "~%Please type two characters:~%")
   (let ((a (read-char))
         (b (read-char)))
        (format t "~a ~a" a b)))
READ-TWO-CHARS

(read-two-chars)
Please type two characters:
no
n o
NIL
```

READ-LINE reads characters until it reaches a #\newline character. It returns the line as a string of characters, without the #\newline.

```
(defun musical-taste-revisited ()
   (format t "~%What kind of music do you like?~%")
   (let ((answer (read-line)))
      (if (search "rock" answer)
          (format t "~%Now we're cooking with gas.~%"))
      (if (search "classical" answer)
          (format t "~%Good, good.~%"))
      (if (search "baroque" answer)
          (format t "~%Here today, Bach tomorrow!~%")))
   (format t "Well, there's plenty of room ~
              for conversation here!~%"))
MUSICAL-TASTE-REVISITED

(musical-taste-revisited)
What kind of music do you like?

Folk, mostly.  I like classical sitar a lot.
Good, good.
Well, there's plenty of room for conversation here!
NIL
```

SEARCH looks for a sequence in another sequence. This example should remind you that it is much more difficult to determine what a user is saying when you allow complex input, such as strings, than it is when there are restrictions.

READ-CHAR and READ-LINE are functions, not variables. If you call either one a second time, it attempts to read a new item, rather than returning the old value. If you wish to use the input in more than one place, then, as usual, you must assign it a name:

```
(setf line (read-line))
```

6.1.1   The Reader

Every time you type an expression, LISP does three things: *reads* the expression, evaluates the expression, and prints the value returned by the expression.

READ is the function that LISP itself uses to get input and create LISP objects. It reads one LISP expression from the screen or file and returns the LISP object that corresponds to that expression. In chapter 2, you were given rules of thumb for distinguishing between different data types:

- A character is marked by #\.
- A string is delimited by double quote marks.
- A number is (as far as possible) anything that looks like a number.
- A symbol is a sequence of "alphabetic" characters that does not qualify as any other LISP object and terminates with either a NEWLINE, a SPACE, a parenthesis, or an END-OF-FILE character.
- A list is delimited by parentheses.

READ is the function that embodies the precise specification of these rules.

One feature worth mentioning now is that strings and symbols can contain any character. For example, LISP normally thinks that it has reached the end of a string when it sees a second double quote mark. However, even the double quote character can be included in a string if you explicitly tell LISP to include it, which is done by preceding the double quote with a special quoting character, \.

```
"This is a string with a quote (\") in it."
"This is a string with a quote (\") in it."
```

The backslash is not actually part of the string. Rather, the print function that LISP uses quotes the " before printing it, so that it can be read in again.

If you use this *escape character* on an ordinary item, the effect is the same as if you hadn't used it at all.

```
"This is a string with a q\uote in it."
"This is a string with a quote in it."
```

To put a backslash inside a string or symbol, you must quote it as well, using the backslash:

```
(format t "\\")
\
NIL
```

You can also quote a whole symbol by surrounding it with vertical bars. Typing MY SYMBOL is equivalent to typing my\ symbol or MY\ SYMBOL.

```
(eq ' MY SYMBOL  'my\ symbol)
T
```

my symbol is not equivalent to my\ symbol because the reader immediately capitalizes all non-quoted characters; however, my symbol is the same as \m\y\ \s\y\m\b\o\l.

When you call READ in your own programs, it behaves exactly as it does when LISP uses it. For example:

```
(defun get-statistics-and-return ()
  (format t "~%Please type a symbol, then ~
             a string, then a list.~%")
  (list (read) (read) (read)))

(get-statistics-and-return)

Please type a symbol, then a string, then a list.
marc "6736 East Boulevard" (skiing sailing bicycling)
(MARC "6736 East Boulevard" (SKIING SAILING BICYCLING))
```

It is not necessary to quote the symbol or the list because READ does not evaluate them.

Quoting a symbol or a list read by READ produces an interesting effect. 'my-symbol appears as (quote my-symbol). That is because the single quote mark is shorthand for the special form QUOTE, which returns its unevaluated argument. The single quote mark is an example of a *reader macro* and is expanded, or converted to "longhand" notation, by the reader.

LISP allows you to make modifications to the reader on several levels, including writing your own reader macros. However, code that uses custom reader macros is hard to read, and another user who wishes to employ it and loads the macros into her own environment may find that her own code no longer loads and reads correctly. Such extensions to the language are discouraged except as carefully designed notation when implementing an embedded language.

6.2   PRINTING

Just as you can call LISP's READ function for yourself, you can call the function that LISP uses to print: PRINT. PRINT takes a LISP object as an argument and prints a newline, the object, and a space. The object is printed in such a way as to be acceptable to READ.

FORMAT, which was introduced earlier, is a generalized mechanism for controlling output. As an option, FORMAT can put its output in a string and return it.

6.2.1   OTHER PRINT FUNCTIONS

FORMAT allows you to maintain elaborate control over what is output. However, by virtue of its complexity, FORMAT is not as fast as single-purpose functions.

PRIN1 is a simpler version of PRINT. It prints the object so that it is acceptable to READ, but does not print either the newline before or the space afterward. Thus it allows you to print several things on the same line.

PRINC differs from PRIN1 in that it does not preserve the LISP "readability" of the object. That is,

```
(princ "This is a string.")
```

produces:

```
This is a string.
"This is a string."
```

while (prin1 "This is a string.") produces

```
"This is a string."
"This is a string."
```

PRINC is intended to print strings in a way that is easy for humans to read. The differences between PRINC and PRIN1 are also noticeable if you call them to print symbols or strings in which quoted characters appear:

```
(prin1 'my\ symbol)
MY\ SYMBOL
(princ 'my\ symbol)
MY SYMBOL
```

The output of PRINC is like that of FORMAT when a ~a directive is used, while the output of PRIN1 is like that of FORMAT when a ~s directive is used.

Another useful function is TERPRI, which prints a #\newline character. Calling TERPRI is equivalent to using the FORMAT directive ~%.

6.3   CONVERTING TYPES

There are reasons for using a particular function to get user input, even though that function does not yield the right type of data for the rest of the program. For example, in some LISPs, READ-CHAR allows the program to react to user input as each character is typed,[1] while READ-LINE allows the user to type in as much as he wants on a line and then erase it. However, READ-LINE returns a string, and READ-CHAR returns a character. If you then want to look at the data as a series of symbols, you must convert them.

COERCE does explicit type conversion. It takes two arguments, an object and a result type, and returns an object of the result type:

```
(coerce "a b c" 'list)
(#\a #\SPACE #\b #\SPACE #\c)
```

[1]In some LISPs, all lines must be followed with a newline to be processed at all, so this consideration doesn't apply. Under these circumstances, programs in this book must have an extra call to READ-CHAR added after a READ-CHAR or READ to absorb the extra newline typed by the user to get anything at all processed.

Not all coercions make sense. For example, you cannot convert the string ''AB'' to a character. Likewise, the following fails to work:

```
(coerce '(1 2 3) 'string)
```

It produces an error because strings cannot contain numbers, but only characters.

When you coerce an object of one type to another type, the type of the object is not really changed; instead, a new object having some important property in common with the old object is created.[2] The important property normally involves the printed representation of the two objects.

In addition to COERCE, functions such as INT-CHAR, CHAR-INT, FLOAT, RATIONAL, ROUND, STRING, and others convert to specific types. You might also like to convert symbols to strings and strings to symbols. One way to obtain a string made up of the print name of a symbol is with the function SYMBOL-NAME, which takes a symbol and extracts its name, as a string, from its print name cell.

```
(symbol-name 'foo)
"FOO"
```

Quite often, you want to produce a string from several objects, perhaps of different types. As you have seen, FORMAT can be used to make strings out of any LISP objects, including other strings. For example,

```
(format nil "~a~a ~a" #\A "nother" 'thing)
```

returns

```
"Another THING"
```

READ-FROM-STRING is an operator that reads one item from a string and returns that item:

```
(read-from-string "another thing")
ANOTHER
(read-from-string "\"More and more\"")
"More and more"
```

You can use READ-FROM-STRING to read all the items from a string, but that is not very convenient, because you have to keep track of the index into the string by yourself.[3]

---

[2]In LISP, a coercion does not merely tell the compiler to treat the object as if it were of a given type, but, rather, it actually produces an object of that type. If the operation does not generate an error, then the result of a coercion is guaranteed to be a well-formed object of the correct type.

In some other languages, if one mistakenly coerces an integer to be a pointer to a string, no error is signalled, but an attempt to reference the pointer would probably result in nonsense or an access violation.

[3]Actually, READ-FROM-STRING returns a *second value*, telling you how much of the string has been read. See the section on multiple values, in Chapter 9, Advanced Constructs.

To be able to read all the objects from a string conveniently, you need to employ a new data type, *streams*, which provide a convenient generalized interface for reading and writing.

6.4   STREAMS

You can use all the facilities for input and output that have been described so far without any knowledge of the underlying mechanisms. However, an important concept has been skirted—that of the stream. *Streams are objects that serve as sources or sinks of data.*

Unlike a list, which has a definite number of elements (unless it is circular), a stream can be indefinitely long. Stream operations cannot access all of the input in a string at once; instead, the data are accessed *sequentially*. Stream processes compute only with the portion of a stream that they have at a given time.

The fact that streams are sequential makes them a little different to work with from most LISP objects; it is much less useful to see the printed representation of a stream than it is to see the printed representation of other objects. In fact, you generally interact with streams exclusively through stream operations, that is, with functions that create, access, or manipulate streams.

Without knowing it, you have been continually relying on streams since starting to work with LISP. All input and output in COMMON LISP is mediated by input and output streams. Anything you type at LISP is read by it through the stream that is the value of the global variable *STANDARD-INPUT*. When LISP prints a value on the screen, it is sent via the stream that is the value of the global variable *STANDARD-OUTPUT*, which is usually a stream directed to the screen. Streams can be thought of as conduits that direct information the way a river directs water.

All the functions introduced in the last few sections read from or write to streams. They take optional second arguments that allow you to specify which stream you want to send to or read from.

By default, READ reads from *STANDARD-INPUT*, which is normally connected to the screen. However, you could specify a stream that led, for example, from a file. FORMAT allows you to specify the name of a stream instead of T or NIL for its first argument; this can be used for writing information into a file. Note that when you have specified T as the first argument to FORMAT, you could have specified *STANDARD-OUTPUT* to exactly the same effect. In that context, T is shorthand for *STANDARD-OUTPUT*.

6.4.1   Streams to Strings

One simple but useful thing you can do is set up a stream from a string and read from that stream. WITH-INPUT-FROM-STRING is an operator that does this.

WITH-INPUT-FROM-STRING has two parts. The first is a clause containing the name that you want the stream to have and the string that the stream should read from. The second part is a body. The variable that names the stream can be referred to from within the body. Therefore, you can read from the stream from within the body.

```
(with-input-from-string
  (my-stream "This is my favorite string.")
    (print (read my-stream))
    (print (read my-stream)))
THIS
IS
IS
```

Here READ is directed by its argument to read from MY-STREAM instead of from *STANDARD-INPUT*. You can write a procedure that reads all the objects in a string and prints them on the screen. However, to do this, you have to use the other two optional arguments to READ in addition to the stream argument. The second optional argument comes after the stream designator and tells LISP what to do if it tries to read past the end of a stream. Normally, an error is generated. However, if the second argument is NIL, then when the end of the stream is encountered, LISP returns the third argument as the result. PRINT-ALL-ELEMENTS shows how multiple calls to read can be used to read an entire string:

```
(defun print-all-elements (string)
  (with-input-from-string (my-stream string)
    (do ((current-object (read my-stream nil 'eof)
                         (read my-stream nil 'eof)))
      ((eq current-object 'eof) t)
      (print current-object))))
(print-all-elements "brother sister mother father")
BROTHER
SISTER
MOTHER
FATHER
T
```

This example illustrates a standard use of multiple calls to READ to read all the elements in a stream, except for one important detail. As written above, the DO-loop in PRINT-ALL-ELEMENTS stops not only in the desired case, but also if the symbol EOF occurs in the stream being read:

```
(print-all-elements "brother eof father")
BROTHER
T
```

This potentially serious problem can be avoided by setting up an end test that the stream being read cannot contain. The standard way to do this is to create a unique cons cell:

```
(defun print-all-elements (string)
  (with-input-from-string (my-stream string)
    (let ((eof (list 'eof)))
      (do ((current-object (read my-stream nil eof)
                           (read my-stream nil eof)))
          ((eq current-object eof) t)
        (print current-object)))))
```

Now DO tests for the unique cons cell created whenever the variable/value section of the LET is evaluated (whenever PRINT-ALL-ELEMENTS is run). If (eof) occurs in the stream, a new and different cons cell, not EQ to the end test, is created. Therefore:

```
(print-all-elements "brother eof father")
BROTHER
EOF
FATHER
T
```

You can also set up streams that write to a string. WITH-OUTPUT-TO-STRING has the same syntax as WITH-INPUT-FROM-STRING, except that if you do not specify a particular string to write to, WITH-OUTPUT-TO-STRING makes one and returns it as its value. We have sometimes used FORMAT to accomplish tasks that might have been done with WITH-OUTPUT-TO-STRING, like putting together strings of symbols.

```
(with-output-to-string (my-stream)
      (princ "This" my-stream)
      (princ "is" my-stream))
"Thisis"
(format nil "~a~a" "This" "is")
"Thisis"
```

A useful trick is to bind *STANDARD-INPUT* or *STANDARD-OUTPUT* in one of these forms. Since they are globally available variables, we need not declare them special here:

```
(setf storage-string (with-output-to-string (*standard-output*)
                        <body>))
```

During the execution of the body of this form, any output that would normally send to *STANDARD-OUTPUT* is sent to the string, which then becomes STORAGE-STRING's value.

6.4.2   File I/O

The function OPEN creates and returns a stream to a file. While a file is open, if the stream is an output stream, output to the stream is written to the file itself. If the stream is an input stream, input is read from the file. CLOSE closes the file and therefore prevents you from writing to or reading from it any further.

Because an open file can cause problems in many operating systems, there is another form besides OPEN, which is more commonly used. Called WITH-OPEN-FILE, it differs from OPEN in that it always tries to close the connection to the file when exited, even when there is an error. This means that if you open a file and lose the pointer to it, it will still be closed before the end of the session with LISP.

The structure of WITH-OPEN-FILE is similar to that of WITH-INPUT-FROM-STRING. Its first part is a list that contains the name of the stream, the file name, and options to the function call. Both OPEN and WITH-OPEN-FILE have a variety of options that specify whether the stream is to be read from or written to and set default parameters for interaction with the file system.

The second part of the form is the body, which contains all the operations you wish to accomplish with the stream open. When the body is exited, either normally or because of an error, the stream is automatically closed, and you can no longer read from or write to it.

The following example creates the stream OUTPUT-STREAM to write to the file whose name is given as the argument to MY-WRITE-LINE. The keyword options specify (a) that the direction is output, (b) that if the file already exists, a new version is to be created (with a higher version number than the previous one if the file system supports version numbers), and (c) that if the file does not exist, it is to be created:

```
(defun my-write-line (output-file)
   (with-open-file (output-stream output-file
                                  :direction :output
                                  :if-exists :new-version
                                  :if-does-not-exist :create)
     (format output-stream
       "Science, sans conscience, n'est que ruine de l'ame.")))
```

The body of the form writes the line "Science, sans conscience, n'est que ruine de l'ame." to OUTPUT-STREAM and then ends, closing the file.

The following example opens an output stream and then an input stream internally. This construction allows programs to operate on the input stream and to write the resulting values to the output stream.

```
(defun copy-line (input-file output-file)
   (with-open-file (output-stream output-file
                                  :direction :output
                                  :if-exists :new-version
                                  :if-does-not-exist :create)
     (with-open-file (input-stream input-file
                                  :direction :input)
        (format output-stream "~a" (read input-stream)))))
```

One additional complication to using WITH-OPEN-FILE in a practical application is a variable scoping problem. As the procedure above stands, the variables OUTPUT-STREAM

and INPUT-STREAM can be referenced only within the textual body of the instances of
WITH-OPEN-FILE. What if you wanted other functions in the program to read from or
write to these streams? There is a choice about how to make these streams accessible
outside the textual body of the procedure.

One way of doing it is to pass them as arguments to the appropriate procedures.
Another way is to declare the variables holding the streams special, that is, dynamically
scoped. A third way is to create the variables that hold them at top level with DEFVAR,
which makes them special and accessible to all the functions. Recall that it is a LISP
convention to name special variables with asterisks on either side.

Every form that we have learned that binds variables has a place for declarations. In
WITH-OPEN-FILE, declarations can be made between the first part and the body:

```
(defun copy-from-other-function (input-file output-file)
  (with-open-file (*output-stream* output-file
                            :direction :output
                            :if-exists :new-version
                            :if-does-not-exist :create)
    (declare (special *output-stream*))
    (with-open-file (*input-stream* input-file
                             :direction :input)
      (declare (special *input-stream*))
      (another-function)))))
(defun another-function ()
  (yet-another-function))

(defun yet-another-function ()
  (declare (special *input-stream* *output-stream*))
  (format *output-stream* "~a" (read *input-stream*)))
```

CLOSE allows you to close files manually:

```
(close stream)
```

However, you hardly ever need this, since WITH-OPEN-FILE does it automatically.

6.5   PATHNAMES

To use the examples above, you have to be able to specify file names. This is easy: all
you need do is type in the name, as a string, in an appropriate format for the operating
system being used.

You may wonder how specific you have to be in specifying file names. The answer
is that, in general, the defaults are set in such a way that you need be no more specific
than you would be if accessing the same file from an editor.

File names can be specified as strings, symbols, streams, or *pathnames*. COMMON
LISP provides pathnames for portability. A pathname is an object that names a file.

Pathname components include host, device, directory, name, type, and version fields, as appropriate, for a particular operating system. You can perform operations on pathnames that would be difficult to perform on the string representation of a file name; for example, you can merge specific names with default names.

For a more detailed discussion of pathnames, see Steele and the reference manual for your particular implementation of LISP.

6.6   AN EXTENDED EXAMPLE: THE ANIMAL PROGRAM

The animal program implements a game similar to Twenty Questions, except that the questions and answers must be about animals. It asks the user to think of an animal and tries to guess what it is. The "knowledge" in the program is held in a list with a tree structure. User directives cause the program to trace a given path through the tree and arrive at a particular leaf.

A sample game of animal looks like this:

```
(init-animal)
Think of an animal and I will try to guess what it is
by asking questions.

Does it sing?
y
Is it a canary?
n
Oh well, I give up.  What was the answer?
nightingale
Please type a question whose answer is yes for a canary
and no for a nightingale.
Is it yellow?
Do you want to play again?
y
Think of an animal and I will try to guess what it is
by asking questions.

Does it sing?
y
Is it yellow?
n
Is it a nightingale?
y
It was nothing, folks.  I knew it all along.

Do you want to play again?
n

Come back soon now, y'hear?
NIL
```

Each node of the tree contains three items: a question, a yes-branch, and a no-branch. The question must be such that its answer distinguishes between the yes-branch and the no-branch. When a node is reached, the question is posed. User response controls whether the yes-branch or the no-branch is chosen. The fundamental selectors QUESTION, YES-BRANCH, and NO-BRANCH extract these elements, as needed.

The leaves contain guesses, which are the names of animals. When a leaf is reached, the program presents the leaf's contents as its answer. The leaf's contents are extracted with the selector ANIMAL. If the answer is correct, that round of the game is over. Otherwise, the program attempts to "learn." Learning is accomplished by posing a series of questions to the user, which extract enough information to call the modifier ADD. ADD replaces the old leaf with a new node containing the old leaf on its no-branch.

One remarkable quality of programs like this is that a very small amount of information and a few tricks can give an impressive superficial appearance of intelligence. Since the knowledge structure and the path through it are completely invisible to the user, it can seem as if the computer is thinking like a person and, more impressively, learning like a person.

Try out the animal game a few times to get an idea of what the user interface is like. The code presented here is very sparse. Read it and try to understand exactly what is going on. LISP's comment character is the semicolon.

```lisp
;;; This is our knowledge tree.
(defvar *animal-data* '("Does it sing" (canary)
                         ("Could it have spots" (dog)
                          ("Does it lay eggs"
                           (chicken)
                           (dolphin)))))
;;; INIT-ANIMAL starts everything.
(defun init-animal ()
  (format t "~%Think of an animal and I will ~
    try to guess what it is ~%by asking questions.~1%")
  ;; We call MAIN-LOOP with our whole, current tree.
  (main-loop *animal-data*))

;;; MAIN-LOOP figures out whether we are at a node or a leaf.
;;; If at a node, it asks the question that is the car of
;;; the node.  Otherwise, it calls GUESS with the animal
;;; that is at the leaf.
(defun main-loop (knowledge)
  (cond ((question-node-p knowledge) (ask knowledge))
        (t (guess knowledge))))

;;; ASK takes a knowledge tree as input.  It extracts the
;;; question from the tree and poses it.  It loops back to
;;; MAIN-LOOP with either the yes-branch or the no-branch
;;; depending on the answer that the user gives.
(defun ask (knowledge)
  (format t "~%~A?~%" (question knowledge))
  (let ((answer (read-line)))
```

```
       (cond ((equalp answer "yes")
              (main-loop (yes-branch knowledge)))
             ((equalp answer "no")
              (main-loop (no-branch knowledge)))
             (t (format t "~%Please type yes or no.~%")
                (ask knowledge)))))
```

```
;;; GUESS makes a guess.  If the guess is correct, this
;;; iteration of the game is over and it asks if the
;;; player wishes to continue.  If the guess is incorrect,
;;; it attempts to add to its knowledge tree.   GUESS
;;; is called only when we are examining a leaf of the
;;; knowledge tree.
(defun guess (knowledge)
  (format t "~%Is it ~A?~%" (a-or-an (animal knowledge)))
  (let ((answer (read-line)))
    (cond ((equalp answer "yes") (gloat) (play-again?))
          ((equalp answer "no") (learn knowledge) (play-again?))
          (t (format nil "~%Please type yes or no.~%")
             (guess knowledge)))))
```

```
;;; LEARN gathers the information to replace the old-node with
;;; a new-node consisting of a question, a yes-branch, and a
;;; no-branch.  Then it calls ADD, which does the actual
;;; replacement.  The old-node should be on the no-branch of
;;; the new-node because that is the way the question is
;;; phrased.
(defun learn (old-node)
  (format t "~%Oh, well, I give up.  What was the answer?~%")
  (let ((new-animal (read)))
    (format t "~%Please type a question whose answer is yes for~
       ~a and no for ~a.~%"
            (a-or-an new-animal)
            (a-or-an (animal old-node)))
    (let ((new-question (read-line)))
      (add new-question
        (animal old-node)
        new-animal
        old-node))))
```

```
;;; ADD replaces the old node with the new node.
;;; ADD is the constructor function for the game.
(defun add (new-question old-animal new-animal node)
  (setf (car node) new-question)
  (setf (cdr node) (list (list new-animal)
                         (list old-animal))))
```

```
(defun a-or-an (symbol)
  (let ((word (format nil "~a" symbol)))
    (cond ((member (char word 0) '(#\A #\E #\I #\O #\U))
           (format nil "an ~a" (string-downcase word)))
          (t (format nil "a ~a" (string-downcase word))))))
```

```
;;; PLAY-AGAIN?  asks the user if he wishes to continue.
(defun play-again? ()
  (format t "~%Do you want to play again?~%")
  (let ((response (read-line)))
```

```
        (cond ((equalp response "yes")
               (init-animal))
              ((equalp response "no")
               (format t "~%Come back soon now, y'hear?~%"))
              (t (format t
                    "~%I guess that's a no.  Well, goodbye.~%")))))
(defun gloat ()
  (format t "~%It was nothing, folks.  I knew it ~
    all along.~%"))
;;; QUESTION, ANIMAL, YES-BRANCH, and NO-BRANCH are the primitive
;;; selectors for the game.  QUESTION and ANIMAL both get the
;;; car of the knowledge tree.  It requires the predicate
;;; QUESTION-NODE-P to tell whether the item is a question
;;; or an animal.
(defun question (knowledge)
  (car knowledge))

(defun animal (knowledge)
  (car knowledge))

(defun question-node-p (knowledge)
  (stringp (question knowledge)))

(defun yes-branch (knowledge)
  (cadr knowledge))

(defun no-branch (knowledge)
  (caddr knowledge))
```

Although this is the largest program presented thus far, it is a minimal implementation of the animal game. One interesting thing to do is to take a program like this and improve it, as you will be asked to do in the exercises.

CHAPTER HIGHLIGHTS

Major Concepts

- READ-CHAR reads one character from the specified stream, or from the terminal if no stream is specified.

- READ-LINE reads one line as a string of characters.

- READ reads one LISP object.

- Complex writing can be accomplished with FORMAT.

- PRINT and PRINC can be used to print without escape characters.

- PRIN1 can be used to print with escape characters.

- Reading and printing are accomplished via objects called streams.

- Streams are sources or sinks of data.

- Stream operations are sequential.

- OPEN allows you to open a stream to file.

- CLOSE allows you to close a stream opened by OPEN.

- WITH-OPEN-FILE should be used instead of OPEN whenever possible.

- WITH-OPEN-FILE is like OPEN, except that it always tries to close your file automatically.

- A pathname is an object that names a file.

Summary of New Syntax

```
(read stream)
(read-line stream)
(read-char stream)
```

```
(princ string)
(prin1 string)
(print string)
(terpri string)
```

```
(coerce obj result-type)
```

```
(with-input-from-string (stream-name string) body)
```

```
(with-open-file (streamvar file-name options) body)
(open filename options)
(close stream)
```

Suggested Reading

The following selections from Steele, *COMMON LISP*, complement this chapter: chapter 4, Type Specifiers, 4.8; chapter 21, Streams, 21.1–21.3; chapter 22, Input/Output, 22.1–22.3; chapter 23, File System Interface, 23.1–23.2.

EXERCISES

1. Write a procedure that asks the user for a number and counts down from that number to one.

2. Now expand that procedure to count up from a negative number to zero, as well as counting down from a positive number.

3. Now improve your procedure so that it checks to see if the user has really typed a number, and, if not, calls itself recursively.

4. Write a version of A-OR-AN that prompts the user for a word and then returns that word together with the appropriate indefinite article.

5. How could you find out whether the backslashes were really in the following string if you were not sure?

    `"The cat is in the \"hat.\""`

6. One obvious problem with the `ANIMAL` program is that it's not very flexible about user responses. If the user types `a chicken` instead of `chicken`, the answer gets recorded as `a`. If the user types in a question mark at the end of his question, the question later appears with two. Don't hesitate to employ any useful functions (previously introduced or not) when making the following improvements:

    a. Check to determine whether the user response starts with ''a'' or ''an'' and take the substring that is the name if it does. (If you are going through these problems in order, don't forget to redefine `A-OR-AN`.)

    b. Sometimes a user might like to type in two or more words to describe the animal, for example, `BROWN HEN`, or `A BROWN HEN`. Extend or change the procedure you just wrote to deal with this more complex situation. Many strategies are possible; an acceptable one is to treat the animal name as a single symbol, `BROWN-HEN`.

    c. Write a procedure that examines the user's input to `ANIMAL` and either adds or deletes a question mark at the end. Make any necessary changes to the rest of the program to produce consistent output. Note that all functions in Steele, chapter 14, Sequences, work on strings as well as lists. Functions in chapter 18, Strings, however, work only on strings.

    d. The animal program is organized recursively. However, the problem is not intrinsically recursive and this structure could mean that a lot of information is retained long after it is needed. Rewrite the control structure iteratively.

    e. After you have reorganized the animal program iteratively, modify it so that it reads in and writes out its information from a file called `ANIMAL.DAT` (or an equivalent name appropriate for your file system).

Chapter 7

MANIPULATING DATA

It is not hard to deduce from LISP's name, which stands for *LISt Processing* language, that its fundamental way of organizing and storing information is the list. Many of LISP's strengths as a language for research accrue from the intrinsic qualities of lists; it's easy to try out new ideas when it's easy to code, and lists make it easy to code because you never have to worry about adding too many elements to them and because they can be decomposed by simple and elegant recursive processes. In fact, function calling in LISP is simple and predictable partly because it employs list structure.

However, over the last twenty-five years, a lot of thought has been given to data structures and their use in programming. One of the most interesting changes in LISP has been the gradual integration into the language of diverse data structures as programmers invented them or came to a consensus that they were necessary. This chapter covers some of the data structures that COMMON LISP provides and the functions that support those structures. The first few sections present higher-level structures built out of lists. In the last sections, new data types: *vectors*, *arrays*, *hash tables*, and *structures* will be introduced.

7.1   DATA ABSTRACTION

You have been now exposed to all the tools you need for storing data in lists and for retrieving them by examining the list's contents. We have even discussed two systems that do this. In chapter 6, the animal game stored its data in a tree, which was implemented as a list. In chapter 4, a set of functions that could be used to create and manipulate objects representing bicycles was introduced.

There are important points to be drawn from these examples, which demonstrate the concept of data abstraction. For example, the tree in the animal program is implemented using lists. However, only a few functions in the program actually depend directly on that: ADD, which constructs nodes, and the selectors QUESTION, ANIMAL, YES-BRANCH, and

135

NO-BRANCH. These functions form a complete interface between whatever implements the tree and the rest of the program; from the point of view of the rest of the program, the actual implementation is a black box, which can be changed as long as each of these functions continues to accept and deliver the same information it used to.

A good data abstraction isolates one conceptual level from another. In part, it means that the main portion of a program refers to data manipulators that are especially designed for the task at hand. These may be built from other task-specific functions or from LISP primitives. However, the level in which the tree is a list is isolated from the level in which it is a series of nodes and leaves. Although the ease of function definition in LISP encourages this kind of programming, identifying and enforcing such situations is a hard part of programming effectively. Most of this chapter is about facts: what functions exist, what structures exist. However, data abstraction is the backdrop against which these facts are presented. It is a discipline which, in addition to helping us write clearer, more maintainable programs, helps us understand the scope of the choices we make about data structures.

7.2   BUILDING MORE COMPLEX STRUCTURES OUT OF LISTS

The bicycle program was an example of a relatively clean data abstraction. It is a list on the inside and a bicycle with three qualities on the outside. A complete interface, including constructors, selectors, and modifiers for each of the bicycle's properties, was developed. For example,

```
(defun make-bike (x-position wheel-size gear-ratio)
   (list x-position wheel-size gear-ratio))
(defun x-position (bike)
   (car bike))
(defun set-x-position (bike x-position)
   (setf (car bike) x-position))
```

A short program, PUMP-PEDALS, took advantage of this abstraction. PUMP-PEDALS demonstrates that this system can be used easily. However, the system has a problem; when you want to add another attribute, if you add it anywhere but at the end of the list, you have to rewrite some of the old selectors and constructors.

The source of this problem is the use of a rule about the *order* of the items in the list to identify each attribute. This means that the selectors and constructors have to know about the order of the items. Rules about order lack modularity because they require that information be distributed between the data and the manipulators that work on the data.

An alternative strategy is to label each piece of data. Although it requires more space, it reduces the complexity of the program. Rules about item order are not always a mistake. Sometimes you can be relatively sure that neither you nor anyone else will want to add or delete attributes on a regular basis. However, when flexibility in adding and deleting items from a list is crucial, you want to label your data.

COMMON LISP provides selectors and modifiers for two ways of grouping together indicators (that is, labels) and values. An *association list* is a list with a structure that looks like this:

```
((indicator . value) (indicator . value) (indicator . value))
```

This can be drawn with a box-and-pointer diagram:

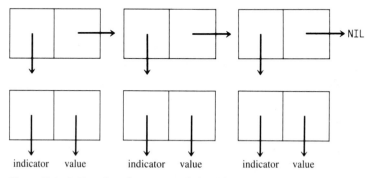

```
indicator    value      indicator    value      indicator    value
```

Figure 7-1. A Template for an Association List

COMMON LISP also provides a set of functions that deal with *property lists*. The data in a property list consist of alternating indicators and values:

```
(indicator value indicator value indicator value)
```

Each indicator/value pair is called a property.

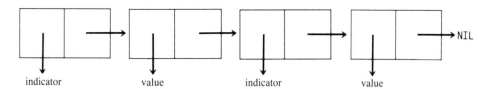

```
indicator          value          indicator          value
```

Figure 7-2. A Template for a Property List

7.3   ASSOCIATION LISTS

Sometimes the term ''association list'' or ''a-list'' is used loosely to refer to any scheme for associating a property and a value in a list. However, in the strict sense an association list is a list whose elements are cons cells. Each cons cell must contain an indicator name in its car and a value in its cdr:

```
((indicator . value) (indicator . value) (indicator . value))
```

Although it is easy to write a fundamental set of functions to manipulate association lists, COMMON LISP provides some built-in functions for convenience.

As an example of the use of association lists, you can define a list of employee names and addresses:

```
(defvar *employees*
  '((john . "62 Walnut St.") (rick . "1066 Umbrella St.")))
```

JOHN and RICK are indicators here; "62 Walnut St." and "1066 Umbrella St." are their associated values.

The function ASSOC, which stands for "associate," extracts items from lists. It is a selector that takes an indicator and an a-list as arguments and searches the a-list for a cons whose car is the indicator.

```
(assoc 'rick *employees*)
(RICK . "1066 Umbrella St.")
```

In previous examples, there was a separate selector function for each property that an object could have: X-POSITION, WHEEL-SIZE, GEAR-RATIO. If you wanted more properties, you had to write more selectors. Now we have one selector that takes a particular property to look for as an argument. ASSOC is independent of the number and order of the properties in the list. This isn't necessarily a good thing; in order to use ASSOC, you must know that the data are in an association list, while to use the old selectors, you didn't need to know anything about how they were stored. Therefore, under some circumstances, you might want to rewrite the selectors to use ASSOC or, alternatively, write a selector called GET-BICYCLE-QUALITY, which would take a bicycle and a quality and call ASSOC internally.

Unlike the bicycle selectors, which return a single value, ASSOC returns the cons cell that contains both the indicator and the value. This turns out to be useful, because the cons cell shares list structure with the larger list. You can make modifications to the parts of the cons cell, and this changes them in the larger list as well.[1]

Naturally, COMMON LISP provides a means to add associations to lists. ACONS takes as arguments an indicator, a value, and the list to put the new association into.

```
(acons 'gregory  "5 Yesterday Lane" *employees*)
((GREGORY . "5 Yesterday Lane") (JOHN . "62 Walnut St.")
 (RICK . "1066 Umbrella St."))
```

---

[1]See section 4.4.1, Using SETF to Change the Value of a Variable.

Like CONS, ACONS is nondestructive. If you want to modify *EMPLOYEES* to have this new value, you have to do so explicitly:

```
(setf *employees*
  (acons 'gregory "5 Yesterday Lane" *employees*))
```

You can now write a function called ADD-EMPLOYEE:

```
(defun add-employee (name address)
  (setf *employees* (acons name address *employees*)))
```

If you had wanted to, you could have created the original employee list like this:

```
(defvar *employees*)

(defun init ()
  (add-employee 'john "62 Walnut St.")
  (add-employee 'rick "1066 Umbrella St."))
```

This way you avoid violating the abstraction and thus, presumably, the temptation to think of *EMPLOYEES* as a list with a certain order that can be accessed with normal list functions.

The function REMOVE, which works on any sequence, can be used to return a list with a pair completely removed:

```
(remove (assoc 'john *employees*) *employees*)
((GREGORY . "5 Yesterday Lane") (RICK . "1066 Umbrella St."))
```

ASSOC returns a cons cell to REMOVE, and REMOVE returns the list (or possibly a copy of it) without any instances of the cons cell. To make this modification permanent, you must change the value of *EMPLOYEES*, as with the following function:

```
(defun remove-employee (employee)
  (setf *employees* (remove (assoc employee *employees*)
                            *employees*)))
```

REMOVE provides a means of eliminating a pair, but sometimes you may want to use the same indicator while changing the value of a pair. Usually you don't actually modify the value but instead rely on the facts that ASSOC always finds the first instance of a cons whose car matches the indicator, and that ACONS always adds on to the front of the list. This allows you to use association lists like push stacks. For example, if you know that Rick is going away for the summer, you add his summer address to the front of the list:

```
(add-employee 'rick "666 Abbey St.")
```

Then the list employees would look like:

```
((RICK . "666 Abbey St.") (GREGORY . "5 Yesterday Lane")
 (JOHN . "62 Walnut St.") (RICK . "1066 Umbrella St."))
```

and

```
(assoc 'rick *employees*)
(RICK . "666 Abbey St.")
```

However, at the end of the summer, you can delete the summer address with REMOVE-EMPLOYEE, and the old address takes over.

Of course, it is also possible to update values by destructively modifying the old ones. If you were sure that ASSOC would not return NIL, you could just type the following phrase:

```
(setf (cdr (assoc 'rick *employees*)) "666 Abbey St.")
```

7.3.1   *Rassoc, Keyword Arguments, and Function*

RASSOC, which stands for "reverse assoc," is another useful function. Instead of taking an indicator and returning the indicator and its value, RASSOC takes a value and returns the indicator and the value.

Two new ideas must be introduced before you can use RASSOC on *EMPLOYEES*. The first is the optional keyword value pair, the second, the operator FUNCTION:

```
(rassoc "666 Abbey St." *employees* :test (function equalp))
(RICK . "666 Abbey St.")
```

The definition of RASSOC allows the use of the optional keyword :TEST. :TEST states that, instead of using EQL, we want RASSOC to use the test that we specify to decide whether the item matches any of the values in the a-list. In this case, we want RASSOC to use EQUALP instead of EQL because the indicator slots in EMPLOYEES are strings, and two strings that look the same are not EQL in most implementations of LISP. :TEST is not quoted, because all symbols that start with colons are keywords, and are self-evaluating. Keywords will be discussed in more detail in chapter 9.

The test specified must follow the keyword. However, RASSOC doesn't take the name of the function as its argument; rather, it wants the *function object* associated with that symbol. The function object is the object actually containing the code that implements the function; it can be passed as data and later called under program control. The function FUNCTION takes a symbol and returns the function object associated with that symbol. Topics associated with this will be developed in chapter 8.

FUNCTION is abbreviated as #', so we would normally write:

```
(rassoc "666 Abbey St." *employees* :test #'equalp)
```

Many of the functions presented in the chapter on writing procedures take optional keyword arguments.

7.4   **PROPERTY LISTS**

Property lists are data structures that alternate indicators and values:

```
(indicator value indicator value indicator value)
```

GETF is a selector that works on property lists.

```
(defvar *phone-list* '(patrick "555-4904" marc "415-555-9989"
  leigh "555-0205"))
*PHONE-LIST*
(getf *phone-list* 'marc)
"415-555-9989"
```

SETF has special knowledge of GETF, which means that you can change values by calling SETF on a call to GETF:

```
(setf (getf *phone-list* 'marc) "555-4483")
"555-4483"
```

You can also use SETF together with GETF to add to the property list once it has been initialized.

One of the chief differences between property lists and association lists is that, unlike ASSOC, GETF returns only the value, not the indicator/value pair. It wouldn't really make sense for GETF to return the entire property, because there is no special unit of list structure associated with the property. A cons would have to be especially created and no useful sharing could be accomplished. Unhappily, this means that you cannot easily examine the value extracted with GETF first, and then change it.[2] That is, the following won't actually change *PHONE-LIST*:

```
(let ((temp (getf *phone-list* 'marc)))
  (if temp (setf temp "555-1106")))
```

REMF removes properties destructively.

```
(remf *phone-list* 'marc)
T

*phone-list*
(PATRICK "555-4904" LEIGH "555-0205" STEVE "555-8797")
```

---

[2]See section 4.4, SETF and Destructive Modification.

7.5 PROPERTY LISTS IN PROPERTY LIST CELLS

Recall that a symbol is a construct made up of different parts: the value is one, the function binding another. The value of a symbol can be accessed under certain conditions, for instance, when typing it in at top level. The function binding is accessed when the symbol is evaluated as the first element in a list or when FUNCTION (#') is used. The property list is another part of a symbol. When a symbol is created, its property list is NIL. Property lists stored in the property list cell of a symbol have the same functionality as property lists stored in the value cell. Thus, operations on them are similar. However, LISP provides functions for manipulating property lists stored in property list cells.

GET parallels GETF. It takes two values, a symbol and an indicator, and returns the value that corresponds to the indicator. Suppose you had already created a property list in the property list cell of the symbol *NEW-PHONE-LIST*. You would be able to use it as follows:

```
(get '*new-phone-list* 'marlene)
"555-6212"
```

You have to quote the symbol whose property list you want to look at because you want to hand GET the symbol itself, not the value of the symbol. GET has special knowledge about how to access the property list of a symbol—you need not find it for GET.

If you had not already created the property list, you would have gotten NIL:

```
(get '*new-phone-list* 'marlene)
NIL
```

If there is no value for the particular indicator, GET also returns NIL. As a consequence, it is impossible to tell the difference between an indicator whose value is null and an indicator that isn't on the list.

You can use a SETF/GET combination to replace old values with new ones. You can also use it to create properties, if no key of the specified name is found.[3]

```
(get '*new-phone-list* 'marlene)
NIL
(setf (get '*new-phone-list* 'marlene) "555-5834")
"555-5834"
(get '*new-phone-list* 'marlene)
"555-5834"
(setf (get '*new-phone-list* 'marlene) "555-4904")
"555-4904"
(get '*new-phone-list* 'marlene)
"555-4904"
```

---

[3]The combination of SETF and GET replaces the PUTPROP function found in older LISPs.

This way of changing the property list encourages a programming style different from that used with association lists. Since updating and adding properties is done destructively, it is difficult to have multiple properties with the same indicator. That means that you don't ordinarily use property lists as push stacks, but rather for situations where unique identifiers are desired.

One way to achieve the effect of deletion is to set the value of a pair to NIL. However, if you wish, you can delete a property altogether from a symbol's property list with REMPROP:

```
(remprop '*new-phone-list* 'marlene)
T

(get '*new-phone-list* 'marlene)
NIL
```

REMPROP returns T if the indicator is present and NIL if no property is found.

7.6   ARRAYS AND VECTORS

The first part of this chapter described different ways to organize lists. Lists, the heart of LISP, provide enormous flexibility and are particularly useful if you are going to add and delete items or deal with small amounts of data. Vectors and arrays are less flexible than lists, but they are faster and more efficient in certain situations. For example, it is more space-efficient to store text in a string than in a list.

In general, vectors and arrays in COMMON LISP behave the way they do in other high-level languages. Arrays are objects with components arranged according to a rectilinear coordinate system. Vectors are special kinds of arrays—arrays of one dimension. Vectors and arrays are zero-based as in C (not like PASCAL) and are defined for zero-dimension and for zero-length. Strings, which you already know about, turn out to be special kinds of vectors, vectors consisting of characters.

Arrays are usually created with the constructor function MAKE-ARRAY. MAKE-ARRAY takes a variable number of arguments. The first must specify the dimensions of the array, but the rest are specified with keyword/value pairs. In the following example the first argument specifies that this is a 3 x 2 x 4 array; these are the number of elements you wish each dimension to be able to hold.

```
(setf my-array
  (make-array '(3 2 4)
              :initial-contents '(((a b c l) (1 2 3 b))
                                  ((d e f j) (3 1 2 g))
                                  ((g h i r) (2 3 1 d)))))
```

The value associated with :INITIAL-CONTENTS is a list whose structure parallels the structure of the array. The list contains first-dimension elements, each sublist contains second-dimension elements, and each sub-sublist has third-dimension elements.

Objects in the array can be referenced by their subscripts, with the AREF command:

```
(aref array subscript1 subscript2 ...)
```

For example,

```
(aref my-array 2 0 1)
```

yields H. The indexes 2, 0, and 1 correspond in order to the dimensions 3, 2, and 4. The 0th index corresponds to the first element in a given dimension of the array.

Array elements can be modified with SETF:

```
(setf (aref my-array 2 0 1) 'apple)
APPLE

my-array
#3A(((a b c 1)    (1 2 3 b))
    ((d e f j)    (3 1 2 g))
    ((g APPLE i r) (2 3 1 d)))
```

When LISP prints arrays on the screen, it starts them with a pound sign, the number of dimensions in the array, and an A. The array is then written as a series of nested lists.

Vectors, as stated above, are arrays of one dimension. All array manipulation functions can be used on vectors; however, COMMON LISP also provides special vector manipulation functions for convenience.

In particular, vectors can be created with the command VECTOR:

```
(vector 'a 'b 'c)
#(a b c)
```

This is an alternative to the wordier call to MAKE-ARRAY. Although you are already familiar with basic string manipulation functions, it is worth noting that all array and vector functions work on strings, in addition to specialized string functions and all sequence functions.

These data types require somewhat more bookkeeping on your part than do lists. For example, if you want to get an element of a list, you examine the list recursively. This takes an amount of time roughly proportional to the length of the list before the item. With an array, you can get any item in constant time, if you know exactly where to look. Otherwise, you can search the array (possibly using DOTIMES); however, you must always be careful not to make references past the end of an array. There is no convenient sign (like NIL) to indicate that you have come to the end.

7.6.1   Fill Pointers, Adjustable Arrays

In part, lists are more flexible and easier to use than arrays because it is a trivial matter to lengthen or shorten them. LISP provides two forms of assistance for this problem handling arrays: *fill pointers* and *adjustable arrays*. Neither of these is a perfect solution, but they do give you more options.

Fill pointers allow you to both set aside ample contiguous space for a vector or array and designate an active portion within it. When working with the array, you can treat it as if it were smaller, yet when the time comes, you can use the space already set aside without the expense of array creation or enlargement. For example, VECTOR-PUSH and VECTOR-POP automatically update the fill pointer and allow you to treat a vector as a stack. LENGTH returns the length of the active portion of the array:

```
(setf things-to-do (make-array '(25) :fill-pointer 0))
(vector-push 'get-a-new-car things-to-do)
0
(length things-to-do)
1
(array-total-size things-to-do)
25
(vector-push 'get-a-job things-to-do)
1
(length things-to-do)
2
(elt things-to-do 0)
GET-A-NEW-CAR
(elt things-to-do 1)
GET-A-JOB
```

Now there are two elements on the push stack. If you decide to you can push more tasks on them as well:

```
(vector-push 'get-a-haircut things-to-do)
2
(length things-to-do)
3
(elt things-to-do 2)
GET-A-HAIRCUT
```

As you accomplish these tasks, you can pop them off again:

```
(vector-pop things-to-do)
GET-A-HAIRCUT
(length things-to-do)
2
(elt things-to-do 1)
GET-A-JOB
```

Sequence operators such as ELT and LENGTH respect the abstraction of the fill pointer and signal an error if you give them an index that is too large. In contrast, operators on arrays such as AREF and ARRAY-TOTAL-SIZE look at the total array. It may be necessary to use ARRAY-TOTAL-SIZE to find out if you can move the fill pointer any more; however, AREF should probably be avoided because you might accidentally refer to items after the fill pointer.

What happens if you have been pushing items onto your vector, and increasing the fill pointer, but you come to the end of the total space allocated for the vector? You have some choice about what to do. One option is to create a new, larger vector and copy the elements of the old vector into it. Another option is to use an adjustable array in the first place. If an array is created with the :ADJUSTABLE option set to non-NIL, you can call ADJUST-ARRAY to make it bigger, or if you are treating it like a push stack, you can use VECTOR-PUSH-EXTEND instead of VECTOR-PUSH. VECTOR-PUSH-EXTEND pushes an item onto the vector, increases the fill pointer, and creates a new, larger vector if the old one is out of space.

Copying the elements of an array by hand may be more expensive than using adjustable arrays; however, this is implementation-dependent. Another consideration is that look-up time may be slightly greater for adjustable arrays, so you should not use them indiscriminately.

7.7   HASH TABLES

Hashing is a clever way of constructing a table so that the data it contains can be accessed relatively quickly via an indicator. COMMON LISP implements hash tables, which allow you to take advantage of hashing without having to implement the algorithm yourself.[4]

Hash tables share some of the advantages of vectors and arrays, and some of the advantages of property lists. As with a property list, a hash table allows you to associate an indicator with a value. As with vectors, access time for items in hash tables is low and does not depend on the size of the hash table.

Unfortunately, hash tables also share some of the disadvantages of vectors. Hash tables grow automatically if you try to add too many elements to them, but such growth may require a substantial amount of time because the entire table has to be recomputed.

Hash tables are created with the function MAKE-HASH-TABLE. When you create a hash table, you can specify whether you want the test for comparison of indicators to be EQ, EQL, or EQUAL. The default is the usual one in COMMON LISP, EQL. Once the hash table is created, the specified test for equality is always used in look-ups.

Items are accessed with the function GETHASH, which takes a key and a hash table as

---

[4]Furthermore, COMMON LISP takes it upon itself to guard against a common problem with hash tables—conflicts in which two data items may be coded the same way.

an argument. Values are changed by calling SETF with a call to GETHASH as a first argument. Items are removed with REMHASH.

As an example, we can write a procedure that takes an association list and converts it to a hash table. It returns the new hash table:

```
(defun initialize-hash-table-from-alist (list)
  (let ((table (make-hash-table :test #'eq)))
    (dolist (pair list)
      (setf (gethash (car pair) table) (cdr pair)))
    table))
```

We can use this on the *EMPLOYEES* a-list defined earlier:

```
(defvar *employees*
  '((john . "62 Walnut St.") (rick . "1066 Umbrella St.")))

(setf *hash-table*
  (initialize-hash-table-from-alist *employees*))
#<Hash Table, Test: EQ, Size: 71, Rehash Size: 1.33, Rehash
Threshold: 1.0, Count: 2, Buckets: #(NIL NIL NIL NIL NIL NIL
NIL NIL NIL NIL NIL NIL NIL NIL NIL NIL NIL NIL NIL NIL NIL
NIL NIL NIL NIL NIL NIL NIL NIL NIL NIL NIL NIL NIL NIL
((JOHN . "62 Walnut St.")) NIL NIL NIL NIL ((RICK . "666
Abbey St.")) NIL NIL NIL NIL NIL NIL NIL NIL NIL NIL NIL NIL
NIL NIL NIL NIL NIL NIL NIL NIL NIL NIL NIL NIL NIL NIL NIL
NIL NIL NIL)>

(gethash 'john *hash-table*)
"62 Walnut St."
```

Look-up in hash tables using EQ comparisons is the least expensive, which is why you want to use them when you are using symbols as keys. Look-up time for hash tables using EQL or EQUAL is greater; however, these tests offer more flexibility. For example, it is necessary to use EQUAL if you wish to have strings as keys.

7.8   STRUCTURES

In addition to vectors, arrays, hash tables, and lists, LISP provides another means of organizing data, called the *structure*. Structures are analogous to records in PASCAL and to structures in C.

Structures, like association lists, property lists, and hash tables, have named slots in which a value can be kept. However, structures are higher-level than these facilities. Structures not only provide the slots themselves, but also organize these slots into types or classes of objects. The structure facility provides a means of creating discrete instances of these objects on demand from a template that you have previously specified. It also creates specialized accessor functions for manipulating each type you define.

Let us start with an example of a situation where you might want to use structures, and then proceed to discuss the syntax in more detail. Assume that you would like to keep some information about your household pets. All household pets have certain properties. For example, any pet has a type, a size, a favorite food, a favorite place to sleep, a birthday, and, possibly, vaccinations.

A pet might therefore be represented as a structure with six components. DEFSTRUCT is the operator that creates these datatypes with named elements:

```
(defstruct household-pet
   kind-of
   size
   favorite-food
   sleep-place
   birthday
   vaccinations)
```

The call to DEFSTRUCT does not create a HOUSEHOLD-PET. Rather, it tells LISP what such an object consists of. A call to DEFSTRUCT creates a template for the data structure. It also creates a new data type called HOUSEHOLD-PET. Finally, it creates a series of functions for manipulating that data type:

- It defines a constructor procedure called MAKE-HOUSEHOLD-PET which, when called, creates an instance of the structure. Therefore, doing:

```
(setf woof (make-household-pet))
#S(HOUSEHOLD-PET :KIND-OF NIL :SIZE NIL :FAVORITE-FOOD NIL
    :SLEEP-PLACE NIL :BIRTHDAY NIL :VACCINATIONS NIL)
```

binds WOOF to a newly created household-pet object.

- It defines the following selectors that take one argument, a household-pet, and return the value in that slot:

```
HOUSEHOLD-PET-KIND-OF
```

```
HOUSEHOLD-PET-SIZE
```

```
HOUSEHOLD-PET-FAVORITE-FOOD
```

```
HOUSEHOLD-PET-BIRTHDAY
```

```
HOUSEHOLD-PET-SLEEP-PLACE
```

```
HOUSEHOLD-PET-VACCINATIONS
```

- It allows you to use SETF to alter the components of a household-pet:

```
(setf (household-pet-size woof) 'big)
```

This updates the information about WOOF's size to BIG.

- A function named HOUSEHOLD-PET-P of one argument is defined; it is a predicate that is true if its argument is of the type household-pet, and is false otherwise.
- A *copier* function, COPY-HOUSEHOLD-PET, which makes a new object that is a copy of an existing pet, is defined.

7.8.1   **Syntax of DEFSTRUCT**

A simple call to DEFSTRUCT, such as that above, specifies a name for the structure and a series of slots. Each slot is either a symbol specifying a slot name or a list. The list has the slot name in the first position and then a default initialization for the slot. The default initialization specifies the value to be given to the slot if none is specified when an instance of the structure is made.

For example, here is a simple call to DEFSTRUCT, specifying one default initialization:

```
(defstruct person
  (age *typical-person-age*)
  sex
  pet
  name)
```

This call does several things. Primarily, it creates a template for a person object. Additionally, the constructor MAKE-PERSON, the selectors PERSON-AGE, PERSON-SEX, PERSON-PET, and PERSON-NAME, the predicate PERSON-P, and the copier COPY-PERSON are automatically defined. You can then create instances of this template:

```
(make-person :age 49 :sex 'F :name 'Ruth :pet nil)
```

If you fail to specify an age, the person-age is *TYPICAL-PERSON-AGE*:

```
(defvar *typical-person-age* 33)

(setf first-person (make-person :name 'ruth :sex 'f))
#S(PERSON :AGE 33 :SEX F :PET NIL :NAME RUTH)

(person-age first-person)
33
```

Note that the default-init is a form that is evaluated each time an instance is to be constructed, so if you change the value of *TYPICAL-PERSON-AGE* and then create a person without overriding the default, the age will be different.

Just as with property lists or hash tables, structure slots can contain any kind of data. For example, if you want   to you can give an instance of HOUSEHOLD-PET as the value of the PERSON-PET slot:

```
(defvar *default-pet-type* 'dog)

(setf my-friend
  (make-person :name 'joe :sex 'm
               :pet (make-household-pet
                        :kind-of *default-pet-type*)))
#S(PERSON :AGE 33 :SEX M
    :PET #S(HOUSEHOLD-PET :KIND-OF DOG :SIZE NIL
               :FAVORITE-FOOD NIL :SLEEP-PLACE NIL
               :BIRTHDAY NIL :VACCINATIONS NIL)
    :NAME JOE)
```

A call to MAKE-HOUSEHOLD-PET might even be a good default value for the PET slot.

A more complex call to DEFSTRUCT could have a name clause instead of just a name. The name clause contains the symbol specifying the name and any options. One important option in the name clause causes DEFSTRUCT to create different names for the structure's accessor functions than it would otherwise. For example, "PERSON-" is the default CONC-NAME for a structure of type PERSON. Ordinarily, "PERSON-" is concatenated onto the slot names in order to make up the names of the selector functions for that structure. However, you can specify:

```
(defstruct (person (:conc-name human-))
  name
  (age *typical-person-age*)
  pets
  sex)
(setf second-person (make-person :name 'abigail :sex 'f))
#S(PERSON :NAME ABIGAIL :AGE 33 :PETS NIL :SEX F)

(human-name second-person)
ABIGAIL
```

The accessors created now are called HUMAN-NAME, HUMAN-AGE, and HUMAN-SEX, and the other functions (PERSON-NAME, PERSON-AGE, and PERSON-SEX) were never created as such.

Another important option is used for building a new structure definition as an extension of an old one:

```
(defstruct person
  age
  sex
  pet
  name)
(defstruct (software-engineer (:include person)
                              (:conc-name se-))
  (hobby 'folk-dancing)
  (favorite-beverage 'coffee)
  number-of-bits-saved)
```

In this example, a software engineer has seven slots: the four defined in PERSON and the three defined in SOFTWARE-ENGINEER itself. The four selector functions defined by the PERSON structure can be applied to instances of the SOFTWARE-ENGINEER structure, and they will work correctly. Additionally, there are seven selector functions specifically for software engineer structures. The following examples illustrate how you can use SOFTWARE-ENGINEER structures:

```
(defvar *staff* nil)
(defun employ (person)
  (push person *staff*))  ; push alters a list by putting an
                          ; item on the front of it
```

```
(employ (make-software-engineer :name 'chuck
                                :age 45
                                :sex 'm
                                :favorite-beverage 'milk))

(person-name (car *staff*))
CHUCK

(se-name (car *staff*))
CHUCK

(se-hobby (car *staff*))
FOLK-DANCING
```

In one way, the facility provided by DEFSTRUCT is more limited than association lists or property lists, and similar to the first bicycle program. There is no simple way to add a slot to a structure. Rather, after you redefine the template, you must recreate your whole data base with the new one. This renders structures unsuitable for situations involving the addition or deletion of attributes. However, there is nothing to stop you from storing an association list, a property list, a vector, an array, or anything else as the value of one of the slots in a structure.

7.9   RECAP

Many different data structures and functions have been presented in this chapter. What order can be found in the different data structures? Data structures in LISP are a bit like organs in the human body; both have evolved over time, and history can be helpful in understanding their current structure.

We can trace some of the changes in LISP. Since 1975 or so, people have started to program differently. In particular, although not everyone approves of object-oriented programming, a more object-oriented approach has crept into the ways in which people talk about LISP itself. That is to say that people increasingly use language that emphasizes not *use* but the metaphorical *presence* of programming objects.

In LISP, people who once talked about "S-expressions" now talk about "LISP objects." Today, LISP allows you to create named structures. When you create a structure, representing, for example, a bicycle, it is not an expression: it doesn't *say* anything; it *is* something—it is an object.

Because there was no other way to create structured objects, people started to use lists when they wanted to do object-oriented programming. Both property lists and association lists can be seen as outgrowths of this direction. Property lists proved useful for some applications and association lists for others; however, lists alone are still somewhat amorphous. Other data types were introduced, partly to allow the extra structure for object-oriented programming and partly for other reasons, such as speed of access.

Structures allow you to create objects of a sort. A structure has a type and private state that can be changed by using its type-specific functions. However, structures do not allow (without embellishments) the *message passing* and private function definitions associated with real object-oriented programming. Most of the other data structures and accompanying functions in LISP were thought over and tried out in various incarnations over periods of roughly ten years before gaining their current form. Right now a lot of work is being done on object-oriented programming, and it is certain that a standard will be created for COMMON LISP; however, objects have not been thought about for quite that length of time, and it is uncertain what form the standard will take.

Nor will the presence of objects make organizing the other information easier—it is like adding the higher functions on top of the cerebellum. How can one keep all this information straight? There are no absolute rules clearly defining what data structure to use in any situation. Yet there is some conventional or summary wisdom.

Lists are a powerful and flexible way to manipulate small amounts of data of any kind and are good for situations that require adding and deleting items easily. Association lists are indicated for modelling stacks. Property lists spring to mind when you wish to have only one occurrence of each indicator. If you have integer indexes into the data for one reason or another, the use of arrays becomes obvious. If you are dealing with characters, strings are most convenient. Hash tables are suggested when it is convenient to access data via a symbol or string but there is too much for an association

TABLE 7-1. Operators on Common Lisp Data Structures

Data Structure	Construction	Selection	Change Value	Remove Slot
Lists	CONS/LIST	CAR, CDR	SETF/CAR SETF/CDR (1)	{REMOVE}
Association lists	ACONS	ASSOC	{SETF/CDR/ ASSOC} (1)	{REMOVE}
Property lists General	SETF/GET	GET	SETF/GET (1)	REMF
Property lists in symbol cells	SETF/GETF	GETF	SETF/GETF (1)	REMPROP
Arrays	MAKE-ARRAY	AREF	SETF/AREF	
Vectors	VECTOR	AREF	SETF/AREF	
Hash tables	MAKE-HASH-TABLE	GETHASH	SETF/GETHASH	REMHASH
Structures	MAKE-⟨name⟩	⟨name-slotname⟩	SETF/⟨name-slotname⟩	

{ } means that the operation is not the usual way of producing the effect
(1) indicates that the operation can add slots to the structure

or property list. Structures are a good way to handle instances of data with a defined number of slots.

One way to remember the various major functions that manipulate these structures is to classify them. Each data structure has a constructor function, one or more accessors, and one or more modifiers, as shown in table 7.1.

CHAPTER HIGHLIGHTS

Major Concepts

- Attaching labels to data inside lists is an alternative to putting the data in a specific order.
- LISP supports two methods of labeling data inside lists—association lists and property lists.
- An association list is a list of dotted pairs.

    –Each dotted pair consists of an indicator and a value.

    –Association lists are often used as stacks.

    –ACONS and ASSOC are the two most important functions for manipulating association lists.

- Property lists consist of alternating indicators and values.

    –Property lists are normally updated destructively.

    –GET and REMF are key functions for manipulating property lists.

    –Property lists can be stored in the property list cell of a symbol and manipulated with GETF and REMPROP.

- Vectors and arrays provide quicker access to each element than do lists. They are particularly useful with data that have a natural index.
- Any function that works on an array works on a vector.
- Any function that works on a vector works on a string.
- The elements of vectors and arrays are referenced by subscripts.
- MAKE-ARRAY and AREF are the constructor and selector for arrays.
- VECTOR is a constructor for vectors.
- Like lists, hash tables allow you to use arbitrary LISP objects as indicators; however, as with arrays, the speed of look-up in a hash table is not dependent on the number of items in the table.

    –Hash tables can use EQ, EQL, or EQUAL as the comparison test when looking up items.

—MAKE-HASH-TABLE, GETHASH, and REMHASH are the three main functions for manipulating hash tables.

• Structures are a facility for creating abstract data structures and the functions to manipulate them.

Summary of New Syntax

```
(acons key value alist)
(assoc key alist)
(remove item sequence)
(rassoc value alist)

(function symbol)

(get symbol key)
(remprop symbol key)

(getf place key)
(remf place key)

(make-array dimensions :initial-contents x)
(aref array subscript1 subscript2 ...)
(vector objects)

(gethash item table)
(make-hash)
(remhash item table)

(defstruct (name option-1 option-2 ...)
           slot-description-1
           slot-description-2
            ...)
```

Suggested Reading

The following sections in Steele, *COMMON LISP*, complement the material covered in this chapter: chapter 10, Symbols, 10.1; chapter 15, Lists, 15.6; chapter 16, Hash Tables, 16.1; chapter 17, Arrays, 17.1–17.3, 17.5–17.6; chapter 19, Structures, 19.1–19.5.

EXERCISES

1. Opposites is a game that maintains data about pairs of opposites. Here is a transcript of a session with the game:

```
(opposite)
What do you like?
candy

What is the opposite of candy?
vegetables

What do you like?
work
```

```
What is the opposite of work?
play

What do you like?
candy

I don't like candy.  I like vegetables.
What do you like?
work

I don't like work.  I like play.
What do you like?
play

What is the opposite of play?
work

What do you like?
play

I don't like play.  I like work.
What do you like?
e
"Bye for now.  Come back soon."
```

Opposite asks the user to type in a word. If the word is in its knowledge list, it prints out that it doesn't like the word, it likes the opposite. If the word is not in its knowledge list, the program asks the user for the opposite of the word and adds the pair to its list.

Load the program into LISP and play the game. Read the code and make sure you understand how it works.

```
;;; This is the beginning of a program that asks questions
;;; about OPPOSITES.
;;; The opposite pairs are stored in an association list
;;; called *OPPOSITE-LIST*.
(defvar *opposite-list* '((new . old) (tall . short)
                          (fat . thin) (right . left)))

;;; OPPOSITE starts the game.
(defun opposite ()
  (get-item-loop))

;;; GET-ITEM-LOOP is the main loop of the program.  It maintains
;;; a local variable called ITEM.  Each time around the loop,
;;; the variable ITEM is updated to the value returned by
;;; GET-NEW-ITEM. If the ITEM is the symbol E, then the loop is
;;; exited.  Otherwise, the ITEM is looked up by GET-PAIR in
;;; *OPPOSITE-LIST*.  If it is found, PRINT-REPLY is called.  If
;;; not, UPDATE-INFO creates a new pair and puts it on
;;; *OPPOSITE-LIST*.
(defun get-item-loop ()
  (do ((item (get-new-item) (get-new-item)))
      ((eql item 'e) (leave))
    (let ((current-property (get-pair *opposite-list* item)))
      (if (null current-property) (update-info item)
          (print-reply current-property)))))
```

```
;;; PRINT-REPLY takes a pair as input and produces a
;;; contradictory response to the user.
(defun print-reply (pair)
    ;; ~( begins lowercasing letters, ~) ends lowercasing
    (format t "~%I don't like ~(~a~).  I like ~(~a~).~%"
            (car pair)
            (cdr pair)))

;;; LEAVE is a message that is called when exiting the
;;; program.
(defun leave ()
    "Bye for now.  Come back soon.")

;;; GET-NEW-ITEM asks the user for input.
(defun get-new-item ()
    (format t "~%What do you like?~%")
    (read))

;;; UPDATE-INFO takes an item that is the object typed in by the
;;; user.  It asks the user for an opposite and installs the
;;; two as a pair in *OPPOSITE-LIST*.
(defun update-info (item)
    (format t "~%What is the opposite of ~(~a~)?~%" item)
    (setf *opposite-list*
          (acons item (read) *opposite-list*)))

;;; GET-PAIR takes an association list and an indicator and
;;; returns the pair found in the list using the key INDICATOR.
(defun get-pair (alist indicator)
    (assoc indicator alist))
```

2. The OPPOSITE program checks its data base only to see if the entry is in the indicator slot of each property. It completely ignores the value slot during the look-up. This results in what looks like strange behavior. For example, if you indicate that you like thin, it will reply, "I don't like thin, I like fat." However, if you then state that you like fat, it will ask you for the opposite of fat.

   This strange behavior comes about because there is a rule about opposites that the program does not account for; opposition is symmetrical. If thin is the opposite of fat, then fat is the opposite of thin.

   Change the program so that it takes advantage of the two pieces of information it gets whenever you type in a pair of opposites.

3. Change OPPOSITE so that the user can type S (for skip) instead of an opposite. Typing S results in moving on to the next item without adding the current one to the data base.

4. Implement a version of ACONS.

5. The famous program ELIZA imitates a therapist giving nondirective psychological aid by taking the sentences the user types in and performing a series of tricks on them that produce stereotypical results. One trick that makes ELIZA startling is that it incorporates the user's own words into its response.

Write a procedure that examines a list and replaces all instances of first-person pronouns with second-person pronouns, and vice versa. For example, if you give the procedure the following input:

```
(I like my mother)
```

It should return:

```
(You like your mother)
```

Once you have the "I-YOU" procedure, it is not at all difficult to put together a credible nondirective response by tacking a few words onto the beginning. For example, the user types in, "I like my mother" and the computer replies, "You say that you like your mother" or "Why do you say that you like your mother?"

Because there is a certain ambiguity in English, your program will not be able to distinguish between the uses of "you" as a subject and an object. For example, "you" is used differently in the phrases "I like you" and "You like me." You have to make an arbitrary choice whether to turn these into "You like me" and "Me like you" or "You like I" and "I like you."

6. Define a structure called manager, with appropriate attributes. Then write and run an initialization procedure that tries to employ some programmers and some managers in a good proportion. Last, write a procedure that produces a list of the type of employee and the age of every employee on *STAFF*.

7. Write a dictionary program that maintains a hash table of words and their definitions. Allow the user to add, remove, and look up items.

8. Change the animal game program in chapter 6 so the knowledge tree is represented using structures rather than lists.

Chapter 8

MANIPULATING PROCEDURES
AS DATA

We have examined the LISP interpreter in some detail in the preceding chapters. This chapter explores a different use for the same information. Not only can your programs be evaluated according to the rules of the interpreter, but you can write programs that call the interpreter while running. This is important because it implies that expressions to be interpreted, that is, "programs," can, like other data, be created and manipulated by your programs.

LISP allows programmers to treat procedures like other data. Procedure objects can be passed as parameters, constructed on the fly, and modified. Then they can be executed when desired, or even compiled and then executed.

This is particularly easy because, in LISP, data and programs are made of the same fundamental data structure, the list. The differences between them are a matter of use rather than of kind. While you can't execute every piece of data, a procedure is only a piece of data if it is not executed.[1]

The following section covers a function that allows you to evaluate expressions under program control. Then comes MAPCAR, one of many LISP functions that take a procedure as input and invoke it on other data. Next, LAMBDA, a construct that can be used for creating procedures under program control, will be introduced. Finally, other functions that are useful for calling procedures under program control are presented, along with a more extensive example.

---

[1]Of course, this is true only of interpreted procedures; compiled procedures are not lists. But they, too, are data; they are stored in modules that are loaded and can be invoked or even examined (as by a disassembler) under program control. Most COMMON LISP compilers are LISP programs that create these compiled code modules.

8.1   EVAL

LISP's process of evaluating expressions is embodied in the function EVAL, which takes a form as input and evaluates it. In practice, this is fairly straightforward, and should do what you expect it to do, given all the rules for evaluation that you have seen in this book. For example,

```
(eval 3)
3

(eval "this string")
"this string"
```

Note, however, that the call to EVAL is mediated by the usual LISP evaluation. EVAL is not a special form. This means that the argument to EVAL is evaluated once normally, just as arguments to functions always are, and once owing to the explicit application of EVAL. For example,

```
(eval '(cons 'a 'b))
(a . b)

(eval (list '+ 3 4 5))
12
```

EVAL allows you to evaluate an expression under program control, that is, when you want to. The need for this may not be immediately obvious. But consider the following example: you have a program that allows the user either to type a word choosing one of a set of actions or to type in a LISP expression and have it evaluated. You write it as follows:

```
(defun interface-message ()
   (format t "
Please type a letter to choose one of the following,
or type a LISP phrase:
         a.   print a file
         b.   show directory
         c.   delete all files~%"))
(defun command-loop ()
   (interface-message)
   (let ((answer (read)))
     (case answer
        (a (sub-procedure-that-prints))
        (b (sub-procedure-that-shows-directory))
        (c (sub-procedure-that-deletes-all-files))
        (t (print answer))))   ;wrong
   (command-loop))
```

However, if you run COMMAND-LOOP and type in the expression (* 3 4), you do not get the desired result. Instead of 12, the list (* 3 4) is printed. This is because the value returned by READ is the expression (* 3 4) and you want the value of that value. You can make this procedure work by using EVAL:

```
(defun command-loop ()
   (interface-message)
   (let ((answer (read)))
      (case answer
         (a (sub-procedure-that-prints))
         (b (sub-procedure-that-shows-directory))
         (c (sub-procedure-that-deletes-all-files))
         (t (print (eval answer)))))
   (command-loop))
```

```
(command-loop)
Please type a letter to choose one of the following,
or type a LISP phrase:
         a.   print a file
         b.   show directory
         c.   delete all files
(* 3 4)
12
```

EVAL evaluates all kinds of LISP objects, not just procedures:

```
(command-loop)
Please type a letter to choose one of the following,
or type a LISP phrase:
         a.   print a file
         b.   show directory
         c.   delete all files
'foo
FOO
```

EVAL allows you to invoke the interpreter recursively. This means that you can construct function calls on the fly. LISP also provides more specific facilities for passing function objects as data and calling them under program control. These will be treated after you are shown how function objects may be used as arguments to various COMMON LISP primitives.

8.2   MAPPING FUNCTIONS

Consider this recursive procedure to square each of the elements in a list:

```
(defun square-each-one (list)
   (if (null list) nil
      (cons (sq (car list))
            (square-each-one (cdr list)))))
```

```
(defun sq (x)
   (* x x))
```

Now consider the following procedure, which takes the absolute value of every element in a list:

```
(defun make-positive (list)
  (if (null list) nil
    (cons (abs (car list))
          (make-positive (cdr list)))))
```

These two procedures have the same form. That is, they both construct a list of the results of invoking a function on each member of another list.

This description could be applied to many procedures written in LISP. Therefore, rather than writing each of these functions as if it performed a task different from the other ones, LISP provides a function that captures the common pattern. MAPCAR "cdrs down" a list, performing the specified operation on every element or car of the list. It returns a list of the results of every operation. For example, you could write the above procedures as follows:

```
(defun square-each-one (list)
  (mapcar #'sq list))
```
```
(defun make-positive (list)
  (mapcar #'abs list))
```

You give MAPCAR a function object as argument. MAPCAR applies the function successively to every element in the list.

MAPCAR can be difficult to understand at first, because it's quite powerful. Such a small expression seems to produce a disproportionate amount of activity. This is true, yet the only difference between MAPCAR and any other recursive function is that the former treats a procedure as data and then uses it. By the end of the chapter, you will see a four-line implementation of a simplified MAPCAR.

Nested MAPCARs (and other mapping functions) are a way to filter lists. For example, if you wanted all the values in an association list that are atoms, you might write:

```
(defun get-all-symbols (association-list)
  (mapcar #'get-if-symbol
     (mapcar #'cadr association-list)))
```
```
(defun get-if-symbol (item)
  (if (symbolp item) item nil))
```
```
(get-all-symbols '((oranges apples)
                   (my-car 57-Buick)
                   (quote-of-the-day
                    "LISP is like a ball of mud.")))
(APPLES 57-BUICK NIL)
```

The inner call to MAPCAR returns a list containing all the values from the association list. The outer MAPCAR filters that list, returning only those items that are symbols. However, the list returned by GET-ALL-SYMBOLS contains a value for every item in the original association list, including one NIL for every item that is not a symbol. You could delete this extra information by using the function MAPCAN, which has the effect of ignoring NIL in coming up with the final list:

```
(defun get-all-symbols (association-list)
  (mapcan #'get-if-symbol (mapcar #'cadr association-list)))
```

MAPCAN uses a different function for combining the elements. Where MAPCAR uses LIST, MAPCAN uses NCONC. Unlike LIST, NCONC needs both of its arguments to be lists. Unfortunately, this requires a small change to GET-IF-SYMBOL:

```
(defun get-if-symbol (item)
  (if (symbolp item) (list item) nil))
```

Now:

```
(get-all-symbols '((oranges apples)
                   (my-car 57-Buick)
                   (quote-of-the-day
                    "LISP is like a ball of mud.")))
(APPLES 57-BUICK)
```

MAPCAR can be used with functions that take more than one argument. However, you must specify one complete set of values for each time the function is called. Thus you would say:

```
(mapcar #'list '(the the the) '(computer language universe))
```

to get:

```
((the computer) (the language) (the universe))
```

If you specified:

```
(mapcar #'list '(the) '(computer language universe))
```

you would get

```
((the computer))
```

You could rewrite SQUARE-EACH-ONE as another example of calling MAPCAR with two arguments:

```
(defun square-each-one (list)
  (mapcar #'* list list))
```

You may want to map over a list not for the returned list, but rather for side effect. MAPC can be used instead of MAPCAR in such cases. The following example recreates the song BINGO by printing it on the screen. The refrain of the song involves substituting one more clap for each letter in the name BINGO every time the refrain is run.

```
(defun bingo ()
    (do ((current-letters '(B I N G O) (cdr current-letters))
         (current-clap-number O (1+ current-clap-number)))
        ((null current-letters)
         (stanza current-letters current-clap-number))
      (stanza current-letters current-clap-number)))
(defun stanza (current-letters current-clap-number)
  (format t "~%There was a farmer had a dog and Bingo ~
was his name-o.~%")
  (refrain current-letters current-clap-number)
  (format t "~%and Bingo was his name-o.~%" ))
(defun refrain (letters number-of-claps)
  (dotimes (i 3)
    (dotimes (j number-of-claps) (format t "(clap) "))
    (mapc #'print-letter letters)))
(defun print-letter (x)
  (format t "~a  " x))
```

If you don't need the list of values returned, it is better to call MAPC than to call MAPCAR because it is more efficient.

The other mapping functions, MAPLIST, MAPL, and MAPCON, are analogous to MAPCAR, MAPC, and MAPCAN, except that they work on successive cdrs of the list instead of successive cars. This means that the first time, the function is called on the whole list, and each successive time it is invoked on the cdr of the time before. For example, you can produce the effect of moving each element in the list over one (including the NIL at the end):

```
(defun shift (list)
  (maplist #'cadr list))

(shift '(a b c d e f))
(b c d e f NIL)
```

The different mapping functions are summarized in table 8-1.

TABLE 8-1. Summary of Mapping Functions

	Operates on CARS	*Operates on* CDRS
Works by side effect	MAPC	MAPL
Returns list	MAPCAR	MAPLIST
Returns list made with NCONC	MAPCAN	MAPCON

8.3   **LAMBDA**

Many one-line functions have been used in this book. For example, SQ, GET-IF-SYMBOL, and PRINT-LETTER, cited in the previous section, were only one line long. Sometimes it can be annoying to have to write a new function and think up a name for every discrete action.

A lambda expression is a list that represents a function without a name. It can be given as an argument to FUNCTION just as the name of a function defined with DEFUN.

Recall the three parts of DEFUN: the name, the variable list, and the body. A lambda expression has two parts: a variable list and a body. For example, we could define a lambda expression that does what SQ does as follows:

```
(lambda (x) (* x x))
```

If we called this by typing:

```
((lambda (x) (* x x)) 4)
```

then X would be bound to 4 in the call and (* X X) would produce 16.

It is worth thinking about what happens when you invoke a lambda expression. Normally, when you call a function, you name the symbol whose function binding performs the operation you want. When you type (sq 4), the first action LISP takes is to retrieve the function binding of SQ. You could draw an imaginary transition state for the code as follows:

```
((Code-that-implements-sq) 4)
```

You can put a lambda expression in place of a symbol name, and it is applied to the value of any arguments that might follow, just as the function binding of the symbol is applied to those arguments. However, when you call a lambda expression, it is as if you are providing the interpreter directly with a function object so that it need not fetch the function binding of a symbol. The use of lambda expressions is the one instance in which an expression can be successfully evaluated with a list in its first position:

```
((lambda (x) (* x x)) 4)
```

You can use lambda expressions where you would have used function calls. For example, you can rewrite the call to MAPCAR that squares each element of a list as follows:

```
(defun square-each-one (list)
  (mapcar #'(lambda (x) (* x x)) list))
```

When SQUARE-EACH-ONE is evaluated with the list '(2 3 4) as an argument, MAPCAR applies the function to each member of the list in turn. Imagine that the series of invocations of the lambda expression looks like this:

```
((lambda (x) (* x x)) 2)
4
((lambda (x) (* x x)) 3)
9
((lambda (x) (* x x)) 4)
16
```

MAPCAR then forms a list of the results, which it returns:

```
(square-each-one '(2 3 4))
(4 9 16)
```

LAMBDA is one of the most fundamental concepts in LISP. McCarthy's original motivation for developing LISP was to implement Alonzo Church's lambda calculus. In early implementations of LISP, DEFUNs were thought of as named LAMBDAs and you had to put a LAMBDA inside each DEFUN explicitly. Now much of the use of LAMBDA is implicit. For example, you can accomplish everything you do with LET with a lambda expression.

Lambda expressions have all the properties associated with functions, except a name. For example, LAMBDAs can have environments, and variables inside a lambda expression are scoped lexically. Unlike DEFUNs, LAMBDAs are not usually written at top level so that there is a greater chance of notable differences between their environment of creation and environment of use. Although this feature can be used to advantage, as illustrated in the next section, it also provides ample room for confusion.

LAMBDA is useful in conjunction with functions like MAPCAR and MAPCAN and for creating functions under program control. But suppose you want to write your own functions that could accept a lambda expression or a function object as an argument and invoke it internally. To do that, you need the primitive functions described next.

8.4   *APPLY AND FUNCALL*

EVAL allows us to invoke the interpreter on expressions we have built. However, precisely because these expressions have been built at run time, the compiler is incapable of transforming them into machine language. Their execution must always be inefficient, always involving the extra step of interpretation.

If we are not actually building expressions, but only want to invoke functions that have been passed as arguments, or functions created locally via LAMBDA, we need not use EVAL; instead we can use FUNCALL or APPLY. The use of these functions is not inherently inefficient as is EVAL; COMMON LISP is designed so that a good compiler can generate machine language for a FUNCALL in the same way that it can generate machine language for the normal occurrence of a function invocation. APPLY is somewhat slower than normal function invocation, but it, too, should be faster than EVAL.

FUNCALL takes a function object as its first argument, and arguments to that function as subsequent arguments.

```
(funcall #'+ 3 7 2 3 4)
19
(funcall #'cons 'a '(b c))
(A B C)
(funcall #'nthcdr 0 '(a b c))
(A B C)
```

FUNCALL evaluates its arguments.[2] Its first argument must evaluate to an acceptable function object. A function object or *lexical closure* is the union of a procedure and the environment in which the procedure was created. As stated in the last chapter, the straightforward way to achieve this is to call FUNCTION on a function name or lambda. #'CAR produces the function object associated with CAR.

We can introduce a degree of indirection to this operation by putting a function object in the value cell of a symbol and then calling FUNCALL on that symbol:

```
(setf my-cons #'cons)
(FUNCTION CONS)
(defun execute ()
  (funcall my-cons 'a '(b c)))
(execute)
(A B C)
```

In this case, you can change the binding of MY-CONS and affect EXECUTE. More generally, you can use any computation to determine a function and then use FUNCALL to call it.

As you were promised at the beginning of this chapter, you should now be able to write a simplified version of MAPCAR, using FUNCALL:

```
(defun mymapcar (function list)
  (if (null list) nil
    (cons (funcall function (car list))
          (mymapcar function (cdr list)))))
(mymapcar #'cadr '((john "66 Sherwood St.")
                   (albert "89 August Ave.")))
("66 Sherwood St." "89 August Ave.")
(mymapcar #'(lambda (x) (* x x)) '(1 2 3 4 5))
(1 4 9 16 25)
```

---

[2] FUNCALL is itself a function and can be called by using FUNCALL. An abstruse but pleasing feature of FUNCALL is that (funcall #'funcall f a b c ...) is equivalent to (funcall f a b c ...).

```
(mymapcar #'(lambda (x) (if (symbolp x) x))
           (mymapcar
             #'cadr
             '((oranges apples)
               (my-car 57-Buick)
               (quote-of-the-day
                 "LISP is like a ball of mud."))))
(APPLES 57-BUICK NIL)
```

The difference between MAPCAR and MAPCAN is the function that is used to glue together the result of the recursive call and the result of the calculation on the current car of the list. MYMAPCAN is a simple variation on MYMAPCAR, differing only in its use of NCONC in place of CONS:

```
(defun mymapcan (function list)
  (if (null list) nil
      (nconc (funcall function (car list))
             (mymapcan function (cdr list)))))
(mymapcan #'(lambda (x) (if (symbolp x) (list x)))
           (mymapcar
             #'cadr
             '((oranges apples)
               (my-car 57-Buick)
               (quote-of-the-day
                 "LISP is like a ball of mud."))))
(APPLES 57-BUICK)
```

As before, we must invoke MAPCAN differently, using (list x) instead of X.

One alternative to FUNCALL is APPLY. Up to this point, we have treated evaluation as an indivisible unit. However, the introduction of LAMBDA suggests that evaluation has two identifiable parts. In the first stage, arguments are evaluated; in the second, the function is applied to the arguments. The overall process is called evaluation, but the second part is called application and is embodied in the function APPLY.

Like FUNCALL, APPLY takes a function object as its first argument. Unlike FUNCALL, APPLY takes a list as a second argument. APPLY applies the function to the arguments contained in the list. APPLY is particularly useful when you don't know how many arguments a function will have. For example,

```
(defun get-max (list)
  (apply #'max list))
(get-max '(2 3 4 10 4))
10
```

In the next example, N-TO-1 produces a list with all the numbers from N down to 1. FUNNY-FACT multiplies all of these together to produce the factorial of N:

```
(defun n-to-1 (n)
  (if (zerop n) nil
      (cons n (n-to-1 (− n 1)))))
```

```
(defun funny-fact (n)
  (apply #'* (n-to-1 n))))
```

This is APPLY's primary purpose; however, as a convenience, APPLY can also take arguments that are not in the list of arguments.[3] Any arguments not in the list must appear between the function object and the list:

```
(apply #'max 3 4 5 '(10 4))
10

(apply #'+ 3 4 '(6 7 8))
28

(apply #'(lambda (x) (* x x)) '(3))
9

(apply #'nthcdr 0 '((a b c)))
(A B C)

(apply #'nthcdr 0 '(a b c) ())
(A B C)
```

8.5   DISPATCHING ON FUNCTIONS

You have seen two common uses for function objects: in implementing abstractions such as MAPCAR and in the construction of everyday LISP functions such as RASSOC, which allow you to specify the test you want them to perform. It is important to realize that you can treat functions exactly as you would treat any other kind of data: you can store them in tables and invoke them when desired. One application for this might be in a text editor: each key, when read, would be looked up in a hash table, and the function found there executed. Modes could be implemented by using the appropriate hash tables.

A less realistic, but easier to demonstrate, example of this technique is a more complete implementation of the simple top-level command language for LISP presented earlier in the chapter. Four commands will be implemented: PRINT-FILE, DELETE-FILE, EXIT, and HELP. DELETE-FILE depends on the COMMON LISP function of the same name. We use the LISP function PROBE-FILE, which returns NIL if the file is not found, and the full pathname of the file if it is.

Also, to initialize the table, we use SYMBOL-FUNCTION to get the contents of the symbol's function call because SYMBOL-FUNCTION is a function and evaluates its arguments, while FUNCTION, a special form, does not.

```
(defvar *command-table* (make-hash-table))
```

[3] This accomplishes what LEXPR-FUNCALL did in some older versions of LISP.

```lisp
(defvar *initial-commands*
   '((print-file . my-print-file)
     (delete-file . my-delete-file)
     (exit . my-exit)
     (help  . my-help)
     (? . my-help)))

;;; PRINT-FILE prompts for a name, and prints out each
;;; line of the file on the screen.
(defun my-print-file ()
   (format t "~%What is the name of the file you ~
          want to see? (Type return after the name.)~%")
   (let ((name (read-line)))
     (if (probe-file name)
         (with-open-file (file-stream name
                              :direction :input)
            (let ((eof (list 'eof)))
              (do ((current-line
                    (read-line file-stream nil eof)
                    (read-line file-stream nil eof)))
                ((eq current-line eof) nil)
                (format t "~A~%" current-line))))
         (format t "~a is not the name of a known file.~%"
                 name))))
;;; MY-DELETE-FILE prompts for the information with which
;;; to call DELETE-FILE.
(defun my-delete-file ()
   (format t "~%What is the name of the file you ~
          would like to delete? (Type return after the name.)~%")
   (let ((name (read-line)))
     (if (probe-file name)
         (when
             (y-or-n-p  ; double check
               (format t "~%Delete the file ~A? " name))
             (delete-file (probe-file name)))
         (format t "~%~a is not the name of a known file.~%"
                 name))))
;;; MY-EXIT is a no-op because it's checked for specially.
(defun my-exit ()
  "no-op")

;;; HELP prints the list of possible commands.
(defun my-help ()
   (format t
     "~%Possible commands for this command language are: ~%")
   (dolist (x *initial-commands*)
     (format t "~(~a~)~%" (car x))))

;;; INIT puts the functions into the hash-table and
;;; calls MAIN-LOOP on that hash-table.
(defun init ()
   (dolist (x *initial-commands*)
     (setf (gethash (car x) *command-table* )
           (symbol-function (cdr x))))
   (format t "Command> ")
   (main-loop *command-table*))
```

```
;;; MAIN-LOOP takes a table and looks up user input in
;;; the table, until the user wishes to exit.  If
;;; the function is found, it is executed.  If not,
;;; help is printed.
(defun main-loop (table)
  (do ((current-command
         (gethash (read) table)
         (gethash (read) table)))
       ;; This end condition lacks elegance.
       ;; We'll do this better in the next chapter.
       ((eq current-command #'my-exit) nil)
     (if current-command
         (funcall current-command)
         (funcall #'my-help))
     (format t "Command> ")))
```

You might wonder why we create a table with the item that the user is expected to type and the item that we want to evaluate rather than just funcalling what the user types in. The reason is that although we would like the user to be able to type ''delete-file,'' we do not actually want the LISP function DELETE-FILE executed. We want our own version, which prompts for input, to be used. By putting this information in a table, we create an interface that guards against inadvertent conflict.

In this program, the function objects, rather than just the names of the functions, are placed directly into the table. This is preferable because it is faster. However, it has a disadvantage; if you redefine a function after initializing the hash table, the old definition is still used because redefining a function means redefining the name of the function to point to different material, yet the table no longer accesses the function through its name. It has a separate pointer to the same material. You must reinitialize the table to get the new definition.

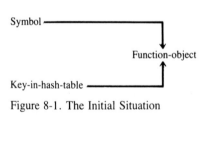

Figure 8-1. The Initial Situation

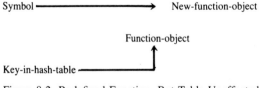

Figure 8-2. Redefined Function, But Table Unaffected

8.6   FURTHER EXPLORATIONS: FUNCTIONS THAT GENERATE FUNCTIONS

Another, more complex kind of program you should now be able to write generates new functions on the fly. A nice way to approach this is through an analogy with machines that make other machines. For example, you can write a program that manufactures gumball machines, complete with its private package of gumballs of different colors. MAKE-GUM-MACHINE takes a package of gumballs and creates a machine that contains those gumballs. Another procedure, GET-GUM, takes one of those machines as an argument and delivers a piece of gum.

Start by writing a procedure that puts together packets of gum. Each package will contain a random number of gumballs under *MAX-NUMBER-OF-GUMBALLS*.

```
(defvar *max-number-of-gumballs* 15)
```

Each gumball will have a color chosen randomly from the list of colors stored in *GUM-COLORS*:

```
(defvar *gum-colors*
   '(brown blue red orange purple green yellow speckled))
```

In the package that MAKE-GUM-PACKAGE returns, each piece of gum is represented by a color name, since color is the only significant property of gumballs for this example. Each occurrence of a color name in a gum package signifies one piece of gum. Therefore, MAKE-GUM-PACKAGE might return something like:

```
(yellow orange orange orange green red brown speckled)
```

MAKE-GUM-PACKAGE itself looks like this:

```
(defun make-gum-package ()
   (put-gum-in-package (random *max-number-of-gumballs*)))

(defun put-gum-in-package (size)
   (if (= size 0) nil
       (cons (nth (random (length *gum-colors*)) *gum-colors*)
             (put-gum-in-package (- size 1)))))
```

Each gum machine is a function object containing a lambda expression. When run, the body of the lambda expression delivers the first item of a list and sets the list to its cdr. Each time the procedure MAKE-GUM-MACHINE is called, it creates a new machine with these properties, that is, it returns a lambda expression in an environment with a private list of pieces of gum.

```
(defun make-gum-machine (pieces-of-gum)
   (function (lambda ()
             (prog1 (car pieces-of-gum)
               (setq pieces-of-gum (cdr pieces-of-gum))))))
```

The symbol PIECES-OF-GUM is lexically scoped. That is, its value inside the lambda expression is determined by its value at the time the function object represented by the lambda expression is created.[4] This is the first instance of a situation in which the environment of use could be significantly different from the environment of creation.

You can call MAKE-GUM-MACHINE, giving a package of gumballs as an argument:

```
(defvar *barber-shop-machine*
  (make-gum-machine (make-gum-package)))

(defvar *grocery-store-machine*
  (make-gum-machine (make-gum-package))))[5]
```

One machine, each with its private stock of gum, has been installed in the barbershop and one in the grocery store. Now you need a procedure that dispenses a piece of gum on request:

```
(defun get-gum (machine)
  (funcall machine))

(get-gum *barber-shop-machine*)
PURPLE

(get-gum *barber-shop-machine*)
YELLOW

(get-gum *grocery-store-machine*)
SPECKLED

(get-gum *barber-shop-machine*)
NIL

(get-gum *grocery-store-machine*)
RED
```

When the machine is empty it gives us NIL.

This is an example of a general sort of process that can be demonstrated with less code (and less motivation) as follows:

```
(defun make-dispenser (list)
  (function (lambda () (prog1 (car list)
                              (setq list (cdr list))))))
```

In this sparser form, it is easy to see that the object created with MAKE-DISPENSER or MAKE-GUM-MACHINE is somewhat like a stream made with WITH-OPEN-FILE. The list or

---

[4] This is a bonus of lexical scoping. The variable PIECES-OF-GUM is private to each lexical closure (function object) returned. PIECES-OF-GUM is like an ALGOL-60 *own* variable, or like a *static internal* variable in C, in that it is completely private to the function (the gum machine), and nothing outside can affect it. Also, it retains its value between invocations of the function. However, this is better than the C construct, in that PIECES-OF-GUM can have multiple existences. There can be more than one gum machine, each with its own instance of the variable.

[5] The value returned has not been specified here, because it will be printed out in a highly implementation-dependent fashion. However, you will probably be able to find the word ''closure'' somewhere in the printout.

stream can be accessed through certain paths that return the next piece of the object they act upon and update the pointer into that object. MAKE-FIB-GENERATOR demonstrates that you do not need to have a finite number of objects, nor must they have been calculated at the beginning:

```
(defun make-fib-generator (last1 last2)
  (function (lambda ()
              (prog1 (+ last1 last2)
                (let ((temp last1))
                  (setq last1 last2)
                  (setq last2 (+ temp last2)))))))
(defun get-fib (fib-generator)
  (funcall fib-generator))

(setf f (make-fib-generator 0 1))

(get-fib f)
1

(get-fib f)
2

(get-fib f)
3

(get-fib f)
5

(get-fib f)
8
```

At the beginning of chapter 7, the concept of data abstraction was introduced: the idea that one should isolate the actual details of the data structure behind a set of functions designed for manipulating it. As you learn about functions like MAKE-GUM-MACHINE and GET-GUM you may feel that the data structure you are dealing with is slipping away. Almost all you can put your finger on are the manipulating functions.

This is absolutely true. The power to pass procedures as data and to create procedures with lexical closures on the fly is elegant and powerful and more natural in LISP than in most other languages.

The power to do this must also cause you to reconsider and broaden your idea of data and data structures. The example that epitomizes the fragility of the distinction between procedures and data is the following implementation of the most fundamental data structure in LISP, the list, without any actual data structures:

```
(defun cons (a b)
  (function
    (lambda (message)
      (cond ((eq message 'car) a)
            ((eq message 'cdr) b)
            (t (format t
                "You can't use the operator ~a on a cons cell."
                message))))))
```

```
(defun car (cons-cell)
  (funcall cons-cell 'car))
(defun cdr (cons-cell)
  (funcall cons-cell 'cdr))
```

Here, as in LISP, CONS takes two inputs, which specify the car and the cdr. It returns something that behaves exactly as you expect a cons cell to behave. If you call CAR on the object returned by CONS, it returns A. If you call CDR on it, it returns B. However, the actual item returned by CONS is not a cons cell, but a lexical closure in which A and B are defined appropriately and which has special information about how to handle the messages CAR and CDR. CAR and CDR are defined to accept a closure and send it the appropriate message.

You would not actually implement a LISP this way, because it is inefficient. However, the potential is there and this example serves to illustrate the richness and flexibility of the tools that LISP gives the programmer.

CHAPTER HIGHLIGHTS

Major Concepts

- LISP lets you pass functions and data and use them later under program control.
- Mapping captures common patterns of use.
- Six mapping functions are summarized in table 8-1.
- Mapping functions take a procedure and apply it successively to each member of a list.
- LAMBDA allows you to create unnamed function objects.
- Each lambda expression has its own environment.
- EVAL, APPLY, and FUNCALL are all ways of evaluating forms under program control.

  –EVAL is the interpreter.

  –In general, calls to EVAL can't be compiled efficiently.

  –FUNCALL takes a function object and some other arguments and calls the function object on the other arguments.

  –APPLY takes a function object, possibly some other arguments, and a list, and applies the function object to the arguments before and in the final list.

  –APPLY is useful when you don't know in advance how many arguments there will be.

  Lexical closures plus the capacity to pass procedures as data provide an elegant means for making functions that create other functions.

SUMMARY OF NEW SYNTAX

```
(mapcar function list)
(mapcan function list)
(mapc function list)
(lambda argument-list body)
(eval form)
(apply function lists)
(funcall function arg)
```

Suggested Reading

The following sections in Steele, *COMMON LISP*, complement the material covered in this chapter: chapter 20, The Evaluator, 20.1; chapter 7, Control Structure, 7.3, 7.8.4.

EXERCISES

1. Write a version of ASSOC that takes a third argument, specifying the test you want applied (e.g., #'EQ, #'EQL, or #'EQUAL). (In fact, ASSOC takes an optional argument that does this; however, optional arguments will not be introduced in detail until the next chapter.)

2. The following is a list of Boston temperatures for a week in February. Write a procedure that produces a list of these temperatures in degrees centigrade by calling MAPCAR on a lambda expression.

   ```
   '(14 15 25 32 50 45 42)
   ```

   The relationship between degrees centigrade and Fahrenheit is that the number of degrees centigrade is equal to the number of degrees Fahrenheit minus 32 times 5/9.

3. Figure out what FOO and BAR will return without running them.

   ```
   (defun bar ()
     (let ((x 4))
       (funcall (foo) 3)))
   (defun foo ()
     (let ((x 5))
       #'(lambda (y) (* x y))))
   ```

4. The bicycle example from chapter 4 employed a set of selectors that worked when given a bicycle object created with MAKE-BIKE:

   ```
   (defun make-bike (x-position wheel-size gear-ratio)
     (list x-position wheel-size gear-ratio))
   ```

```
(defun x-position (bike)
   (car bike))

(defun wheel-size (bike)
  (cadr bike))

(defun gear-ratio (bike)
   (caddr bike))
```

Create a list of bicycles such as:

```
(defvar *bicycle-rack* (list (make-bike 0 2 3)
                             (make-bike 1 1 2)
                             (make-bike 5 2 1)))
```

Now write a procedure that takes any selector as argument, applies it to every bicycle in the list in turn, and returns a list of that item.

5. Add a command that allows the user to add commands to the top-level command loop on the fly (for the duration of the session with the command loop). The commands must have been previously defined as LISP functions with no arguments. (An additional improvement would be to allow the user to define things in LISP, perhaps even a general facility for evaluating LISP expressions.)

6. When people load candy machines, they usually load each hopper of the machine with one type of candy. However, if they run out, they load that hopper with another kind of candy. Write a program that simulates a candy machine with two hoppers. Write a procedure similar to MAKE-GUM-PACKAGE that loads the hoppers with one kind of candy until the stock of that kind of candy has run out. Then it should pick a new kind of candy and continue loading the hopper. The candy stock should consist of different types of candy in different amounts. Finally, write a procedure that gets candy from the machine and hopper that the user specifies.

Chapter 9

ADVANCED CONSTRUCTS

This chapter presents some more advanced constructs that will be useful when you begin to write larger programs in LISP. Conceptually, most of the items discussed here are refinements of material presented earlier.

Six areas are covered. They are optional arguments, "dynamic non-local exits," signalling errors, packages, multiple values, and documentation strings and conventions for commenting.

9.1 LAMBDA LISTS AND KEYWORDS

One way to help people manage complex systems is to reduce the number of facts and relationships they have to remember in order to use the system. Of course, the chief way to make a system manageable is through good design, which involves writing modular functions with meaningful names. However, at a somewhat lower level, there are a few things LISP does to make handling lists of variables easier for the user.

In a large system, even if you remember a function's name, you may not remember what arguments it takes; if you remember what arguments it takes, you may not remember their order; and, if you remember all these details, you may care about the values of only some of the arguments. Why should you have to know how to specify the default values for esoteric features in order to use simple features? For example, you should not need to know about streams in order to use READ to get information from the terminal.

To help with these issues, LISP allows functions to have optional arguments. From a user's point of view, there are three different kinds of optional arguments: optional arguments like those to READ, optional arguments like those to +, and optional arguments that require a keyword like :INITIAL-CONTENTS in MAKE-ARRAY.

9.1.1   *Writing Procedures with Optional Arguments*

To write procedures with optional arguments you must look at the variable or *lambda* list specified in a function's definition. Until now, you have written only functions that used the first part of the lambda list. In fact, there are a number of possible parts to the lambda list, any or all of which may be specified. Four of them are the required, optional, rest, and key parameters.

What do you already know about lambda lists? If you type in a list of parameters when defining a function, they will be bound to values specified at run time, in order, from left to right. When defining a function, you can specify as many arguments as you like, from none to an implementation-dependent limit, which you can find out by looking at the value of the constant LAMBDA-PARAMETERS-LIMIT.

These are the required arguments; if they are not given when the function is called, an error is signalled. Even when you have optional arguments, any required arguments must be typed first, and in order; otherwise, you wouldn't be able to tell if the actual parameters were intended for the required or optional formal parameters. For example, here is a standard function with three required parameters:

```
(defun poem (x y z)
  (format nil "Because I do not ~a to turn again~
              ~%Because I do not ~a~
              ~%Because I do not ~a to turn~%" x y z))
(poem "want" "care" "like")
"Because I do not want to turn again
Because I do not care
Because I do not like to turn
"
```

The second part of a lambda list is set off from the first by the presence of the &OPTIONAL lambda-list keyword. Although it is called a keyword, it is different from the keywords that begin with colons, such as :INITIAL-CONTENTS and :TEST. Keywords that begin with colons are employed by the user to indicate something about the variables in the function call. Lambda-list keywords begin with an ampersand and are employed by the writer to set up certain conditions for the variable list. One way a function writer can *use* lambda-list keywords is to specify normal keywords for the lambda list of a function.

The parameter specifiers that follow &OPTIONAL in the lambda list are optional arguments, like those to READ. Remember that READ takes several optional arguments: a stream name, a symbol to tell it what to do if the end of the stream is reached during the call to read, and a symbol to be returned if the second argument is NIL and the end of the stream is reached during a call. Optional parameters may or may not be present when the function is called. If they are not present, their default value is NIL:

```
(defun poem (x &optional y z)
   (format nil "Because I do not ~a to turn again~
                ~%Because I do not ~a~
                ~%Because I do not ~a to turn~%" x y z))

(poem "care" "care" "care")
"Because I do not care to turn again
Because I do not care
Because I do not care to turn
"

(poem "hope" "want")
"Because I do not hope to turn again
Because I do not want
Because I do not NIL to turn
"
```

Happily, the writer of a function using &OPTIONAL parameters can specify other default values by grouping together in a list the parameter name and an expression that computes the desired default value:

```
(defun poem (x &optional (y "hope") (z y))
   (format nil "Because I do not ~a to turn again~
                ~%Because I do not ~a~
                ~%Because I do not ~a to turn~%" x y z))

(poem "hope" "want")
"Because I do not hope to turn again
Because I do not want
Because I do not want to turn
"

(poem "hope")
"Because I do not hope to turn again
Because I do not hope
Because I do not hope to turn
"
```

The expression that computes the default value is evaluated only if the default value is actually needed (because no argument was passed explicitly). The expression may refer to previous parameters. When calling functions with optional parameters, in order to specify a value for a later variable, you must specify the values that precede it.

In READ, optional arguments are employed to allow a user to specify complex instructions if and when they are desired, but to ignore them if they're not necessary. This is a very desirable characteristic in a system or function because it allows a user to learn about the system or function incrementally.

After any required and &OPTIONAL parameters have been processed, the evaluator processes the third part of the lambda list, the *rest* parameter. If &REST is present, the variable whose name follows it is bound to a list of all the arguments left in the lambda list. This allows the user to type in as many arguments as he or she might wish to a function like +, without typing the arguments in as a list.

```
(defun my-add (&rest list-of-arguments)
 (do ((left-to-add list-of-arguments (cdr left-to-add))
      (running-sum 0 (+ (car left-to-add) running-sum)))
     ((null left-to-add) running-sum)))
(my-add)
0

(my-add 2 4)
6

(my-add 2 4 6 8 10 12 -15)
27
```

&REST makes a list of all the arguments passed after the required and &OPTIONAL parameters. Therefore, a procedure like the following one does not work:

```
(defun my-add1 (&rest list-of-args)
 (if (null list-of-args) 0
   (+ (car list-of-args)
      (my-add1 (cdr list-of-args))))) ; bug!
```

If you call this procedure initially with (my-add1 2 3 4 5), &REST causes a list to be made of the arguments. Therefore, when you call it recursively on the cdr of the list, the call looks like (my-add1 '(3 4 5)). &REST then causes a list to be made from this single argument, which is not what you wanted to happen. You can use APPLY to rewrite this procedure and make it work:

```
(defun my-add1 (&rest list-of-args)
 (if (null list-of-args) 0
   (+ (car list-of-args)
      (apply #'my-add1 (cdr list-of-args)))))
```

The fourth part of a lambda list starts with the &KEY keyword, which interprets all the remaining arguments as keywords followed by values. For example, when you type

```
(make-array '(3 2 4) :initial-contents '(((a b c l) (1 2 3 b))
                                         ((d e f j) (3 1 2 f))
                                         ((g h i r) (2 3 1 d))))
```

the first argument is interpreted as specifying the dimensions of the array: a required parameter. Then &KEY comes into play. The interpreter (or compiler) looks at the rest of the lambda list:

```
:initial-contents '(((a b c l) (1 2 3 b))
                    ((d e f j) (3 1 2 f))
                    ((g h i r) (2 3 1 d)))
```

and interprets the first element, :INITIAL-CONTENTS, as a keyword and the second element, the actual contents, as a value. Keywords do not have to be quoted because, as will be shown later in this chapter, they belong to the keyword package, and all members of the keyword package evaluate to themselves.

```
(defun complain (&key (times 1))
    (dotimes (i times)
      (format t "~%HURRY UP PLEASE IT'S TIME~%")))

(complain)
HURRY UP PLEASE IT'S TIME
NIL

(complain :times 3)
HURRY UP PLEASE IT'S TIME

HURRY UP PLEASE IT'S TIME

HURRY UP PLEASE IT'S TIME
NIL
```

Inside the function definition, keyword arguments are referred to without the colon before them, that is, as normal symbols, not keywords. This is necessary because keywords evaluate to themselves and could not be bound to the actual parameters. Keywords exist for the user's convenience in calling the function.

If both &KEY and &REST are present, they process the same arguments. They both get all the arguments that are not required and not optional.

```
(defun test (&rest a &key b)
  (format t "A: ~A~%B: ~S" a b))

(test)
A: NIL
B: NIL
NIL

(test :b 4)
A: (B 4)
B: 4
NIL
```

9.2   CATCH, THROW, AND UNWIND-PROTECT

CATCH and THROW provide a way to respond to certain conditions with a "non-local" exit of the current function. For example, you could change the way the top-level command language presented in chapter 8 worked. Instead of the main loop testing for the symbol EXIT as its end test, you could have the function MY-EXIT throw to a catch placed outside the loop:

```
(defun my-exit ()
  (throw 'exit nil))

;;; MAIN-LOOP takes a table and looks up user input in
;;; the table.  If a function is found, it is executed.
;;; If not, help is printed.
(defun main-loop (table)
  (catch 'exit
```

```
(do ((current-command
       (gethash (read) table)
       (gethash (read) table)))
     ()
  (if current-command
      (funcall current-command)
      (funcall help))
  (format t "~%Command> "))))
```

If the user types EXIT, it is executed like any other command the user gives, and THROW gets called. Since this THROW is throwing to the tag EXIT, the CATCH 'EXIT in MAIN-LOOP catches it. CATCHes catch only THROWs whose tags match their tags. The effect of the THROW is to exit both EXIT and the DO-loop.

This design is cleaner and more easily extensible than the previous arrangement. For instance, one improvement to the command language would be to change the way DELETE-FILE works so that it keeps a list of the files you have asked to delete until you exit the system, and deletes them only at that time. You would extend EXIT to delete the files. You might want to have a quit as well as an exit command: QUIT would do just the throw; EXIT would delete the files first. Other extensions are also possible.

The above example does not do anything interesting with THROW's second argument; however, this argument provides a mechanism for passing back information based on the environment of the THROW. Although the second argument is evaluated in the environment of the THROW, it is returned as the value of the CATCH. You might use this argument in a situation where you were THROWing to a CATCH with the tag ERROR from many different places in a program, but specifying different actions to be taken, depending on the information passed back by the THROW.

When the THROW exits both EXIT and the DO-loop, it is performing a non-local exit. It stops evaluation of the enclosing contexts completely. For example,

```
(catch 'foo (print (throw 'foo nil)))
```

never prints anything. The THROW breaks out of the current context and any other enclosing contexts until it reaches the matching CATCH. Aborting execution of a function in LISP is accomplished via a THROW, as is exiting from the debugger.

UNWIND-PROTECT is a form that allows you to make sure that a piece of code gets executed *whenever* another form is executed. This is important because errors, interrupts, and user programs can all do THROWs that cause an immediate return to an enclosing CATCH. This means that a situation can arise where an action is begun, but not finished, because of a THROW.

For example, suppose you were writing a program to direct a mobile robot to perform covert operations. If the robot was interrupted while committing the crime and had to escape, the program might do a THROW out of the crime-committing routine so that the robot would leave immediately:

```
(defun spy ()
  (catch 'run-away
         (commit-crime))
  (make-good-escape))
(defun commit-crime ()
  (take-valuable-information)
  (if (someone-in-room?) (throw 'run-away nil))
  (destroy-evidence))
```

But what if it simply ran away, leaving incriminating evidence behind? You must make sure that, no matter what happens, the robot destroys the evidence before leaving. You can accomplish this with an UNWIND-PROTECT. The syntax of UNWIND-PROTECT is:

```
(unwind-protect
   protected-form
   cleanup-forms)
```

If no THROW occurs while the protected form is being executed, the cleanup forms are executed after the protected form, just as in PROGN; however, if a THROW is executed in the course of evaluating the protected form, even if it is a THROW to a CATCH in some context enclosing the UNWIND-PROTECT, the cleanup forms are executed before control passes to the CATCH.

You can use UNWIND-PROTECT to coerce the robot into better priorities by rewriting COMMIT-CRIME as follows:

```
(defun commit-crime ()
  (unwind-protect
    (progn
      (take-valuable-information)
      (if (someone-in-room?)
          (throw 'run-away nil)))
    (destroy-evidence)))
```

This program guarantees that the hapless mobile robot will put your interests ahead of its own, regardless of the circumstances.

On a more mundane level, the most obvious example of a situation in which you would want UNWIND-PROTECT is with the OPEN command:

```
(defun test (file-name)
  (let ((input-stream nil))
    (unwind-protect
      (progn ;protected form
        (setf input-stream (open file-name))
        (print (read-line input-stream)))
      (when input-stream
        (close input-stream)))))   ;cleanup form
```

This ensures that the file is closed when the PROGN is exited. In fact, this is almost exactly what the form WITH-OPEN-FILE does, and is why it is ordinarily preferable to OPEN.

9.3   ERROR SIGNALLING

COMMON LISP leaves error handling up to the specific implementation but provides a standard way to signal errors. ERROR is a function that signals a fatal error, that is, an error that halts the execution of a form or function. CERROR signals a continuable error, one in which execution stops but may be continued.

ERROR takes as arguments a format string and format arguments. The string is formatted and printed to the stream *DEBUG-IO* when the function is invoked.

CERROR's syntax is like error's except that it takes an additional argument; it takes two format strings and a set of arguments. The first string is a message stating what will happen if the program is continued; the second is the error message itself. Only one set of arguments is used for both strings. For example,

```
(defun my-divide (&rest args)
  (do ((argument-list args (cdr argument-list))
       (running-count
         (car args)
         (if (null (cadr argument-list))
             running-count
           (/ running-count
              (check-for-zero (cadr argument-list))))))
      ((null argument-list) running-count)))
(defun check-for-zero (number)
  (cond ((zerop number) (cerror "Substituting 1 for the 0."
                                "Attempt to divide by zero.") 1)
        (t number)))
```

A common mistake in handling errors, either with CATCH and THROW or with an error-signalling function, is to solicit user input but forget to check for its acceptability. To avoid this problem, write a loop that calls the checking function until the condition is satisfied:

```
(defun check-for-zero (number)
  (cond ((zerop number)
         (cerror "Type a new number."
                 "Attempt to divide by zero.")
                 (check-for-zero (read)))
        (t number)))
```

9.4   PACKAGES AND MODULES

You may have wondered what prevents you from accidentally redefining an internal function used by the system designers, thus breaking the LISP system. This is just a dramatic version of a problem anyone working on a large programming project has:

How do you prevent one programmer from accidentally using a name that somebody else has already used?

COMMON LISP provides a mechanism for solving this problem by allowing you to group a set of symbols together in a given *namespace*. Every symbol is owned by a particular *package*.[1] The package name is thus a kind of second, or family, name for the symbol, allowing you to tell the difference between John Smith and John Jones.

You are prevented from accidentally redefining an internal system function because system functions are kept in a different package. In fact, the parts that make up LISP are all in separate packages. If the LISP includes an editor, the symbols in the editor are typically all in the package called EDITOR. The symbols in the rest of the system are in the package LISP or SYSTEM. Keywords are in the KEYWORD package, and, finally, the symbols you create are, by default, in the USER package.

When you type a symbol to the LISP reader, if you do not specify a package name, and the symbol doesn't already exist, it is created in the package that is the value of *PACKAGE*, which is usually the USER package.

Assume, for the moment, that you know how to create symbols in a particular package. Assume, too, that you have created a package called FORMATTER, which contains a program that does text formatting. Formatter contains several symbols; in particular, FORM invokes the program.

If you are a user of the program FORM, working in package USER, you are thus protected against inadvertently redefining constructs used in FORM. However, this leaves you with a problem; if you are in the package USER, and the symbols for the formatter are in the package FORMATTER, you cannot invoke the formatter by simply typing (form "myfile").

The brute-force way to get around this difficulty is to specify the package name along with the symbol name:

```
(formatter::form "myfile")
```

The two colons are the way of specifying that the symbol is an *internal* symbol named FORM in the FORMATTER package.

A more elegant solution is for the creator of the formatter to identify symbols that should be externally available. To do this, the program writer inserts the line at top level into her file:

```
(export '(form))
```

EXPORT allows the program writer to make a clearly defined interface between her program and any others. If a symbol appears in the EXPORT list, it is all right for others to use it. If a symbol does not appear in the EXPORT list, others can use it, either by

---

[1] It is possible to create uninterned symbols, that is, symbols not owned by any package. This capacity is important, but does not require discussion here.

importing it with the function IMPORT or by specifying its package name and two colons; however, such use is clearly marked as dabbling with internals.

Once this is done, you still cannot access FORM by typing FORM while you are in package USER. Instead, you can access it by referring to it in a special way meant for exported symbols:

```
(formatter:form 'myfile)
```

One colon between the package name and the symbol name allows you to refer to symbols exported from a package, but does not allow you to refer to nonexported symbols.

In fact, when you use keyword arguments as defined with &KEY, you are referring to symbols exported from the keyword package. However, the keyword package has several strange properties. First, all keywords present in the package are exported. Second, all keywords evaluate to themselves. Third, you do not have to specify the package name to refer to a symbol in the keyword package. Instead, any symbol with only a colon before it is considered to belong to the package KEYWORD. That is, although you could type KEYWORD:INITIAL-CONTENTS, typing :INITIAL-CONTENTS has the same effect.

Sometimes it is sufficient to export symbols and leave them accessible, as above. This allows the user of your package to have the symbol named FORM of her own in her package without conflict. However, if that user so desires, she can make the symbols exported from a package available from the current package as if they were part of it by using the command USE-PACKAGE. Thus, the creator of the format program might write an initialization file that loads in the formatter, and then has the line:

```
(use-package 'formatter)
```

Now, the user can simply type:

```
(form "myfile")
```

If there is a symbol named FORM in the current package and a symbol named FORM in the FORMATTER package, and (use-package 'formatter) is called, there will be a name conflict. In this case, a continuable error is probably signalled[2] and the user is asked which symbol should take precedence.

The function IMPORT allows the user to import specific symbols rather than all the

---

[2] Under some circumstances, that is, if the symbol in the current package is a shadowing symbol, an error will not be signalled. The interested reader is referred to Steele, pages 178–181.

external symbols of a package. Therefore, you could accomplish the effect of (use-package 'formatter) for the symbol FORM by calling:

```
(import '(formatter:form))
```

The program writer could also produce this effect by taking advantage of IMPORT's second argument. IMPORT allows you to specify the package that the symbol should be imported to. To specify packages, use the function FIND-PACKAGE and specify the name of the package. Therefore, if you were working in the package FORMATTER and wished to export FORM to the USER package, you could write:

```
(import '(form) (find-package 'user))
```

LISP probably makes its symbols available in just this way. Certain symbols, including CAR, CDR, and CONS, are present in the USER package (and by default in all other packages); however, the auxiliary functions used to implement them are quite invisible.

The discussion so far has concerned itself with preventing access to most of the symbols in a package. However, how do you arrange to put symbols in a package? The step-by-step way to do so is to make the package with the function MAKE-PACKAGE:

```
(make-package 'my-package)
```

and then type symbols into it:

```
(defun my-package::foo (my-package::x)
  (* my-package::x my-package::x))
```

By default, new packages have (use-package 'LISP) run in them, so you can use DEFUN and *.

A more convenient way to put symbols in MY-PACKAGE is to make MY-PACKAGE the current one by typing:

```
(setf *package* (find-package 'my-package))
```

Now all symbols typed will be created in the package MY-PACKAGE. Setting the value of *PACKAGE* is useful when you are writing a program and working in the interpreter. However, you also want to make sure that, when the file that contains the program is loaded into LISP, the symbols are created in the correct package. Inserting the command IN-PACKAGE at the top of a file causes the symbols in that file to be created in the package specified. If the package does not already exist, IN-PACKAGE will make it and then set the value of *PACKAGE* to it. After the file has been loaded, the value of *PACKAGE* is reset to whatever it was before loading started.

Suppose you were writing a text formatter, normally invoked by calling the function FORM, with the name of a file to be formatted as an argument. If you wanted the formatter to be in a package called FORMATTER, you would put the line

```
(in-package 'formatter)
```

at the top of each file containing a part of the formatter.

COMMON LISP allows you to label a file or group of files as part of a *module*. The purpose of creating a module is so that other programs can state a dependency on it and load it if it is not already present in LISP. Module creation is done in an implementation-dependent fashion, which you should look up in the documentation for your LISP system.

To load in a module, use the function REQUIRE, which looks to see if the module is already present. If it is not, REQUIRE determines where it is (in an implementation-dependent way) and loads it in.

The function PROVIDE is used to update LISP's knowledge of whether or not a module is present. A call to PROVIDE with the module name as an argument should appear at the beginning of the module. This adds the module name to the list stored in the variable called *MODULES*. REQUIRE consults *MODULES* to determine whether or not the module is present.

Causing a module to be loaded into LISP may interact with the desired manipulation of packages in the current module, because modules typically contain one or more packages of their own, each of which may REQUIRE other modules that undoubtedly contain exported symbols. For this reason, REQUIRE should be placed after local symbols are established with IN-PACKAGE and EXPORT (and SHADOW, see below) but before USE-PACKAGE and IMPORT.

In fact, in many cases it is crucial to put the commands presented in this section in the right order. Otherwise, it is very hard to tell which symbol in what package is being referred to. For this reason, package instructions are put at the top of a file, next to one another.

PROVIDE should appear first, to make sure that LISP knows that the current package is, in fact, present. IN-PACKAGE appears next. IN-PACKAGE sets the default package; therefore, if the next command is EXPORT, it is quite clear that the symbols are being exported from the package named by IN-PACKAGE. Calls to REQUIRE must come after calls to EXPORT because the REQUIREd modules may refer to exported symbols. USE-PACKAGE must come after REQUIRE because to use a package it must be loaded in. Calls to IMPORT, which import symbols from other packages, come next. These could come before USE-PACKAGE, but it's probably best to perform the more general operation first.

EXPORT, IMPORT, and USE-PACKAGE can all take a package as an optional second argument. In the case of EXPORT, the package signifies which package the symbols should be exported from. In the case of IMPORT and USE-PACKAGE, it specifies which package gains access to the symbols.

9.4.1   **Shadow**

Imagine that the package MY-PROGRAM uses many of the external symbols of the package HELP, so it is convenient to do (use-package 'help). Yet one symbol, HELP-USER, is already present in MY-PROGRAM and is also imported from HELP. You want to keep the HELP-USER in MY-PROGRAM, so that when you change the definition of HELP-USER, you change the definition of MY-PACKAGE::HELP-USER and leave HELP::HELP-USER alone.

You can specify this behavior by including a SHADOW command in your file:

```
(shadow 'help-user)
```

Now when you refer to HELP-USER inside MY-PACKAGE, you get MY-PACKAGE::HELP-USER; however, if you wish to refer to HELP::HELP-USER, you can still do so by specifying HELP:HELP-USER.

The call to SHADOW must be made before the call to USE-PACKAGE because USE-PACKAGE looks at the list provided to SHADOW and modifies its behavior accordingly.

9.5   **MULTIPLE VALUES**

Until now, all LISP functions have been treated as if they return exactly one value. However, just as you have choices about many other behaviors in LISP, you have options about how many values are returned.

There are two parts to returning multiple values: writing functions that return multiple values and writing functions that accept multiple values.

You have already seen functions that return multiple values. For example, FLOOR takes a number as argument and returns as a first value the truncated portion of that number. As a second value, it returns the remainder. If a second argument is specified, that number is used as a divisor.

Most often when you use FLOOR, you are interested in only the first value returned, and when a call to FLOOR is used to provide an argument to another function, only the first value is used. Subsequent values are ignored:

```
(floor 3.5 3)
1
; 0.5
(+ (floor 3.5 3) 4)
5
```

How would you arrange to look at subsequent values? MULTIPLE-VALUE-BIND is one useful special form for receiving multiple values. MULTIPLE-VALUE-BIND takes a list of variable names, a function call that is supposed to return multiple values, and a body. Variables in the variable list are matched up in order, with values returned by the function call. The first variable is bound to the first value returned by the function, the second variable is bound to the second value, and so forth. The body is evaluated while the variables are bound to the values.

Thus, MULTIPLE-VALUE-BIND is a lot like LET, but for variables bound to the results of a single evaluation, which returns multiple values. Here is a function called TABINDENT that uses both parts of FLOOR to "tab over" from the left margin to column N, using ASCII tabs and spaces in the optimal fashion:

```
(defconstant spaces-per-tab 8)

(defun tabindent (n &optional (stream *standard-output*))
  (multiple-value-bind (tabs spaces)
      (floor n spaces-per-tab)
    (dotimes (i tabs)
       (format stream "~a" #\tab))
    (dotimes (j spaces)
       (format stream "~a" #\space)))))

(defun test ()
 (tabindent 12)
 (format t "test"))

(test)
              test
NIL
```

The list (tabs spaces) in this example contains the names of the variables. The call (floor n spaces-per-tab) is expected to return two values, the first named TABS and the second SPACES. In the sample call, TABS is bound to 1 and SPACES to 4 within the body of MULTIPLY-PARTS. If more values are returned than there are variables, the extra values are ignored. If there are more variables than there are values returned, the extra variables are bound to NIL.

You might also want multiple values when using the function READ-FROM-STRING, which first returns the item read, and then the index of the first character not read. If you want to read more of the string, you can use the index number to specify where to start reading next.

```
(defun list-from-string (string)
  (list-from-string-index string 0))

(defun list-from-string-index (string start)
  (if (= start (length string)) nil
      (multiple-value-bind (item index)
                     (read-from-string string nil 'eof
                                       :start start)
          (cons item (list-from-string-index string index)))))
```

The construct MULTIPLE-VALUE-LIST can be useful when you don't know how many values will be returned but want all of them. MULTIPLE-VALUE-LIST takes a form and returns a list containing the values that the form returns. For example, the LISP interpreter never knows how many values it will have to print. Imagine that it was written like this:

```
(defun read-eval-print-loop ()
  (do () ()
    (mapc #'print (multiple-value-list (eval (read))))
    (terpri)))
```

Returning multiple values is comparatively simple. The function VALUES returns all its arguments as separate values.

```
(defun proportion (number portion)
  (values (* number portion)
          (* number (- 1 portion)))))
```

You can see both values if you call the function from top level[3]:

```
(proportion 9 1/3)
3
; 6
(proportion 9 1/4)
9/4
; 27/4
```

VALUES called with no arguments allows you to return no value from a function. The top-level loop prints nothing if it receives no values, so you can use it to avoid returning unnecessary values that seem messy.

In the following example, CENTER-LINE prints a line centered with respect to the value of *TEXT-WIDTH*. It does all the printing itself, but figures out how many spaces and tabs to print by calling CALCULATE-SPACES. CALCULATE-SPACES figures out how many spaces have to be filled and calls NEW-TABINDENT, which no longer prints the spaces and tabs itself but calls FLOOR and returns the values. CALCULATE-SPACES and NEW-TABINDENT have no special constructs for returning multiple values; however, a function defined with DEFUN returns the values returned by the last form in its body.

```
(defvar *text-width* 65)

(defun center-line (string &optional (stream *standard-output*))
  (multiple-value-bind (tabs spaces)
      (calculate-spaces string)
    (unless (null tabs)
      (dotimes (i tabs)
        (format stream "~a" #\tab))
      (dotimes (j spaces)
        (format stream "~a" #\space))
      (format stream "~a" string))))
```

---

[3] Values after the first may be printed slightly differently in different implementations of LISP.

```
(defun calculate-spaces (text-string)
  (cond ((<= (length text-string) *text-width*)
         (new-tabindent (/ (- *text-width*
                              (length text-string))
                           2)))
        (t nil)))
(defun new-tabindent (n)
  (floor n spaces-per-tab))
```

Forms with implicit PROGNs (DEFUN, LET) just pass along the values returned. Many other constructs, such as APPLY, FUNCALL, and IF also do this; however, if you decide to rely on this behavior, you should look up the exact rules in Steele, section 7.9.2. Be aware that some forms are slightly tricky; they pass multiple values back under some conditions but not under others. For example, COND always passes multiple values except when the predicate is the only item in the clause.

Multiple values are particularly useful when a subfunction can give two distinct pieces of information that the calling function needs. Multiple values are never essential because their information can be returned in a list; however, using multiple values is less expensive and more convenient if you are creating a list to use only as a sort of envelope that will be opened and discarded by the caller.

9.6   COMMENTS AND DOCUMENTATION STRINGS

A LISP comment begins with a semicolon. The LISP reader ignores anything on a line that appears after a semicolon. By convention there are four levels of comments:

```
;;;; Four semicolons are treated as a heading.  Thus, comments
;;;; at the beginning of a file or of a major section of a file
;;;; should be preceded by four semicolons.

;;; Three semicolons are treated as a comment on a particular
;;; function.  Such comments usually appear on the lines
;;; just before the function.

;; Two semicolons are used to comment on the line of code
;; immediately below them.

;One semicolon refers to the line of code it is on.
;Usually one doesn't leave a space between
;the semicolon and the comment if using only one semicolon.
```

Editors with pretty-printers treat different numbers of semicolons differently. For example, a line with two semicolons is printed with the same indentation as the line below it. A line with one semicolon is printed with the comment indented some number of spaces from the end of the row it is on.

```
;;; This is a general comment on a form.
(defun foo (x)
  ;; This is a comment on the line below.
  (bar baz))  ;this is a comment on the current line.
```

Many LISP editors have a command that moves the cursor to the proper place on a line for adding comments.

9.6.1   **Documentation Strings**

When DESCRIBE was introduced in chapter 3, you were told that you could give it a LISP object, and it would return interesting information about that object. In particular, if you call DESCRIBE on a symbol, such as NTHCDR, you might get information like this:

```
The symbol NTHCDR
Package:  SYSTEM
Value:    unbound
Function: a compiled-function
    NTHCDR number list

      This function returns the nth cdr of the list.
```

The line "This function returns the nth cdr of the list." is a documentation string.

You were also told that DESCRIBE can be called on user-defined objects as well as on system-provided ones. If the object is a symbol, DESCRIBE, without any further effort on your part, tells you which package it belongs to, its value, and whether or not it is compiled. DESCRIBE prints the symbol's lambda list if it has a function binding.

An important option in COMMON LISP is to provide documentation strings as part of object definitions. These documentation strings are printed by DESCRIBE, providing a kind of on-line documentation. Documentation strings are usually located just before the body of a form that allows them. For example,

```
(defun my-complicated-function (x)
  "This claims to be a complicated function, but isn't."
  (print x))

(describe 'my-complicated-function)
It is the symbol MY-COMPLICATED-FUNCTION
Package:  USER
Value:    unbound
Function: a cons
    This claims to be a complicated function, but isn't.
```

It can be particularly valuable to use documentation strings along with DEFVAR and DEFSTRUCT. For example,

```
(defvar *fish* '(pike bass bluefish)
  "All the types of fish at the market today.")

(defstruct fish
    "An instance of a fish that might be available
at the market today."
    (type 'halibut)
    (salt-water? t))
```

If you type (describe '*fish*) or (describe 'fish), you receive the documentation.

You can call DESCRIBE on an instance of a structure or list as well as on symbols. For example, you might get a response like this:

```
(describe (make-fish))
The object at <XXXX> is of type FISH.
SLOTS:
    TYPE: type is T, value is the symbol HALIBUT
    SALT-WATER?: type is T, value is the symbol T
```

The function DOCUMENTATION may also be used to examine the documentation string for a symbol. DOCUMENTATION takes a symbol and a documentation type and returns the string for the symbol for that type of object. For example,

```
(documentation 'fish 'structure)
"An instance of a fish that might be available
at the market today."
```

DOCUMENTATION is especially useful because you can call SETF on it to change the documentation string.

9.6.1.1   THE TOP-LEVEL LOOP

DESCRIBE is primarily useful when you are working from top-level LISP. As a programmer, you may also find some variables associated with the top-level READ-EVAL-PRINT loop useful.

LISP stores the last three items read and the last three items returned. You can retrieve and use any of these items. Table 9-1 shows which variables are bound to which items.

These variables are of assistance if you want to use the result of one evaluation as input while typing at the top-level loop.

TABLE 9-1. The Top-level Loop

Variables	Items
+	the last item read by LISP
*	the last result printed by LISP
++	the next to last item read by LISP
**	the next to last result printed by LISP
+++	the item read by LISP the time before ++
***	the item printed as a result by LISP the time before **

```
(caadr '(apples (oranges (peaches)) mangoes kiwi))
ORANGES
```

```
(cons * '(my-favorite-fruit))
(ORANGES MY-FAVORITE-FRUIT)
```

They are also useful if you want to repeat an action:

```
(print (car *some-variable-with-a-long-name*))
```

```
(eval +)
```

9.7   EXTENDED EXAMPLE: TEXT FORMATTING

FORM is a simple, one-pass text formatter. It opens an input file, reads it line by line, processes each line, and writes text to an output file.

Like most text formatters, FORM allows you to put commands that affect the output in the input file. As presented here, FORM has nine commands; they begin with a % and must occur at the beginning of a line. Many FORM commands take arguments, which follow them on the line.

The commands %FILL and %NO-FILL allow you to choose between FORM's two modes. In fill mode, FORM ignores all line breaks. Instead of printing a return, it prints as many words on a line as will fit and then generates a line break. In no-fill mode, FORM outputs all lines literally, without regard to whether they fit on the page.

%LEFT-MARGIN, %TEXT-WIDTH, and %PAGE-LENGTH can be used to set up the default size for a page. %LEFT-MARGIN specifies the number of spaces to be put on each line before printing begins. %TEXT-WIDTH is the number of characters that can be accommodated after printing begins in fill mode. %PAGE-LENGTH specifies the number of lines that can be put on a page.

%NEW-PAGE and %BREAK allow the user to ask for a new page or a new line at a particular place in the text.

%HEADER takes a string and arguments. When a new page is started, the string and arguments are evaluated, and the result is given to FORMAT. The value returned by FORMAT is printed at the top of the page by a recursive invocation of the formatter.

Last, %EVAL allows you to have arbitrary LISP functions evaluated so that, if you want, you can change the value of FORM variables while the program is running. For example, you could temporarily set *FORM-COMMAND-CHARACTER*, the variable that normally specifies that commands begin with %, to something else if you were printing a lot of words that begin with % signs.

Exhibits 9-1 and 9-2 illustrate a sample input file for FORM and its output.

```
%no-fill
%text-width 45
%left-margin 30
%header "%left-margin 15~%SAMPLE LETTER~%%break 2~%"
Cambridge, MA
February 28, 1986
%left-margin 8
Dear Lenny,
%fill
%break 2
Thank you for your letter which arrived last Thursday. I haven't replied
before this because of a series of small tragedies that beset my week:
my car broke down, the dog ate it, the page was torn out, the alarm
clock didn't go off. Nothing serious, but all time consuming.
%break 2
I will be out in California for two months starting June 1.
My address there will be:
%break 2
%no-fill
%left-margin 15
4545 Big View Canyon
Overlook, CA 95404
%break
%left-margin 8
%fill
After that I'll be in Germany for 3 weeks, and then back home for
the semester.
%break 2
Everything is going quite well here, "all projects are go," as they say,and the
winter is proving less brutal than usual.
%break 2
Thanks again for your letter!
%break 3
%left-margin 30
Sincerely,
%break
%new-page
%left-margin 8
P.S. By the way, the chapter titles for my book are:
%left margin 20
%no-fill
Chapter 1: Introduction
Chapter 2: Datatypes and Evaluation
Chapter 3: Writing Procedures
Chapter 4: Variables
Chapter 5: Recursion and Iteration
Chapter 6: Interactions with the Outside World
Chapter 7: Manipulating Data
Chapter 8: Manipulating Procedures as Data
Chapter 9: Advanced Topics
%break
%fill
%left-margin 8
and that's as far as I've gotten!
```

Exhibit 9-1. Sample Input to FORM

```
                                      Cambridge, MA
                                      February 28, 1986
        Dear Lenny,

        Thank you for your letter which arrived last
        Thursday. I haven't replied before this
        because of a series of small tragedies that
        beset my week: my car broke down, the dog
        ate it, the page was torn out, the alarm
        clock didn't go off. Nothing serious, but all
        time consuming.

        I will be out in California for two months
        starting June 1. My address there will be:

              4545 Big View Canyon
              Overlook, CA 95404

        After that I'll be in Germany for 3 weeks,
        and then back home for the semester.

        Everything is going quite well here, "all
        projects are go," as they say, and the winter
        is proving less brutal than usual.

        Thanks again for your letter!

                                      Sincerely,
```

```
                    SAMPLE LETTER

        P.S. By the way, the chapter titles for my book
        are:
                    Chapter 1: Introduction
                    Chapter 2: Datatypes and Evaluation
                    Chapter 3: Writing Procedures
                    Chapter 4: Variables
                    Chapter 5: Recursion and Iteration
                    Chapter 6: Interactions with the Outside World
                    Chapter 7: Manipulating Data
                    Chapter 8: Manipulating Procedures as Data
                    Chapter 9: Advanced Topics

        and that's as far as I've gotten!
```

Exhibit 9-2. Sample Output from FORM

9.7.1   **The Implementation of FORM**

The formatter is invoked by calling the function FORM, which has one required parameter: a string indicating the file containing the material to be formatted. FORM also has one optional argument. If the user does not specify a particular output file, the material is written to FORMED.TXT.[4]

FORM-DRIVER-LOOP is the main loop of the program. It reads a line and decides whether to call FORM-EXECUTE-COMMAND, FORM-FILL-OUTPUT-LINE, or FORM-NO-FILL-OUTPUT-LINE on the basis of (a) whether the line is a command line and (b) the value of the *FILL-MODE?* variable:

```
;;; main loop
(defun form-driver-loop ()
    (do ((current-line (read-line *input-stream* nil
                                    'form-driver-loop-eof)
                        (read-line *input-stream* nil
                                    'form-driver-loop-eof)))
        ;; current-line will be the symbol FORM-DRIVER-LOOP-EOF
        ;; at end-of-file.
        ((eq current-line 'form-driver-loop-eof))
        ;; a blank line can't be a command line
        (cond ((and (> (length current-line) 0)
                    (equal (char current-line 0)
                           *form-command-char*))
               (form-execute-command current-line))
              (t (if *fill-mode?*
                  (form-fill-output-line current-line)
                  (form-no-fill-output-line current-line)))))))
```

FORM-EXECUTE-COMMAND deciphers the command line and executes it. It uses the construct LET*, which sets the value of its variables in sequences instead of in parallel. Therefore, COMMAND and ARGS are always set to the value of the car and cdr of the current COMMAND-LIST instead of that of the previous one.

```
;;; form-execute-command executes a user command
(defun form-execute-command (current-line)
    (let* ((command-list
            (list-from-string (subseq current-line 1)))
           (command (car command-list))
           (args (cdr command-list)))
      (case command
            ;; It would be better to make this data driven
            ;; but for a small number of commands, CASE will do.
            (fill (setf *fill-mode?* t))
            (no-fill (form-newline) (setf *fill-mode?* nil))
            (left-margin (setf *left-margin* (car args)))
            (new-page (apply #'form-newpage args))
            (header (setf *header-text-list* args))
```

---

[4] This default may not work on a machine that does not run the VMS operating system.

```
(text-width (setf *text-width* (car args)))
(page-length (setf *page-length* (car args)))
(break (apply #'form-newline args))
(eval (mapc #'eval args))
(t (format t "~&Warning: ~A is not a known FORM command.~%"
    command))))))
```

FORM-NO-FILL-OUTPUT-LINE simply outputs the left margin and the line. If a line is too long for the page (or screen), it runs off the edge, without warning. No-fill mode outputs text exactly as the user typed it in. FORM-NO-FILL-OUTPUT-LINE also calls a function that checks to see whether the end of the page has been reached.

```
;;; Output a line of input text in no-fill mode.
(defun form-no-fill-output-line (line)
    (form-output-left-margin) ;first output the left margin
    (format *output-stream* "~A" line) ;then the text
    (form-newline))                      ;then a new line,
                                         ;and page
                                         ;if necessary
```

Inside FORM-NO-FILL-OUTPUT-LINE, FORM-NEWLINE is sufficient to update the two state variables that the system uses to keep track of where it is printing on the page. These variables are *CURRENT-LINE* and *CURRENT-COLUMN*. FORM-NEWLINE increments *CURRENT-LINE*, starting a new page if necessary, and sets *CURRENT-COLUMN* to 0. *CURRENT-COLUMN* is always zero after printing a line in no-fill mode because the last thing that no-fill mode prints is a new line.

FORM-FILL-OUTPUT-LINE is considerably more complex. When filling text you cannot simply translate one line of input into one line of output. Instead the basic idea is:

• Get a word from the input line.

• Check whether there is room for it on the output line.

• If there is, print it with a trailing space and update the *CURRENT-COLUMN*.

• If there isn't, issue a return, a left margin, and then print it.

• Repeat these steps until you have processed all the words on the input line.

```
;;; Output a line of input text in fill mode.
(defun form-fill-output-line (line)
    (do ((pointer 0)) (nil)
      (multiple-value-bind (word char-pointer)
          (form-get-word pointer line)
          (if (null word) (return))
          ;; see if the word fits on this line,
          ;; and do a newline if it doesn't
          (if (>= (+ *current-column* (length word)) *text-width*)
            (form-newline))  ;output new line, check for new page
          ;; output the margin spacing if at beginning of new line
          (if (zerop *current-column*) (form-output-left-margin))
```

```
;; now print the word
(format *output-stream* "~A" word)
  ;; and the trailing space, if there's room
  (unless (= *text-width*
             (+ *current-column* (length word)))
          (format *output-stream* " "))
(setf *current-column*
      (+ *current-column* (length word) 1))
  ;; next call to form-get-word should start after last word
  (setf pointer char-pointer))))
```

FORM-FILL-OUTPUT-LINE calls the auxiliary function FORM-GET-WORD, which returns a word from a string. FORM-GET-WORD begins by looking for the word, starting at the index POINTER, ignoring all white-space characters, that is, all spaces and tabs, until it comes to something that is not a white-space character. Then it starts accumulating, and does so until it comes to another white-space character. It returns two values: the word found, or NIL if no word is found, and a pointer to the white-space character after it.

```
(defun form-get-word (pointer line)
  ;; Strip any leading white space.
  (let ((word-beginning
          (position-if-not #'white-space-char?
                           line :start pointer)))
    ;; Now find the end of the word
    ;; i.e., the first char not in it.
    (if word-beginning      ;if we found a word
        (let ((word-end (position-if #'white-space-char?
                                     line :start word-beginning)))
          ;; If word-end's nil, it's the end of string.
          (if (not word-end) (setf word-end (length line)))
          (values (subseq line word-beginning word-end)
                  word-end))
        nil)))
```

Most of the functions that implement the commands perform fairly straightforward tasks. However, FORM-OUTPUT-HEADER demands some explanation. As stated above, the *HEADER-TEXT-LIST* is evaluated and the result formatted to create a string. Then dynamic shadows are created for the variables *FILL-MODE?* and *LEFT-MARGIN*. That is, the variables created inside the LET shadow the variables of the same name outside the LET. Since both *FILL-MODE?* and *LEFT-MARGIN* have been proclaimed special by DEFVAR, this shadowing is dynamic and affects all references to them in any function called inside the LET. Any changes made to these variables while the header text is being printed are in effect only until the LET is exited. This means that you can give instructions about formatting the header in the command %HEADER and not worry about changing defaults in the rest of the text. This is one of the most important uses for dynamic scoping.

```
(defun form-output-header ()
  (let ((header-string (apply #'format nil
                               (mapcar #'eval *header-text-list*)))
        (*fill-mode?* *fill-mode?*)
        (*left-margin* *left-margin*))
    (with-input-from-string (*input-stream* header-string)
      (declare (special *input-stream*))
      (form-driver-loop)))))
```

This is a complete printout of FORM, a toy text formatter.

```
;;; some internal parameters
(defparameter *form-command-char* #\%)
(defvar *input-stream*)
(defvar *output-stream*)

;;; some user-interface parameters
(defvar *current-line-number*)
(defvar *current-column*)
(defvar *page-number*)
(defvar *fill-mode?*)
(defvar *page-length*)
(defvar *left-margin*)
(defvar *text-width*)
(defvar *header-text-list*)

;;; Initialize the user-interface parameters to nice defaults.
(defun form-initialize ()
  (setf *current-line-number* 0)
  (setf *current-column* 0)
  (setf *page-number* 1)
  (setf *fill-mode?* nil)
  (setf *page-length* 47)
  (setf *left-margin* 8)
  (setf *text-width* 70)
  (setf *header-text-list* '("")))

;;; This is the function the user calls.
(defun form (filename &optional (output-filename "formed.txt"))
  (declare (special *output-stream*) (special *input-stream*))
  (form-initialize)
  (with-open-file (*output-stream* output-filename
                   :direction :output :if-exists :supersede)
    (with-open-file (*input-stream* filename
                     :direction :input)
      (form-driver-loop))))

;;; main loop
(defun form-driver-loop ()
  (do ((current-line (read-line *input-stream* nil
                                'form-driver-loop-eof)
                     (read-line *input-stream* nil
                                'form-driver-loop-eof)))
      ;; current-line will be the symbol FORM-DRIVER-LOOP-EOF
      ;; at end-of-file.
```

```
       ((eq current-line 'form-driver-loop-eof))
       ;; a blank line can't be a command line
       (cond ((and (> (length current-line) 0)
                   (equal (char current-line 0)
                          *form-command-char*))
              (form-execute-command current-line))
             (t (if *fill-mode?*
                    (form-fill-output-line current-line)
                  (form-no-fill-output-line current-line)))))))

;;; output a line of input text in no-fill mode
(defun form-no-fill-output-line (line)
  (form-output-left-margin)  ;first output the left margin
  (format *output-stream* "~A" line);then the text
  (form-newline))                    ;then a new line,
                                     ;and page if necessary

;;; Output a line of input text in fill mode.
(defun form-fill-output-line (line)
  (do ((pointer 0)) (nil)
    (multiple-value-bind (word char-pointer)
        (form-get-word pointer line)
      (if (null word) (return))
      ;; see if the word fits on this line,
      ;; and do a new line if it doesn't
      (if (>= (+ *current-column* (length word))
              *text-width*)
          ;; output new line, check for new page
          (form-newline))
      ;; output the margin spacing
      ;; if at beginning of new line
      (if (zerop *current-column*)
          (form-output-left-margin))
      ;; now print the word
      (format *output-stream* "~A" word)
      ;; and the trailing space, if there's room
      (unless (= *text-width*
                 (+ *current-column* (length word)))
        (write-char #\space *output-stream*))
      (setf *current-column*
            (+ *current-column* (length word) 1))
      ;; The next call to form-get-word should start
      ;; after the last word.
      (setf pointer char-pointer))))
(defun form-get-word (pointer line)
  ;; Strip any leading white space.
  (let ((word-beginning
          (position-if-not #'white-space-char?
                           line :start pointer)))
    ;; Now find the end of the word
    ;; i.e., the first char not in it.
    (if word-beginning      ;if we found a word
        (let ((word-end (position-if #'white-space-char?
                         line :start word-beginning)))
          ;; If word-end's nil, it's the end of string.
          (if (not word-end) (setf word-end (length line)))
```

```
                    (values (subseq line word-beginning word-end)
                                    word-end))
            nil)))
;;; Output the left margin spacing.
(defun form-output-left-margin ()
  (dotimes (i *left-margin*)
    (write-char #\space *output-stream*)))

;;; Output a new line and a new page (including any header)
;;; if necessary.
(defun form-newline (&optional (times 1))
  (dotimes (i times)
    (setf *current-column* 0)
    (incf *current-line-number*)
    ;; Have we reached the maximum number of lines for a page?
    ;; If so, begin a new page.
    (if (= *current-line-number* *page-length*)
        (form-newpage)
        ;; otherwise, just output a new-line char
        (format *output-stream* "~%"))))

;;; Output a new page and header, if any.
(defun form-newpage (&optional (times 1))
  (dotimes (i times)
    (format *output-stream* "~|")
    (incf *page-number*)
    (setf *current-line-number* 0)
    (setf *current-column* 0)
    (form-output-header)))

;;; Output the header text, which is a list containing a
;;; format control string (which may contain FORM commands)
;;; and a set of args.  FORMAT will be called on the control
;;; string and args, and the resulting string will be treated
;;; as input text in a recursive invocation of the driver loop.
;;; Before formatting the header text, the values of
;;; *fill-mode?* and *left-margin* are saved and they are restored
;;; after the header text is output.
(defun form-output-header ()
  (let ((header-string (apply #'format nil
                              (mapcar #'eval *header-text-list*)))
        (*fill-mode?* *fill-mode?*)
        (*left-margin* *left-margin*))
    (with-input-from-string (*input-stream* header-string)
      (declare (special *input-stream*))
      (form-driver-loop))))

;;; form-execute-command executes a user command
(defun form-execute-command (current-line)
  (let* ((command-list
           (list-from-string (subseq current-line 1)))
         (command (car command-list))
         (args (cdr command-list)))
    (case command
        ;; It would be better to make this data driven
        ;; but for a small number of commands, CASE will do.
```

```
      (fill (setf *fill-mode?* t))
      (no-fill (form-newline) (setf *fill-mode?* nil))
      (left-margin (setf *left-margin* (car args)))
      (new-page (apply #'form-newpage args))
      (header (setf *header-text-list* args))
      (text-width (setf *text-width* (car args)))
      (page-length (setf *page-length* (car args)))
      (break (apply #'form-newline args))
      (eval (mapc #'eval args))
      (t (format t
            "~&Warning: ~A is not a known FORM command.~%"
            command))))))

;;; some utility functions

(defun white-space-char? (char)
  (or (char-equal char #\space)
    (char-equal char #\tab)))

;;; LIST-FROM-STRING creates a list of the tokens read from a
;;; string and returns it.
(defun list-from-string (string)
  (with-input-from-string (stream string)
    (do ((token (read stream nil 'list-from-string-eof)
                (read stream nil 'list-from-string-eof))
         (list))
        ((eq token 'list-from-string-eof) (nreverse list))
      (push token list))))
```

CHAPTER HIGHLIGHTS

Major Concepts

- Lambda lists can have optional arguments.

  –&OPTIONAL allows you to write functions like READ, that is, functions with a specific set of optional arguments.

  - Arguments after &OPTIONAL must occur in the right order if at all specified by the caller.

  - The writer can specify default values.

  –&REST allows you to write functions like +.

  - The variable whose name appears after &REST is bound to a list of all the arguments left after processing the required and optional arguments.

  –&KEY allows you to write functions with optional arguments that can be specified out of order.

- Keywords start with colons.
- Keywords are self-evaluating.
- Keywords must be followed by values.
- The function writer can specify default values for keyword arguments.
- CATCH and THROW allow you to do dynamic non-local exits.
  - —A CATCH stops a THROW with the same tag.
  - —THROW's second argument is evaluated in the environment of the THROW; it is returned as the value of the CATCH.
- UNWIND-PROTECT makes sure that its cleanup form is executed whenever the protected form is exited, whether normally, because of a THROW, or because of an error.
- ERROR signals a fatal error, that is, one which halts execution of a form or function.
- CERROR signals a continuable error.
- Packages are separate name spaces for symbols.
  - —IN-PACKAGE tells LISP that the symbols in the file that follow should be considered to be in a particular package.
  - —EXPORT is called with a list of symbols as argument; it is used to tell LISP to make the symbols in the argument list externally available.
  - —USE-PACKAGE tells LISP to make the external symbols of a package accessible in another package.
  - —IMPORT is used to import specific symbols from a package.
  - —FIND-PACKAGE accepts a package name as argument and returns the package object itself.
- REQUIRE can be used to load modules that are files grouped together in some convenient way.
  - —PROVIDE tells LISP which modules are loaded.
- Multiple values can be returned using VALUES.
- They can be received using MULTIPLE-VALUE-BIND or MULTIPLE-VALUE-LIST.
- Semicolons are used to begin comments in LISP.
- Documentation strings provide a way of creating self-commenting objects.
  - —DESCRIBE prints the documentation string for an object along with other information.
  - —DOCUMENTATION returns the documentation for a particular documentation type for a symbol.
  - —SETF can be called on a call to DOCUMENTATION to change a documentation string.

Summary of New Syntax

```
(defun name (required &optional (arg default-val)
             &rest arg &key (arg default-val))
   documentation-string
   body)
```

```
(multiple-value-bind (var-name-1 var-name-2 ...)
   (values-form)
   body)
```

```
(multiple-value-list form)
```

```
(values form1 form2 ...)
```

```
(catch tag body)
(throw tag result)
(unwind-protect protected-form cleanup-form)
```

```
(error format-string args-for-format-string)
(cerror continue-format-string format-string args-for-strings)
```

```
(in-package package-name)
(export symbols &optional package)
(import symbols &optional package)
(use-package package-name &optional package)
(find-package package-name)
(require module-name)
(provide module-name)
(shadow symbols &optional package)
```

```
(documentation symbol documentation-type)
```

Suggested Reading

The following sections from Steele, *COMMON LISP*, complement the material in this chapter: chapter 5, Program Structure, 5.2.2; chapter 7, Control Structure, 7.9–7.10; chapter 11, Packages, 11.1–9; chapter 24, Errors, 24.1.

EXERCISES

1. Turn back to the gumball machine example in chapter 8. Change the gumball machines so they can receive refills, and write a procedure for loading refills.

2. Write a general procedure that can return a list of all the attributes of a given kind from a list of bicycles and also update all the attributes of a given kind in a list of bicycles. For example, you might want to find out the x-position of all the bicycles:

```
(defvar *bike-rack*)
```

```
(defun init-bike-rack (number-of-bikes)
   (dotimes (x number-of-bikes)
     (setf *bike-rack*
           (cons (make-bike (random 4) (random 6) (random 7))
                 *bike-rack*))))
```

```
(init-bike-rack 4)
```

```
(do-in-turn 'x-position *bike-rack*)
(0 1 3 1)
(do-in-turn 'set-x-position *bike-rack* 0)
NIL

(do-in-turn 'x-position *bike-rack*)
(0 0 0 0)
```

3. Use CATCH and THROW to change the following procedure so that it checks to see whether each element in the list is a number. If it is not, give the user the option of providing another number and continuing.

```
(defun my-average (list)
  (do ((yet-to-do list (cdr yet-to-do))
       (accumulator 0 (+ accumulator (car yet-to-do)))
       (counter 0 (+ counter 1)))
    ((null yet-to-do) (/ accumulator counter)))))
```

4. The last change to the animal program (exercise 6.d. in chapter 6) made it read in its information tree from a file. Now change this latest version so it takes an optional argument specifying which file is to be used as data.

5. Read FORM's code and make sure you understand it. Try writing and running a sample input file.

    You will notice that a different number of BREAK commands are needed to skip a line in fill and no-fill modes. This is because the formatter simply prints the user's text in no-fill mode; any command (including %break) must come after a line break, but, in fill mode, returns are treated just like spaces. Therefore, %break may come in the middle of a line, causing a genuine dilemma that many real-text formatters handle by having two commands, break and blank (or skip). You might think that this could be resolved by having every command issue a break as %no-fill does; however, it would have unfortunate consequences if all you were trying to do was change the indentation or alter a font.

6. Have FORM-NO-FILL-OUTPUT-LINE call CERROR when it encounters a line that is longer than *TEXT-WIDTH*.

7. Make the formatter skip two spaces after a period. Be careful to do it in such a way that the formatter knows that another space on the line has been taken up.

8. Now extend the last exercise to make the formatter skip two spaces after a word if the last character, excepting any),],', or '', is a ?, !, or .. An example is shown in figure 9-1.

```
"WAS IS DAS?"     ("WHAT IS THAT?")
```

two spaces

Figure 9-1. Skip Two Spaces After a Question Mark

9. Write an autoparagraph mode that starts a new paragraph whenever it sees a null line. Add commands to turn autoparagraphing on and off.

10. Write a command that centers the next line; if necessary, break the line at a word boundary.

11. Make the formatter print out page numbers. You can do that with a formatter command rather than by rewriting the code of the formatter.

Chapter 10

COMPILATION

A compiler is a program that reads source code and produces a sequence of machine instructions that, when executed, have the result the source program "intended." In most languages, the compiler plays a somewhat different role than it does in LISP. If there is a document defining the language specifications, then the compiler is the mechanism by which those specifications are implemented. If there is no document, then the compiler is the definition of the language. LISP, however, has an interpreter that can execute the source code, and the compiled code is expected to produce the same behavior that the interpreted code does.

Compiled LISP code is intended to be loaded into LISP and run from the LISP environment. The compiled and interpreted versions of a function are usually interchangeable.

It is easiest to debug code by running it interpreted first. Once it has been debugged, you can compile it so that it will be faster. Compiled code can be executed much faster than interpreted code if the source code is written in such a fashion that the compiler can easily produce machine instructions to duplicate its actions. Declarations provide a way of giving the compiler more information, allowing it to generate code that runs faster.

10.1   SIMPLE COMPILATION

You can compile a function quite easily with the function COMPILE:

```
(defun sq (x)
  (* x x))
(compile 'sq)
```

This procedure calls the compiler on the source code for the function, and the symbol's function cell is changed to point to the compiled code produced. This definition exists only during the current LISP session.

An entire file of source code can be compiled with COMPILE-FILE:

```
(compile-file input-pathname :output-file output-name)
```

If no output file is specified, then the code produced by the compiler is output to a file with the first name of the source code file and an implementation-dependent second name. For example, if you are working in VAX LISP, and the name of your file of source code is FOO.LSP, the code produced by the compiler is output to a file called FOO.FAS. If the :OUTPUT-FILE keyword is specified, its argument must be either a string, a symbol, or a stream, which is the name of the file that the code will be output to.

After the file has been compiled, you must load it to use the compiled code. The LOAD function can be used to load a file of compiled code the same way that it can be used to load interpreted code. Loading compiled code is usually faster than loading interpreted code.

10.2   DECLARATIONS

A declaration is a statement to the LISP system *about* a program or some part of a program. A declaration is not usually *part* of the program. It is not evaluated, it performs no action, and it returns no value. Declarations can occur only in certain places in LISP programs, commonly before a body of code in a special form that binds variables. DEFUN, LET, DO, and DEFMACRO are all examples of such forms. There are others as well.[1]

Most declarations exist to provide advice to the compiler. The advice is often information the compiler might need to produce more efficient code. One exception is the one kind of declaration already introduced in this book: special declarations. Special declarations differ from other declarations in two respects: they are essential rather than optional, and they are important to the interpreter as well as to the compiler.

10.3   MAKING DECLARATIONS

There are four major types of declarations: special declarations, type declarations, in-line declarations, and optimization declarations.

Of these, only special declarations alter the meaning of code. Special declarations tell LISP that a variable is to be scoped dynamically instead of lexically. This affects both interpreted and compiled code and causes the interpreter to pay attention to special declarations.

In compiled code, a variable that is local to a function cannot be referred to anywhere outside of that function; therefore, whenever possible, the compiler produces code that

---

[1] See Steele, page 154, for a complete list.

models local variables with machine registers, making access to the value of a local variable very fast. A special declaration tells the compiler that it cannot do this; the value of a special variable can be found only by looking in the value cell of the atom which is that variable.

Type declarations are used to tell the compiler that it can produce code that depends on those types, without having to check for others. For example, the function + adds two numbers, no matter what their types. These numbers might be floating-point numbers, integers, or even complex numbers. + can add these different kinds of numbers only by first determining their types. If you use + inside a function, and know that this function will call only + with integer arguments, you might want to avoid the overhead of checking the types of its arguments. A type declaration can be used to tell the compiler what the types of variables are so it can eliminate type checks when the arguments to a function like + are variables. You can use type declarations to declare the types of variables, including formal parameters to functions, and the types of values returned by functions.

You may also use a declaration to ask the compiler to produce in-line code for a function. When the compiler works on a function, it produces a machine-language subroutine that can be called with a call-subroutine instruction. Normally, when the compiler encounters a function call, it produces code that, when executed:

- puts the arguments to the call somewhere;
- saves any current state it has to;
- executes an instruction that dispatches to the function's code;
- runs the function's code;
- executes an instruction that returns from the function's code;
- restores any state that might have been saved.

If you were executing a compiled function whose source code looked like:

```
(defun get-member (x y)
  (cond ((endp y) y)
        ((eq (car y) x) y)
        (t (get-member x (cdr y)))))
```

you might want to avoid some of the overhead involved in calling functions as simple as ENDP, EQ, CAR, and CDR. Were the compiler to code these calls in-line, it would put code that would do the same things as calling the subroutines right into the subroutine for GET-MEMBER. This would speed up GET-MEMBER a good deal.

In many systems, in-line coding is useful only for calls to simple system-provided functions like CAR, CDR, or +. In larger functions, the overhead of function calling is insignificant compared to the time spent in execution of the function. Such large functions are rarely called as often as functions like CAR and CDR.[2]

There are disadvantages to producing in-line code. If a function call is coded in-line, then compiled calls to the function cannot be detected by TRACE, which can make the code difficult to debug. Just as you can ask the compiler to try to produce in-line code for functions, you can also ask it *not* to produce in-line code for functions. This feature is useful because some implementations code functions like CAR and CDR in-line by default. The compiler may ignore INLINE requests if it does not know how to handle them, but must always listen to a NOTINLINE declaration.

The last major category of declarations is optimization declarations, which are used to instruct the compiler on which qualities to emphasize during compilation. For example, if you are confident that your code works, you may instruct the compiler to sacrifice safety (amount of checking done) for speed whenever possible. If you are concerned about the space that the compiled code takes up in the LISP workspace, you can ask the compiler to make the code as small as possible. Other tradeoffs can be made as well.

Optimizing declarations require emphasis of an important point. Not all compilers can use all of the information you give them with declarations. All COMMON LISP compilers must recognize SPECIAL declarations and NOTINLINE declarations. Beyond that, it is up to the particular implementation.

Even if your compiler does not do much with declarations, it is a good idea to include as much information as you can. Code written in COMMON LISP is meant to be transportable, and new versions of a compiler may include features that earlier releases did not. In addition, declarations provide valuable documentation for the maintainer of the code.

10.4   DECLARATION SYNTAX

Declarations are made either with the DECLARE form or with PROCLAIM:

```
(declare declaration-form...)
(proclaim declaration-form)
```

Any number of declaration forms can be specified in a single DECLARE; however, PROCLAIM allows only one declaration form.

DECLARE and PROCLAIM differ in several respects, one being that DECLARE is a special

---

[2] In other COMMON LISP systems, INLINE declarations are viewed differently. They have a great effect on the compiler and are used widely to produce SUBSTs—that is, objects which behave like functions in interpreted code but like macros in compiled code. There is no other way of simulating DEFSUBST, the facility that creates SUBSTs in older versions of LISP, in COMMON LISP.

form and does not evaluate its arguments. PROCLAIM, on the other hand, is a function, so its arguments must be quoted.

Another difference is that DECLARE is used inside another form. You can specify declarations locally, in DEFUN, DO, LET, and MULTIPLE-VALUE-BIND by placing a DECLARE just before the body. The declarations made in the DECLARE remain in effect for all code in the body of the form but are not in effect outside the body.

PROCLAIM, on the other hand, is used at top level and therefore affects behavior pervasively throughout a session with LISP. Therefore, you can have DEFCONSTANTs and DEFVARs in one file and code that uses them in another.

10.4.1   Declaring a Variable Special

As demonstrated in chapter 4, LISP gives the user fine control over variable access.

```
(defun add-1-to-n (n)
   (declare (special n))
   (add1))
(defun add1 ()
   (declare (special n))
   (1+ n))
```

In particular, the special declarations state that N is dynamically scoped, and therefore ADD1 can legally refer to it, even though N is not one of its formal parameters. You need two special declarations: one to tell COMMON LISP that N should be set up as a special variable during the execution of ADD-1-TO-N, and another to state that the references to N in ADD1 are special. You can think of this more simply as being a result of the scope of declarations: a declare form is usually in effect only in the body of the form in which it occurs.

This turns out to be particularly useful in dealing with I/O streams. In chapter 9, we relied on dynamic scoping to implement FORM-OUTPUT-HEADER. To process the header text, a stream to the header text was temporarily allowed to shadow the stream to the file that was being processed. Since this shadowing was dynamic, we were able to call FORM-DRIVER-LOOP and have it print the header text, employing all the facilities available in the rest of the formatter. When FORM-OUTPUT-HEADER was exited, the former value of *INPUT-STREAM* took over once more.

10.4.2   Type Declarations

A *type* declaration form, to let the compiler know the kinds of variables used in functions, looks like:

```
(type <type> var1 var2 ....)
```

where $<$type$>$ is any type defined in this version of COMMON LISP. (See Steele, chapter 4, *Type Specifiers*, for a list of predefined types.) Here is an example of such a declaration:

```
(defun square (x)
  (declare (type fixnum x))
  (* x x))
```

The declaration promises that, inside SQUARE, the variable X refers only to objects of type *fixnum* (that is, small integers), and that the compiler is free to produce code for SQUARE that relies on this fact.

If you were sure that the result of the multiplication would also be a fixnum, to really speed up the process, you might want to add a declaration for the result type of the multiplication operation. The construct THE lets you make type declarations about results of an unnamed form:

```
(defun square (x)
  (declare (type fixnum x))
  (the fixnum (* x x)))
```

If the compiler were to produce in-line code for *, it might find these declarations especially useful, as then it could simply use the hardware multiplication instruction for small integers, rather than checking for the kinds of numbers provided as arguments. Thus a type declaration to a sophisticated compiler can sometimes speed things up considerably.

If the type you are declaring is one of LISP's predefined types, like FIXNUM, you can specify the declaration in an abbreviated form without saying ''type'':

```
(defun square (x)
  (declare (fixnum x))
  (* x x))
```

You can also declare the types of arguments you expect a function to be called on, and the type of value you expect it to return, with a *function* declaration form, which looks like

```
(function <function> (<arg-type1> <arg-type2>...) <result-type>)
```

where $<$function$>$ is the name of the function you're providing the compiler with information about, the $<$arg-typeN$>$s are the types of the arguments you expect to call it with, and $<$result-type$>$ is the type of the value that $<$function$>$ returns. If you do not want to specify any of these, you can provide a type specification of T.

If you want to specify which kinds of objects you expect the function NTH to be called on, and which kinds of values you expect it to produce, you could type something like:

```
(declare (function nth (integer list) t))
```

This declaration tells the compiler that the function NTH is called with two arguments, the first of which is an integer, and the second of which is a list. NTH is declared to return a value that may be of any type whatsoever, which makes sense because a list may contain any LISP object. This declaration tells the compiler that it may produce code for NTH that depends on these type declarations.

The declaration appears either in the function that called NTH or as a proclamation at top level.

Obviously, you must be quite sure that these declarations are correct. Overspecification may lead to bewildering errors if the compiler omits type checks and the code produced is given the wrong type of object as argument.

10.4.3   In-line Declarations

In-line declarations are syntactically as simple as special declarations. Like a function-type declaration, an in-line declaration may be made at top level, or locally. A function declared in-line at top level may also be declared not in-line locally if desired.

```
(defun get-member (x y)
  (declare (inline endp eq car cdr))
  (cond ((endp y) y)
        ((eq (car y) x) y)
        (t (get-member x (cdr y)))))
```

10.4.4   Optimization Declarations

Optimizing declarations have the syntax:

```
(optimize (quality1 value1) (quality2 value2) ...)
```

The qualities are implementation-dependent, but probably include size, speed, and safety. The values usually range between 0 and 3 (inclusive), where 0 means that the quality is not at all important and 3 means that it is essential. The usual value is 1. Therefore, to make very fast code with a minimal amount of type checking, you might put the proclamation (optimize (speed 3) (safety 0)) at the beginning of your file.

A potential source of problems is that bugs may arise when you reduce the amount of checking. Compiled code should do what interpreted code did; however, if the interpreted code isn't actually doing precisely what you thought it was, problems may arise upon compilation.

10.5   DISASSEMBLE

You may occasionally want to look at the output of the compiler, possibly to see how efficient its code is. COMMON LISP provides the function DISASSEMBLE to allow you to do so.

For example, if you define FACT as follows:

```
(defun fact (n) (cond ((zerop n) 1) (t (* n (fact (1- n)))))))
FACT
```

and compile it, you can disassemble it:

```
(disassemble 'fact)
  0:  WORD 1024                      ;Save register(s) FLP
  2:  MOVAL 1^_416,FLP
  9:  PUSHL b^CL$QC_CCFRAME(SLP)
 12:  CMPL SP,b^CL$STACK_ALARM(SLP)
 16:  BLEQ +22
 18:  BLBC b^CL$TM_POLLP(SLP),+25
 22:  MINICALL CL$MS_INTERRUPT
 25:  CMPB s^#4,(AP)
 28:  BEQLU +33
 30:  MINICALL CL$MS_WNA_ERR
 33:  MOVL b^16(AP),AR1
 37:  MINICALL CL$MS_ZEROP
 41:  BEQLU +46
 43:  BRW +50
 46:  MOVL s^#4,AR1
 49:  RET
 50:  PUSHL b^16(AP)
 53:  MOVL b^16(AP),AR1
 57:  MINICALL CL$MS_SUB1
 61:  PUSHL AR1
 63:  ADDL3 SLP,b^_4(FLP),R0   ;#'FACT
 68:  PUSHL @b^0(R0)
 71:  PUSHL b^_4(FLP)          ;#'FACT
 74:  PUSHL s^#6
 76:  CALLS s^#4,@b^8(SP)
 80:  MINICALL CL$MS_TIMES2
 84:  RET
NIL
```

This example is from VAX LISP. Obviously, the output of the disassembler is highly implementation-dependent. However, a good disassembler produces relatively readable code, even including comments.

CHAPTER HIGHLIGHTS

Major Concepts

- Compilation in LISP is integrated into the LISP environment.

- Compiled and interpreted code can be mixed freely.

- Compiled code, except in a few cases, should produce the same effect as source code.

- DECLARE is good for making local declarations.

- PROCLAIM is good for making global declarations.
- Special declarations instruct the interpreter and compiler to scope variables dynamically.
- Other kinds of declarations give the compiler information about assumptions it can make in compiling the code. These assumptions usually result in faster code.
- Type declarations tell the compiler which data type input or output to a function will have.
- THE can be used to declare the type of an unnamed form.
- INLINE declaration asks the compiler to code the function without a special subroutine call.
- INLINE declarations can make code hard to debug.
- NOTINLINE forces the compiler to make a special subroutine call.
- OPTIMIZE declarations ask the compiler to adjust the tradeoffs it makes during compilation.
- DISASSEMBLE lets you see the output of the compiler.

Summary of New Syntax

```
(compile function-name)
(compile-file input-pathname :output-file output-name)

(declare declaration-form ...)
(proclaim declaration-form ...)
(special var1 var2 ...)
(type type var1 var2 ...)
(function function-name (arg1 arg2 ...)
    return-value1 return-value2 ...)
(the type form)
(inline function1 function2 ...)
(notinline function1 function2 ...)
(optimize (quality number) ...)

(disassemble function-name)
```

Suggested Reading

The following sections from Steele, *COMMON LISP*, document the features outlined in this chapter: chapter 9, Declarations, 9.1–9.2; chapter 25, Miscellaneous Features, 25.1.

EXERCISES

1. Choose a program from one of the earlier chapters in the course. Go through it and add declarations. Compile the program and run it.

2. Add declarations to the following procedure:

```
(defun fib (n)
  (if (< n 2) n
      (+ (fib (1- n)) (fib (- n 2)))))
```

Compile it, once optimizing for speed and once for safety. Run the two procedures. You can use the special form TIME to find out how long different invocations take to run.

3. Disassemble both the version of FIB compiled for speed and the version compiled for safety. Compare the source code.

Chapter 11

MACROS

Macros, like functions, are forms which allow you to group actions together and give them a name. However, instead of simply being evaluated by the interpreter or compiled by the compiler, macros are first *expanded* and then the result of the expansion is evaluated or compiled. Since LISP treats macros in a more complex way than it does functions, macros can be somewhat tricky to use. Additionally, compiled code that contains a lot of macros can be hard to debug. On the other hand, macros allow you to create constructs that do not evaluate their arguments, and which are faster in compiled code than functions.

11.1   THE NEED FOR MACROS

You may have noticed that there are functions in COMMON LISP whose behavior you cannot reproduce. For example, if you try to write your own version of IF, it might look like this:

```
(defun my-if (predicate then-clause &optional else-clause)
   (cond (predicate then-clause)
         (t else-clause)))
```

Outwardly, it appears to be a perfectly reasonable implementation. If the predicate evaluates to T, the value of THEN-CLAUSE is returned. Otherwise, the value of ELSE-CLAUSE is returned. If the ELSE-CLAUSE was not provided, ELSE-CLAUSE will have been bound to NIL, so MY-IF returns NIL.

In fact, if you call MY-IF like this

```
(my-if t 3 4)
```

3 is returned, whereas if you do

```
(my-if nil 3 4)
```

219

4 is returned. But what happens if you call MY-IF like this?

```
(my-if t (format t "~%True.~%") (format t "~%False.~%"))
```

First "True" is printed, then "False" is printed, and finally NIL is returned. Was this the behavior you wanted? Certainly IF does not do this. What happened was that the printing of "True" and "False" took place before MY-IF ever got called. MY-IF never had a chance to do what IF does; it was given only the values that the calls to FORMAT returned; both, as it happened, were NIL, so MY-IF returned NIL.

This happens because of the evaluator's behavior when it encounters a function: first it evaluates the function's arguments, then it binds those values to the variables in the function's formal parameter list, and only then does it execute the body of the function.

How, then, is a form like IF implemented? It could be a special form or it could be a macro. Special forms are recognized as such by the compiler and the interpreter, and evaluated specially. The compiler produces the appropriate conditional code; the interpreter executes the subforms appropriately. You cannot write your own special forms; they are interesting here only because IF could be implemented as a special form in your version of LISP.

However, IF could also be implemented as a macro displaying the same behavior. Unlike a function, a macro is a thing that is first expanded and then evaluated. During expansion LISP takes the macro and its arguments and produces another piece of LISP code, which it then treats exactly as if it had been there instead of the macro-invoking form.

In interpreted code, the effect is mostly syntactic; depending on how the macro definition is written, invoking a macro may look exactly like invoking a function, or you may not have to quote all the arguments, or there may be a template into which arguments should be typed.

In compiled code, the expansion is done at compile time, leaving the expanded code where the macro was, so that the compiler produces code as if there had been no macro invocation, and the result of the expansion had been where the macro-invoking form was in the source code. In compiled code, calling a group of statements that is defined as a macro is faster than calling a group of statements that is defined as a function, because the function-calling instructions are never generated by the compiler or executed. However, the code produced is bulkier and far harder to debug.

There are three drawbacks to using macros: (1) Macro calls in compiled code cannot be detected by TRACE. (2) Unlike redefining a function, when you redefine a macro, you must recompile every function whose source contains a call to the macro. Failure to do so can lead you to believe that a new definition works, when in fact it is faulty. Then, when you do recompile, your program suddenly ceases to work for mysterious reasons. (3) Macros are not functions; they cannot be used with FUNCALL, APPLY, or any of the mapping functions. This may remind you of in-line coding (see chapter 10). There is a similarity, and many of the tradeoffs are the same.

To gain further understanding, look at the LISP macro WHEN. If the first argument to WHEN is true, it evaluates the succeeding arguments and returns the value of the last one. If the first argument to WHEN is NIL, none of the other arguments are evaluated.

```
(when t 2 3 4)
4
(when nil 2 3 4)
nil
```

You can see what a macro expands into, without evaluating the resulting form, by using the function MACROEXPAND. MACROEXPAND accepts one argument, a form to expand. MACROEXPAND is a function, so its argument must be quoted here:

```
(macroexpand '(when (oddp x) (print x) 3))
```

The result of the call to MACROEXPAND is probably much like:

```
(cond ((oddp x) (print x) 3))¹
```

The execution of this code will, by definition, produce exactly what you want WHEN to produce. Suppose you had used WHEN in a procedure.

```
(defun print-and-square-if-odd (number)
  (when (oddp number) (print number) (* number number)))
```

This expands into

```
(defun print-and-square-if-odd (number)
  (cond ((oddp number) (print number) (* number number))))
```

and, when PRINT-AND-SQUARE-IF-ODD is executed, this is what is evaluated.

The process of macro expansion is recursive—if a macro expands into a macro, that thing is expanded, until the expansion produces something that is not a macro call. If you want to see only the result of the first expansion, you can use the function MACROEXPAND-1.

11.2   DEFINING MACROS

Macros are most easily defined using the DEFMACRO macro, which is similar in form to DEFUN and DEFSTRUCT. Its arguments include a name, a lambda list, and a body:

```
(defmacro sq (x)
  (list '* x x))
```

---

¹ It may not look exactly like the example because COND itself might be a macro in your implementation of LISP.

The name of this macro is SQ. Its lambda list has one member, X. Its body contains one form, (list '* x x). An invocation of SQ might look like:

```
(sq (+ 3 4))
```

The following occurs during the expansion of this macro call:

- An environment is created in which X is bound to the argument to SQ, which is the list (+ 3 4). This differs from the binding of arguments in a function call in that the argument form is not evaluated, but is itself the argument.
- The body of the macro SQ (that is, (list '* x x)) is evaluated in this environment. The result of that evaluation is the result of the macro expansion. For this example, the result is (* (+ 3 4) (+ 3 4)).
- The environment in which the body of the macro was evaluated is then discarded. It is not used in the evaluation of the result of the macro expansion. It was only the environment in which the code to be executed was produced.

After expansion, normal LISP evaluation or compilation of the result of the expansion can take place. (If the result of the expansion is itself a macro call, that call is expanded in turn.)

In interpreted code, the expansion takes place when the macro-invoking form is encountered by the evaluator in the course of evaluating an expression. In compiled code, it happens in the compiler. As a result, macros are amoung the few places where compiled code may behave differently than interpreted code. In both cases, the code that is executed or compiled is the *result* of the expansion.

Consideration of a common bug in the definition and use of macros can help you to focus better on the process. The bug occurs when a macro expands into a form that, when evaluated, evaluates one of the arguments to the macro more than once. For example, if you define SQ as above and then call SQ with a call to PRINT as an argument,

```
(sq (print 3))
```

3 is printed twice, rather than once. Why? Try MACROEXPANDing the call to SQ; you will see that two calls to PRINT actually show up in the expansion.

Here is one way you might solve this problem.

```
(defmacro sq (x)
  (list 'let (list (list 'x-val x))
        '(* x-val x-val)))
```

When SQ is called with (+ 3 4) as its argument, it produces an expression that looks like this

```
(let ((x-val (+ 3 4)))
   (* x-val x-val))
```

and is what you wanted.

The lambda list used to specify the arguments to the macro can contain all the keywords that lambda lists for functions can, and more. For example, &BODY is like &REST, except that it may give LISP information about how to format the macro nicely.

Armed with this new knowledge of macros, you can again try to define MY-IF, this time as a macro.

```
(defmacro my-if (predicate then-clause &optional else-clause)
   (list 'cond (list predicate then-clause)
         (list 't else-clause)))
```

This definition solves the problem and behaves appropriately in every case. However, it is not easy to tell what it will expand into by looking at the code. Before exploring what can be done with macros, some syntax that makes macro definition more convenient must be introduced.

11.3   BACKQUOTE-COMMA SYNTAX

Backquote-comma syntax allows you to treat writing macros as creating a template for the thing that the macro will expand into. Thus, the macro,

```
(defmacro my-if (predicate then-clause &optional else-clause)
   (list 'cond (list predicate then-clause)
         (list 't else-clause)))
```

which, when called as follows,

```
(my-if (< 10 3) (print 4) (print 5))
```

expands into

```
(cond ((< 10 3) (print 4))
      (t (print 5)))
```

can also be written:

```
(defmacro my-if (predicate then-clause &optional else-clause)
   `(cond (,predicate ,then-clause)
      (t ,else-clause)))
```

This definition of MY-IF expands into the same form as the previous one; however, it is easier to see the form it takes by looking at the macro definition.

The backquote is an instruction to LISP to quote everything in the list except items beginning with a comma.[2] Backquote (`` ` ``) is similar to quote (`'`), except that it looks for commas and treats items beginning with a comma differently from other items. A useful rule of thumb for remembering which is quote and which is backquote on your keyboard is that usually quote is more conveniently located. Items beginning with a comma are evaluated. Items that must have commas in front of them in the second definition of MY-IF are those not quoted in the first.

Although it is not necessary, macros are almost always written with backquote-comma syntax because it is so convenient. Backquote-comma syntax can also be used outside of macros to make better-looking code. For example,

```
`(apple ,pear)
```

is equivalent to (`list 'apple pear`).

11.3.1   Comma-Atsign and Comma-Dot

Two other useful parts of backquote-comma syntax are ,@ and ,. (comma-atsign and comma-dot) notation. Both are used to "splice" lists into macros.

Suppose you wanted to write a macro to add numbers. In chapter 9, a procedure was written that did this.

```
(defun my-add (&rest list-of-arguments)
  (do ((running-sum 0 (+ (car left-to-add) running-sum))
       (left-to-add list-of-arguments (cdr left-to-add)))
      ((null left-to-add) running-sum)))
```

However, you could reduce the complexity of this program by using a macro and splicing the list of arguments into the call to +:

```
(defmacro my-add (&rest list-of-arguments)
  `(+ ,@list-of-arguments))
```

,@ tells LISP to insert the elements of a list into the enclosing list. ,. does this as well, but makes the further statement that the list to be inserted can be destructively modified. Therefore, to produce more efficient code, you might use ,. in the example above:

```
(defmacro my-add (&rest list-of-arguments)
  `(+ ,.list-of-arguments))
```

11.4   MACRO-DEFINING MACROS

Macros commonly expand into simple procedures that do only one thing. However, from time to time you may want to make significantly more complex macros. One task that you might like to perform is writing macros that define other macros.

---

[2] Like quote, backquote is a kind of reader macro. Reader macro characters are expanded by the reader, not by the compiler or the evaluator.

Macro-defining macros bring up the topic of nested backquotes. When you have a backquote nested inside another one, and a comma occurs inside the nested backquote, when is the item after the comma evaluated?

For example, suppose you want to write a macro-defining macro that, when called with a symbol as argument, defines a macro whose name is that symbol, and which expands into a call to PRINT, which prints the symbol. That is, if you name the macro-defining macro MAKE-MACRO-NAMED and type:

```
(make-macro-named fish)
```

the macro

```
(defmacro fish () `(print 'fish))
```

would be defined.

You can define MAKE-MACRO-NAMED as follows:

```
(defmacro make-macro-named (name)
  `(defmacro ,name ()
     `(print ',name)))
```

This macro is not particularly different from other macros; it simply happens to expand into a macro definition.

However, suppose you want to provide an argument to the macro defined by MAKE-MACRO-NAMED; say that you want the defined macro to print the list of its name and this argument. Then the body of the defined macro could no longer be constant; it would have to start with a backquote instead of a quote. You would want the macro created by (make-macro-named fish) to look like:

```
(defmacro fish (arg)
  `(print '(fish ,arg)))
```

The body must begin with a backquote because the argument has to start with a comma, that is, the argument must be substituted in.

You could try modifying MAKE-MACRO-NAMED to do this, as follows:

```
(defmacro make-macro-named (name)
  `(defmacro ,name (arg)
     `(print '(,name ,arg))))
```

However, if you call (make-macro-named fish) now, the macro defined will look like:

```
(defmacro fish (arg)
  `(print '(,name ,arg)))
```

and an attempt to invoke FISH will result in an error, because NAME will not be bound when FISH is expanded.

But ARG could be printed without problems; a single comma inside two backquotes means "evaluate this once, when the form quoted by the innermost backquote is expanded," that is, the comma matches the inner backquote.

You also want NAME to be evaluated once, but in the context of the outer backquote. You could try redefining MAKE-MACRO-NAMED as follows,

```
(defmacro make-macro-named (name)
  `(defmacro ,name (arg)
     `(print '(,,name ,arg))))
```

thinking that the second comma before NAME will match the outermost backquote. In fact, it does, but the result is not what you want. Now (make-macro-named fish) expands into

```
(defmacro fish (arg)
  `(print '(,fish ,arg)))
```

That is, the second comma matched the outer backquote, and NAME was evaluated in the outer context, but that did not make the first comma go away, so an attempt to expand (fish 3) still results in an error, because the variable FISH is not bound when the macro FISH is expanded.

It seems then that two commas inside two backquotes mean "evaluate what follows once when the thing that starts with the outer backquote is expanded, and then evaluate the result of that when the thing that starts with the inner backquote is expanded." Once again, the left comma matches the inner backquote.

What you really want is for the name to be evaluated only once, in the outermost context. You can get this effect with a sort of trick, by quoting the result of an evaluation in the outermost context so that its reevaluation in the inner context produces the thing itself. That is, FISH can look like

```
(defmacro fish (arg)
  `(print '(,'fish ,arg)))
```

Then the expansion of (fish 3) would be (print '(fish 3)), because the comma before 'FISH causes 'FISH to be evaluated and the value of 'FISH is FISH.

You can incorporate this into MAKE-MACRO-NAMED as follows:

```
(defmacro make-macro-named (name)
  `(defmacro ,name (arg)
     `(print '(,',name ,arg))))
```

When you expand (make-macro-named fish), the ,',NAME turns into the ,'FISH in the above definition of FISH.

You now have three combinations that allow you to control the order in which things inside two nested backquotes are evaluated. A single comma matches the inner backquote; it means evaluate the thing following once, when the form starting with the inner backquote is expanded. Two commas match both backquotes; they mean evaluate the following thing once, when the form starting with the outer backquote is expanded, and then evaluate the result when the form starting with the inner backquote is expanded. A comma, a quote, and another comma mean evaluate the thing following once, when the form starting with the outer backquote is expanded.

11.4.1 **DEFSTRUCT**

In COMMON LISP, DEFSTRUCT produces functions, not macros; however, we can implement a simplified version of DEFSTRUCT which creates macros instead of functions. In addition, MYDEFSTRUCT doesn't accept any options in the NAME part and accepts only limited options in the slot descriptions. However, invoking MYDEFSTRUCT with a call such as (mydefstruct fish (dorsal-fin-length 4) habitat) produces a constructor, (MAKE-FISH), two selectors, (FISH-DORSAL-FIN-LENGTH and FISH-HABITAT), a definition for the type FISH, and a predicate, (FISH-P), which returns T if its argument is a fish.

```
(defmacro make-name (&rest args)
  `(intern (format nil "~{~A~}" (list ,@args))))
(defun get-slot-name (item)
  (cond ((atom item) item)
        ((listp item) (car item))
        (t (error "Bad format for slot ~S." item))))
(defmacro mydefstruct (name &body body)
  `(progn
     (defmacro ,(make-name "MAKE-" name)
       (&key ,@body)
       `(make-array ,',(1+ (length body))
          :initial-contents
          ',(list ',name ,@(mapcar #'get-slot-name body))))
     (defun ,(make-name "VECTOR-HAS-NAME-" name) (vector)
       (eq (svref vector 0) ',name))
     (deftype ,name ()
       `(and (simple-vector ,',(1+ (length body)))
             (satisfies
               ,',(make-name "VECTOR-HAS-NAME-" name))))
     (defmacro ,(make-name name "-P") (object)
       `(typep ,object ',',name))
     ,.(mapcar
         #'(lambda (x counter)
             `(defmacro
                ,(make-name name "-" (get-slot-name x))
                (structure)
                `(svref ,structure ,',counter)))
           body
           (do ((counter (length body) (- counter 1))
                (list () (cons counter list)))
               ((zerop counter) list)))
     ',name))
```

Two new constructs are introduced in this example, but before they are discussed, note that the call (mydefstruct fish (dorsal-fin-length 4) habitat) expands into

```
(progn
  (defmacro make-fish (&key (dorsal-fin-length 4) habitat)
    `(make-array ,'3 :initial-contents
       ',(list 'fish dorsal-fin-length habitat)))
  (defun vector-has-name-fish (vector)
    (eq (svref vector 0) 'fish))
  (deftype fish ()
    `(and (simple-vector 3)
          (satisfies vector-has-name-fish)))
  (defmacro fish-p (object)
    `(typep ,object ','fish))
  (defmacro fish-dorsal-fin-length (structure)
    `(svref ,structure ,'1))
  (defmacro fish-habitat (structure)
   `(svref ,structure ,'2))
  'fish)
```

Placing these forms inside a PROGN at top level is equivalent to typing the four DEFMACROs, the DEFUN, and the DEFTYPE directly at top level. You need the PROGN as an envelope because a macro can expand into only one form.

Two unfamiliar items are the function INTERN, used in MAKE-NAME, and the use of DEFTYPE, to define a new type. Normally, you create symbols merely by using them; however, INTERN allows you to create a symbol, give the name as a string, and put it in a package under program control.

DEFTYPE allows you to create new types for LISP, recognizable by the function TYPEP. In using DEFTYPE, you employ the type-specifying language described in chapter 4 of Steele's book. The phrase above means that the object is of type FISH if it is a simple vector with length 3, and if its 0th element is the symbol FISH.

11.5   **DESTRUCTURING**

Macros allow you to create constructs that do not evaluate their arguments. Because of this, it is particularly easy to require that the arguments to macros be presented in a special pattern such as that of DEFUN, LET, COND, or WITH-OPEN-FILE.

Creating special patterns can be done in the ordinary way, by giving each input a name and decomposing it later.

```
(defmacro my-with-open-file (list &rest body)
  (let ((stream-name (car list))
        (file-name (cadr list)))
    `(let ((,stream-name nil))
       (unwind-protect
           (progn (setf ,stream-name (open ,file-name))
                  ,@body)
         (if ,stream-name (close ,stream-name))))))
```

However, LISP also provides an easier way to make such patterns. Called *destructuring*, it is one of the properties of the lambda list of a macro. The destructuring facility automatically does pattern matching between the lambda list of the macro and the arguments in the calling form. It also allows you to treat each sublist of the lambda list as a lambda list in its own right. For example, MY-WITH-OPEN-FILE can be rewritten as follows:

```
(defmacro my-with-open-file ((stream-name file-name) . body)
  `(let ((,stream-name nil))
     (unwind-protect
         (progn (setf ,stream-name (open ,file-name))
                ,@body)
         (if ,stream-name (close ,stream-name)))))
```

You use destructuring to state that you expect arguments to MY-WITH-OPEN-FILE to consist of an initial list, which is the name clause, and some other forms, which constitute the body. The name clause is made up of the stream-name and the file-name. The body is a list of everything after the name clause. The dot between the name clause and the body should remind you of dotted pairs. The body is whatever is consed together with the name clause in the invocation of the macro.

```
(my-with-open-file (my-stream "example.txt")
    (dolist (x 3)
      (print (read my-stream))))
```

In this call to MY-WITH-OPEN-FILE, the name clause is (my-stream "example.txt") and the body is (dolist (x 3) (print (read my-stream))). During the expansion of this call to MY-WITH-OPEN-FILE, STREAM-NAME will be bound to MY-STREAM. FILE-NAME will be bound to "example.txt", and BODY will be bound to ((dolist (x 3) (print (read my-stream)))).

You can improve on this to include the options that WITH-OPEN-FILE usually includes:

```
(defmacro my-with-open-file
  ((stream-name file-name . options) . body)
  `(let ((,stream-name nil))
     (unwind-protect
         (progn
           (setf ,stream-name (open ,file-name ,.options))
           ,.body)
         (if ,stream-name (close ,stream-name)))))
```

CHAPTER HIGHLIGHTS

Major Concepts

• Macro calls are first expanded, and then the result of the expansion is either evaluated or compiled.

Expansion may be iterated.

- Three drawbacks of using macros are:

  1. Macros cannot be detected by TRACE or the stepper in compiled code.

  2. Macros cannot be used in FUNCALL, APPLY, or any mapping functions.

  3. Whenever you redefine a macro, you must recompile every function whose source contains a call to the macro for the redefinition to have an effect on them.

- Two advantages of macros are:

  1. Arguments to macros are not evaluated; thus new syntactic constructs can be defined with macros.

  2. Macros produce faster code than functions because they avoid the overhead of function calls.

- MACROEXPAND lets you look at the expansion of a macro call.

- MACROEXPAND-1 lets you look at one level of expansion of a macro call.

- Backquote-comma syntax lets you define macros more conveniently.

  –Backquote means, "quote this object, except evaluate items inside it with commas before them."

  –Backquote-comma syntax lets you think of macro definitions as templates, in which values can be substituted at expansion time to produce the code that will run.

  –,@ means, "The next item evaluates to a list; get that list and splice it into the current list."

  –Inside nested backquotes, the leftmost comma causes the item after it to escape from the innermost backquoted context.

  –Nested backquotes are useful for writing macro-defining macros.

  –A single comma matches the inner backquote. The form following it will be evaluated once, when the form starting with the inner backquote is expanded.

  –Two commas match two backquotes. Therefore, the following item is evaluated when the form starting with the outer backquote is expanded, and then evaluates the result when the form starting with the inner backquote is expanded.

  –Comma-quote-comma means "evaluate the following item once, when the form starting with the outer backquote is expanded."

- INTERN allows you to create new symbols under program control.

- DEFTYPE allows you to define new types.

- Lambda lists of macros defined by using DEFMACRO can be destructured.

  –The lambda list can be set up to do pattern matching with the macro call.

  –Each sublist is treated as a lambda list on its own.

Summary of New Syntax

```
(defmacro name lambda-list form1 form2 ...)
(macroexpand form)
(macroexpand-1 form)
(intern string)
(deftype name arg-list body)
```

Suggested Reading

The following sections from Steele, COMMON LISP, complement the material covered in this chapter: chapter 5, Program Structure, 5.1.4.; chapter 8, Macros, 8.1–8.2; chapter 22, Input/Output, 22.1.3.

EXERCISES

1. Implement a version of the macro PUSH. It should take an item and a place and add an item to the front of a list kept in the place.

2. Implement a version of POP. MY-POP should take a place, remove the first item from the list found in the place, and return the former first item as a value.

3. Implement a simplified version of LET that expands into a LAMBDA expression. Your LET does not have to accept singleton variables, but only variable value pairs.

4. Implement a macro that takes a name and a symbol designating an arithmetic operator and defines a macro that takes numbers as arguments and performs the operation on them. This macro can be used to implement MY-ADD. Thus,

```
(make-arithmetic-combinator my-add +)
MY-ADD

(my-add 1 2 3 4)
10
```

5. Implement a macro called WARN that takes a string, possibly with format directives, and a series of arguments to the format directives and prints the string to the stream *ERROR-OUTPUT*.

6. Write a macro called MY-UNLESS which evaluates its second argument if the first returns NIL.

7. Modify MY-UNLESS so that it takes more than one consequent argument.

8. Modify MYDEFSTRUCT to include the creation of a copying macro for the structure (COPY-FISH, for example).

9. Write a destructured version of MYDEFSTRUCT that allows you to specify the keyword option CONC-NAME. In the real DEFSTRUCT, the structure name may appear alone or

in a list with options. Don't worry about the case where the structure name appears as a lone symbol. You should be able to call it

```
(mydefstruct (fish) (dorsal-fin-length 4))
```

or

```
(mydefstruct (fish :conc-name fishy-) (dorsal-fin-length 4))
```

Don't forget to write the code to implement CONC-NAME.

10. Enlarge the destructured version of MYDEFSTRUCT to include the option :CONSTRUCTOR, which specifies a name for the constructor function created by MYDEFSTRUCT.

Chapter 12

AN EXTENDED EXAMPLE: A TOY EXPERT SYSTEM

The major purpose of this chapter is to give you a chance to look at a more complex program than those presented elsewhere in the book. A secondary purpose is to provide a brief introduction to expert systems by means of an example. It is hoped that working through the code of a real, if simple, expert system will be a helpful supplement to the ample theoretical discussions to be found elsewhere.[1]

The example is Otto, a toy expert system for diagnosing simple problems with four-stroke, carbureted automobile engines. It is named after Nikolaus August Otto, who invented the four-stroke internal combustion engine. Otto consists of a backward-chaining inference engine that acts on weighted rules. Otto also has a second expert, which works together with the first.

Otto is first shown from the point of view of a user. Then its three major parts—the rule base, the inference engine, and the second expert—are discussed. These must be understood at a theoretical level. A TRACE of some major functions is used to introduce the code and demonstrate the outline of the program. Another level of knowledge about how Otto works involves adding new rules to the system. Next comes a discussion of the second expert and how to add to its knowledge. The final section in the chapter is a listing of the entire program.

12.1   A SESSION WITH OTTO

Otto is invoked with (run-otto):

(run-otto)

Welcome to Otto, an expert system for diagnosing problems with engines.
Otto knows only about four-stroke, piston-driven, carbureted,
gasoline engines.

---

[1] See the Annotated Bibliography.

233

```
The engine won't start: ?
```

Legal responses are yes, y, no, n, or a number between 0 and 1, inclusive,
where 0 indicates that the condition is certainly not the case,
and 1 means that it certainly is the case. Therefore,
yes means 1, and no means 0.

```
The engine won't start: n
```

Otto prints a description of a condition, and the user responds with a value that indicates
her certainty of the validity of the statement. Most users will wish to type only "yes"
or "no" in response to the description of a condition, because the resolution of the
numeric values is rather rough. Above, the user typed ? to request help.

The user continues to respond to Otto's questions in this fashion until Otto prints out
a list of possible causes of the problem:

```
The engine won't start: n
The engine misfires while running: y
The engine hesitates on acceleration: y
One cannot see jets of gasoline entering the throttle bore
when the accelerator pedal is depressed: n
The engine sometimes stalls at full throttle: y
The engine runs on ('diesels') after the ignition is turned
off: n
The engine pings or knocks while running: n
A compression gauge shows low compression in one or more
 cylinders: y
A compression gauge shows low compression in two adjacent
cylinders: y
Squirting oil into the cylinders with low compression causes
their compression readings to rise: y
The spark plug electrodes are fouled with oil: y
Spark is evident at all spark plug wires when the engine is
cranking: y
Crimping the vacuum line to the distributor does not cause
motion of the timing marks under a timing light while the
engine is running: n
Use of a timing light shows that the timing marks do not match
while the engine is running: n
The engine turns over normally when starting is attempted: y

These are the interesting conclusions and values associated with them:
1. The piston rings may be corroded, causing low compression. (0.8)
2. The head gasket may be blown, causing low compression. (0.8)
3. The spark plugs are fouled with oil.
 Possible cause:
 The piston rings leaking oil into the cylinders. (0.6)
4. The spark plugs are fouled with oil.
 Possible cause:
 The valve seals leaking oil into the cylinders. (0.6)
5. The spark plugs are fouled with oil.
 Possible cause:
 The head gasket leaking oil into the cylinders. (0.6)
```

```
6. The air and/or fuel filters are clogged and in need of
replacement. (0.5)
7. The carburetor idle mixture is misadjusted. (0.5)
NIL
```

The possible causes are ranked from most to least likely; the numbers next to them are *validity measures*. If any of the questions had been answered with a lack of certainty (such as a 0.5 answer), the validity measure of the final answers would have been affected.

Two kinds of causes are listed. Some of them, such as

```
1. The piston rings may be corroded, causing low compression. (0.8)
```

are descriptions produced by the inference engine. Others, such as

```
3. The spark plugs are fouled with oil.
 The cause may be:
The piston rings leaking oil into the cylinders. (0.6)
```

are generated by a second expert, the seals expert. Because several seals may leak a substance into a place, several conclusions may be generated by the seals expert. In the case of the problem described above, three seals can leak oil into the cylinders, and three descriptions were produced by the seals expert.

In the event that Otto is unable to find a plausible cause for the problem, it will say so, as in the case of a problem that defies description.

```
The engine won't start: n
The engine misfires while running: n
The engine hesitates on acceleration: n
The engine sometimes stalls at full throttle: n
The engine runs on ('diesels') after the ignition is turned
off: n
The engine pings or knocks while running: n
The engine turns over normally when starting is attempted: y

This program can't conclude anything useful about the problem you've
described.
NIL
```

12.2   **RULES IN OTTO**

Most, but not all, expert systems attempt to characterize the knowledge they possess in terms of rules. The term "rule" means the knowledge in the program embodied in a conditional "if-then" statement; however, rules differ from conditional statements in traditional programming languages in that rules are intended to be independent of the control structure of the expert system that operates on them.[2] In an imaginary very

---

[2] Rules may be written in such a way as to take advantage of the control structure, but they are not part of it.

simple system, the following might be used to create a rule:

```
(defrule engine-wont-start (out-of-gas))
```

It says, "If the engine won't start, then there may not be fuel in the fuel tank." This states a global relationship or truth not related to the way the particular system works. The diagnosis of the problems of a particular car is made by determining which conditions are true in the car under consideration.

Rules with syntax as simple as that of the one above are not very useful for most problems. For example, the rule states a true relationship, but it doesn't lead to a system that helps the layman distinguish between the possibilities that the car is out of gas, the battery is malfunctioning, and the starter is broken. All are good reasons for an engine not to start. One thing we can do to make rules more useful is to assign a number to them, representing the chance that the consequent is actually true if the predicate is true. This number is usually referred to as a weight or validity measure. A rule with a weight might look like this:

```
(defrule engine-wont-start
  (out-of-gas 0.2))
```

Now this says, "If the engine won't start, we attach a weight of 0.2 to the idea that there may not be fuel in the fuel tank." This is a useful piece of information.

Weights play a part in giving credibility and usefulness to an expert system; most experts have a variety of possibilities in mind and pursue them according to some ranking based on likelihood and ease of proof. Note that weights such as that above are not probabilities in the mathematical sense. However, they are supposed to be a rough indication of what the user or rule writer thinks the likelihood is that the consequent of the rule is true if the predicate for the rule is completely true.

The rule above is still simple. It takes one piece of evidence and makes one conclusion. Most expert systems allow you to construct more sophisticated predicates by combining descriptions with the help of what in Otto are called *predicate functions* or *predfuns*. For example,

```
(defrule (and engine-wont-start
              no-fuel-to-carb
              fuel-pump-works)
  (out-of-gas 0.7))
```

This says, "If all three condition descriptors are completely true, there is a 0.7 likelihood that you're out of gas." In Otto, the actual descriptions in predicate and consequent clauses are called *condition descriptors*, or *CDs*. Rules are if-then statements, using both predicate functions and weights in addition to condition descriptors.

Rules stand in isolation from the control structure but not from one another. The consequents of one rule are very likely the predicates of others. For example, the predicate FUEL-PUMP-WORKS may be supported by the truth of the following rule or contra-indicated if it is not true:

```
(defrule
  (and fuel-pump-suction)
  (fuel-pump-works 1))
```

This says, "if suction is noticed when one holds a finger over the fuel pump inlet while the engine is cranking, there is a likelihood of 1 out of 1 that the fuel pump is operating normally."

What happens if you're not quite sure that there is suction, or if there is only a little bit of suction? The weight specified by the rule writer represents a general truth. In a specific session with Otto, the chances that the predicate leads to the consequent must be combined with the chance that the predicate is in fact true to determine the overall likelihood that the rule is true. The likelihood that the predicate is true in the particular session is determined by the predicate function, which has a rule for combining the weights of some or all of the component predicate cds.

Otto has three types of predicate functions: AND, OR, and NOT. Do not confuse these with the LISP functions that have the same names! Like the LISP functions, predicate functions may play a role in determining the path through the graph of rules. However, their primary task is to help propagate likelihoods.

The predicate function contains a rule for combining the weights of the component clauses of a predicate. For example, if, in a session with Otto, there is a .6 probability that the engine really doesn't start, a .4 probability that the fuel is really not reaching the carburetor, and a .8 probability that the fuel pump is operating normally, then AND will cause a weight of $.4 * .6 * .8$ or .19 to be associated with the idea that the total predicate is correct or a weight of $.7 * .19$ or .13 to be associated with the conclusion of the rule. AND multiplies the weights of the individual condition descriptors in the predicate because the likelihood of a combined event being true is the chance that one event is true multiplied by the chances that the others are true.

Had the predicate function been OR, rather than multiplying the uncertainties within the predicate, it would have chosen the highest weight and multiplied that together with the rule's intrinsic weight. The likelihood that any one of a nonexclusive group of things is true is as high as the probability that the most likely one of them is true.

AND and OR are useful because they allow us to describe situations in which several things need to be true, or in which only one of several things need be true. The use of NOT may be less clear. Unlike AND and OR, NOT is unary. It behaves like "NOT AND" and is used to calculate the likelihood that its clause is not true. This allows rule writers to phrase condition descriptors conveniently. NOT is defined to subtract the weight of a cd from 1. Thus, if the probability that a condition descriptor is true is 1, its inverse would have a weight of 0.

AND, OR, and NOT also direct the flow of control. For example, the cutoff value for AND is 0. If one condition descriptor in a predicate with the predfun AND has a likelihood in the given session of 0, then there is no use in evaluating the other condition descriptors in the predicate. The value of the total predicate must be 0. Therefore, the function returns without examining the other predicate clauses.

The predicate functions in Otto are based on those for MYCIN, one of the first and most important backward-chaining expert systems. These behaviors were felt to be more natural for the user than exactly probabilistic ones.

Rules in Otto have one more part—a section for options. Two are possible: :GOAL and :FUNCTION. :GOAL states that this rule is one whose success will be of interest to the user, and should be reported at the end of the session. This is consonant with the idea that the rule represents a universal truth about the problem at hand. If the state of the spark plugs becomes less interesting to a user, it will be because something about cars has changed, not because Otto changes its structure. Instead of identifying goal rules explicitly, we could have written the inference engine so that all the rules whose consequences were not predicates of other rules would be treated as goals. However, this would have prevented interesting intermediate results from ever being reported.

```
(defrule
   (and engine-wont-start
        no-fuel-to-carb
        fuel-pump-works)
 (out-of-gas .7)
 :GOAL)
```

The seond option, :FUNCTION is not as neat. It is the interface to a second expert, which is invoked when rules with this option are fired. Thus, in fact, its presence in the rule has nothing to do with automobiles, but rather with the limits of Otto as an expert system.

The links between the predicate condition descriptors of one rule and the consequent condition descriptor of another cause Otto to form what is called a *directed acyclic graph*, which is like a tree, except that it may have more than one root and more than one node may point down to a given node or leaf. The Figure 12-1 shows the connections between Otto's rules about fuel.

Directed acyclic graphs are an appropriate structure for problems about car engines, because, as above, many different pieces of information may be contributing to the same diagnosis, or there may be several different independent problems with overlapping evidence for each one. For example, if the spark plugs are fouled with oil it could

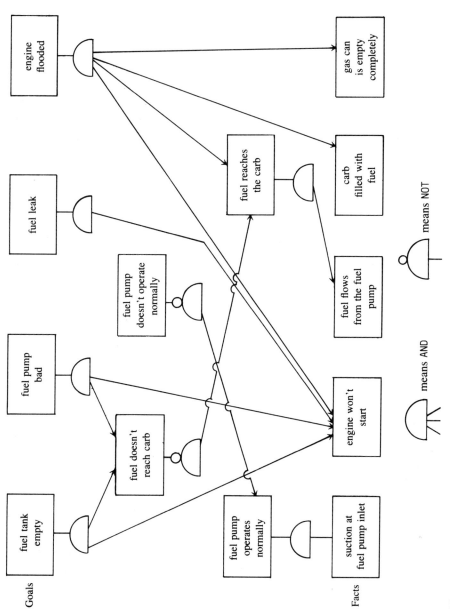

Figure 12-1. Connections Between Rules in Otto

be because the piston rings are leaking oil into the cylinders, or because the valve seals are leaking oil into the cylinders, or for both reasons.

12.3   **THE INFERENCE ENGINE**

To come up with a solution, an expert system must have an order for searching through the rules, evaluating or *firing* them, and figuring out what the consequence of one rule's truth is for all the other rules. Two possible ways of proceeding are *backward chaining* and *forward chaining*. In forward chaining, the truth of rules that are not consequences of other rules, i.e., facts, are determined first. In backward chaining, the attempt is to prove *goal* rules true.

Forward chaining is "fact driven." In a forward-chaining system, the user is asked, in some program-dependent fashion, to volunteer as much information as possible initially. For example, the user types in that fuel is not reaching the carburetor normally but that the fuel pump is working. Then the rules are searched for ones with predicates that match the assertions the user made. Any such rules are run, and they produce an augmented set of assertions. The chaining process continues until there are no more rules all of whose predicates are determined. Goal rules whose predicates are determined are reported to the user.

Backward chaining is "goal driven." This means that the system starts with the set of possible goal rules, or solutions, and checks which of these can be supported by the facts. Otto is a backward-chaining system. In other words, when Otto encounters the goal rule whose consequent is OUT-OF-GAS, it tries to determine whether the engine will start, whether fuel is reaching the carburetor, and whether the fuel pump is operating normally. To do so, it looks for the rules whose consequents were the condition descriptors of these predicates. When Otto wants to prove that a predicate is true, and the predicate is not the consequent of another rule, it asks the user for information.

The method of chaining is determined partly by its convenience in problem representation, partly by its convenience in user interface matters, and it is partly arbitrary. In terms of abstract design, there is no reason not to implement Otto in a forward-chaining manner. However, backward chaining springs to mind because it is easy to think about a system that diagnoses what's wrong as holding a hypothesis (a goal) and then checking whether the facts support it or not.

Additionally, backward chaining creates a natural user interface for the problem. Although combinations of backward and forward chaining are possible, in general, the user must volunteer all information at the beginning of a session in a forward-chaining system. In a backward-chaining system, the user waits until the system asks for the information. Therefore, forward chaining is often used in expert systems where it makes sense for the user to specify all information first. For example, XCON, an expert system which configures VAX computer systems, takes a user order as input and generates a configuration. In that case, the user presumably has some sort of specification already in mind, and it is easy to specify all the information to the system at the beginning of a session.

Backward chaining is most often used in systems where it might be difficult for the user to present all the information right away, either because he might not know what information is useful to the system, because he might not have thought to ask a particular question, or because it might not be worth while to find out the answer unless there is already a reason to believe that the particular question is worth answering. MYCIN is the most famous example of a backward-chaining system. MYCIN attempts to model a human internist diagnosing a medical problem. Obviously, you do not want your doctor to order all possible tests to find out all possible facts about you every time you go to her with a problem. The function of an internist is to eliminate possibilities and then perform tests to discriminate between the remaining possibilities.

One advantage of forward chaining is that the user has the comfortable feeling of having told all he knows in a coherent order. In backward-chaining systems, the user is asked for information in the order in which rules are fired. Under the best of circumstances, this models what a real expert would do and leads the user along in quite specific ways; the questions an internist asks may not at first seem related to a problem, but they gradually narrow down. However, in an expert system, backward chaining sometimes leads merely to a confusing progression of questions.

The control structure, or inference engine, embodies the chaining mechanism used to determine the order in which rules are fired. Since firing rules produces consequents that are also rules, the inference engine performs a recursive walk of the directed graph that constitutes the data base. Many expert systems go to great lengths to avoid doing a complete walk of the tree. Indeed, Otto's tree is pruned when the user makes a categorical statement. For example, if the predicate function for the rule is OR, and the user states that one of the clauses is true with a certainty of 1, then none of the other clauses are evaluated.

12.4   OTTO'S OTHER EXPERT

One feature of Otto is a second expert. The seals expert is a second repository for knowledge in the program. However, this knowledge is not represented in terms of rules, but rather in terms of objects. A seal is defined rather broadly as anything that can leak a substance from one area to another. A list of all possible seals, the substances they can leak, and the destinations to which they can leak the substances is kept by the system. The :FUNCTION option in a rule allows the inference engine to call in the seals expert when certain rules are fired. The seals expert looks at every seal and compiles a list of those which could be responsible for the leakage.

A rule that invokes the seals expert contains a function call to that expert in its consequent. For example,

```
(defrule
   (and engine-wont-start
        no-fuel-to-carb
        gasoline-odor)
   ((seals :substance "fuel" :leaks-to "world" :prefix
    "A fuel leak is preventing fuel from reaching the carburetor."))
   :goal :function)
```

When this rule is fired, the inference engine notices the option :FUNCTION. Therefore, it evaluates the consequent, and the function SEALS is called to produce one or more condition descriptors. SEALS is the function that embodies the second expert. Each condition descriptor produced by SEALS corresponds to a seal that could be leaking the substance specified to the place specified.

It is convenient to put knowledge about seals in a different place than knowledge about other matters, because other knowledge represented by the system is knowledge about causal relations, whereas knowledge of seals is information about the objects themselves.

12.5   A TRACE OF OTTO'S PATH

In backward chaining, the inference engine sequentially considers the list of rules, and when it finds a goal rule, attempts to evaluate its predicate, by seeing if they are already asserted in the data base of assertions. If they are, then it can assign a value to the consequent without searching any further. If one or more of the predicates is not asserted, then it has to try to determine their values by searching for a rule whose consequent is one of these predicates. If there is no such rule, it invokes the rule of last resort; it asks the user to assign a value to the predicate.

In other words, Otto recursively walks the directed graph of rules until it has a value for the goal rule and then it assigns the goal rule's consequent a value and goes on to the next goal rule.

Otto does not necessarily do a complete walk of the tree. Predicate functions, such as AND, OR, and NOT, have information about when it is appropriate to prune branches from a node. For example, if the predicate has the predicates function AND, and one of the predicate condition descriptors is found to have a value of 0, then the predicate as a whole must have a weight of 0, and other condition descriptors do not have to be evaluated.

Walking the part of the tree that actually is explored turns out to be less onerous than we might imagine because by the time Otto has gone through a few goal rules, the remaining ones will often have been completely determined. That is, Otto won't have to query the user anymore because the predicates that determine the values of the other goal rules will have been completely determined by the user's responses to earlier queries. Once all the goal rules have been evaluated, those assertions with a significantly high value will be reported to the user.

A good technique for getting a picture of Otto's inference engine is to TRACE its most interesting functions, follow the process through its course, and compare it with the code that implements the process. The forms watched are: RUN-OTTO, INFER, DETERMINE, DETERMINE-CD-VALUE, DETERMINE-IF-RULE, DETERMINE-BOTTOM, and DETERMINE-BOTTOM-QUERY.

Unfortunately, a complete walk-through requires many thousands of lines, so it is impractical to reproduce in a book. However, we can look at the beginning of a run through the program. Even here, we abbreviate the list of rules in the system with ..., since printing out all fifty or so of the rules in the system takes too much space.

```
;;; Dribble file "otto.txt" started
T
> (run-otto)
1 Enter RUN-OTTO


Welcome to Otto, an expert system for diagnosing problems with engines.
Otto knows only about four-stroke, piston-driven, carbureted,
gasoline engines.

  2 Enter INFER (((#<CD MIXTURE-BAD> .5)
                 (#<PREDFUN AND> #<CD ENGINE-RUNS-BUT-MISFIRES>) T NIL)
                ((#<CD ENGINE-STALLS-OR-SLUGGISH> 1)
                 (#<PREDFUN OR> #<CD ENGINE-STALLS>
                                #<CD ENGINE-HESITATES>) NIL NIL)
                ((#<CD ADJUST-ACCELERATOR-PUMP> .9)
                 (#<PREDFUN AND> #<CD ENGINE-DOES-START>
                                 #<CD ENGINE-HESITATES>
                                 #<CD PUMPING-GAS-NO-JETS>) T NIL)
                ((#<CD REPLACE-AIR-AND-OR-FUEL-FILTERS> .5)
                 (#<PREDFUN AND> #<CD ENGINE-DOES-START>
                                 #<CD ENGINE-STALLS-OR-SLUGGISH>) T NIL)
                 ...)
```

RUN-OTTO is the function we call. It initializes everything, prints the welcome message, and calls INFER on *RULES*. The rules that appear here are not in the format presented earlier, which we use to enter rules into the system because the TRACE represents the rule objects as created by calling DEFRULE. When INFER returns, RUN-OTTO calls REPORT-CONCLUSIONS.

```
(defun run-otto ()
  (format t "~2%~
Welcome to Otto, an expert system for diagnosing problems with ~
engines.  Otto knows only about four-stroke, piston-driven, ~
carbureted, gasoline engines.~2%")
  (setq *cd-values* nil);    No cd values known yet.
```

```
(setq *conclusions* nil)    ;No conclusions yet
(infer *rules*)
(report-conclusions *conclusions*))
```

CD-VALUES is an association list of condition descriptors and their weights in this particular session. *CONCLUSIONS* is also an a-list, containing all the goal rules that have been determined and their weights in this session.

INFER is the main loop of the program. It embodies the overall backward-chaining behavior of the system by looking at every rule in the system, checking whether it is a goal rule, and, if so, calling DETERMINE on the rule. DETERMINE takes a second argument—the list of RULES-BEING-RUN. This is NIL, because no rules are being run. However, when DETERMINE is called recursively, RULES-BEING-RUN has a value.

```
(defun infer (rule-list)
  (dolist (rule rule-list)
    (if (goal-rule? rule)
        ;; The second arg is NIL because no rules have been run yet.
        (determine rule nil)))))

    3 Enter DETERMINE ((#<CD MIXTURE-BAD> .5)
                       (#<PREDFUN AND> #<CD ENGINE-RUNS-BUT-MISFIRES>)
                       T NIL)
                      NIL
       4 Enter DETERMINE-CD-VALUE #<CD ENGINE-RUNS-BUT-MISFIRES>
               (((#<CD MIXTURE-BAD> .5)
                 (#<PREDFUN AND> #<CD ENGINE-RUNS-BUT-MISFIRES>)
                 T NIL))
          5 Enter DETERMINE-IF-RULE #<CD ENGINE-RUNS-BUT-MISFIRES>
                  (((#<CD MIXTURE-BAD> .5)
                    (#<PREDFUN AND> #<CD ENGINE-RUNS-BUT-MISFIRES>)
                    T NIL))
             6 Enter DETERMINE
                     ((#<CD ENGINE-RUNS-BUT-MISFIRES> 1)
                      (#<PREDFUN AND> #<CD ENGINE-DOES-START>
                                      #<CD ENGINE-MISFIRES>)
                      NIL NIL)
                     (((#<CD MIXTURE-BAD> .5)
                       (#<PREDFUN AND> #<CD ENGINE-RUNS-BUT-MISFIRES>)
                       T NIL))
```

DETERMINE first checks to see whether the current rule is a member of RULES-BEING-RUN. In this case, it cannot be, since no rules are being run. However, if the rule were found, Otto would generate an error because it would mean that the rule was dependent on itself. This enforces the idea that rules in Otto are part of a directed acyclic graph, rather than a semantic network. There cannot be any pointers back up the graph. DETERMINE calls DETERMINE-1 (which is not traced here) and DETERMINE-1 calls the predicate function. A secondary part of DETERMINE is what it does with the values returned by `DETERMINE-1`. `SET-CONSEQUENT-VALUE-AND-CONCLUSION` makes a pair out of the consequent condition descriptor for the rule and its value and puts it on `*CD-VALUES*`, which contains all the condition descriptors and values determined for this session with Otto. It also puts the rule on `*CONCLUSIONS*` if it is a goal rule.

```
(defun determine (rule rules-being-run)
    (if (member rule rules-being-run :test #'eq) (error nil "~
The rule ~s
was encountered while it was being run.  This means that this rule is
recursively dependent on itself.  The list of rules being run when it
was encountered was ~s." rule rules-being-run)
        (multiple-value-bind (consequents value more-than-one?)
            (determine-1 rule rules-being-run)
          (if more-than-one?
              (dolist (consequent consequents)
                (set-consequent-value-and-conclusion
                  consequent value rule))
              (set-consequent-value-and-conclusion
                consequents value rule)))))
```

`DETERMINE-1` returns three values: a consequent condition descriptor or list of consequent condition descriptors that have been supported, a value generated from the values of the predicates condition descriptors, and a truth value that tells whether the first value returned is one or more condition descriptors. This last value is returned only for convenience: the information it contains could be deduced by examination; however, only an invocation of the seal expert produces more than one consequent condition descriptor.

`DETERMINE-1` is the function that calls the predicate function on the predicate condition descriptors. When the value of the predicate has been determined, `DETERMINE-1` either invokes the seals expert or simply returns the rule consequent, its likelihood, and a third value indicating whether one or more consequents has been produced.

```
(defun determine-1 (rule rules-being-run)
  (let ((pred (rule-predicate rule)))
    (let ((value (funcall (predfun-evaluation-function
                            (predicate-predfun pred))
                          (predicate-cds pred)
                          (cons rule rules-being-run))))
      ;; Now we have the value to be associated with rule's
      ;; cd in VALUE.
      (if (generate-cd? rule)
          (values
            (apply (symbol-function (car (rule-consequent rule)))
                   (cdr (rule-consequent rule)))
                   value t)
          (values (rule-consequent rule) value nil)))))
```

In this case, the function associated with `AND` calls `DETERMINE-CD-VALUE` to find the value of #<CD ENGINE-RUNS-BUT-MISFIRES>:

```
(defun and-predicate-evaluator (cds rules-being-run)
  (let ((accumulated-value 1))
    (dolist (cd cds accumulated-value)
      (let ((value-pair (determine-cd-value cd rules-being-run)))
        ;; See if we can cut off here — AND of anything with 0 is 0.
        (when (= (cdr value-pair) 0) (return 0))
        ;; otherwise continue accumulating a value
        (setq accumulated-value
          (* (cdr value-pair) accumulated-value))))))))
(defun determine-cd-value (cd rules-being-run)
  (let ((value-pair (cd-value cd)))
    ;; If it hasn't been set yet, determine its value.
    (if (not value-pair)
        (progn (determine-if-rule cd rules-being-run)
               (cd-value cd))          ;return the value
        value-pair)))
```

DETERMINE-CD-VALUE first checks to see whether the value has already been calculated. If not, as in this case, it calls DETERMINE-IF-RULE. DETERMINE-IF-RULE looks to see whether there is a rule whose consequent is the predicate. If it finds such a rule, as it does in this case, it recursively calls DETERMINE on that rule. This time DETERMINE's second argument does have a value. The rule being run is the top-level rule that the top-level call to DETERMINE is working on. This process continues until a predicate is found which is not the consequent of another rule. We omit some data in the following example:

```
7 Enter DETERMINE-CD-VALUE #<CD ENGINE-DOES-START> ...)
  8 Enter DETERMINE-IF-RULE #<CD ENGINE-DOES-START> ...)
    9 Enter DETERMINE ((#<CD ENGINE-DOES-START> 1)
                       (#<PREDFUN NOT>
                        #<CD ENGINE-WONT-START>) NIL NIL)
                       ...)
      10 Enter DETERMINE-CD-VALUE #<CD ENGINE-WONT-START>
                                  ...)
        11 Enter DETERMINE-IF-RULE #<CD ENGINE-WONT-START>
                                   ...)
          12 Enter DETERMINE-BOTTOM
                   #<CD ENGINE-WONT-START>
            13 Enter DETERMINE-BOTTOM-QUERY "~&~a: "
"The engine won't start"
The engine won't start: n
```

A predicate that is not the consequent of another rule is called a fact. It is something that cannot be deduced, but must be known. DETERMINE-BOTTOM is responsible for getting a value for the predicate and putting that information in the right places. DETERMINE-BOTTOM-QUERY is the function that actually prompts the user for input.

```
          13 Exit DETERMINE-BOTTOM-QUERY O
        12 Exit DETERMINE-BOTTOM
                  (#<CD ENGINE-WONT-START> . O)
        11 Exit DETERMINE-IF-RULE
                  (#<CD ENGINE-WONT-START> . O)
      10 Exit DETERMINE-CD-VALUE
                  (#<CD ENGINE-WONT-START> . O)
     9 Exit DETERMINE NIL
    8 Exit DETERMINE-IF-RULE NIL
   7 Exit DETERMINE-CD-VALUE (#<CD ENGINE-DOES-START> . 1)
```

Since the user has typed NO in response to the query, a value of 0 is associated with the condition descriptor. Then, DETERMINE-BOTTOM, DETERMINE-IF-RULE, DETERMINE-CD-VALUE, and this invocation of DETERMINE all return. Other recursive invocations may also return if the consequent is the last condition descriptor in the predicate they are trying to determine.

When a predfun receives a value for a condition descriptor, it may prune the tree. When it receives values for all the relevant condition descriptors in a predicate, it determines the total likelihood of the predicate. This result is then combined with the likelihood of the consequent if the predicate is completely true to get the likelihood that the consequent is true in this particular session. This information is put onto the list *CD-VALUES*, and, if the rule is a goal rule, also onto the list *CONCLUSIONS*.

12.6   RULES, CONDITION DESCRIPTORS, AND PREDFUNS

As stated earlier, a rule contains three parts: a predicate, a result, and any options that may be specified. For example, a rule may be specified as follows:

```
(defrule (and engine-wont-start
    no-fuel-to-carb
    fuel-pump-works)
  (out-of-gas .7)
  :GOAL)
```

In fact, neither condition descriptors nor predfuns are merely symbols. Instead, they are objects. Condition descriptors consist of a name and a string. The name is the way we refer to the symbol when writing rules. The string is what the symbol uses when it prints information out to the user. Matching of predicate and consequent condition descriptors is done by checking whether the object itself is the same. Predfuns consist of a name and a function. The name is used for writing rules, and the function implements the action implied by the predicate name.

The fact that condition descriptors are objects rather than just strings that describe the condition prevents a serious problem. It is very hard to make sure that the rules in the system work as expected. What happens when you define a rule with the predicate

NOT-FUEL-IN-CARB instead of NO-FUEL-IN-CARB? In this system, DEFRULE, the macro that
creates rules, generates an error, because there is no object whose name is NOT-FUEL-
IN-CARB. Were condition descriptors simply strings, no such checking would be possible, and even small typos would produce a rule that did nothing (except slow the
system down). Of course, condition descriptors must have strings, because symbols do
not provide an adequate user interface.

DEFDESCRIPTOR is used to define condition descriptors. The condition descriptor is
stored in the property list of the symbol that is its name.

```
(defmacro defdescriptor (name string)
  `(let ((cd
          (make-condition-descriptor :name ',name :string ,string)))
     ;; make it fetchable for writing rules with it.
     (setf (get ',name 'condition-descriptor) cd)))
```

It is much less likely that you would want to add a predicate function to the system
than that you would want to add a condition descriptor. However, the function that
allows you to do so is DEFPREDFUN, which makes the object and pushes it onto the list
PREDICATE-FUNCTIONS. Writing the function that implements a predfun is relatively
complex. The function must accept two arguments: the predicate cds and the list of
rules being run. It must decide which of the predicate cds to evaluate and how to
combine their responses. Here is the function associated with the predfun AND.

```
(defun and-predicate-evaluator (cds rules-being-run)
  (let ((accumulated-value 1))
    (dolist (cd cds accumulated-value)
      (let ((value-pair (determine-cd-value cd rules-being-run)))
        ;; See if we can cut off here — AND of anything with 0 is 0.
        (when (= (cdr value-pair) 0) (return 0))
        ;; otherwise continue accumulating a value
        (setq accumulated-value
          (* (cdr value-pair) accumulated-value))))))
```

Although there is nothing to prevent you from making the predicate evaluator perform
any arbitrary action, an interesting one will have a cutoff value and a cutoff return
value. If the value specified for any predicate condition descriptor is equal to the
predicate function's cutoff value, then the tree is pruned. Most predicate functions have
their own cutoff return value. When the tree is pruned like this, the cutoff return value
is returned. The remaining condition descriptors in the predicate are not evaluated.
AND's cutoff return value is 0. This makes sense, because if one clause has a likelihood
of 0, then the weights of the others are irrelevant. OR's likelihood is 1. If one clause is
absolutely true, then no other can imply the consequent more strongly. NOT does not
have a cutoff return value because it can have only one clause.

DEFRULE creates rules. At compile time (or run time for rules created on the fly), it
expands into DEFRULE-INTERNAL, which does the work. DEFRULE-INTERNAL makes sure

that the specified options exist. It then performs several substitutions. It replaces the
name of the predicate function with the predfun object and the names of all condition
descriptors in the predicate with condition descriptor objects. If the consequent is not
a function, the condition descriptor is also replaced with an object. FIND-CD-WITH-NAME
generates an error if no condition descriptor object is found, which means that the user
has warning at load time about this potentially major problem in the data base. DEFRULE-
INTERNAL also puts the new rule on *RULES*, a list of all the rules in the system.

```
(defmacro defrule (predicate consequent &rest options)
  ;; Options are self-evaluating keywords.
  `(defrule-internal ',predicate ',consequent ,.options))

;;; This will run when the rules are defined; usually at load time.
(defun defrule-internal (predicate consequent &rest options)
  ;; Process the options.
  (let ((goal nil) (function nil))
    (dolist (option options)
      (cond ((eq option :goal) (setq goal t))
            ((eq option :function) (setq function t))
            (t (error nil "The option ~s is not a recognized option ~
                           for defrule."
                      option))))
    ;; Substitute in the condition descriptor for the
    ;; name in the consequent, unless the consequent is
    ;; to be a function call.  We purposely cons
    ;; instead of bashing the list structure the user gave us.
    (when (not function)
      (setq consequent (cons (find-cd-with-name (car consequent))
                             (cdr consequent))))
    ;; Now do the same thing for the cd names in the predicate,
    ;; at the same time replacing the predfun symbol with the
    ;; predfun object.
    (setq predicate
          (cons (find-predfun-with-name (car predicate))
                (mapcar #'find-cd-with-name (cdr predicate))))
    (push (list consequent predicate goal function) *rules*)))
```

Entering rules is usually tedious and ongoing and considerable work is done in real
expert systems to make rule entry as simple and expedient as possible. Even with this
load-time checking, there are potential programming problems in writing rules for Otto.
Consider the rule:

```
(defrule
  (and engine-does-start
       engine-misfires)
  (engine-runs-but-misfires 1))
```

The system has no idea what rules are basic; therefore, if the two condition descriptors
in the predicate are switched, the user is first asked if the engine misfires while running,
then if the engine starts. This would be particularly annoying if you had told the system

that the engine didn't start because of a previous rule (and then were asked whether it misfired while running).

The inference engine could be modified to check whether any of the predicate condition descriptors had already been evaluated and, if so, whether one of those values completely determined the value of the rule's consequent. If so, it could perform a cutoff right away without checking the values of the other predicate condition descriptors. This would eliminate the particular sensitivity to predicate condition descriptor ordering just described.

In fact, the entire rule above is an example of another weakness in Otto. The rule exists only as a way of combining those two statements. If there were a more powerful representation language, combinations like that could be inferred automatically.

12.7   **SEALS**

Otto has another expert in addition to the inference engine. The second engine works together with the first. When DETERMINE-1 encounters a rule with the :FUNCTION option set to T, it calls the car of the consequent on the cdr of the consequent. In theory the call could be to any function; however, the only acceptable alternative is SEALS. SEALS looks for every seal that matches the arguments given to it. It then returns one condition descriptor for every such seal. Since the inference engine expects consequences to be condition descriptors, the only additional difference its presence makes to the inference engine is that DETERMINE must be prepared to accept more than one consequent condition descriptor for a rule.

The seals expert knows about the engine's seals. In Otto, seals are parts of the engine that can leak one or more substances to one or more places. You define a seal as follows:

```
(defseal "head gasket"
  '("oil" "coolant")
  '("cylinders" "world"))
```

The name of this seal is head gasket; it can leak either oil or coolant to either cylinders or world. If there is only one substance leaked or only one place leaked to, a list need not be used.

```
(defseal "piston rings"
  "oil"
  "cylinders")
```

In the one session presented as an example, the seals expert was invoked by the following rule:

```
(defrule (and engine-wont-start-or-misfires
              spark-plugs-electrodes-fouled-with-oil)
```

```
((seals :substance "oil" :leaks-to "cylinders"
        :prefix "The spark plugs are fouled with oil.") 0.6)
 :goal :function)
```

This call to the seals expert caused it to generate three condition descriptors: one for every seal that can leak oil into the cylinders.

Like DEFRULE, DEFSEAL can be invoked at run time, in the interpreter. A seal is a structure with three slots: a descriptor, a substance, and a list of where they leak to. Defining a seal causes it to be put on the list of all the seals that Otto knows about.

```
(defmacro defseal (descriptor substance leaks-to)
  `(push (make-seal :descriptor ,descriptor :substance ,substance
                    :leaks-to ,leaks-to)
         *seals*))
```

The function SEALS is called when Otto wants to know what seals could be leaking. It takes any of four arguments: a descriptor, a substance, a list of places leaked to, and a statement of the problem to be prefixed to the explanation of what seals might be at fault.

```
(defun seals (&key descriptor substance leaks-to prefix)
  (mapcan
    #'(lambda (seal)
        (generate-seal-assertions
          (seal-descriptor seal)
          (seal-substance seal)
          (seal-leaks-to seal)
          descriptor substance leaks-to prefix))
        *seals*))
```

SEALS does pattern matching between its arguments and the set of all seals in the system. Thus, if you call SEALS, specifying just a substance, say coolant, you will get back a list with one condition descriptor for each seal in the system which satisfies the constraint that the substance it leaks is coolant. If you specify that the substance is coolant and the place leaked to the cylinders, you will get back only one condition descriptor with the string ''The head gasket may be leaking coolant into the cylinders.'' If you call SEALS with no constraints, you will get back all of the seals in the system.

SEALS calls GENERATE-SEAL-ASSERTION on every seal in the list of seals to see if it satisfies the constraints.

```
(defun generate-seal-assertions (seal-desc seal-subst seal-leaks-to
                                 descriptor substance leaks-to prefix)
  ;; Spread the seal properties if they're lists.
  (cond ((listp seal-subst)
         (mapcan #'(lambda (seal-subst)
                     (generate-seal-assertions
                       seal-desc seal-subst
                       seal-leaks-to descriptor
                       substance leaks-to prefix))
                 seal-subst))
```

```
((listp seal-leaks-to)
 (mapcan #'(lambda (seal-leaks-to)
             (generate-seal-assertions seal-desc
               seal-subst seal-leaks-to descriptor
               substance leaks-to prefix))
         seal-leaks-to))
(t (let ((assertion (generate-1-seal-assertion
                      seal-desc seal-subst seal-leaks-to
                      descriptor substance leaks-to prefix)))
     (if assertion (list assertion) nil)))))
```

Most of the code in GENERATE-SEAL-ASSERTIONS is concerned with mapping over items that may be lists. For example, a seal could leak more than one substance or it could leak to more than one place. If any of its substances and any of its places match the problem, then that seal could be the problem. When GENERATE-SEAL-ASSERTIONS is finally called with atomic arguments for SEAL-SUBST and SEAL-LEAKS-TO, it calls GENERATE-1-SEAL-ASSERTIONS. If this subprocedure returns NIL, no match was found. If it returns an assertion, that assertion might be a problem with the car.[3]

GENERATE-1-SEAL-ASSERTION does the pattern matching. It says, "Can the specified seal leak the specified substance to the specified place?" If there are no contradictions, it generates a condition descriptor just like all the strings that one finds in rules. If no match was found, it returns NIL.

```
(defun generate-1-seal-assertion (seal-desc seal-subst seal-leaks-to
                                  descriptor substance
                                  leaks-to prefix)
  ;; Candidates must be null or match targets.
  (if (and (or (null descriptor) (equal descriptor seal-desc))
           (or (null substance) (equal substance seal-subst))
           (or (null leaks-to) (equal leaks-to seal-leaks-to)))
      ;; then write a nameless CD for this seal and return it
      (if prefix      ;if a prefix was provided, use it
          (make-condition-descriptor
            :string
            (format nil
                    "~A~% Possible cause:~% The ~A leaking ~
                     ~A into the ~A"
                    prefix seal-desc seal-subst seal-leaks-to))
          (make-condition-descriptor
            :string
            (format nil "The ~A leaking ~A into the ~A"
                    seal-desc seal-subst seal-leaks-to)))
      nil))
```

The seals expert allows us to specify rules that automatically generate additional information about possible sources of a leak. It provides a simple model of some of a mechanic's knowledge of the geometry of an engine.

---

[3] This is probably the reader's only opportunity to confuse cars with CARs legitimately.

12.8   **OTTO'S STRENGTHS AND WEAKNESSES**

It is as hard to assess the competence of an expert system as it is to assess that of an expert. All we can say is that Otto is successful in that it appears to work well—it successfully diagnoses automobile engine maladies. We can test it on different situations; in the session presented at the beginning of this chapter, the responses to Otto's questions described the symptoms exhibited by a 1977 Honda Civic. The car had its engine rebuilt and, as predicted, the piston rings were worn and the head gasket blown between two cylinders. The carburetor was also in need of adjustment. Otto was wrong only in that the car did not need either a new fuel filter or a new air filter. A number of other ad hoc test cases have been tried on it; it was successful, except, of course, when dealing with cases that its rules did not cover, and in these cases it did state that it had nothing to say.

Otto is a toy for several reasons. First, the domain was chosen in part because the problems are relatively simple, and a set of troubleshooting techniques have long since been worked out. An expert system is a program that contains the knowledge that a human expert would have about a particular, specialized domain of knowledge. Its usefulness is dependent on capturing knowledge that is otherwise hard to come by. The tasks of gathering information and determining procedural heuristics are typically major problems in writing an expert system. In contrast, it is not at all difficult for a person to gain the knowledge that Otto has.

One limitation of this particular implementation of Otto is that information flows in only one direction. There is no convenient way to write a rule whose predicate includes a condition descriptor that is the output of another expert. Thus, the inference engine does not see the output of the seals expert. A backward-chaining expert system depends on being able to find rules whose evaluation will give a value for a precursor of the rule being evaluated; however, the inference engine does not know how to get another expert to produce them when it's trying to run a rule that would have such an assertion in its predicate. Although Otto keeps a list of possible assertions the inference engine might make, it does not keep a list of possible assertions the seals expert might make. Because the program producing the condition descriptor may not yet have run when the search is done, Otto interrogates the user about the condition, rather than invoking an expert that might generate it.[4]

You could make Otto more powerful by adding more rules and seals to it, to the point where it covers most things that could go wrong with an automobile engine. It would not, however, be that much more powerful than it is now. Its knowledge of what might go wrong in an automobile engine would still be limited to common cases

---

[4] This has been a problem with real-world expert systems that make use of more than one expert.

that mechanics have run into again and again. You would not really be using the abilities that computers have that humans don't.[5]

One approach that promises more is modelling the engine. A sufficiently detailed model of an automobile engine could simulate interactions between, say, mixture composition and load that would lead to stalling. We could elicit a description of the problem from the user and perturb the model in ways that might be likely to produce the behavior described by the user. This approach is interesting in part because an automobile engine is sufficiently complex that a human being would have a hard time doing this sort of simulation. It would also be useful to be able to directly meter parameters like manifold vacuum pressure, RPM, and exhaust composition, rather than asking the user to describe them, because this would give the system a better idea (higher bandwidth, greater resolution with respect to time) of the state of the engine than a user typing at a keyboard could.

However, modelling an automobile engine is a very complex task. A useful model would need to include the dynamics of the pistons, crankshaft, and valve train; a model of the behavior (including flow) of lubricants under different temperatures and pressures; and an electrical model of the ignition system, at the very least.

While Otto is the most complex program presented in this book, and has some interesting properties, it ranks second out of list of eleven steps of ''successful architectural embellishments appropriate to increasingly complex problems'' described in *Building Expert Systems*.[6] We have not even skimmed the surface of the problems and possibilities in writing expert systems.

12.9   A PRINTOUT OF OTTO

```
;;; A toy expert system called Otto.
(in-package 'otto)
(import '(run-otto) (find-package 'user))
;;; All the rules Otto knows about are kept on this list.
;;; A sample element of *RULES* looks like:
;;; (#<cd engine-stalls-or-sluggish> 1)
;;;   (#<predfun OR>
;;;     #<cd engine-stalls>
;;;     #<cd engine-hesitates>)
;;;   NIL NIL)
(defparameter *rules* nil)

;;; *CD-VALUES* is an a-list containing all the condition descriptors
;;; that have values in Otto, and their values in the current session.
```

---

[5] Except for an infallible memory.

[6] Frederick Hayes-Roth, Donald A. Waterman, and Douglas B. Lenat, eds, *Building Expert Systems* (Reading, MA: Addison-Wesley, 1983), p. 91.

```
;;; A typical element of this list is:
;;; (#<starter-malfunction> . 0.0)
;;; *CD-VALUES* is reset on entering Otto.
(defvar *cd-values* nil)

;;; *CONCLUSIONS* is the a-list of goals worked over so far and
;;; their likelihoods as an answer to the given problem.  Elements
;;; in it look just like elements in *CD-VALUES*.
;;; *CONCLUSIONS* is reset each time OTTO is
;;; re-entered.
(defvar *conclusions* nil)

;;; *INTERESTING-CONCLUSION-CUTOFF* is the minimum truth value
;;; that must be associated with a conclusion so that it is
;;; reported by REPORT-CONCLUSIONS.
(defparameter *interesting-conclusion-cutoff* 0.25)

;;; A predicate-function (predfun) is composed of a name
;;; (the symbol used in the rule), and an evaluation function.
(defparameter *predicate-functions* nil)

(defstruct (predfun (:print-function predfun-print-fn))
  name
  evaluation-function)

(defun predfun-print-fn (predfun stream ignore)
  (declare (ignore ignore))
  (format stream  "#<PREDFUN ~s>" (predfun-name predfun)))

(defmacro defpredfun (name evaluation-function)
  `(push (make-predfun :name ,name
                       :evaluation-function ,evaluation-function)
         *predicate-functions*))

;;; predicate function evaluators.

;;; The predicate evaluator for AND, which returns the product
;;; of the values of its cds.
(defun and-predicate-evaluator (cds rules-being-run)
  (let ((accumulated-value 1))
    (dolist (cd cds accumulated-value)
      (let ((value-pair (determine-cd-value cd rules-being-run)))
        ;; see if we can cut off here — and of anything with 0 is 0.
        (when (= (cdr value-pair) 0) (return 0))
        ;; otherwise continue accumulating a value
        (setq accumulated-value
              (* (cdr value-pair) accumulated-value))))))

;;; The predicate evaluator for OR, which returns the maximum of
;;; the values of its cds.
(defun or-predicate-evaluator (cds rules-being-run)
  (let ((greatest-so-far 0))
    (dolist (cd cds greatest-so-far)
      (let ((value-pair (determine-cd-value cd rules-being-run)))
        ;; See if we can cut off here — OR of anything with 1 is
        ;; 1 (1 is the greatest value in our universe).
        (when (= (cdr value-pair) 1) (return 1))
        ;; Otherwise continue computing a value.
        (setq greatest-so-far
              (max (cdr value-pair) greatest-so-far))))))
```

```
;;; The predicate evaluator for NOT, which is unary, and
;;; inverts the value of its cd.
(defun not-predicate-evaluator (cds rules-being-run)
  (let ((cd (car cds)))
    (when (not (null (cdr cds)))
      (error "Only one argument condition descriptor should be ~
              specified for the NOT predfun, but the list ~S ~
              was specified." cds))
    (- 1 (cdr (determine-cd-value cd rules-being-run)))))

;;; Predicate function definitions.
(defpredfun 'and #'and-predicate-evaluator)
(defpredfun 'or #'or-predicate-evaluator)
(defpredfun 'not #'not-predicate-evaluator)

(defun find-predfun-with-name (name)
  (find name *predicate-functions* :key #'predfun-name))

;;; A condition-descriptor (CD) is an object that associates the
;;; name of a condition with a string describing it in English, which
;;; is used in interacting with the user.  CD's are Otto's basic
;;; increments of knowledge about a problem.
(defstruct (condition-descriptor (:print-function cd-print-fn))
  name
  string)

(defun cd-print-fn (cd stream ignore)
  (declare (ignore ignore))
  (format stream "#<CD ~s>"
          (condition-descriptor-name cd)))

;;; Note that the descriptor string should be a string, and
;;; especially must not be nil.
(defmacro defdescriptor (name string)
  `(let ((cd (make-condition-descriptor :name ',name
                                        :string ,string)))
     ;; Make it fetchable for writing rules with it.
     (setf (get ',name 'condition-descriptor) cd)))

(defun find-cd-with-name (name)
  (let ((cd (get name 'condition-descriptor)))
    (if (null cd)
        (error "~S is not the name of a condition descriptor." name)
        cd)))

;;; A rule has predicates and an assertion.  One can also indicate
;;; that the rule is a goal rule with the presence of :GOAL; :GOAL
;;; means that the rule is one whose success should be reported to
;;; the user. Another "keyword" that can be specified is :FUNCTION;
;;; :FUNCTION means that, instead of an assertion, a function and a
;;; set of arguments are provided, and the function should be run to
;;; generate the cd or list of cds that are to be asserted.
(defmacro defrule (predicate consequent &rest options)
  ;; Options are self-evaluating keywords.
  `(defrule-internal ',predicate ',consequent ,.options))

;;; This will run when the rules are defined, usually at load time.
(defun defrule-internal (predicate consequent &rest options)
```

```lisp
;; Process the options.
(let ((goal nil) (function nil))
  (dolist (option options)
    (cond ((eq option :goal) (setq goal t))
          ((eq option :function) (setq function t))
          (t (error nil "The option ~s is not a recognized option ~
                         for defrule."
                    option))))
  ;; Substitute in the condition descriptor for the name in
  ;; the consequent, unless the consequent is to be a function
  ;; call.  We purposely cons instead of bashing the list structure
  ;; the user gave us.
  (when (not function)
    (setq consequent (cons (find-cd-with-name (car consequent))
    (cdr consequent))))
  ;; Now do the same thing for the cd names in the predicate,
  ;; at the same time replacing the predfun symbol with the
  ;; predfun object.
  (setq predicate
        (cons (find-predfun-with-name (car predicate))
              (mapcar #'find-cd-with-name (cdr predicate))))
  (push (list consequent predicate goal function) *rules*)))

(defmacro rule-consequent (rule)
  `(first (first ,rule)))

(defmacro rule-consequent-weight (rule)
  `(second (first ,rule)))

(defmacro rule-predicate (rule)
  `(second ,rule))

(defmacro predicate-predfun (pred)
  `(first ,pred))

(defmacro predicate-cds (pred)
  `(rest ,pred))

(defmacro goal-rule? (rule)
  `(third ,rule))

(defmacro generate-cd? (rule)
  `(fourth ,rule))

;;; For serious speed improvement, we would want to hash this list.
;;; Since this system is not going to run into any speed problems
;;; just yet, we don't.
(defmacro cd-value (cd)
  `(assoc ,cd *cd-values*))

;;; Returns the pair.
(defmacro set-cd-value (cd value)
  `(let ((pair (cons ,cd ,value)))
     (push pair *cd-values*) pair))

(defun find-rule-with-consequent (consequent)
  (assoc consequent *rules*
         :test #'(lambda (item rule-car)
                   (eq item (first rule-car)))))
```

```
;;; Run otto.  Perform necessary initializations.
(defun run-otto ()
  (format t "~2%~
Welcome to Otto, an expert system for diagnosing problems with ~
engines.  Otto knows only about four-stroke, piston-driven, ~
carbureted, gasoline engines.~2%")
  (setq *cd-values* nil)           ;No cd values known yet.
  (setq *conclusions* nil)               ;No conclusions yet.
  (infer *rules*)
  (report-conclusions *conclusions*))

;;; The top loop in the inference engine.  Find a goal rule in
;;; the rule list and try to determine its truth.  Keep going
;;; until there are no more goal rules.

(defun infer (rule-list)
  (dolist (rule rule-list)
    (if (goal-rule? rule)
        ;; Second arg is NIL because no rules run yet.
        (determine rule nil))))

(defun set-consequent-value-and-conclusion
        (consequent value rule)
  (let ((pair
          (set-cd-value consequent
              (* (rule-consequent-weight rule) value))))
    (if (goal-rule? rule) (push pair *conclusions*))))

;;; DETERMINE "runs" a rule.  If the rule is a goal rule, it adds
;;; the result(s) of running it to *CONCLUSIONS*.  In any case, it
;;; adds the results of running the rule to *CD-VALUES*.
;;; RULES-BEING-RUN is a list of the rules that DETERMINE is
;;; in the course of running.  It allows for circularity checks,
;;; which are done with EQ, so pass the rule itself.
(defun determine (rule rules-being-run)
  (if (member rule rules-being-run :test #'eq) (error nil "~
The rule ~s
was encountered while it was being run.  This means that this
rule is recursively dependent on itself.  The list of rules being
run when it was encountered was ~s." rule rules-being-run)
      (multiple-value-bind (consequents value more-than-one?)
          (determine-1 rule rules-being-run)
        (if more-than-one?
            (dolist (consequent consequents)
              (set-consequent-value-and-conclusion
                  consequent value rule))
            (set-consequent-value-and-conclusion
                consequents value rule)))))

;;; DETERMINE-1 checks the values of the condition descriptors
;;; in the rule's predicate, and, if they do not yet have values,
;;; calls itself recursively on them.  DETERMINE returns the
;;; consequent or consequents, a value generated from the values
;;; of the predicates, and a value that is T if it is returning a
;;; list of consequents, NIL if returning just one consequent.
(defun determine-1 (rule rules-being-run)
  (let ((pred (rule-predicate rule)))
```

```
(let ((value (funcall (predfun-evaluation-function
                        (predicate-predfun pred))
                      (predicate-cds pred)
                      (cons rule rules-being-run))))
  ;; Now we have the value to be associated with rule's cd
  ;; in VALUE.
  (if (generate-cd? rule)
      (values
        (apply (symbol-function (car (rule-consequent rule)))
               (cdr (rule-consequent rule)))
        value t)
      (values (rule-consequent rule) value nil)))))

;;; DETERMINE-IF-RULE tries to find a rule whose consequent is
;;; the same as the cd that is DETERMINE-IF-RULE's arg.  If it
;;; finds one, it runs DETERMINE on it.  If it doesn't find one,
;;; it calls  DETERMINE-BOTTOM on the cd.
(defun determine-if-rule (cd rules-being-run)
  (let ((rule (find-rule-with-consequent cd)))
    (if (null rule) (determine-bottom cd)
      (determine rule rules-being-run))))

;;; DETERMINE-BOTTOM is the function called to associate a
;;; value with a cd that is not the consequent of any rule.
;;; It queries the user and sets the cd's value.
(defun determine-bottom (cd)
  ;; SET-CD-VALUE because we know it's only a cd, not
  ;; necessarily a consequent of a rule.
  (set-cd-value cd (determine-bottom-query
                     "~&~a: " (condition-descriptor-string cd))))

;;; Gets a numeric value between 1 and 0, inclusive, from
;;;  the user.  yes => 1, no => 0.
(defun determine-bottom-query (format-string &rest format-args)
  (apply #'format *query-io* format-string format-args)
  ;; Set the package to avoid problems with reading.
  (let ((*package* (find-package 'otto)))
    (let ((response (read *query-io*)))
      (case response
        ((yes y) 1)  ; translate YES to 1
        ((no n) 0)   ; translate NO to
        (t (cond ((and (numberp response)
                       (<= response 1) (>= response 0))
                  response) ; if it's an acceptable number, return it.
                 (t (format t "~%~
Legal responses are yes, y, no, n, or a number between 0 and 1,
inclusive, where 0 indicates that the condition is certainly not
the case, and 1 means that it certainly is the case.  Yes means 1,
and no means 0.~2%")
                    (apply #'determine-bottom-query
                           format-string format-args)))))))))

;;; Determines the value of a CD, invoking determine-1 and querying
;;; the user if necessary.
(defun determine-cd-value (cd rules-being-run)
  (let ((value-pair (cd-value cd)))
```

```
  ;; If it hasn't been set yet, determine its value.
  (if (not value-pair)
     (progn (determine-if-rule cd rules-being-run)
            (cd-value cd))           ;return the value
     value-pair)))
;;; Report conclusions to the user.
(defun report-conclusions (conclusions)
  (setq conclusions
     (sort (remove *interesting-conclusion-cutoff*
                         conclusions
                         :test #'>
                         :key #'cdr)
        #'> :key #'cdr))
  (if (null conclusions)
     (format t
"This program can't conclude anything useful about the problem ~
you've described.")
     (progn
      (format t
"These are the interesting conclusions and values associated with ~
them:")
      (do ((conclusion conclusions (cdr conclusion))
           (i 1 (+ i 1)))
          ((null conclusion) nil)
        (format t "~%~d. ~a. (~a)"
                   i
                   ;; Format it to get out any stuff that the typist
                   ;; put in to make it fit on lines.
                   (format nil
                       (condition-descriptor-string
                           (caar conclusion)))
                   (cdar conclusion))))))
;;; The seals expert.

;;; A seal is a thing that can leak.  Certain objects are seals in Otto
;;; although they are not seals in the real world, because there is no
;;; reason to model them more closely.  For example, the radiator is a
;;; seal, and the exhaust system is a seal.

;;; A seal can leak one or more substances.  The seal is described by a
;;; string, which is used for identifying potentially losing seals to the
;;; user.  Finally, the seal can leak these substances into one or more
;;; places.
(defstruct (seal :conc-name)
  descriptor
  substance
  leaks-to)

;;; All the seals that Otto knows about.
(defparameter *seals* nil)

;;; Use DEFSEAL to make seals and tell Otto of them.
(defmacro defseal (descriptor substance leaks-to)
  `(push (make-seal :descriptor ,descriptor :substance ,substance
                    :leaks-to ,leaks-to)
      *seals*))
```

```
;;; Find the seals that inclusively match the args and assert
;;; cds in the database for them.  Return a list of
;;; condition-descriptor/value pairs asserted.
(defun seals (&key descriptor substance leaks-to prefix)
  (mapcan
    #'(lambda (seal)
        (generate-seal-assertions
          (seal-descriptor seal)
          (seal-substance seal)
          (seal-leaks-to seal)
          descriptor substance leaks-to prefix))
      *seals*))

(defun generate-seal-assertions (seal-desc seal-subst seal-leaks-to
                                  descriptor substance leaks-to prefix)
  ;; Spread the seal properties if they're lists.
  (cond ((listp seal-subst)
         (mapcan #'(lambda (seal-subst)
                     (generate-seal-assertions
                       seal-desc seal-subst
                       seal-leaks-to descriptor
                       substance leaks-to prefix))
                 seal-subst))
        ((listp seal-leaks-to)
         (mapcan #'(lambda (seal-leaks-to)
                     (generate-seal-assertions
                       seal-desc seal-subst
                       seal-leaks-to descriptor
                       substance leaks-to prefix))
                 seal-leaks-to))
        (t (let ((assertion (generate-1-seal-assertion
                              seal-desc seal-subst seal-leaks-to
                              descriptor substance leaks-to prefix)))
             (if assertion (list assertion) nil)))))

(defun generate-1-seal-assertion (seal-desc seal-subst seal-leaks-to
                                  descriptor substance
                                  leaks-to prefix)
  ;; Candidates must be null or match targets.
  (if (and (or (null descriptor) (equal descriptor seal-desc))
           (or (null substance) (equal substance seal-subst))
           (or (null leaks-to) (equal leaks-to seal-leaks-to)))
      ;; then write a nameless CD for this seal and return it
      (if prefix ;if a prefix was provided, use it
          (make-condition-descriptor
            :string
            (format nil
                    "~A~% Possible cause:~% The ~A leaking ~
                    ~A into the ~A"
                    prefix seal-desc seal-subst seal-leaks-to))
          (make-condition-descriptor
            :string
            (format nil "The ~A leaking ~A into the ~A"
              seal-desc seal-subst seal-leaks-to)))
      nil))
```

```
;;; Descriptors for Otto.
(defdescriptor engine-doesnt-turn-over
  "The engine doesn't turn over at all when starting is attempted")

(defdescriptor engine-turns-over-slowly
  "The engine turns over slowly when starting is attempted")

(defdescriptor engine-turns-over-slowly-or-not-at-all
  "The engine turns over slowly or doesn't turn over when starting
is attempted")

(defdescriptor engine-turns-over-normally
  "The engine turns over normally when starting is attempted")

(defdescriptor engine-doesnt-turn-over-normally
  "The engine doesn't turn over normally when starting is attempted")

(defdescriptor engine-wont-start
  "The engine won't start")

(defdescriptor battery-malfunction
  "The battery is malfunctioning")

(defdescriptor headlights-dim
  "The headlights are dim")

(defdescriptor battery-leads-loose-or-charge-low
  "The battery leads are loose or the battery charge is low")

(defdescriptor cracks-in-battery-case
  "There are cracks in the battery case")

(defdescriptor replace-battery
  "The battery needs to be replaced because the case is cracked")

(defdescriptor starter-malfunction
  "The starter is malfunctioning")

(defdescriptor jump-between-battery-and-starter
  "Placing a jumper directly between the battery and the starter
solenoid makes the engine turn over")

(defdescriptor ignition-malfunction
  "The ignition switch system is malfunctioning")

(defdescriptor not-jump-between-battery-and-starter
  "Placing a jumper directly between the battery and the starter
solenoid does not make the engine turn over")

(defdescriptor no-hydrostatic-lock
  "Hydrostatic lock is not indicated")

(defdescriptor replace-starter
  "The starter is broken and should be replaced")

(defdescriptor engine-doesnt-fire-when-starting
  "The engine doesn't fire when starting is attempted")

(defdescriptor engine-wont-fire
  "The engine doesn't fire")

(defdescriptor engine-does-fire
  "The engine does fire")
```

```
(defdescriptor engine-does-start
  "The engine does start")

(defdescriptor engine-misfires
  "The engine misfires while running")

(defdescriptor engine-runs-but-misfires
  "The engine runs, but misfires while running")

(defdescriptor engine-wont-start-but-does-fire
  "The engine won't start but does fire")

(defdescriptor engine-wont-start-or-misfires
  "The engine won't start or misfires while running")

(defdescriptor no-spark-at-spark-plug-wires
  "No spark is evident at any spark plug wires when the engine
is cranking")

(defdescriptor no-spark-at-high-tension-lead
  "No spark is evident at the coil high tension lead when the
engine is cranking")

(defdescriptor ignition-coil-or-high-tension-lead-defective
  "The ignition coil or high tension lead is defective")

(defdescriptor high-tension-lead-cracked-or-too-much-resistance
  "The ignition coil high tension lead has cracked insulation, or
has excessive resistance")

(defdescriptor replace-high-tension-lead
  "The ignition coil high tension lead should be replaced")

(defdescriptor high-tension-lead-ok
  "The ignition coil high tension lead is in good condition")

(defdescriptor replace-ignition-coil-or-high-tension-lead
  "The ignition coil or high tension lead is defective")

(defdescriptor replace-ignition-coil
  "The ignition coil is defective and should be replaced")

(defdescriptor spark-at-some-spark-plug-wires
  "Spark is evident at some spark plug wires when the engine is
cranking")

(defdescriptor spark-at-all-spark-plug-wires
  "Spark is evident at all spark plug wires when the engine is
cranking")

(defdescriptor not-spark-at-all-spark-plug-wires
  "Spark is not evident at all spark plug wires when the engine is
cranking")

(defdescriptor distributor-cap-or-spark-plug-wires-bad
  "The distributor cap or spark plug wires may be faulty")

(defdescriptor spark-plug-wires-cracked-or-too-much-resistance
  "The spark plug wires have cracked insulation, or excessive
resistance")

(defdescriptor replace-spark-plug-wires
  "The spark plug wires should be replaced")
```

```
(defdescriptor distributor-cap-cracked-or-burned-or-rotor-bad
  "The distributor cap is cracked or burned, or the rotor
contacts are corroded")

(defdescriptor replace-distributor-cap-and-rotor
  "The distributor cap and rotor should be replaced")

(defdescriptor coolant-in-oil
  "A look at the dipstick shows that there is coolant in the oil")

(defdescriptor coolant-in-cylinders
  "There is coolant in one or more of the cylinders")

(defdescriptor hydrostatic-lock
 "Hydrostatic lock is indicated")

(defdescriptor fuel-to-carb
   "Fuel is reaching the carburetor")

(defdescriptor throttle-bore-of-carb-filled-with-fuel
  "The throttle bore of the carburetor is filled with fuel")

(defdescriptor gasoline-odor
  "There is a strong gasoline odor in the engine compartment")

(defdescriptor engine-flooded
  "The engine is flooding, and should be allowed to dry before
restarting is attempted")

(defdescriptor fuel-flows-from-pump
  "Disconnection of the carburetor fuel line shows that fuel flows
smoothly from the fuel pump while the engine is cranking")

(defdescriptor no-fuel-to-carb
  "Fuel is not reaching the carburetor")

(defdescriptor fuel-pump-suction
  "Suction is noticed when one holds a finger over the fuel pump
inlet while the engine is cranking")

(defdescriptor fuel-pump-works
  "The fuel pump is operating normally")

(defdescriptor out-of-gas
  "There may not be fuel in the fuel tank")

(defdescriptor fuel-pump-doesnt-work
  "The fuel pump is not operating normally")

(defdescriptor replace-fuel-pump
  "The fuel pump is defective and should be replaced")

(defdescriptor timing-marks-off
  "Use of a timing light shows that the timing marks do not match
while the engine is running")

(defdescriptor adjust-timing
  "The timing is off; the distributor should be adjusted until the
timing is correct")

(defdescriptor crimping-vacuum-line-makes-no-difference
  "Crimping the vacuum line to the distributor does not cause
motion of the timing marks under a timing light while the
engine is running")
```

```
(defdescriptor replace-vacuum-advance
  "The vacuum advance mechanism is broken and should be replaced or
 rebuilt")
(defdescriptor spark-plug-electrodes-fouled-with-oil
  "The spark plug electrodes are fouled with oil")
(defdescriptor low-compression
  "A compression gauge shows low compression in one or more
 cylinders")
(defdescriptor squirting-oil-raises-compression
  "Squirting oil into the cylinders with low compression causes
 their compression readings to rise")
(defdescriptor piston-rings-corroded
  "The piston rings may be corroded, causing low compression")
(defdescriptor squirting-oil-doesnt-raise-compression
  "Squirting oil into the cylinders with low compression does not
 cause their compression readings to rise")
(defdescriptor burned-or-sticking-valves
  "There may be a burned or sticking valve causing low compression")
(defdescriptor low-compression-two-adjacent-cylinders
  "A compression gauge shows low compression in two adjacent
 cylinders")
(defdescriptor head-gasket-blown
 "The head gasket may be blown, causing low compression")
(defdescriptor engine-pings-or-knocks
  "The engine pings or knocks while running")
(defdescriptor timing-advanced
  "The ignition timing is excessively advanced, causing predetonation")
(defdescriptor engine-diesels
  "The engine runs on ('diesels') after the ignition is turned
 off")
(defdescriptor detonation
  "Detonation is indicated")
(defdescriptor carbon-on-cylinder-head
  "There is excessive carbon build-up on the cylinder head, causing
 detonation")
(defdescriptor engine-stalls-or-sluggish
  "The engine stalls or performs sluggishly on acceleration")
(defdescriptor replace-air-and-or-fuel-filters
  "The air and/or fuel filters are clogged and in need of
 replacement")
(defdescriptor engine-hesitates
  "The engine hesitates on acceleration")
(defdescriptor pumping-gas-no-jets
  "One cannot see jets of gasoline entering the throttle bore
 when the accelerator pedal is depressed")
```

```
(defdescriptor adjust-accelerator-pump
  "The accelerator pump is malfunctioning, and should be
overhauled or adjusted")

(defdescriptor engine-stalls
  "The engine sometimes stalls at full throttle")

(defdescriptor mixture-bad
  "The carburetor idle mixture is misadjusted")

;;; rules for Otto.

;;; engine starting disjunctions
(defrule
  (or engine-doesnt-turn-over
      engine-turns-over-slowly)
  (engine-turns-over-slowly-or-not-at-all 1))

(defrule (not engine-turns-over-normally)
  (engine-doesnt-turn-over-normally 1))

;;; battery
(defrule (and engine-wont-start
              engine-doesnt-turn-over-normally
              engine-turns-over-slowly-or-not-at-all)
  (battery-malfunction 0.6))

(defrule (and battery-malfunction
              headlights-dim)
  (battery-leads-loose-or-charge-low 0.9)
  :GOAL)

(defrule (and battery-malfunction
              cracks-in-battery-case)
  (replace-battery 0.9)
  :GOAL)

;;; starter lossage
(defrule
  (and engine-doesnt-turn-over-normally
       engine-doesnt-turn-over)
  (starter-malfunction 0.8))

(defrule
  (and engine-wont-start
       starter-malfunction
       jump-between-battery-and-starter)
  (ignition-malfunction 0.9)
  :GOAL)

(defrule
  (not jump-between-battery-and-starter)
  (not-jump-between-battery-and-starter 1))

(defrule
  (and starter-malfunction
       not-jump-between-battery-and-starter
       no-hydrostatic-lock)
  (replace-starter 0.9)
  :GOAL)
```

```
;;; starter and battery eliminated
(defrule (and engine-wont-start
               engine-turns-over-normally
               engine-doesnt-fire-when-starting)
  (engine-wont-fire 1))

(defrule (not engine-wont-fire)
  (engine-does-fire 1))

(defrule (not engine-wont-start)
  (engine-does-start 1))

(defrule (and engine-does-start
               engine-misfires)
  (engine-runs-but-misfires 1))

(defrule (and engine-wont-start
               engine-does-fire)
  (engine-wont-start-but-does-fire 1))

(defrule (or engine-wont-start-but-does-fire
             engine-runs-but-misfires)
  (engine-wont-start-or-misfires 1))

;;; coil or high tension lead
(defrule
  (and engine-wont-fire
       no-spark-at-spark-plug-wires
       no-spark-at-high-tension-lead)
  (ignition-coil-or-high-tension-lead-defective 1))

(defrule
  (and ignition-coil-or-high-tension-lead-defective
       high-tension-lead-cracked-or-too-much-resistance)
  (replace-high-tension-lead 1)
  :GOAL)

(defrule
  (not high-tension-lead-cracked-or-too-much-resistance)
  (high-tension-lead-ok 1))

(defrule (and ignition-coil-or-high-tension-lead-defective
              high-tension-lead-ok)
  (replace-ignition-coil 1)
  :GOAL)

;;; plug wires
(defrule
  (not spark-at-some-spark-plug-wires)
  (no-spark-at-spark-plug-wires 1))

(defrule
  (not spark-at-all-spark-plug-wires)
  (not-spark-at-all-spark-plug-wires 1))

(defrule
  (and engine-wont-start-or-misfires
       not-spark-at-all-spark-plug-wires
       spark-at-some-spark-plug-wires)
  (distributor-cap-or-spark-plug-wires-bad 0.9))
```

```
(defrule (and distributor-cap-or-spark-plug-wires-bad
               spark-plug-wires-cracked-or-too-much-resistance)
             (replace-spark-plug-wires 0.9)
             :GOAL)

(defrule (and distributor-cap-or-spark-plug-wires-bad
               distributor-cap-cracked-or-burned-or-rotor-bad)
         (replace-distributor-cap-and-rotor 0.9)
  :GOAL)

;;; hydrostatic lock
(defrule
  (or coolant-in-oil
      coolant-in-cylinders)
  (hydrostatic-lock 1))

(defrule (not hydrostatic-lock)
  (no-hydrostatic-lock 1))

(defrule
  (and starter-malfunction
       not-jump-between-battery-and-starter
       hydrostatic-lock)
  ((SEALS :SUBSTANCE "coolant" :LEAKS-TO "cylinders"
          :PREFIX
          "Hydrostatic lock is preventing the engine from ~
          turning over.") 1)
  :GOAL :FUNCTION)

;;; fuel delivery
(defrule (and engine-wont-start
              fuel-to-carb
              throttle-bore-of-carb-filled-with-fuel
              gasoline-odor)
  (engine-flooded 0.9)
  :GOAL)

(defrule
  (and fuel-flows-from-pump)
  (fuel-to-carb 1))

(defrule (not fuel-to-carb)
  (no-fuel-to-carb 1))

(defrule (and engine-wont-start
              no-fuel-to-carb
              gasoline-odor)
  ((SEALS :SUBSTANCE "fuel" :LEAKS-TO "world"
     :PREFIX
  "A fuel leak is preventing fuel from reaching the carburetor.")
  0.6)
  :GOAL :FUNCTION)

(defrule
  (and fuel-pump-suction)
  (fuel-pump-works 1))

(defrule (and engine-wont-start
              no-fuel-to-carb
              fuel-pump-works)
```

```
      (out-of-gas 0.7)
      :GOAL)

(defrule (not fuel-pump-works)
   (fuel-pump-doesnt-work 1))

(defrule (and engine-wont-start
        no-fuel-to-carb
        fuel-pump-doesnt-work)
   (replace-fuel-pump 1)
   :GOAL)

;;; timing
(defrule
   (and engine-runs-but-misfires
        spark-at-all-spark-plug-wires
        timing-marks-off)
   (adjust-timing 1)
   :GOAL)

(defrule
   (and engine-runs-but-misfires
        spark-at-all-spark-plug-wires
        crimping-vacuum-line-makes-no-difference)
   (replace-vacuum-advance 0.9)
   :GOAL)

;;; oil on plugs
(defrule (and engine-wont-start-or-misfires
             spark-plug-electrodes-fouled-with-oil)
             ((SEALS :SUBSTANCE "oil" :LEAKS-TO "cylinders"
             :PREFIX
             "The spark plugs are fouled with oil.") 0.6)
   :GOAL :FUNCTION)

;;; low compression
(defrule
   (and engine-wont-start-or-misfires
        low-compression
        squirting-oil-raises-compression)
   (piston-rings-corroded 0.8)
   :GOAL)

(defrule
   (not squirting-oil-raises-compression)
   (squirting-oil-doesnt-raise-compression 1))

(defrule
   (and engine-wont-start-or-misfires
        low-compression
        squirting-oil-doesnt-raise-compression)
   (burned-or-sticking-valves 0.8)
   :GOAL)

(defrule (and engine-wont-start-or-misfires
             low-compression
             low-compression-two-adjacent-cylinders)
   (head-gasket-blown 0.8)
   :GOAL)
```

```
;;; predetonation and dieselling
(defrule  (and engine-does-start
                engine-pings-or-knocks)
  (timing-advanced 0.8)
  :GOAL)

(defrule (or engine-diesels
             engine-pings-or-knocks)
  (detonation 1))

(defrule (and engine-does-start
              detonation)
  (carbon-on-cylinder-head 0.8)
  :GOAL)

;;; carburetion
(defrule (and engine-does-start
              engine-stalls-or-sluggish)
  (replace-air-and-or-fuel-filters 0.5)
  :GOAL)

(defrule (and engine-does-start
              engine-hesitates
              pumping-gas-no-jets)
         (adjust-accelerator-pump 0.9)
         :GOAL)

(defrule (or engine-stalls
             engine-hesitates)
  (engine-stalls-or-sluggish 1))

(defrule (and engine-runs-but-misfires)
  (mixture-bad 0.5)
  :GOAL)

;;; seals
(defseal "piston rings"
         "oil"
         "cylinders")

(defseal "valve seals"
         "oil"
         "cylinders")

(defseal "head gasket"
         '("oil" "coolant")
         '("cylinders" "world"))

(defseal "radiator"
         "coolant"
         "world")

(defseal "water pump"
         "coolant"
         "world")

(defseal "exhaust system"
         "exhaust fumes"
         "world")
```

```
(defseal "radiator hoses"
         "coolant"
         "world")
(defseal "fuel tank"
         "fuel"
         "world")
(defseal "fuel hoses"
         "fuel"
         "world")
```

CHAPTER HIGHLIGHTS

Major Concepts

- Expert systems are programs that contain knowledge that a human expert would have about a domain.

- Most expert systems consist of rules containing their knowledge and an inference engine, which searches the rules.

- The two most common strategies for searching through rules are forward chaining and backward chaining.

  –Forward chaining is fact driven.

  –Forward chaining is best for systems in which the user can easily specify all pertinent information at the beginning of the session.

  –Backward chaining is goal driven.

  –Backward chaining is best for situations in which information needs to be drawn from the user step by step.

EXERCISE

1. Modify Otto so that after it prints out a question the user can ask it what it is currently trying to prove.

Annotated Bibliography

This bibliography is selective rather than exhaustive; it cites books and articles whose connection to the current book is very clear. The truly curious reader is referred to the excellent and complete bibliographies in many of these books.

Guy L. Steele Jr., COMMON LISP: *The Language* (Bedford, MA: Digital Press, 1984) specifies the language used in this book and is necessary for anyone wishing to learn more. The NIL language, which is currently a super-set of COMMON LISP and was an influence on its design, is documented in Glenn S. Burke, George J. Carrette, and Christopher R. Eliot, *The* NIL *Reference Manual* (Technical Report 311, MIT Laboratory for Computer Science, 1984).

Documentation of other implementations of LISP that were influences on COMMON LISP includes: David Moon, Richard Stallman, and Daniel Weinreb, *LISP Machine Manual, Sixth Edition* (Technical Report, MIT Artificial Intelligence Laboratory, 1984); Harold Abelson et al., *The Revised Revised Report on Scheme or an UnCommon Lisp* (AI Memo 848, MIT Artificial Intelligence Laboratory, 1985); Kent M. Pitman, *The Revised MACLISP Manual* (Technical Report, MIT Laboratory for Computer Science, 1983); Warren Teitelman, *INTERLISP Reference Manual*; (Technical Report, Xerox Palo Alto Research Center, 1974); and Utah Symbolic Computation Group, *The Portable Standard LISP* (Technical Report 10, Department of Computer Science, University of Utah, 1982). Most of these dialects are still in use and new reports are issued from time to time.

The best book about programming in LISP (and possibly in any language) is Harold Abelson and Gerald J. Sussman, *Structure and Interpretation of Computer Programs* (Cambridge, MA: MIT Press, 1985). This book is written in the SCHEME dialect. Engineering and design principles are presented clearly and in depth, and a case is made for their importance in practical programming. John Allen, *Anatomy of LISP* (New York: McGraw-Hill, 1978), has an excellent exposition of programming techniques, although the LISP implementation techniques described are somewhat out of date.

273

Important survey books about artificial intelligence include: Avron Barr, Edward A. Feigenbaum, and Paul R. Cohen, *The Handbook of Artificial Intelligence*, 3 vols. (Los Altos, CA: William Kaufmann, 1981); Frederick Hayes-Roth, Donald A. Waterman, and Douglas B. Lenat, eds., *Building Expert Systems* (Reading, MA: Addison-Wesley, 1983), Nils J.Nilsson, *Principles of Artificial Intelligence* (Palo Alto, CA: Tioga Press, 1980); and Patrick Henry Winston, *Artificial Intelligence*, 2d ed. (Reading, MA: Addison-Wesley, 1984).

Papers and articles about related topics include: Alan Kay, "Computer Software," *Scientific American* 251, 3 (September 1984) and Joseph Weizenbaum, "Eliza—A Computer Program for the Study of Natural Language Communication Between Man and Machine," *Communications of the ACM* 9, 1 (January 1965).

LOGO is a LISP-like language intended for use by people with little computer experience. Many of the examples in this book are influenced by the wealth of thought about writing examples collected at the MIT LOGO Group and reflected in Harold Abelson, *Logo for the Apple II* (Peterborough NH: BYTE/McGraw-Hill, 1982), and Cynthia Solomon, Margaret Minsky, and Brian Harvey, eds., *Logoworks* (New York: McGraw-Hill, 1986).

Appendix

Solutions to the Exercises

CHAPTER 2

1.   a. symbol
    b. list of 4 symbols
    c. list of 4 symbols
    d. list of 2 lists
    e. number
    f. list of 1 number
    g. list of a symbol and a number
    h. list of three elements
    i. malformed expression
    j. string
    k. character
    l. malformed expression
    m. string
    n. list
    o. list
    p. list
    q. malformed expression
    r. malformed expression

2. Sample explanation: A is a symbol, LISP will return its value (unless it doesn't have one, in which case LISP will signal an error). 'A is a quoted symbol. LISP will return A, the symbol itself. #\A is of a different data type, a character. LISP will return #\A, the character itself.

3. a. 2
    b. 15
    c. 4

4. a. d

  b. (g r s)

  c. (purple 1)

  d. ((size-of-hall 250))

  e. (oil vinegar)

  f. (#\b)

  g. (("marsh" 43))

  h. b

  i. 4th

  j. CLASSICAL

  k. (rent (+ (* 1/3 actual-rent) parking-space))

  l. (cdr ((a b) (c d) (e f)))

  m. car

  n. (car (car (cdr (cdr ((strawberry-protein-drink)
                         (vitamin-d) (acerola))))))

  o. (#\return #\tab)

  p. 6

  q. pears

  r. QUOTE

5. the second

6. a. (car (cdr (cdr '(table lamp chair shelf))))

  b. (car (car (cdr '((table lamp) (chair terminal)))))

  c. (car (car (car (cdr (cdr '(terminal (shelf)
                                ((chair)) (((sofa))))))))))

  d. (car (cdr (car '((((table) file-cabinet)
                      chair) telephone))))

7. a. yes

  b. yes

  c. no

  d. no

8. a. Figure A-1. (apples . (bananas . (strawberries . nil)))

  b. Figure A-2. (values . ((first-value . (second-value . nil)) . nil))

  c. Figure A-3. ((my-symbol . ("my-string" . nil)) . (#\C . nil))

9. a. Figure A-4.

  b. Figure A-5.

10. a. Figure A-6.

  b. Figure A-7.

  c. Figure A-8.

    d. Figure A-9.
    e. Figure A-10.
    f. Figure A-11.
    g. Figure A-12.
    h. Figure A-13.
    i. Figure A-14.
    j. Figure A-15.
    k. Figure A-16.
    l. Figure A-17.

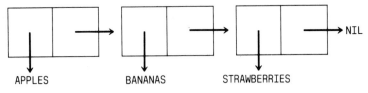

Figure A-1

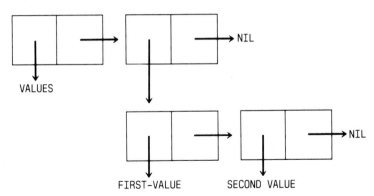

Figure A-2

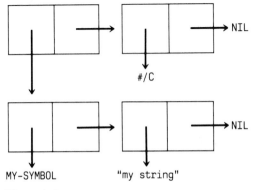

Figure A-3

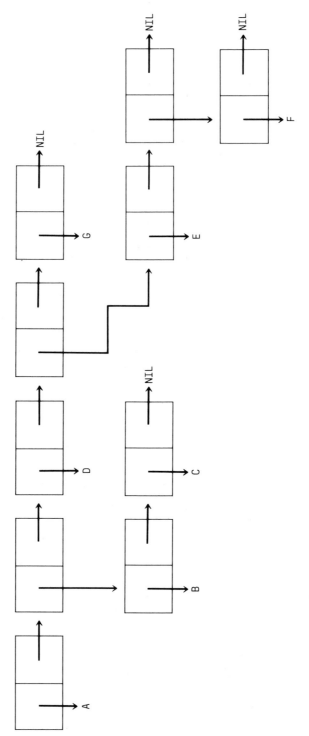

Figure A-4

279

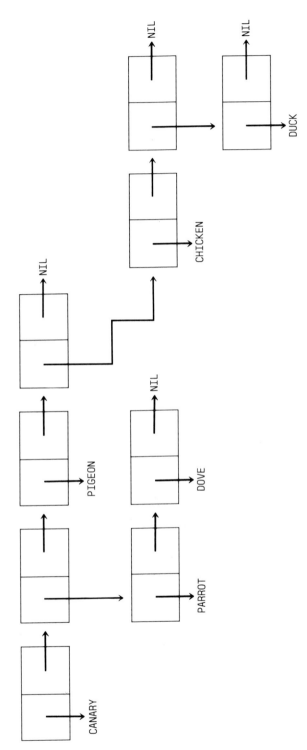

Figure A-5

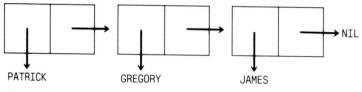

Figure A-6

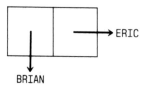

Figure A-7

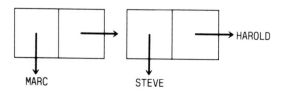

Figure A-8

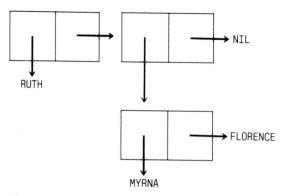

Figure A-9

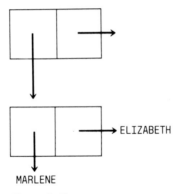

MARLENE

Figure A-10

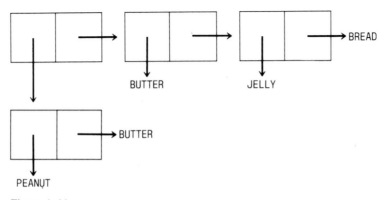

PEANUT

Figure A-11

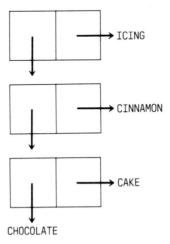

CHOCOLATE

Figure A-12

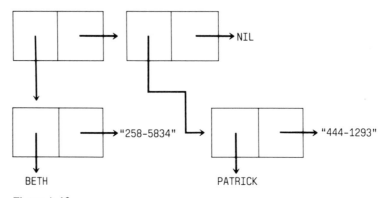

Figure A-13

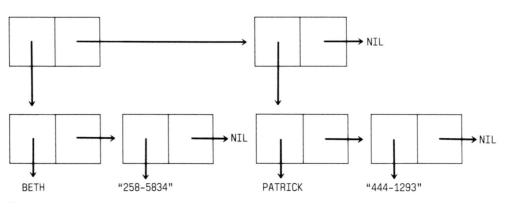

Figure A-14

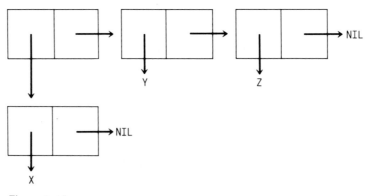

Figure A-15

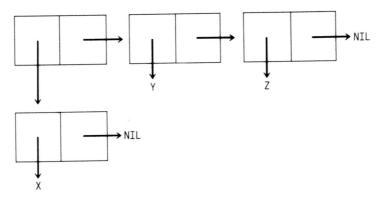

Figure A-16

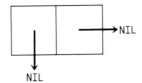

Figure A-17

11. (a)(car . ((quote . (a . nil)) . nil)) <=> (car (quote a))
    (b)(+ . (3 . (4 . nil))) <=> (+ 3 4)

CHAPTER 3

1. a. This will result in the signalling of an error, since it doesn't make sense to ask
   if two symbols are numerically equal.
   b. NIL
   c. NIL
   d. T
   e. NIL
   f. T
   g. NIL
   h. T
   i. T
   j. T
   k. T
   l. NIL
   m. 3
   n. T

    o. NIL

    p. 0

2.
```
(defun list-circle-facts (r)
    (list r (circumference r) (circle-area r)))

(defun circle-area (r)
  (* pi (sq r)))

(defun circumference (r)
  (* 2 pi r))

(defun sq (x)
  (* x x))
```

3.
```
(defun average (x y)
  (/ (+ x y) 2))
```

4. The original arguments look like Figure A-18. (a (b c) (e ((f)))) and
   ((g h) i r)

   The new list returned looks like Figure A-19. (a (b c) (e ((f))) (g h) i r)

5.
```
(defun schedule (day)
   (case day
      ((monday wednesday friday) '((vector-calculus "9:30-11:00")
                                   (physics "11:00-12:00")
                                   (phys-ed "3:00-4:00")))
       (tuesday '((economics "10:00-11:00")
                  (physics-lab "5:30-7:00")))
       (thursday '((economics "10:00-11:00")))
       ((saturday sunday) nil)))
```

6.
```
(defun dress-for-success (list-of-attributes)
    (if (and (member 'dress-shoes list-of-attributes)
             (not (member 'socks list-of-attributes)))
        (format t "Don't wear white socks!~%"))
    (if (member 'striped list-of-attributes)
        (format t "Don't wear plaids too.~%"))
    (if (member 'plaids list-of-attributes)
        (format t "Don't wear stripes too.~%"))
    (if (and (member 'pink list-of-attributes)
             (member 'purple list-of-attributes))
        (format t "Have you thought about ~
                   more subdued colors?~%")))
```

   The interesting thing about these conditions is that they are not mutually exclusive,
   as they would be if COND had been used.

7.
```
(defun a-or-an (string)
    (case (char string 0)
       ((#\a #\e #\i #\o #\u #\y) (format nil "an ~a" string))
       ((#\A #\E #\I #\O #\U #\Y) (format nil "an ~a" string))
       (t (format nil "a ~a" string))))
```

8. This answer does not reflect the most elegant way to solve the problem in LISP;
   however, it does confine itself to constructs already introduced.

```
(defun lookup-cost (weight zone)
  (case zone
    ((1 2) (close-zone-lookup weight))
    (3 (zone-3-lookup weight))
    (4 (zone-4-lookup weight))
    (5 (zone-5-lookup weight))
    (6 (zone-6-lookup weight))
    (t "Information about that zone
is temporarily unavailable.")))

(defun close-zone-lookup (weight)
  (cond ((<= weight 1) "First class: 2.24, Fourth class: 1.55")
        ((<= weight 2) "First class: 2.54, Fourth class: 1.55")
        ((<= weight 3) "First class: 3.01, Fourth class: 1.63")
        ((<= weight 4) "First class: 3.49, Fourth class: 1.71")
        (t "Information about weights over 4 lb. is unavailable")))

(defun zone-3-lookup (weight)
  (cond ((<= weight 1) "First class: 2.24, Fourth class: 1.61")
        ((<= weight 2) "First class: 2.54, Fourth class: 1.63")
        ((<= weight 3) "First class: 3.01, Fourth class: 1.73")
        ((<= weight 4) "First class: 3.49, Fourth class: 1.84")
        (t "Information about weights over 4 lb. is unavailable.")))

(defun zone-4-lookup (weight)
  (cond ((<= weight 1) "First class: 2.24, Fourth class: 1.70")
        ((<= weight 2) "First class: 2.70, Fourth class: 1.70")
        ((<= weight 3) "First class: 3.25, Fourth class: 1.86")
        ((<= weight 4) "First class: 3.81, Fourth class: 2.02")
        (t "Information about weights over 4 lb. is unavailable.")))

(defun zone-5-lookup (weight)
  (cond ((<= weight 1) "First class: 2.24, Fourth class: 1.83")
        ((<= weight 2) "First class: 2.88, Fourth class: 1.83")
        ((<= weight 3) "First class: 3.53, Fourth class: 2.06")
        ((<= weight 4) "First class: 4.18, Fourth class: 2.29")
        (t "Information about weights over 4 lb. is unavailable.")))

(defun zone-6-lookup (weight)
  (cond ((<= weight 1) "First class: 2.34, Fourth class: 1.99")
        ((<= weight 2) "First class: 3.09, Fourth class: 1.99")
        ((<= weight 3) "First class: 3.85, Fourth class: 2.30")
        ((<= weight 4) "First class: 4.60, Fourth class: 2.61")
        (t "Information about weights over 4 lb. is unavailable.")))
```

CHAPTER 4

1. a. "Oh no!"

   b. I want 3 ORANGES

   c. 3, because the assignment of variables inside a LET is done in parallel, so the special (global) value of X is seen. None of the assignments are available to the others.

   d. "I have 3 Cortland apples."

   APPLE-STATISTICS is called in an environment in which Y is 4; however, it was

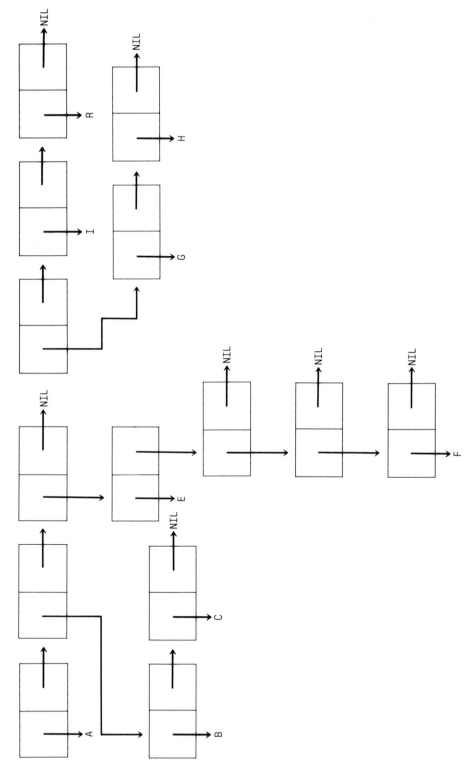

286

Figure A-18

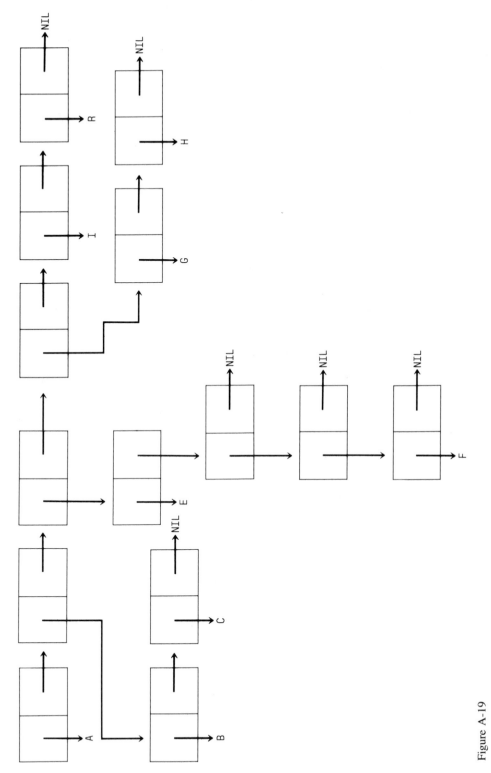

Figure A-19

defined in an environment in which Y was 3. In a lexically scoped system, the environment of definition is the crucial factor.

2.
```
(defun test1 ()
   (let  ((a 3))            ; gives A the value 3
     (let ((a 4) (b 1))     ; gives A the value 4 and B the value 1
       (print (+ a b)))     ; prints 5
     (print a)))            ; prints 3, returns 3

(defun test2 ()
   (let ((a 3))             ; gives A the value 3
     (let ((a 4)(b 1))      ; gives A the value 4 and B the value 1
       (setf a 16)          ; gives the inner A the value 16
       (print (+ a b)))     ; prints 17
     (print a)))            ; prints and returns 3
```

The inner one binding is changed.

3. Figure A-20.

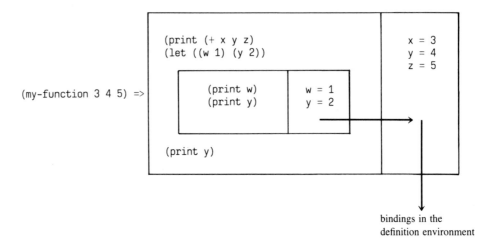

```
(my-function 3 4 5)
12
1
2
4
4
```

4.
```
(defun bow (arrow)
   (defun shoot ()
      (print arrow)))
BOW

(bow "my-arrow")
SHOOT
```

```
(shoot)
"my-arrow"

(shoot)
"my-arrow"
```

ARROW is in the environment in which SHOOT was defined, and therefore always accessible by SHOOT. SHOOT is defined at top level because DEFUN by definition affects the top-level environment.

Note that this is not usually done in quite this way. It is possible to make local definitions with FLET (function let) and with LOCAL. It is also possible to make functions on the fly using LAMBDA. LAMBDA will be presented in chapter 8.

5. a. CHOCOLATE

   b. CHOCOLATE

   c. (vanilla chocolate strawberry mint-chocolate-chip)

   d. (mint-chocolate-chip)

6. The easy way to make this change is to add the item at the end:

   Constructor:

   ```
   (defun make-bike (x wheel-size gear-ratio color)
       (list x wheel-size gear-ratio color))
   ```

   Selector:

   ```
   (defun color (bike)
       (car (cdr (cdr (cdr bike)))))
   ```

   Modifier:

   ```
   (defun set-color (bike newcolor)
       (setf (cadddr bike) newcolor))
   ```

   The hard ways to make this change happen if you add the new attribute anywhere but at the end because you then have to rewrite some or all of the other selectors and constructors.

CHAPTER 5

1. ```
   (trace tower-of-hanoi)
   (TOWER-OF-HANOI)
   ```

   ```
   (tower-of-hanoi 3 'a 'b 'c)
   ```

   ```
   #11: (TOWER-OF-HANOI 3 A B C)
   . #27: (TOWER-OF-HANOI 2 A C B)
   . . #43: (TOWER-OF-HANOI 1 A B C)
   Move a disk from A to B.
   . . #43==> NIL
   Move a disk from A to C.
   . . #43: (TOWER-OF-HANOI 1 B C A)
   ```
   ```

```
Move a disk from B to C.
. . #43==> NIL
. #27==> NIL
Move a disk from A to B.
. #27: (TOWER-OF-HANOI 2 C B A)
. . #43: (TOWER-OF-HANOI 1 C A B)
Move a disk from C to A.
. . #43==> NIL
Move a disk from C to B.
. . #43: (TOWER-OF-HANOI 1 A B C)
Move a disk from A to B.
. . #43==> NIL
. #27==> NIL
#11==> NIL
NIL
```

2. ```
(defun my-nth (list item)
   (cond ((= item 0) (car list))
         (t (my-nth (cdr list) (- item 1)))))
```

3. ```
(defun get-member (object list)
   (cond ((null list) nil)
         ((equal object (car list)) list)
         (t (get-member object (cdr list)))))
```

4. ```
(defun filter (list item)
   (cond ((null list) nil)
         ((eql (car list) item) (filter (cdr list) item))
         (t (cons (car list) (filter (cdr list) item)))))
```

5. ```
(defun my-append (list1 list2)
   (cond ((null list1) list2)
         (t (cons (car list1) (my-append (cdr list1)
                                          list2)))))
```

Note that it might be nice to be able to call MY-APPEND with an atom and a list. It would simple to enlarge it as follows:

```
(defun my-append (list1 list2)
   (cond ((null list1) list2)
         ((atom list1) (cons list1 list2))
         (t (cons (car list1) (my-append (cdr list1)
                                          list2)))))
```

6. ```
(defun my-reverse (list)
   (cond ((null (cdr list)) list)
         (t (append (my-reverse (cdr list))
                    (cons (car list) nil)))))
```

7. ```
(defun my-reverse (list)
   (do ((current-list list (cdr current-list))
        (accumulator '() (cons (car current-list)
                               accumulator)))
       ((null current-list) accumulator)))
```

8. (defun my-average (list)
     (do ((yet-to-do list (cdr yet-to-do))
          (accumulator 0 (+ accumulator (car yet-to-do)))
          (counter 0 (+ counter 1)))
         ((null yet-to-do) (/ accumulator counter))))

9. (defun pump-all-pedals (bike-list)
      (do ((current-list bike-list (cdr current-list)))
          ((null current-list) nil)
        (pump-pedals (car current-list))))

10. (defun race-bikes (bike-list)
       (do ((current-list bike-list (cdr current-list)))
           ((null current-list) nil)
         (iterate-pump (car current-list))))

    (defun iterate-pump (bike)
       (do ((counter (random 10) (- counter 1)))
           ((zerop counter) nil)
         (pump-pedals bike)))

Another way to do this involves the DOTIMES construct:

    (defun iterate-pump (bike)
       (dotimes (i (random 10)) (pump-pedals bike)))

CHAPTER 6

1. (defun get-and-count ()
     (format t "Please type a number greater than 0.~%")
     (let ((answer (read)))
       (cond ((<= answer 0) (get-and-count))
             (t (do ((current-number answer (- current-number 1)))
                    ((= current-number 0) nil)
                  (print current-number))))))

2. (defun get-and-count ()
     (format t "Please type in a number.~%")
     (let ((answer (read)))
       (if (> answer 0) (count-down answer) (count-up answer))))

   (defun count-down (answer)
      (do ((current-number answer (- current-number 1)))
          ((= current-number 0) nil)
        (print current-number)))

   (defun count-up (answer)
      (do ((current-number answer (+ current-number 1)))
          ((= current-number 0) nil)
        (print current-number)))

Another way to solve this problem is to replace the constant 1 in the solution to the
previous problem with (signum answer). SIGNUM returns -1 if its argument is negative,
1 if it is positive, and 0 if it is zero.

3. ```
(defun get-and-count ()
   (format t "Please type in a number.~%")
   (let ((answer (read)))
    (if (not (numberp answer)) (get-and-count)
      (if (> answer 0) (count-down answer) (count-up answer)))))
```

In general, you should avoid many levels of nested conditionals. These are very simple, so it's reasonable to have two, but any more complexity would be stretching things.

4. ```
(defun read-with-a-or-an ()
   (format t "Please type in a word.~%")
   (let ((string (read-line)))
    (case (char string 0)
      ((#\a #\e #\i #\o #\u #\y) (format nil "an ~A" string))
      (t (format nil "a ~A" string)))))
```

5. By printing it with PRIN1 or by examining the characters at indexes 20 and 26.

6. a. Here is one good answer:

```
(defun learn (old-node)
   (format t "~%Oh well, I give up.  ~
What was the answer?~%")
   ;; examine-animal must return a symbol
   (let ((new-animal (examine-animal (read-line))))
     (format t "~%Please type a question whose answer
is yes for ~A and no for ~A.~%"
               (a-or-an new-animal)
               (a-or-an (animal old-node)))
     (let ((new-question (read-line)))
        (add new-question
           (animal old-node)
           new-animal
           old-node))))

;;; EXAMINE-ANIMAL takes a string and returns the symbol that is
;;; most likely to contain the actual name of the animal.
(defun examine-animal (string)
  (let ((list (list-from-string string)))
    (cond ((= 1 (length list)) (car list))
          ((or (eq (car list) 'a) (eq (car list) 'an))
           (cadr list))
          (t (car list)))))

;;; LIST-FROM-STRING returns a list with all the
;;; contents read from a string.
(defun list-from-string (string)
  (with-input-from-string (my-stream string)
     (let ((eof (list 'eof)))
        (do ((current-object (read my-stream nil eof)
                             (read my-stream nil eof))
             (accumulator nil))
            ((eq current-object eof) (nreverse accumulator))
          (push current-object accumulator)))))
```

b.
```
(defun examine-animal (string)
    (let ((list (list-from-string string)))
      (cond ((= 1 (length list)) (car list))
            ((or (eq (car list) 'a) (eq (car list) 'an))
             (put-together-name (cdr list)))
            (t (put-together-name list)))))
;;; PUT-TOGETHER-NAME takes a list of symbols and returns
;;; one symbol, whose name consists of all the
;;; old symbols stuck together with separating hyphens.
(defun put-together-name (list)
    (do ((current-list (cdr list) (cdr current-list))
         (accumulator (format nil "~a" (car list))
            (format nil "~a-~a" accumulator (car current-list))))
        ((null current-list)
         (with-input-from-string (my-stream accumulator)
           (read my-stream)))))
```

To make this nicer, you can make symbols print out without the hyphens. However, before you do that, you would probably want to start storing the animal's
name as a string. COMMON LISP contains many string functions that make this
type of manipulation easy, including, for example, STRING-TRIM, STRING-UPCASE,
STRING-DOWNCASE, SUBSEQ, SEARCH, and REMOVE.

c.
```
(defun learn (old-node)
    (format t "~%Oh well, I give up.  ~
What was the answer?~%")
      ;; EXAMINE-ANIMAL returns a symbol.
      (let ((new-animal (examine-animal (read-line))))
        (format t "~%Please type a question whose answer
is yes for ~A and no for ~A.~%"
              (a-or-an new-animal)
              (a-or-an (animal old-node)))
        (let ((new-question (remove-question-marks (read-line))))
          (add new-question
              (animal old-node)
              new-animal
              old-node))))
;;; REMOVE-QUESTION-MARKS returns a string with any question
;;; marks removed
(defun remove-question-marks (string)
    (delete #\? string))
```

d.
```
(defun init-animal ()
        (format t "~%This is a game.  Think of an animal and I
will try to guess what it is by asking questions.~1%")
        (do () ((main-loop *animal-data*))))

(defun play-again? ()
    (format t "~%Do you want to play again?~%")
    (let ((response (read-line)))
      (cond ((equalp response "yes") nil)
            ((equalp response "no")
```

```
                    (format t "~%Come back soon now, y'hear?~%")
                    t)
                   (t (format t "~%I guess that's a no.  ~
    Well, goodbye.~%")
                      t))))
```

Note that MAIN-LOOP is also recursive and could be made iterative.

e. ```
   ;;; *KNOWLEDGE-FILE* will hold the name of the file
   ;;; where the knowledge list is stored.

   (defconstant *knowledge-file* "ANIMAL.DAT")

   ;;; INIT-ANIMAL starts everything.
   (defun init-animal ()
     (format t "~%This is a game. Think of an animal and I
   will try to guess what it is by asking questions.~1%")
     (do () ((let ((*knowledge*
                     (if (open "animal.dat" :direction :probe)
                         (with-open-file (input-file *knowledge-file*
                                                     :direction :input)
                           (read input-file))
                         animal-data)))
               (main-loop *knowledge*)
               (with-open-file (output-file *knowledge-file*
                                            :direction :output
                                            :if-exists :supersede)
                 (format output-file "~S" *knowledge*))
               (play-again?)))))
```

```
(defun guess (knowledge)
  (format t "~%Is it ~A?~%" (a-or-an (animal knowledge)))
    (let ((answer (read-line)))
      (cond ((equalp answer "yes") (gloat))
            ((equalp answer "no") (learn knowledge))
            (t (format nil "~%Please type yes or no.~%")
               (guess knowledge)))))
```

CHAPTER 7

2. ```
   (defun get-pair (list indicator)
     (let ((forward-search (assoc indicator list)))
       (if (null forward-search)
           (reverse-pair (rassoc indicator list))
         forward-search)))
   ```

```
   (defun reverse-pair (property)
     (if (null property) nil
       (cons (cdr property) (car property))))
```

Another approach would be to have it keep a list with the pairs each way.

3. ```
   (defun update-info (item)
     (format t "~%What is the opposite of ~(~a~)?~%(Type
   ~s if you want to skip this one.)~%" item)
   ```
   ```

```
         (let ((response (read)))
           (if (eq response 's) nil
             (setf *opposite-list* (acons item response
                                          *opposite-list*)))))))
```

4. `(defun my-acons (item value list)`
   `(cons (cons item value) list))`

5. Here is one good solution:

```
(defvar *pronouns* '((I . you) (me . you) (my . your)
   (you . I) (your . my)))

(defun I-you (list)
  (if (null list) nil
    (cons (switch-or-return (car list))
          (I-you (cdr list)))))

(defun switch-or-return (item)
  (or (cdr (assoc item *pronouns*))
      item))
```

It is not necessary to give a name to the list of words to be switched since the list is so short. Nonetheless, it's a good idea to give it a name so that you can change it on the fly if you find it unsatisfactory.

It might also be reasonable to search the list of pronouns both normally and in reverse and reduce its length by half.

6. ```
(defstruct (manager (:conc-name important-)
                     (:include person))
           reports-written
           (former-engineer t))

(defun initialize-project ()
  (dotimes (i (random 7)) ; make up to seven employees
    (if (eql (random 2) 0)   ; one time in two make a manager
        (employ (make-manager :age (+ 27 (random 20))))
        ;; the other time, make a programmer
        (employ
         (make-software-engineer :age (+ 22 (random 20)))))))

(defun who-is-on-staff? (list)
  (do ((remainder list (cdr remainder))
       (accumulator nil (acons
                          (if (manager-p (car remainder))
                              'manager 'software-engineer)
                          (person-age (car remainder))
                          accumulator)))
      ((null remainder) accumulator)))
```

7. ```
;;; *WORDS* is the default table used by the dictionary.
(defvar *words*)

;;; *INITIAL-LIST* contains the words and definitions loaded by
;;; the dictionary initially.
```

```
(defvar *initial-list*
        '((intend "to have in mind")
          (list "the basic combinatory unit of LISP")
          (symbol "something that represents something else")
          (yclept "known as or called")))

;;;; INIT initializes the dictionary program.  It assumes that
;;;; you want the table *WORDS* with the words in *INITIAL-LIST*.
(defun init ()
  (format t "~%Welcome to the dictionary program.~%")
  (setf *words* (make-hash-table))
  (init-dictionary *words* *initial-list*)
  (how-to)
  (main-loop *words*))

;;; Recursively put all the elements from the initial list
;;; into the hash table.
(defun init-dictionary (table list)
  (dolist (item list)
   (put-word table (car item) (cadr item))))

;;; GET-WORD takes a table and a word and gets the definition
;;; of the word from the table.  If the word is not found, it
;;; returns a message.
(defun get-word (table word)
  (or (gethash word table)
      (format nil "The word ~a is not in the dictionary."
              word)))

;;; PUT-WORD takes a table, a word, and a definition and puts
;;; the word and the definition into the table.
(defun put-word (table word definition)
  (setf (gethash word table) definition))

;;; REMOVE-WORD takes a table and a word and removes the
;;; word from the table.
(defun remove-word (table word)
  (remhash word table))

;;; MAIN-LOOP runs the program.  It gets a command, looks it up,
;;; executes it and loops.   This can be done more concisely
;;; using the Common LISP function LOOP.
(defun main-loop (table)
  (format t "~%Command> ")
  (let ((answer (read-char)))
    (case answer
      (#\a (put-word table (prompt-for-word)
                           (prompt-for-definition))
           (main-loop table))
      (#\e nil)
      (#\l (print (get-word table (prompt-for-word)))
           (main-loop table))
      (#\r (remove-word table (prompt-for-word))
           (main-loop table))
      (#\? (how-to) (main-loop table))
      ((#\newline #\space #\tab) (main-loop table))
      (t (format t "~%~a is not a known command. ~%  Please ~
```

```
      type a command or ? for a list of commands.~%" answer)
            (main-loop table)))))

;;; HOW-TO is help for the program.
(defun how-to ()
  (format t "~%Please type one of the following: ~%~
             A to add a word~%~
             E to exit~%~
             L to look up a word~%~
             R to remove a word~%~
             or ? for this list.~%"))

;;; PROMPT-FOR-WORD gets a word from the user and returns it.
;;; It checks to make sure that the thing typed is, in fact,
;;; a symbol.

(defun prompt-for-word ()
  (format t "What word are you interested in? ~%")
  (let ((word (read)))
    (if (symbolp word) word
        (prompt-for-word))))

;;; PROMPT-FOR-DEFINITION gets a string from the user.
(defun prompt-for-definition ()
  (format t "~%Please type a definition and push <RETURN>:~%")
  (read-line))
```

8.
```
   ;;; This is a game called ANIMAL
   (defstruct (node (:conc-name nil))
      (question)
      (yes-branch)
      (no-branch))

   (defun animal (node)
      (question node))

   (defvar *animal-data*
     (make-node
         :question "Does it sing"
         :yes-branch (make-node
                         :question 'canary)
         :no-branch (make-node
                         :question
                         "Could it have spots"
                         :yes-branch (make-node :question 'dog)
                         :no-branch
                         (make-node
                             :question "Does it lay eggs"
                             :yes-branch (make-node :question
                                                     'chicken)
                             :no-branch (make-node :question
                                                    'dolphin)))))

   (defun add (new-question old-animal new-animal node)
     (setf (question node) new-question)
     (setf (yes-branch node) (make-node :question new-animal))
     (setf (no-branch node) (make-node :question old-animal)))
```

CHAPTER 8

1. ```
(defun my-assoc (item a-list test)
   (cond ((null a-list) nil)
         ((funcall test item (caar a-list)) (car a-list))
         (t (my-assoc item (cdr a-list) test))))
```

2. ```
(defun convert-to-centigrade (list)
   (mapcar #'(lambda (degrees-fahrenheit)
                (* (- degrees-fahrenheit 32)
                   5/9))
           list))
```

This solution prints out the numbers as rational numbers. You can convert them to floating point with the function FLOAT.

3. FOO will return a lexical closure that contains the lambda expression and in which X is bound to 5 because that was its binding when the function object was created. BAR will return 15, since X is bound to 5 inside the lambda expression, and Y is bound to 3 inside BAR. Remember that LISP evaluates the arguments to FUNCALL before actually executing it; this means that FUNCALL acts not upon FOO, but rather upon the lexical closure produced by the call to FOO.

4. Both of these work:

```
(defun get-bicycle (method list)
   (mapcar method list))
```

```
(defun get-bicycle (method list)
   (if (null list) nil
       (cons (funcall method (car list))
             (get-bicycle method (cdr list)))))
```

5. ```
(defvar *initial-commands*
    '((print-file . my-print-file)
      (delete-file . my-delete-file)
      (exit . my-exit)
      (help . my-help)
      (? . my-help)
      (add-command . add-command)))

(defun add-command ()
  (format t "~% What do you want the command called? ~% ~
          It must be one word. Type return to end.~%")
  (let ((name (read-from-string (read-line))))
    (format t "~%Type the name of the LISP procedure you want ~
            executed.~%")
    (let ((function-name (read-from-string (read-line))))
      ;; Put it on the command table.
      (setf (gethash name *command-table*)
            (symbol-function function-name))
      ;; Put it on the list so HELP will show it.
```
```

```
            (setf *initial-commands*
                 (acons name function-name *initial-commands*)))))

6. (defvar *candy-stock* '((mars-bars . 10) (peanuts . 5)
                          (reeses . 8) (necco-wafers . 4)
                          (twinkies . 12)))

  (defvar *candy-hopper-size* 7)

  (defun allot-candy-for-column (size)
    (if (not (= 0 (length *candy-stock*)))
        (let ((candy-type (car (nth (random
                                      (length *candy-stock*))
                                    *candy-stock*))))
          (do ((counter size (- counter 1))
               (accumulator nil))
              ;; stop if you've finished the column
              ;; or you've run out of that type of candy
              ((or (= counter 0)
                   (= (cdr (assoc candy-type *candy-stock*))
                      0))
               ;; if you haven't finished loading the column
               (cond ((not (zerop counter))
                      ;; delete the type of candy
                      (setq *candy-stock*
                        (delete (assoc candy-type *candy-stock*)
                          *candy-stock*))
                      ;; get more candy for the column
                      (append (allot-candy-for-column counter)
                              accumulator))
                     ;; if you've finished loading the
                     ;; column, return the stuff
                     (t accumulator)))
            ;; add to the column
            (setq accumulator (cons candy-type accumulator))
            ;; delete the item from the stock.
            (decf (cdr (assoc candy-type *candy-stock*)))))))

  (defun make-candy-machine (column-one column-two)
    (function (lambda (button-pressed)
                (cond ((= button-pressed 1)
                       (prog1 (car column-one)
                         (setf column-one (cdr column-one))))
                      ((= button-pressed 2)
                       (prog1 (car column-two)
                         (setf column-two (cdr column-two))))
                      (t (print "That's not one of my buttons."
                         nil))))))

  (defun get-candy (candy-machine button-pressed)
    (funcall candy-machine button-pressed))

  (setq my-candy-machine
    (make-candy-machine
      (allot-candy-for-column *candy-hopper-size*)
      (allot-candy-for-column *candy-hopper-size*)))
```

CHAPTER 9

1. ```
(defun make-gum-machine (gumballs)
    (function (lambda (&optional new-stuff)
                (if (not new-stuff)
                    (prog1 (car gumballs)
                        (setf gumballs (cdr gumballs)))
                    (setf gumballs (append new-stuff gumballs))))))

(defun load-gum-machine (machine)
    (funcall machine (make-gum-package)))
```

2. ```
(defun do-in-turn (method list &rest other-arg)
    (if (null other-arg) (get-bicycle method list)
        (set-bicycle method list other-arg)))

(defun set-bicycle (method list new-value)
    (cond ((null list) nil)
          (t (funcall method (car list) (car new-value))
             (set-bicycle method (cdr list) new-value))))

(defun get-bicycle (method list)
    (mapcar method list))
```

3. ```
(defun my-average (list)
    (catch 'bad-item
        (do ((yet-to-do list (cdr yet-to-do))
             (accumulator 0 (+ accumulator
                              (get-next-element (car yet-to-do))))
             (counter 0 (+ counter 1)))
            ((null yet-to-do) (/ accumulator counter)))))

(defun get-next-element (item)
    (cond ((numberp item) item)
          (t (get-correction item))))

(defun get-correction (item)
    (cond ((y-or-n-p (format nil "~%~a is not a number.
Do you wish to continue anyway?~%" item))
           (format t "~%What number do you wish to ~
substitute?~%'')
           (get-next-element (read)))
          (t (throw 'bad-item))))
```

4. ```
(defun init-animal (&optional (file-name "ANIMAL.DAT"))
    (format t "~%This is a game.  Think of an animal and I
will try to guess what it is by asking questions.~1%")
    (do ()
        ((let ((knowledge
                  (if (open file-name :direction :probe)
                      (with-open-file (input-file
                                          file-name
                                          :direction :input)
                          (read input-file))
                      '(("Does it sing" (canary)
                        ("Could it have spots" (dog)
                         ("Does it lay eggs"
                          (chicken)
                          (dolphin)))))))
```

```
          (main-loop knowledge)
          (with-open-file (output-file file-name
                                        :direction :output
                                        :if-exists :supersede)
            (format output-file "~S" knowledge))
          (play-again?)))))
```

5. Answers vary according to input.

6.
```
;;; output a line of input text in no-fill mode
(defun form-no-fill-output-line (line)
  (form-output-left-margin)    ;first output the left margin
  (check-length line)
  (format *output-stream* "~A" line)     ;then the text
  (form-newline))                        ;then a new line, and page
                                         ;if necessary

;;; CHECK-LENGTH checks the length of the line and asks the
;;; user if he or she wants to continue
(defun check-length (line)
  (if (> (length line) *text-width*)
      (cerror "Will print rest of line on next line"
        "Line: ~a is wider than ~a, does not fit on page."
        line *text-width*)))
```

7.
```
;;; output a line of input text in fill mode
(defun form-fill-output-line (line)
  (do ((pointer 0)) (nil)
    (multiple-value-bind (word char-pointer)
        (form-get-word pointer line)
      (if (null word) (return))
      (let ((spaces
              (if (eql
                    (char word (- (length word) 1)) #\.)
                  2 1)))
        ;; see if the word fits on this line,
        ;; and do a newline if it doesn't
        (if (> (+ (length word) *current-column*)
               *text-width*)
            (form-newline))          ;output new line
        ;; output the margin spacing if
        ;; at beginning of new line
        (if (zerop *current-column*)
            (form-output-left-margin))
        ;; print the word
        (format *output-stream* "~a" word)
        ;; increment the column counter
        (incf *current-column* (length word))
        ;; output the spaces
        (dotimes (i (min spaces
                         (- *text-width*
                            *current-column*)))
          (format *output-stream* "~a" #\space)
          (incf *current-column*))
        (setf pointer char-pointer)))))
```

8.
```
;;; output a line of input text in fill mode
(defun form-fill-output-line (line)
  (do ((pointer 0)) (nil)
    (multiple-value-bind (word char-pointer)
      (form-get-word pointer line)
      (if (null word) (return))
      (let ((spaces (form-fill-examine-for-spaces word)))
        ;; see if the word fits on this line,
        ;; and do a newline if it doesn't
        (if (> (+ (length word) *current-column*)
               *text-width*)
            (form-newline))        ;output new line
        ;; output the margin spacing if
        ;; at beginning of new line
        (if (zerop *current-column*)
            (form-output-left-margin))
        ;; print the word
        (format *output-stream* "~a" word)
        ;; increment the column counter
        (incf *current-column* (length word))
        ;; output the spaces
        (dotimes (i (min spaces
                         (- *text-width*
                            *current-column*)))
          (format *output-stream* "~a" #\space)
          (incf *current-column*))
        (setf pointer char-pointer)))))

(defun form-fill-examine-for-spaces (word)
  (let ((ignore-for-spacing '(#\) #\ #\' #\"))
        (follow-with-two-spaces '(#\? #\! #\.)))
    (do* ((char-no-to-examine (- (length word) 1)
                              (- char-no-to-examine 1))
          (char-to-examine (char word char-no-to-examine)
                           (char word char-no-to-examine)))
        ;; Return one space if you've gotten to zero
        ;; and it's still not resolved, because you're not
        ;; dealing with a proper word.
        ((= char-no-to-examine 0) 1)
      (unless (member char-to-examine ignore-for-spacing)
        (if (member char-to-examine follow-with-two-spaces)
            (return 2)
            (return 1))))))
```

9.
```
(defvar *autoparagraph?*)

;;; Initialize the user-interface parameters to nice defaults.
(defun form-initialize ()
  (setf *current-line-number* 0)
  (setf *current-column* 0)
  (setf *page-number* 1)
  (setf *fill-mode?* nil)
  (setf *page-length* 47)
  (setf *left-margin* 8)
  (setf *text-width* 70)
  (setf *header-text-list* '(""))
  (setf *autoparagraph?* nil))
```

```lisp
;;; Output a line of input text in fill mode.
(defun form-fill-output-line (line)
  (if (and *autoparagraph?* (string= line ""))
      (form-new-paragraph)
      (do ((pointer 0)) (nil)
        (multiple-value-bind (word char-pointer)
            (form-get-word pointer line)
          (if (null word) (return))
          ;; See if the word fits on this line,
          ;; and do a newline if it doesn't.
          (if (>= (+ *current-column* (length word))
                  *text-width*)
              ;; Output new line, check for new page.
              (form-newline))
          ;; Output the margin spacing if at
          ;; beginning of new line.
          (if (zerop *current-column*)
              (form-output-left-margin))
          ;; now print the word
          (format *output-stream* "~A" word)
          ;; and the trailing space, if there's room
          (unless (= *text-width*
                     (+ *current-column* (length word)))
            (write-char #\space *output-stream*))
          (setf *current-column*
                (+ *current-column* (length word) 1))
          ;; The next call to form-get-word should start
          ;; after last word.
          (setf pointer char-pointer)))))

(defun form-new-paragraph ()
  (form-newline 2))

;;; Form-execute-command executes a user command.
(defun form-execute-command (current-line)
  (let* ((command-list
          (list-from-string (subseq current-line 1)))
         (command (car command-list))
         (args (cdr command-list)))
    (case command
      ;; It would be better to make this data-driven
      ;; but for a small number of commands, CASE will do.
      (autoparagraph (setf *autoparagraph?* t))
      (no-autoparagraph (setf *autoparagraph?* nil))
      (fill (setf *fill-mode?* t))
      (no-fill (form-newline) (setf *fill-mode?* nil))
      (left-margin (setf *left-margin* (car args)))
      (new-page (apply #'form-newpage args))
      (header (setf *header-text-list* args))
      (text-width (setf *text-width* (car args)))
      (page-length (setf *page-length* (car args)))
      (break (apply #'form-newline args))
      (eval (mapc #'eval args))
      (t (format t
                 "~&Warning: ~A is not a known FORM command.~%"
                 command)))))
```

Notice how easy it would be to change FORM-NEW-PARAGRAPH so that it indents the new paragraph correctly.

10.
```
;;; FORM-CENTER is a loop that reads all the lines to be
;;; centered and checks for the end of file.
(defun form-center (&optional (times 1))
   (dotimes (i times)
      (let ((current-line (read-line *input-stream* nil
                                     'form-center-eof)))
         (if (eq current-line 'form-center-eof) (return nil)
           (form-center-line current-line)))))

(defun form-center-line (line)
   ;; if you're not at the beginning of a line,
   ;; do a new line
   (unless (= *current-column* 0) (form-newline))
   ;; Is the line is too wide?
   (cond ((> (length line) *text-width*)
          (let* ((place2
                   ;; If there's a white-space-char in the line
                   ;; before *text-width* find that place.
                   (or (position-if #'white-space-char?
                                     line :end (+ *text-width* 1)
                                     :from-end t)
                      ;; otherwise, just break at *text-width*
                      *text-width*))
                 ;; Find the last place before place2 where
                 ;; you are printing a character.
                 (place1
                   (or (position-if-not #'white-space-char?
                            line :end place2 :from-end t)
                       place2)))
             ;; Print the part of the line you've identified.
             ;; You have to add to one to include that place.
             (form-pad-output-line (subseq line 0 (+ place1 1)))
             ;; Center the rest of the line.
             (form-center-line (subseq line place2))))
         ;; If the line's not too long, pad it and print it.
         (t (form-pad-output-line line))))

;;; FORM-PAD-OUTPUT-LINE does the same thing as
;;; FORM-NO-FILL-OUTPUT-LINE except that it also
;;; prints the padding characters
(defun form-pad-output-line (line)
   ;; print left margin
   (form-output-left-margin)
   ;; print padding characters
   (dotimes (i (round (/ (- *text-width* (length line)) 2)))
      (write-char #\space *output-stream*))
   ;; print line
   (format *output-stream* "~a" line)
   ;; make sure everything is updated
   (form-newline))

;;; Form-execute-command executes a user command.
(defun form-execute-command (current-line)
```

```
        (let* ((command-list
                (list-from-string (subseq current-line 1)))
               (command (car command-list))
               (args (cdr command-list)))
          (case command
            ;; It would be better to make this data-driven
            ;; but for a small number of commands, CASE will do.
            (fill (setf *fill-mode?* t))
            (no-fill (form-newline) (setf *fill-mode?* nil))
            (left-margin (setf *left-margin* (car args)))
            (new-page (apply #'form-newpage args))
            (header (setf *header-text-list* args))
            (text-width (setf *text-width* (car args)))
            (page-length (setf *page-length* (car args)))
            (break (apply #'form-newline args))
            (eval (mapc #'eval args))
            (center (apply #'form-center args))
            (t (format t
                 "~&Warning: ~A is not a known FORM command.~%"
                 command)))))
```

11. Include the command:

    ```
    %header "~a~%~%%break" *page-number*
    ```
    in your file.

CHAPTER 10

1. No single answer.

2.
   ```
   (proclaim '(function fib (fixnum) fixnum))
   (proclaim '(inline 1- < - +))

   (defun fib (n)
     (if (< n 2) n
         (+ (fib (1- n)) (fib (- n 2)))))
   ```

3. Answers vary.

CHAPTER 11

1.
   ```
   (defmacro my-push (item list-place)
     '(setf ,list-place (cons ,item ,list-place)))
   ```

2.
   ```
   (defmacro my-pop (list-place)
     '(prog1 (car ,list-place)
             (setf ,list-place (cdr ,list-place))))
   ```

3.
   ```
   (defmacro my-let (variable-value-pairs &body body)
     '((lambda ,(mapcar #'car variable-value-pairs) ,.body)
       ,.(mapcar #'cadr variable-value-pairs)))
   ```

4.
   ```
   (defmacro make-arithmetic-combinator (name operator)
     '(defmacro ,name (&rest list-of-numbers)
        '(,',operator ,list-of-numbers)))
   ```

```
5. (defmacro my-warn (string &rest args)
     '(format *error-output* ,string .,args))

6. (defmacro my-unless (predicate consequent)
      '(cond ((not ,predicate) ,consequent)))

7. (defmacro my-unless (predicate &rest consequents)
      '(cond ((not ,predicate) ,.consequents)))

8. (defmacro mydefstruct (name &body body)
    '(progn
       (defmacro ,(make-name "MAKE-" name)
                 (&key ,@body)
         '(make-array ,',(1+ (length body))
              :initial-contents
              ',(list ',name ,@(mapcar #'get-slot-name body))))
       (defun ,(make-name "VECTOR-HAS-NAME-" name) (vector)
         (eq (svref vector 0) ',name))
       (deftype ,name ()
         '(and (simple-vector ,',(1+ (length body)))
               (satisfies
                 ,',(make-name "VECTOR-HAS-NAME-" name))))
       (defmacro ,(make-name name "-P") (object)
         '(typep ,object ',',name))
       ,.(mapcar
            #'(lambda (x counter)
                '(defmacro ,(make-name name "-"
                                (get-slot-name x))
                   (structure)
                   '(svref ,structure ,',counter)))
             body (do ((counter (length body) (- counter 1))
                       (list () (cons counter list)))
                      ((zerop counter) list)))
       (defmacro ,(make-name "COPY-" name) (structure)
         ;; You could do '(copyseq ,structure) here,
         ;; but if you don't know about copyseq, here's
         ;; how you could do it.
         '(let ((newstruct (make-array ,',(1+ (length body)))))
            (copy-vector ,structure newstruct)))
       ',name))

  (defun copy-vector (vector newvector)
    (dotimes (i (length vector) newvector)
      (setf (svref newvector i) (svref vector i))))

9. (defmacro mydefstruct
        ((name &key (conc-name (make-name name "-")))
         . body)
    '(progn
       (defmacro ,(make-name "MAKE-" name)
                 (&key ,@body)
         '(make-array ,',(1+ (length body))
              :initial-contents
              ',(list ',name ,@(mapcar #'get-slot-name body))))
       (defun ,(make-name "VECTOR-HAS-NAME-" name) (vector)
```

```
        (eq (svref vector 0) ',name))
    (deftype ,name ()
      '(and (simple-vector ,',(1+ (length body)))
            (satisfies
              ,',(make-name "VECTOR-HAS-NAME-" name))))
    (defmacro ,(make-name name "-P") (object)
      '(typep ,object ',',name))
    ,.(mapcar
        #'(lambda (x counter)
            '(defmacro ,(if conc-name
                            (make-name
                              (string-upcase conc-name)
                              (get-slot-name x))
                            (get-slot-name x))
                  (structure)
                '(svref ,structure ,',counter)))
          body
          (do ((counter (length body) (- counter 1))
               (list () (cons counter list)))
              ((zerop counter) list)))
    ',name))
```

10. ```
    (defmacro mydefstruct
        ((name &key (conc-name (make-name name "-"))
                    (constructor (make-name "MAKE-" name)))
         . body)
      '(progn
         (defmacro ,constructor (&key ,@body)
           '(make-array ,',(1+ (length body))
                 :initial-contents
                 ',(list ',name
                     ,@(mapcar #'get-slot-name body))))
         (defun ,(make-name "VECTOR-HAS-NAME-" name) (vector)
           (eq (svref vector 0) ',name))
         (deftype ,name ()
           '(and (simple-vector ,',(1+ (length body)))
                 (satisfies
                   ,',(make-name "VECTOR-HAS-NAME-" name))))
         (defmacro ,(make-name name "-P") (object)
           '(typep ,object ',',name))
         ,.(mapcar
             #'(lambda (x counter)
                 '(defmacro ,(if conc-name
                                 (make-name
                                   (string-upcase conc-name)
                                   (get-slot-name x))
                                 (get-slot-name x))
                       (structure)
                     '(svref ,structure ,',counter)))
               body
               (do ((counter (length body) (- counter 1))
                    (list () (cons counter list)))
                   ((zerop counter) list)))
         ',name))
    ```
    ```

CHAPTER 12

```
1. (defun determine-if-rule (cd rules-being-run)
     (let ((rule (find-rule-with-consequent cd)))
       (if (null rule) (determine-bottom rules-being-run cd)
         (determine rule rules-being-run))))

   (defun determine-bottom (rules-being-run cd)
     ;; SET-CD-VALUE because we know it's only a cd, not necessarily a
     ;; consequent of a rule.
     (set-cd-value cd (determine-bottom-query rules-being-run
                  "~&~a: " (condition-descriptor-string cd))))

   (defun determine-bottom-query
       (rules-being-run format-string &rest format-args)
     (apply #'format *query-io* format-string format-args)
     ;; Set the package to avoid problems with reading.
     (let ((*package* (find-package 'otto)))
       (let ((response (read *query-io*)))
         (case response
           ((yes y) 1)   ; translate YES to 1
           ((no n) 0)    ; translate NO to 0
           ((w why) (print-justification
                       rules-being-run format-string format-args)
            (apply #'determine-bottom-query
                 rules-being-run format-string format-args))
           (t (cond ((and (numberp response) (<= response 1)
                          (>= response 0))
                     response) ; if it's acceptable, return it.
                    (t (format t "~%~
Legal responses are yes, y, no, n, or a number between 0 and 1, inclusive,
where 0 indicates that the condition is certainly not the case, and 1 means
that it certainly is the case. Yes means 1, and no means 0.~2%")
                       (apply #'determine-bottom-query
                              format-string format-args)))))))))

   (defun print-justification
       (rules-being-run format-string format-args)
     (format t "~%~%The system is presently trying to ~
prove the following rules:~%")
     (do ((rules rules-being-run (cdr rules)))
         ((null rules) nil)
       (let ((pred (rule-predicate (car rules))))
         ;; If there are more rules
         (if (cdr rules)
             ;; Print them out.
             (format t "~%The goal: ~s~% would be proved by the predicate:
~s~%"
                     (condition-descriptor-string
                       (rule-consequent (car rules)))
                     (cons (predfun-name (predicate-predfun pred))
                           (do ((cds (predicate-cds pred) (cdr cds))
                                (list ()))
                               ((null cds) list)
                             (push (condition-descriptor-string (car cds))
                                   list)))))))))
```

Index of Defined Procedures
and Macros

ABS, 58–59
ADD, 131, 297
ADD-COMMAND, 298–299
ADD-EMPLOYEE, 139
ADD1, 213
ADD1-TO-N, 213
ADD-SOME, 70
ALLOT-CANDY-FOR-COLUMN, 299
ALMOST-A-PALINDROME, 45
AND-PREDICATE-EVALUATOR, 246, 248
ANIMAL, 132, 297
ANOTHER-FUNCTION, 128
ANY-SHORT-FUNCTION, 70–71
ANYTHING-TO-CHOMP-LEFT, 114–115
ANYTHING-TO-CHOMP-RIGHT, 114–115
A-OR-AN, 54–55, 131, 284
APPLE-STATISTICS, 92
ASK, 130–131
AVERAGE, 284

BACKWARD, 98, 99
BAR, 78, 175
BARBER-SHOP-MACHINE, 8–9
BINGO, 163
BOTH-START-WITH-VOWELS?, 57
BOTTOM-LINE-ON-SHAKESPEAREAN-PLAY, 55
BOW, 288–289
BUGGY-HAMLET, 75

CALCULATE-SPACES, 192
CAR, 174
CD-PRINT-FN, 256
CDR, 174
CD-VALUE, 257

CENTER-LINE, 191–192
CHECK-FOR-ZERO, 184
CHECK-LENGTH, 301
CHOMP, 113–115
CHOMPER-GOING-WHERE?, 114
CHOMPER-POINT, 115
CHOMP-ONCE, 114
CIRCLE-AREA, 69, 284
CIRCUMFERENCE, 284
CLOSE-ZONE-LOOKUP, 285
COLOR, 289
COMMAND-LOOP, 159, 160
COMMIT-CRIME, 183
COMPLAIN, 181
CONS, 173
CONSTRUCTOR, 307
CONTAINED-IN?, 52
CONVERT-TO-CENTIGRADE, 298
COPY-FROM-OTHER-FUNCTIONS, 128
COPY-LINE, 127
COPY-VECTOR, 306
COUNT-DOWN, 291
COUNT-EVERYTHING, 101
COUNT-UP, 291

DEFDESCRIPTOR, 256
DEFPREDFUN, 255
DEFRULE, 249, 256
DEFRULE-INTERNAL, 249, 256–257
DEFSEAL, 251, 260–261
DEFUN-MY-ADD, 224
DETERMINE, 245, 258
DETERMINE-BOTTOM, 259, 308
DETERMINE-BOTTOM-QUERY, 259, 308

DETERMINE-CD-VALUE, 246, 259–260
DETERMINE-IF-RULE, 259, 308
DETERMINE-1, 245, 258–259
DO-IN-TURN, 300
DRESS-FOR-SUCCESS, 284

EMPLOY, 150
EXAMINE-ANIMAL, 292–293
EXECUTE, 166

FACT, 216
FACTORIAL, 101
FEED-ME-NUMBERS, 52
FIB, 218, 305
FILTER, 5–6, 290
FILTER-OUT-THE, 102
FIND-CD-WITH-NAME, 256
FIND-GREATER, 112–113
FIND-PREDFUN-WITH-NAME, 256
FIND-RULE-WITH-CONSEQUENT, 257
FISH, 225, 226
FISH-DORSAL-FIN-LENGTH, 228
FISH-HABITAT, 228
FISH-P, 228
FLUSH-UNTIL-CHOMPER, 115
FOO, 175, 192
FORM, 201
FORM-CENTER, 304
FORM-CENTER-LINE, 304
FORM-DRIVER-LOOP, 198, 201–202
FORM-EXECUTE-COMMAND, 198–199, 203–204,
    303, 304–305
FORM-FILL-EXAMINE-FOR-SPACES, 302
FORM-FILL-OUTPUT-LINE, 199–200, 301–302,
    303
FORM-GET-WORD, 200, 202
FORM-INITIALIZE, 201, 302
FORM-NEWLINE, 203
FORM-NEWPAGE, 203
FORM-NEW-PARAGRAPH, 303
FORM-NO-FILL-OUTPUT-LINE, 199, 202, 301
FORM-OUTPUT-HEADER, 203, 213
FORM-OUTPUT-LEFT-MARGIN, 203
FORM-PAD-OUTPUT-LINE, 304
FUNNY-FACT, 168

GEAR-RATIO, 7, 88, 176
GENERATE-CD?, 257
GENERATE-GUM-SUPPLY, 8
GENERATE-1-SEAL-ASSERTION, 252, 261
GENERATE-SEAL-ASSERTIONS, 251–252, 261
GET-ALL-SYMBOLS, 161, 162

GET-AND-COUNT, 291, 292
GET-BICYCLE, 298, 300
GET-CANDY, 299
GET-CORRECTION, 300
GET-FIB, 173
GET-GUESS, 95
GET-GUM, 9, 171, 172
GET-IF-SYMBOL, 161, 162
GET-ITEM-LOOP, 155–156
GET-LENGTH, 100, 112
GET-MEMBER, 211, 215
GET-NEW-ITEM, 156
GET-NEXT-ELEMENT, 300
GET-NUMBER, 290
GET-PAIR, 156, 294
GET-STATISTICS-AND-RETURN, 121
GET-WORD, 296
GLOAT, 132
GOAL-RULE?, 257
GROCERY-STORE-MACHINE, 8–9
GUESS, 94, 131, 294
GUESS-THE-AGE-OF-MY-CAR, 52–53
GUM-MACHINE, 8–9

HAMLET, 74–75
HI, 40
HOWL, 72
HOW-TO, 297

INFER, 244, 258
INIT, 139, 169, 296
INIT-ANIMAL, 130, 293, 294, 300–301
INIT-BIKE-RACK, 206
INIT-DICTIONARY, 296
INITIALIZE-HASH-TABLE-FROM-ALIST, 147
INITIALIZE-PROJECT, 295
INTERFACE-MESSAGE, 159
IS-IT-TALL?, 53–54
ITERATE-PUMP, 291
I-YOU, 295

LEARN, 131, 292, 293
LEAVE, 156
LESS-SIMPLE, 68
LESS-THAN-10, 52
LIST-CIRCLE-FACTS, 284
LIST-FROM-STRING, 190, 204, 292
LOAD-GUM-MACHINE, 300
LOOK-FOR, 112
LOOKUP-COST, 285

MAIN-LOOP, 30, 170, 181–182, 296–297

MAKE-ARITHMETIC-COMBINATOR, 305
MAKE-BIKE, 7, 87–90, 136, 175–176, 289
MAKE-CANDY-MACHINE, 299
MAKE-DISPENSER, 172
MAKE-FIB-GENERATOR, 173
MAKE-FISH, 228
MAKE-GUM-MACHINE, 171, 300
MAKE-GUM-PACKAGE, 171
MAKE-MACRO-NAMED, 225, 226
MAKE-POSITIVE, 161
MOVE-DISK, 108
MOVE-LEFT, 115
MOVE-RIGHT, 115
MUSICAL-TASTE, 118–119
MUSICAL-TASTE-REVISITED, 119
MY-ABS, 58–59
MY-ACONS, 295
MY-ADD 180
MY-ADD1, 180
MY-APPEND, 290
MY-ASSOC, 298
MY-AVERAGE, 207, 291, 300
MY-COMPLICATED-FUNCTION, 193
MY-COUNT, 96, 111
MYDEFSTRUCT, 227, 306–307
MY-DELETE-FILE, 169
MY-DIVIDE, 184
MY-EXIT, 169, 181–182
MY-FUNCTION, 76, 77, 92
MY-HELP, 169
MY-IF, 219, 223
MY-LAST, 44
MY-LET, 305
MYMAPCAN, 167
MYMAPCAR, 166–167
MY-NTH, 290
MY-OTHER-FUNCTION, 76, 77
MY-POP, 305
MY-PRINT-FILE, 169
MY-PUSH, 305
MY-REVERSE, 290
MY-UNLESS, 306
MY-WARN, 306
MY-WITH-OPEN-FILE, 228, 229
MY-WRITE-LINE, 127

NAME, 206, 231
NEWGUESS, 95, 96
NEW-TABINDENT, 192
NO-BRANCH, 104, 132
NOT-PREDICATE-EVALUATOR, 256
N-TO-1, 167–168

OPPOSITE, 155–156
OR-PREDICATE-EVALUATOR, 255

PALINDROME, 45
PHRASE, 73
PLAY-AGAIN?, 131–132, 293–294
POEM, 178–179
PREDFUN-PRINT-FN, 255
PREDICATE-CDS, 257
PREDICATE-PREDFUN, 257
PRINT-ALL-ELEMENTS, 125–126
PRINT-AND-SQUARE-IF-ODD, 221
PRINT-JUSTIFICATION, 308
PRINT-LETTER, 163
PRINT-NUMBER, 110
PRINT-REPLY, 156
PRINT-SOMETHING, 61
PRINT-SQUARES, 110
PRINT-TWO-RETURN-ONE, 41
PROMPT-FOR-DEFINITION, 297
PROMPT-FOR-WORD, 297
PRONOUNS, 295
PROPORTION, 191
PUMP-ALL-PEDALS, 117, 291
PUMP-PEDALS 7, 90
PUT-GUM-IN-PACKAGE, 171
PUT-TOGETHER-NAME, 293
PUT-WORD, 296

QUESTION, 104, 132
QUESTION-NODE-P, 132

RACE-BIKES, 291
READ-EVAL-PRINT-LOOP, 191
READ-TWO-CHARS, 119
READ-WITH-A-OR-AN, 292
REFRAIN, 163
REMOVE-EMPLOYEE, 139
REMOVE-QUESTION-MARKS, 293
REMOVE-WORD, 296
REPORT-CONCLUSIONS, 260
REVERSE-PAIR, 294
RULE-CONSEQUENT, 257
RULE-CONSEQUENT-WEIGHT, 257
RULE-PREDICATE, 257
RUN-OTTO, 243, 258

SCHEDULE, 284
SEALS, 251, 261
2ND, 41
SELECT-A-OR-AN, 61
SET-BICYCLE, 300

SET-CD-VALUE, 257
SET-COLOR, 289
SET-CONSEQUENT-VALUE-AND-CONCLUSION, 258
SET-GEAR-RATIO, 7, 88, 89
SET-WHEEL-SIZE, 7, 88
SET-X-POSITION, 7, 88, 90, 136
SHIFT, 163
SIMPLE, 68
SIZE-OF-PACKAGE, 54
SIZE-OF-PARCEL, 59, 69
SOCIAL-INTERACTION, 72
SPY, 183
SQ, 78, 160, 209, 221, 222
SQUARE, 214
SQUARE-EACH-ONE, 160, 161, 162, 164
STANZA, 163
START-GUESS, 95
STARTS-WITH-VOWEL-P, 57
SUM-OF-SQUARES, 40
SWITCH-OR-RETURN, 295

TABINDENT, 190
TALK, 72

TEST, 51, 181, 183, 190
TEST1, 92, 288
TEST2, 92, 288
TOWER-OF-HANOI, 107, 117

UPDATE-INFO, 156, 294–295

VECTOR-HAS-NAME-FISH, 228

WHAT-IS-IT, 51
WHEEL-SIZE, 7, 88, 176
WHITE-SPACE-CHAR?, 204
WHO-IS-ON-STAFF?, 295

XANADU-PHRASE, 73–74
X-POSITION, 7, 88, 89, 136, 176

YES-BRANCH, 104, 132
YET-ANOTHER-FUNCTION, 77, 128

ZONE-N-LOOKUP, 285

General Index

A, 144
Abstraction, 173
  animal program example of, 135–136
  conceptual issues of, 136
  example of, 6–8
  labeling as technique in, 136–137
  and rules of order, 136
  usefulness of, 89–90
Accessors. *See* Selectors
ACONS, 138–139
  template for, 154
ADJUST-ARRAY, 146
A-list. *See* Association lists
Ampersands (&) as indicators in keywords, 178
AND, 56–57
  evaluation of, 57
  in predicate functions, 237–238
  template for, 64
Animal program, 129–132, 292–294
APPEND, 45
  destructive versions of, 86
  template for, 64
APPLY, 167–168, 174
  advantages of, 165–166
  vs. FUNCALL, 167, 174
  macros in, 230
  template for, 175
APROPOS, 46
  template for, 154
AREF, 146
  template for, 154
Arguments, 178. *See also* Functions
  evaluation of, 178, 179, 180
  &KEY, 180
  keywords as, 178
  lambda lists, 178

  of macros, 223, 229, 230
  optional, 124, 177–181, 204
  packages as, 188
  &REST, 179, 180
  structure of, 178, 179, 180
Arithmetic operators, 23
  prefix notation for, 18
Arrays
  and ADJUSTABLE option, 146
  advantages and disadvantages of, 143, 144, 152
  creation of, 143
  definition of, 143
  end tests for, 144
  functions for, 144, 153
  modifying elements of, 144
  modifying length of, 144–145
  names of, 144
  operators on, 145–146, 152, 153
  printed form of, 144
  referencing objects in, 144
  space allocation for, 146
  zero-basis of, 143
ARRAY-TOTAL-SIZE, 146
Artificial intelligence, 130
  tree searches in, 104
ASSOC
  advantages and disadvantages of, 138
  template for, 154
  in updating a-lists, 139–140
  value returned by, 138
Association lists, 137–140, 153
  advantages of, 152
  definition of, 137–138
  example of, 138
  functions for, 138
  operators on, 152, 153

Association lists (*continued*)
  vs. property lists, 141
  as push stacks, 139
  template for, 137
Asterisks (*), 79, 128
ATOM, 47
  template for construction, 64
Atsign (@). See Comma-atsign (,@)

Backquote (`), 224
  nested, 225–227, 230
Backquote comma (`,), 230
  usefulness of, 223–224
Backquote comma-atsign (`,@), 224
Backquote comma-dot (`,.), 224
Backslash (\), 120
Backward chaining systems, 240, 241, 271. *See
    also* Expert systems
  evaluation in, 242–243
  limitations of, 253
Bicycles, modeling, 6–8, 87–90
BIGNUMS
  EQ vs. EQL tests for, 50
Binary choices
  in animal program, 130
  with multiple consequents, 112–113
  in tree structure, 103–104
Binding
  definition of, 67
  order of, 178, 179
  pretty-printer display of, 23
&BODY, 223
BREAK, 207
%BREAK, 195

CALCULATE-SPACES, 191–192
CAR, 20
  acronym basis of, 26
  in cons cells, 28–30
  evaluation of, 24, 25
  function of, 30
  nesting with, 25, 26–27
  NIL, 26
  operators on, 163
  replacing with value, 86–87
  template for, 34
Case
  with characters, 12
  vs. COND, 54
  directives converting, 61
  in EQUAL vs. EQUALP tests of equality, 48–49
  EQL as default for, 55

  in reader, 121
  with symbols, 15
  template for, 54, 64
CATCH, 181, 182, 205
  template for, 206
CDR
  acronym basis of, 26
  in cons cells, 28–30
  evaluation of, 24, 25
  function of, 30
  of last cons cell, 30–31
  nesting with, 25, 26–27
  NIL, 26
  operators on, 163
  replacing with value, 86–87
  template for, 34
CDs. *See* Condition descriptors
CERROR, 205
Characters
  Case in tests of equality of, 48–49
  case of, 12
  conversion of, 123
  from decomposition of strings, 45
  designation of, 120
  evaluation of, 11–12, 27
  printed form of, 12, 122
  in strings or symbols, 12–13, 120
  testing equality of, 48
  value returned by, 275
CHAR=, 48
  template for, 64
CHAR-INT, 123
Chomper, 113–115
CLOSE, 126, 128, 133
  template for, 133
Code
  compiled vs. interpreted, 209, 215, 216
  complied vs. interpreted for macros, 222
  expanded, 220
  for function calls, 211
  in-line, 211–212, 217
  for local variables, 210–211
COERCE, 122–123
  template for, 133
Coercion
  compiler results of, 123
Colon (:)
  as package marker, 140, 178, 181, 186, 205
Colons (::), as indicators of internal symbols, 185
Comma (,), in backquote notation, 223–224, 230
Comma-atsign (,@), 224
Comment character, 130

Comments, 130, 192–193, 194, 205
COMMON LISP
  vs. other LISPS, 3–4
  specification of, 4
Compilation, 209–212
  and checking, 211, 215
  examining output of, 215–216
  and execution, 211
  and in-line coding, 211–212
  of local variables, 210–211
  selecting tradeoffs for, 212
COMPILE, 209
  template for, 217
COMPILE-FILE, 210
  template for, 217
Compilers
  definition of, 209
  purpose of, 209
COND, 53–54
  vs. CASE, 54
  predicate for last clause in, 53
  template for, 53, 64
  value returned by, 192
Conditional expressions, 51–55
Conditional operators, 56–59. *See also* Logical
    operators
  selecting, 58–59
  usefulness of, 51
Condition descriptors (CDs), 236
  defining, 248
  elements of, 247
  as objects, 247–248
  ordering of, 249–250
CONS, 43
  arguments for, 24
  function of, 30
  object constructed by, 28
  space for, 85–86
  template for, 34
  usefulness of, 24
Cons cells, 28–30, 33
  in association lists, 137–138
  contents of, 31
  dotted-pair notation of, 30–32, 33–34
  modifying, 138
Consequents, 53, 54
Conses, 10
Constants
  global, 78
  redefining, 80
Constructors, 7, 143
  for data structures, 152

DEFSTRUCT definition of, 148, 149
  examples of, 87
Control
  conditional operators in, 56–57
  directing flow of with predicate functions, 238
  recursive techniques for, 6, 97
  tracing flow of, 99
Control stack, 72, 73
Conversion
  of case, 61
  of data type, 122–124
  to floating point numbers, 298
Copiers, DEFSTRUCT definition of, 148, 149
COPY, template for, 91
Copying
  vs. destructive modification, 85–86
  with sharing, 84–85
COPY-LIST, 84

`d, 60
Data abstraction. *See* Abstraction
Data structures, 147–151
  adding slots to, 151
  advantages and disadvantages of, 147, 152
  association lists, 137–140
  creating, 148
  directed acyclic graphs, 238–240
  documentation on, 194
  functions for, 152
  in LISP vs. other systems, 147
  modifying components of, 148
  procedures as, 173–174
  property lists, 141
  values allowed as slots for, 151
Data type, conversion of, 122–124
Debugger, 3
  exiting from, 27, 56, 72, 182
  value returned by, 72–73
Debugging. *See also* Errors
  control stacks in, 72, 73
  of macros, 220
  of recursive functions, 99
  running interpreted code for, 209
  sharing as problem for, 84
  testing predictions in, 70
  tools for, 2–3, 70–73
Declarations, 77, 91
  abbreviated form of, 214
  definition of, 210
  function form of, 214–215
  implementation as factor with, 212
  in-line, 211–212, 215, 217

Declarations (*continued*)
  local specification of, 213
  NOTINLINE, 217
  for optimization, 212, 215, 217
  position of, 210
  purpose of, 209, 210
  scope as factor in, 213
  special, 77, 91, 210–211, 217
  template for, 212
  template for function form of, 214
  template for optimization form of, 215
  template for type form of, 213–214
  type, 211, 213–214, 217
  types of, 210, 216–217
  for WITH-OPEN-FILE, 128
DECLARE, 216
  vs. PROCLAIM, 212–213
  template for, 91, 217
DEFCONSTANT, 80
  template for, 91
DEFDESCRIPTOR, 248
DEFMACRO, 220–221, 230
  template for, 231
DEFPARAMETER, 78, 79–80
  redefining with, 79, 80
  template for, 91
DEFPREDFUN, 248
DEFRULE, 248–249
DEFSETF, 90
  template for, 91
DEFSTRUCT
  in creation of macros, 227
  functions created by, 148
  initialization for, 149
  options for, 150
  template created by, 149–151
  template for, 154
DEFTYPE, 228
  template for, 231
DEFUN, 63
  calling function defined with, 40
  declaration for, 77
  evaluation of, 41–42
  execution of, 40
  as macro, 42
  to redefine functions, 41
  side effects of, 39
  syntax for, 42
  template for, 39, 64, 206
  value returned by, 39, 40, 191
  variables created inside, 68, 91
  writing, 39

DEFVAR, 78–79, 80
  calling to change value, 82
  defining with, 79, 80
  shadowing with, 78
  template for, 91
DELETE-FILE, modifying, 182
Deletion, 143
DESCRIBE, 46, 193–194, 205
  template for, 64
Destructive modification
  vs. copying, 85–86
  dangers of, 84
  definition of, 81
  with DEFUN, 82
  with REMF, 141
  with SETF, 81–82, 141
  with SET/GET, 142
Destructuring, 228–229, 230
Device, in pathnames, 129
Directed acyclic graphs, 238–240
Directives, 60
Directory, in pathnames, 129
DISASSEMBLE, 215–216
  template for, 217
DO, 110–112, 116
  diagram of, 112
  iteration-variable specifiers in, 111
  operations performed by, 110
  other DO-loop forms, 110
  return in, 112
  template for, 116
Documentation, 130, 192, 194, 205
  self-documentation functions, 46
DOCUMENTATION, 194, 205
  with SETF, 205
  template for, 206
DOLIST, 110, 116
  template for, 116
DO-loops
  vs. DO, 110
  end tests in, 110, 111
  initializing in, 111
  parts of, 110, 116
Dot. *See* Comma-dot
DOTIMES, 116, 291
  Optional evaluation with, 110
  template for, 109, 116
Dotted pairs, 30–32, 33–34
  in association lists, 137–140, 153
  notation for, 31, 32
  printed form of, 36
DRIBBLE, 99

Dynamic scoping, 76–78, 91
  declarations for, 77, 91, 210–211, 213
  naming for, 79
  relying on, 213
  in text formatting, 200

Editors, features of, 62–63
ELIZA, 156–157
ELT, 45–46
  template for, 64
Empty lists (()), 15, 25, 47
  as last CDR of list, 29
  testing for, 47–48
ENDP, 48
Endtests, 100, 101, 116
  for arrays, 144
  in DO-loops, 110, 111
  modifying, 181–182
  unique cons cell as, 125–126
Environments, 2–3
  definition of, 67, 288, 289
  diagrams of, 73–74
  differences in, 172
  elements of, 67
  with LAMBDA, 165
  in lexically-scoped systems, 288
  of macro evaluation, 222
  with recursive calls, 97, 98, 106, 107
EQ, 49–50
  vs. EQL, 49–50
  template for, 64
  in tests of sharing, 84
EQL, 49–50
  as default test, 50
  vs. EQ, 49–50
  template for, 64
  as test for strings, 140
EQUAL, 48–49
  case and type in, 48–49
  vs. EQUALP, 48–49
  template for, 64
Equality
  default for, 50
  degrees of, 48
  error messages with tests of, 283
  function for, 48
  in hash tables, 146, 147, 153
  vs. same place in memory, 49
  template for function for, 64
  tests of, 48–50
EQUALP, 48
  case and type in, 48–49

  vs. EQUAL, 48–49
  as test for strings, 140
ERROR, 205
  as tag, 182
  template for, 206
Errors. *See also* Debugging
  from calling operator on inappropriate
    argument, 56
  with coercions, 123
  commonly found, 56
  with COND, 56
  continuing execution after, 182–184
  with dependent rules in expert systems, 244
  with ELT, 145
  with end of streams, 125
  with ENDP, 48
  with equality tests, 283
  in evaluation of lists, 20
  functions signalling, 184
  from incorrect specifications of condition
    descriptors, 248, 249
  with LENGTH, 145
  from macroexpansion, 222–223
  from missing sequence in LENGTH, 44
  from name conflicts, 186
  from names of symbols, 22
  from nested backquotes, 225, 226
  from overspecification, 215
  with redefined macros, 220
  for required arguments, 178
  resuming control after, 56
  returning to normal state after, 27
  specifying response to, 182
  with symbols, 27, 275
  usefulness of, 55–56
  and user input, 184
  with variables created with DEFUNS, 68
Escape characters, 120
  controlling in printing, 132
EVAL, 159–160, 174
  disadvantages of, 165, 174
  evaluation of, 159, 160
  template for, 175
%EVAL, 195
Evaluation, 2, 10, 11
  of AND, 57
  application as stage in, 167
  of backquote-comma syntax, 225–227, 230
  of CAR, 24, 25
  of CDR, 24, 25
  cutoff of in expert systems, 241, 242–243, 248
  of DEFUN, 41, 42

Evaluation (*continued*)
  of DOTIMES, 110
  exceptions to rules for, 42
  of FUNCALL, 166, 298
  of functions, 17–18
  of LAMBDA, 164
  of LET, 69
  of lists, 16–21, 23, 27, 41
  of macro, 222, 225–227
  of nested lists, 19
  of NIL, 15, 25, 47
  of numbers, 11–12, 27
  of OR, 57
  order of, 219–220
  preventing, 19–22
  under program control, 158–160, 174
  of QUOTE, 27
  quoting result of, 226
  rules for, 27, 33, 41
  of SETF, 80, 83
  of strings, 11–12, 27
  of symbols, 14–15, 27
  of T, 47
  of THROW, 182
  values returned by, 32–33
Execution, aborting, 182–184
Exiting
  from debuggers, 182
  from functions, 182
  from LISP, 27, 34
  non-local, 182–184
  WITH-OPEN-FILE, 127, 128, 133
Expansion, 219, 220
  effect of on code, 220
  iteration with, 229
  recursive nature of, 221
  results of, 222
Expert systems, 233, 236
  adding to, 248
  backward-chaining in, 238, 240, 241
  backward-chaining evaluation in, 242–243
  cutting off evaluation in, 248
  definition of, 271
  efficient evaluation in, 241, 242–243
  facts in, 246
  forward-chaining in, 240, 241
  independence of rules in, 244
  limitations of, 253
  ordering of rules in, 249–250
  predicate functions in, 236, 237
  rules of, 271
  TRACE of, 243

  usefulness of, 253
  user interaction as factor in design of, 240–241
  weights in, 236
EXPORT, 185–186, 205
  placement of, 188
  template for, 206

Factorials, with APPLY, 167–168
Facts, 246
  in forward-chaining systems, 240, 271
File names, 62, 128–129
Files, 210
  loading, 62
  loading compiled code in, 210
  as modules, 188
  opening and closing, 126–127, 128, 133,
    183–184
  saving, 62
  searches for, 168
  writing to, 127
%FILL, 195
Fill pointers, 145
Filtering
  example of, 4
  of lists, 161–162
FIND-PACKAGE, 187, 205
  template for, 206
FIRST, 26
FIXNUMS
  in declaration statements, 214
  EQ vs. EQL tests of, 50
FLET, 289
FLOAT, 298
FORM
  commands for, 195–204
  output file for, 198
  printout of, 201–204
  sample input to, 196
  sample output from, 197
  directives in, 60
  vs. PRINC, 122
  vs. PRIN1, 122
  print to screen arguments for, 61
  streams in, 60
  for string output, 121, 123, 126, 132
  template for, 60, 64
  vs. TERPRI, 122
  value returned by, 195
  for writing file, 124
FORMAT (FORTRAN), 60
Form-feed character, 60
FORM-OUTPUT-HEADER, 200–201

Forms
    definition of, 42
    predicting value returned by, 192
    special, 220
Forward-chaining systems, 240, 241, 271. *See also* Expert systems
Free variables, 75. *See also* Variables
    references to, 91
Funarg problem, 76
FUNCALL, 174
    advantages of, 165–166
    vs. APPLY, 167, 174
    calling FUNCALL with, 166
    evaluation of, 166, 298
    macros in, 230
    template for, 175
FUNCTION, 140–141
    abbreviation of, 141
    vs. SYMBOL-FUNCTION, 168
    template for, 154, 217
    value returned by, 140
:FUNCTION, 238, 241–242
Function binding
    definition of, 67
    order of, 178, 179
    pretty-printer display of, 23
Function declarations, 214–215
Function objects
    creating unnamed types of, 164, 174
    definition of, 140, 166
    LAMDBA expressions in, 171
    manipulation of, 173–174
    passing and calling, 160
    redefining functions as factor with, 170
    uses for, 168
Functions. *See also* Arguments; Procedures
    aborting execution of, 182–184
    avoiding duplicate names for, 184–188
    definition of, 42
    evaluation of, 17–18, 219–220
    execution of, 211
    multiple values returned by, 189–192
    names for, 45
    optional arguments for, 124, 177–181
    passing, 8–9
    private definitions of, 152
    redefining and reinitializing of, 170
    for self-documentation, 46
    type declarations for, 214–215

Garbage collection, 85–86
Generalized variables. *See* Variables

GET
    quoting with, 142
    template for, 154
    value returned by, 142
GETF, 141
    and SETF, 141
    template for, 154
    value returned by, 141
GETHASH, 146–147
    template for, 154
Global variables, 68–80. *See also* Dynamic scoping; Variables
:GOAL, 238
Grouping, 94
    constructs for, 112–113

Hash tables, 146–147, 153
    advantages and disadvantages of, 146, 152–153
    changing values in, 147
    duplicate coding problem with, 146
    initializing, 168, 1170
    keys for, 147
    operators on, 152, 153, 154
    tests for equality with, 146, 147, 153
%HEADER, 195
Host, in pathnames, 129

IF, 51–53
    limitations of, 52
IMPORT, 186–187, 205
    placement of, 188
    template for, 206
Indentation
    for arguments to functions, 23
    for comments, 192–193
    LINEFEED, 23
    with steppers, 71
Index numbers, ELT in, 45, 46
Inference engine, 240–231
:INITIAL-CONTENTS, 143–144
Initializing, 95–96
    for DEFSTRUCT, 149
    in DO-loops, 111
    of hash tables, 168, 170
    and redefining, 170
    for stepping forms, 111
INLINE, 212, 217
    template for, 217
In-line declarations, 211–212, 215, 217
IN-PACKAGE, 187, 205
    placement of, 188
    template for, 206

Input. *See also* Output; Streams
    function for, 118–121
    newline character in, 122
    quoting in, 120–121
    reader macros in, 121
INT-CHAR, 123
Interactions. *See also* Streams
    printed copy of, 99
INTERLISP, 3
INTERN, 230
    template for, 231
Interpreters, 209
    calling, 158
I/O. *See* Input; Output; Streams
Iteration, 94, 97
    constructs for, 109–112, 116
    in DO-loops, 110, 111
    ELT in, 45, 46
    with expansion, 229
    with LENGTH, 44
    and return, 112
    stepping forms in, 111

&KEY, 180, 204
Keyforms, 54
Keylists, 54
Key objects, 54
Keywords, 205
    evaluation of, 140, 180, 181, 186, 205
    in function calls, 178, 181
    for lambda lists, 178–180
    properties of package for, 186
Keyword value pair, 140
    for MAKE-ARRAY, 143

LAMBDA, 164–165, 174, 289
    environment as factor with, 165
    evaluation of, 164
    as function object, 171–172
    properties of, 165
    template for, 175
Lambda lists. *See* Arguments
LAMBDA-PARAMETERS-LIMIT, 178
LAST, 44
    end of list for, 44
    template for, 64
    program attempts at, 130
%LEFT MARGIN, 195
LENGTH, 44
    template for, 64
    value returned by, 145
LET, 68–70
    declaration for, 77
    evaluation of variables list in, 69

vs. MULTIPLE-VALUE-BIND, 190
    parallel binding in, 70, 74–75, 285
    setting values in sequence with, 198
    specifying variables in, 73–74
    template for, 69, 91
    variable assignment in, 69–70
Lexical closures, 66, 172, 173, 174. *See also*
        Function object
    definition of, 166
Lexical scoping, 75–78, 91
    advantages of, 172
    as default, 75–76, 77, 91
    in DEFUNS, 68, 75–76
    in LET, 69, 75–76, 91
LEXPR-FUNCALL, APPLY as substitute for, 168
Line breaks, 195
    in different modes, 207
LINEFEED, 23
LISP
    compiled and interpreted versions of, 209
    integration of data structures into, 135
    as *LISt Processing* language, 135
    object-oriented programming in, 151–152
    usefulness of, 1–2
LISP MACHINE LISP, 3
LIST, 43
    template for, 64
LISTP, 47
    template for, 64
Lists
    adding associations to, 138–139
    advantages and disadvantages of, 143, 144, 152
    box-and-pointer diagrams of, 28–30, 33
    to call functions, 16–19
    circular, 102
    coding conventions for, 23
    concatenating, 45
    constructing, 10
    documentation on, 194
    dotted-pair notation of, 30–32, 33–34
    elements of, 15
    end of, 25
    evaluation of, 16–21, 23, 27, 41
    extracting items from, 138
    filtering, 161, 162
    iteration with, 110, 116
    labeling data inside, 136–137, 153
    last cdr of, 25
    manipulating, 24–25
    modifying, 82–85, 86–87
    vs. multiple values, 192
    nested structures of, 19
    NIL in, 15, 25–26

Lists (*continued*)
  with no elements, 15
  operators on, 42–44, 152, 153
  preventing evaluation of, 20–22
  printed form of, 36
  recursive decomposition of, 100–101, 103–104
  sample types of, 16, 17
  as series of cons cells, 28–30, 33
  splicing of into macros, 224
  storing data in, 15
  syntax of, 15, 120
  as trees, 102, 103–104
  usefulness of, 15
LOAD, 62, 210
  template for, 64
LOCAL, 289
Logical operators. *See also* conditional operators
  selecting, 58–59
Looping, 97

MACLISP, 3
MACROEXPAND, 221, 230
  template for, 221, 231
MACROEXPAND-1, 221, 230
  template for, 231
Macros, 42, 219–227
  advantages and disadvantages of, 219, 220–221,
    230
  in APPLY, 230
  backquote-commas in, 223–224, 230
  common errors with, 222–223
  compiled vs. interpreted versions of, 222
  creation of with DEFSTRUCT, 227
  defining, 221–222
  evaluation of, 222
  expansion of, 229
  inspecting expansion of, 221
  lambda lists of, 229, 230
  pattern for arguments to, 228, 229
  inside PROGN, 228
  redefining, 220, 230
  splicing lists into, 224
  as template, 223–224, 230
Macros-defining-macros, 224–227
  common errors with, 225, 226
  nested backquotes for, 230
  order of evaluation in, 225–227
MAKE-ARRAY
  arguments for, 143
  template for, 154
  VECTOR as alternative to, 144
MAKE-HASH, 15
MAKE-HASH-TABLE, 146

MAKE-PACKAGE, 187
MAPC, 163
  template for, 175
MAPCAN, 162–163
  vs. MAPCAR, 167
  NIL with, 162
  template for, 175
  value returned by, 161
MAPCAR, 161–162
  vs. MAPCAN, 167
  NIL with, 162
  template for, 175
  value returned by, 161, 163
MAPCON, 163
MAPL, 163
MAPLIST, 163
Mapping functions, 160–163, 174
  summary of, 163
Margins, specifying, 195
  specifying, 195
MAX, 23
MEMBER, 50
  EQL as default for, 50
  template for, 64
Message passing, 152
MIN, 34
Modification, destructive
  vs. copying, 85–86
  dangers of, 84
  definition of, 81
  with DEFUN, 82
  with REMF, 141
  with SETF, 80–82, 141
  with SETF/GET, 142
Modification, nondestructive, 138–139
Modules, 188
  placement of commands as factor with, 188
MULTIPLE-VALUE-BIND, 189–190, 205
  vs. LET, 190
  template for, 206
MULTIPLE-VALUE-LIST, 190–191, 205
  template for, 206
Mutators, 7
MYCIN, 238

Names
  advantages of, 295
  with ampersands, 178
  of arrays, 144
  avoiding duplication of, 184–188
  with colons, 178, 205
  conversion of to strings, 123
  errors from conflict in, 186

Names (*continued*)
  of files, 62, 128–129
  of functions, 45
  for internal symbols, 185–186
  for keywords, 181, 186
  for package names, 184–188
  in pathnames, 129
  for predicates, 47
  of procedures, 41
  of streams, 125
  of symbols, 61, 185–186
  of variables, 45, 74, 79
NCONC, 86
  arguments with, 162
  template for, 91
Newline characters, 60
  for input processing, 122
  in output, 121, 122
%NEW-PAGE, 195
NEW-TABINDENT, 191–192
NIL, 15, 27
  at end of lists, 25
  evaluation of, 15, 25, 47
  as last CDR, 29, 30–31
  meaning of, 63
  as member of list, 26
  multiple meanings of, 47
  as value returned from GET, 142
%NO-FILL, 195
NOT, 47–48
  in predicate functions, 237–238
  template for, 64
NOTINLINE, 217
  declaration for, 212
  template for, 217
NREVERSE, 86
  template for, 91
NTHCDR, 43
  vs. items in lists, 117
  template for, 64
  zero-based index for, 44
NULL, 47–48
  template for, 64
NUMBERP, 47
  template for, 64
Numbers, 120
  converting to floating point, 298
  evaluation of, 11–12, 27
  testing equality of, 48

Objects
  creation of, 11

ONE-STARTS-WITH-A-VOWEL?, 58
OPEN, 126–127, 133
  template for, 133
  UNWIND-PROTECT, 183–184
Operators, 42
  template for, 34
OPPOSITE program, 155–156
Optimization. *See also* Speed
  declarations for, 212, 215, 217
  with tail-recursion, 108–109
OPTIMIZE, 217
&OPTIONAL, 178
  placement of arguments to, 204
Optional arguments, 124, 177–181, 204
OR, 56–58
  evaluation of, 57
  in predicate functions, 237–238
  template for, 64
Otto program, 233–271
  as backward-chaining system, 240
  condition descriptors in, 236
  descriptors for, 262–266
  evaluation of inference engine in, 241, 242–243
  following path through, 243–247
  limitations of, 253–254
  modeling engine as improvement on, 254
  predicate functions in, 236, 237, 238
  printout of, 254–271
  rules of, 238–243, 253–252, 253–257, 260–270
  seals expert in, 241–242, 250–252
  user session with, 233–235
  validity measures in, 235–236
Output. *See also* Input; Streams
  functions for, 121–122
  strings of, 121, 126–127, 132
:OUTPUT-FILE, 210

PACKAGE, 185
  value of, 187
Packages
  as arguments, 188
  definition of, 205
  exporting and importing with, 185–187
  importing specific symbols to, 187
  names in, 184–188
  putting symbols in, 187
%PAGE-LENGTH, 195
Pages
  lines too long for, 199
  numbering, 208
  setting default size for, 195
Pairs. *See* Dotted pairs

Parameters, 178. *See also* Arguments
  creating of with DEFPARAMETER, 79–80
Parentheses, 42
Pathnames, 128–129
  definition of, 128, 133
  operations on, 129
PI, 27
Pound sign, to represent arrays, 144
Precedence rules, 19. *See also* evaluation
Predicate functions, 236–240, 242
  combining weights in, 237–238
  defining, 248
  elements of, 247
  in rules, 236, 237
  types of, 237
Predicates
  for equality, 48–50
  names for, 47
  in procedures, 51
  for types of arguments, 47–51
  usefulness of, 63
Prefix notation, 18
Pretty-printing, 23
  for nested arguments to functions, 23
  treatment of semicolon comments in, 192
  usefulness of, 23
PRINC, 122, 132
  vs. FORMAT, 122
  vs. PRIN1, 122
  template for, 133
PRIN1, 132
  vs. FORMAT, 122
  vs. PRINC, 122
  vs. PRINT, 121
  template for, 133
PRINT, 40, 121, 132
  vs. PRIN1, 121
  template for, 133
PRINTF, 60
Printout. *See* Text formatting
PROBE-FILE, 168
Procedures, 42
  abstraction in 89–90
  arguments in, 40
  calls to in lists, 16
  compiled, as data, 158
  as contracts, 5, 8
  as data, 173
  defining, 39–41
  interpreted, as lists, 158
  mutual support in, 7
  names of, 41

  passing under program control, 150, 174
  purpose of, 39
  structure of, 38–39
  using predicates in, 51
Procedure-writing procedures
  example of, 8–9, 171–172
  as powerful tool, 173–174
PROCLAIM, 217
  vs. DECLARE, 212–213
  template for, 217
PROGN
  macros inside, 228
  template for, 116
PROGN-type forms, 112–113
  values returned by, 112, 113, 116
PROG1
  template for, 116
  values returned by, 113, 116
PROG2, 116
Programming, object-orientation in, 151, 152
Programs, 38. *See also* Data abstraction;
    Procedures
  modularity of, 63, 135–136
  rules of order in, 136–137
Prompts, 11, 27
Properties
  creating with SETF/GET, 142–143
  definition of, 137
Property lists, 137, 141–143, 153
  advantages of, 152
  vs. association lists, 141
  deletion from, 143
  operators on, 152, 153
  of symbols, 142
  template for, 137, 141
PROVIDE, 188, 205
  placement of, 188
  template for, 206
Push stacks
  association lists as, 139
  vectors as, 145
PUTPROP, replacement of with SETF/GET, 142

QUIT
  as command, 182
QUOTE
  abbreviation of, 21
  vs. backquote, 224
  evaluation of, 27
  guidelines for, 22
  with lists, 21–22
  reader macro for, 121

QUOTE (*continued*)
  as special form, 22
  with symbols, 22
  template for, 34
Quoting
  character for, 120
  with GET, 142
  in input, 120–121

RASSOC, 140–141
  arguments with, 140
  template for, 154
  value returned by, 140
RATIONAL, 123
READ, 118, 120–121, 132
  default values with, 124, 178, 179
  extra calls to, 122
  optional arguments with, 125, 178, 179
  output for, 121–122
  template for, 133
READ-CHAR, 118–119, 132, 133
  assigning name to, 119
  extra calls to, 122
  value returned by, 118, 122
Reader macros, 224
READ-EVAL-PRINT, 194–195
READ-FROM-STRING, 123–124
  multiple values from, 190
  value returned by, 123
READ-LINE, 118, 119, 132
  assigning name to, 119
  template for, 133
  value returned by, 119, 122
Recursion, 6, 8, 94–109
  cybernetic example of, 113–115
  definition of, 95, 115
  diagram of, 96–97, 98
  disadvantages of, 108, 134
  end tests in, 100, 101, 116
  in evaluation of lists, 19
  flow of control in, 97
  of functions calling functions, 98–99
  operations on values returned by, 101–102
  steps in procedures using, 100, 116
  with tail-recursive situations, 108–109
  Tower of Hanoi problem, 105–108
  types of procedures for, 115–116
  values returned in, 97, 98–99
REMF, 141
  template for, 154
REMHASH, 147
  template for, 154

REMOVE, 139–140
  template for, 154
  values returned by, 139
REMPROP, 143
  template for, 154
  values returned by, 143
REQUIRE, 188, 205
  placement of, 188
  template for, 206
REST, 26
&REST, 179, 180, 204
RETURN, 27, 60
  in DO-loops, 112
REVERSE, 45
  destructive versions of, 86
  template for, 64
ROUND, 123
RPLACA, 86–87
  template for, 91
RPLACD, 86, 87
  template for, 91
Rules, 244, 271
  definition of, 235
  directed acyclic graphs in 238–240
  elements of, 236
  :FUNCTION option in 241–242
  independence of in expert systems, 244
  interrelationship of, 237, 238
  options with, 238
  ordering of, 249–250
  of Otto, 243–247, 266–270
  parts of, 247
  recursive dependence of, 258
  searching through, 240–241, 271
  validity measures in, 236

-S, 60
Saving files, 62
SCHEME, 3
Scoping, 75–78, 91
  advantages of lexical, 172
  default in, 75–76, 77, 91
  in DEFUNS, 68, 76
  dynamic, 76–78, 91
  dynamic in text formatting, 200
  and funarg problem, 76
  in LET, 69, 76, 91
  and lexical closures, 166, 172, 173, 174
  LISP dialect differences in, 68, 76
  relying on dynamic, 213
  special declarations for, 77, 91, 210–211, 213
  and variable names, 79

SEARCH, 119

Selectors, 7, 24–25, 33, 50, 141
  for data structures, 152
  DEFSTRUCT definition of, 148, 149
  examples of, 88
  selecting, 138

Self-documentation functions, 46

Semicolons, as comment character, 130, 192, 205

Sequence functions, 44–46

SETF, 144
  changing documentation string with, 194
  with DOCUMENTATION, 205
  efficiency of, 83
  explicit commands for functions of, 86–87
  and GETF, 141
  modifying values of symbols with, 80–82
  operators used in first argument of, 83
  setting values of objects with, 82–83
  template for, 91
  usefulness of, 82
  values returned by, 81

SETQ, 86
  template for, 91

SHADOW
  placement of, 189
  purpose of, 189
  template for, 206

Shadowing, 73–75, 91
  with DEFVAR, 78
  diagram of, 74
  in FORM, 200–201

Sharing
  copying vs. destructive modification with, 84–86
  EQ in test for, 84

Side effects, 82, 91, 112
  dangers of, 84
  of DEFUN, 39
  with MAPC, 163
  with MAPL, 163
  of recursive procedures, 97

SIGNUM, 291

Space, as factor with vectors, 146

SPECIAL
  template for, 217

Special declarations, 77, 91, 210–211, 213, 217

Special forms, 220
  definition of, 42
  QUOTE as, 22

Speed. *See also* Optimization
  checking with TIME, 218
  as compilation tradeoff, 212

  from declarations, 217
  and DEFCONSTANT, 80
  in-line coding for, 211–212
  of local variable accessing, 210–211
  of macros, 230
  of macros vs. functions, 219, 220
  optimization declarations for, 212, 215
  type declarations for, 214

SQRT, 34

STANDARD-INPUT, 124, 126

STANDARD-OUTPUT, 124, 126

STEP, 71
  template for, 91
  values returned by, 71

Steppers, 3, 70
  for compiled macros, 230
  identation with, 71
  with recursive functions, 99
  sample interaction with, 71

Stepping forms
  initializing, 111
  in iteration, 111

Streams, 124–128, 132–133. *See also* Input; Output
  accessibility of, 124, 127–128, 133
  as arguments, 128
  definition of, 118, 124, 133
  using DEFVAR with, 128
  as input and output, 127
  naming, 125
  outputting to file, 127
  printed form of, 124
  setting up from string, 124–125
  as special variables, 128
  writing to string from, 126

STRING, 123

Strings, 120
  binding standard input and output to, 126
  characters in, 12–13, 120
  constructing from data, 59–61
  conversion of, 123
  decomposing, 45
  evaluation of, 11–12, 27
  format output for, 121, 126–127, 132
  operations on, 123
  printed form of, 12
  printing, 122
  as special vectors, 143
  stream input from, 124–125
  stream output to, 126

Structures. *See* Data structures

Subscripts, 144

SYMBOL-FUNCTION, 168
  vs. FUNCTION, 168
SYMBOL-NAME, 123
Symbols, 13, 120
  accessing, 142
  calling, 185–186
  case of, 15
  changing value of, 86
  characters in, 120
  converting, 123
  creation of with INTERN, 228, 230
  default names of, 61
  defining parts for, 13
  documentation as, 193
  evaluation of, 14–15, 27
  exporting, 185–186
  face values of, 14
  as first element in lists, 15
  function binding vs. value of, 45
  identifying, 14
  importing, 185–186
  modifying value of, 80–82
  package names for, 184–188
  preventing evaluation of, 22
  printed form of, 14
  printing, 122
  property list of, 142
  putting in packages, 187
  quoted versions of, 275
  uninterned, 185
  values returned by, 275
  values of, 14

T, 27
  evaluation of, 47
  meaning of, 63
  as shorthand for *STANDARD-OUTPUT*, 127
Tags
  in CATCH and THROW, 182
Tail recursion. See Recursion
TERPRI, 122
  vs. FORMAT, 122
  template for, 133
TEST, 140–141
Text formatting, 195–204
%TEXT-WIDTH, 195
THE, 214, 217
  template for, 217
THROW, 181, 182, 205
  evaluation of, 182
  template for, 206
Throws, continuing execution with, 182–184

Tilde (˜), 60
Tower of Hanoi, 105–108
TRACE, 71–72
  of compiled macros, 220, 230
  example of, 99
  of expert systems, 243
  and in-line code, 212
  of Otto, 243–247
  template for, 91
Tracers, 3, 71–72
  with recursive functions, 99
Translation, 11
Trees
  in animal program, 129–132
  depth-first searches of, 102–104
  lists as, 102, 103–104
  searches of in artificial intelligence, 104
  structure diagrams of, 102, 103, 104
Type, in pathnames, 129
Type declarations, 211, 213–214, 217
TYPE, 217
TYPEP, 228

UNTRACE, 71, 72
  template for, 91
UNWIND-PROTECT, 182–184
  template for, 183, 206
Updating
  with ASSOC, 139–140
  with destructive modification, 140, 142–143
  with REMPROP, 143
  with SETF/GET, 142–143
USE-PACKAGE, 186, 205
  placement of, 188, 189
  template for, 206

VALUES, 191, 205
Variable creation
  with DEFCONSTANT, 80
  with DEFUNS, 68
  with DEFVAR, 78–79, 80
  with LET, 69–70
Variables, 128. See also Scoping
  advantages of lexical scoping of, 172
  binding multiple values to, 189–192
  binding of in DO-loops, 111
  binding of in recursive procedures, 98
  default for, 111
  diagram representing changes in, 81
  free, 75, 78, 91
  generalized, 83
  global, 68–80

Variables (*continued*)
  in LET statements, 73–74
  local, 68, 69, 75–76, 91
  as locators, 83
  modifying, 80–87, 141, 142
  modifying values of objects as, 82–85
  names for, 45, 74, 79
  parallel binding of, 70, 74–75
  pointers of, 81
  sequential binding of, 70
  setting values of in sequences, 198
  specifying values of, 179
  top-level loop binding of, 194–195
  types of, 67, 75, 91, 172
  usefulness of, 90
VECTOR, 144
  template for, 154
VECTOR-POP, 145
VECTOR-PUSH, 145
VECTOR-PUSH-EXTEND, 146
Vectors
  advantages and disadvantages of, 143, 144
  creating, 144
  definition of, 143, 144
  functions for, 144, 153
  modifying length of, 144–145
  operators on, 152, 153
  as push stacks, 145
  space allocations for, 146
Version fields, in pathnames, 129

Walking the tree, 102–104
WITH-INPUT-FROM-STRING, 124–125, 127
  template for, 133
WITH-OPEN-FILE, 127
  template for, 133
  variable scoping problem with, 127–128

WITH-OUTPUT-TO-STRING, 126

XCON, 240–241

YES-OR-NO-P, 50–51
  as input, 118
  template for, 64
Y-OR-N-P, 50–51
  as input, 118
  template for, 64

SPECIAL CHARACTERS
" (double quote), 120
' (# quote), 141
\ (# backslash), 120, 122
#nA (#, number array designator), 144
% (percent text formatter character), 195
& (ampersand), 178
' (single quote), 121
((left parenthesis), 42
) (right parenthesis), 42
() (empty list), 15, 25
* (asterisk), 79, 128
, (comma), 223–224, 230
,. (comma-dot), 224
,@ (comma-atsign), 224
: (colon), 140, 178, 181, 186, 205
; (semicolon), 130, 192, 205
= (equals sign), 48
\ (backslash), 120
` (backquote), 223–227, 230
| (vertical bar), 120–121
˜ (tilde), 60
˜% (tilde percent) 60, 122
˜((tilde left parenthesis), 61
˜| (tilde vertical bar), 60
˜⟨RETURN⟩ (tilde return), 60

ORDERING INFORMATION

To order additional copies of this book and Guy L. Steele Jr., COMMON LISP, fill in and mail this form or call the toll-free telephone number below. Orders under $50 must be prepaid by check or charge card; postage and handling are free on prepaid orders. There is a 10 percent discount on orders of two or more copies of each title.

Digital Press/Order Processing
Digital Equipment Corporation
12A Esquire Road
Billerica, MA 01862

QTY.	TITLE	ORDER NO.	PRICE*	TOTAL
	Tatar, Programmer's Guide	EY-6706E-DP	$23.00	
	Steele, COMMON LISP	EY-00031-DP	30.00	
			Total	
			Discount	
			Add state sales tax	
			Total remitted	

METHOD OF PAYMENT

_____ Check included (Make checks   _____ MasterCard/Visa

payable to Digital Equipment   Charge Card Acc't No. _____

Corporation)   Expiration Date _____

_____ Purchase order (Please attach)   Authorized Signature _____

Name _____ Phone _____

Address _____

City _____ State _____ Zip _____

TOLL-FREE ORDER NUMBER

To order books by MasterCard or VISA, call 1-800-343-8321. In Massachusetts, call 1-800-462-8006. Phone lines are open from 8:00 A.M. to 4:00 P.M., Eastern time.

*Price and terms quoted are U.S. only and are subject to change without notice. For prices outside the U.S., contact the nearest office of Educational Services, Digital Equipment Corporation.